Theoretical Approaches to Participatory Communication

INTERNATIONAL ASSOCIATION FOR MEDIA AND COMMUNICATION RESEARCH

This series consists of books arising from the intellectual work of IAMCR sections, working groups, and committees. Books address themes relevant to IAMCR interests; make a major contribution to the theory, research, practice and/or policy literature; are international in scope; and represent a diversity of perspectives. Book proposals are submitted through formally constituted IAMCR sections, working groups, and committees.

Series Editors
IAMCR Publication Committee

Coordinator: Annabelle Sreberny

Members:
Naren Chitty
John Downing
Elizabeth Fox
Virginia Nightingale

Theoretical Approaches to Participatory Communication

edited by
Thomas L. Jacobson
State University of New York at Buffalo

Jan Servaes
Catholic University of Brussels

HAMPTON PRESS, INC.
CRESSKILL, NEW JERSEY

Printed in the United States of America

Library of Congress Cataloging-in-Publication Data

Theoretical approaches to participatory communication / edited by
 Thomas L. Jacobson, Jan Servaes.
     p.   cm. -- (IAMCR book series)
   Includes biobraphical references and indexes.
   ISBN 1-57273-169-9. -- ISBN 1-57273-170-2
   1. Communication in community development. 2. Community
development--Citizen participation. I. Jacobson, Thomas L., 1952-
. II. Servaes, Jan, 1952-   . III. Series.
HN49.C6T457 1999
307.1'4--dc21   99-32613
                                                        CIP

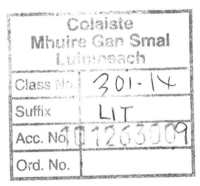

Hampton Press, Inc.
23 Broadway
Cresskill, NJ 07626

Contents

Introduction

Thomas Jacobson
State University of New York at Buffalo
Jan Servaes
Catholic University of Brussels

It is long past time since citizen participation in the planning of national development efforts could be called a new idea. It is an idea that has experienced multiple waves of interest in recent decades, both practical and theoretical. Each time, it has been redefined and reemphasized in a new form. Each form has suffered perhaps a short fate, being eclipsed in each case by a new approach with new theoretical and practical concerns. Nevertheless, the idea of local citizen participation in planning for improvement in the conditions of life, and the idea of localities as the context in which promises for betterment must be conceived, is durable. It remains and, in connection with development communication, is the subject of this book.

Within the field of development communication, the first wave of interest in participation occurred in connection with classical modernization theory during the post-World War II period. This was the theory of national modernization applied to the study of Third World countries by political scientists such as Pye and Verba (1965) and Almond and Coleman (1960). Also involved were sociologists such as Eisenstadt (1966), Hoselitz (1960), and Parsons (1960), as well as economists such as Rostow (1960). Participation in this theory mainly referred to citizen participation in representative democratic party processes, especially voting. Communication was considered an important element of participation. Apter (1965) argued that communication was an essential process through which information was utilized in modern institutions, in place of authority, and Lerner's (1958) work is well known for having emphasized the role of media participation in facilitating political participation.

During the 1970s, widespread criticism of modernization theory appeared, based initially in studies of economic dependency that emphasized the marginalization of large portions of developing countries populations. Even when economic policy led to national growth, benefits of this growth has usually concentrated in numerically small wealthy classes. Under modernization regimes, development programs were managed by experts from developed countries rather than by the local populations themselves. It eventually became clear that political participation was unlikely to develop where localities themselves did not have the capacity to participate in planning their own futures.

As a result, a richer notion of participation was advanced to replace the earlier notion associated with representative party politics. In this notion, exogenous, expert knowledge was downplayed, whereas indigenous knowledge and local aspirations were of more central concern (Riano, 1994; Salmen, 1987). In studies of communication, Beltran (1980) argued that horizontal communication among local community members was of central importance and should take precedence over, or complement, vertical patterns of communication through which experts transmitted their modernization plans. Freire's (1970) notion of conscientization highlighted the importance of dialogue as a process essential to community development because it is first essential to the development of self-actuated, self-determining individuals.

Dialogic processes have since assumed more importance in the study of development communication.

1. One such dialogic process, or context, concerns communication among community members themselves, for self-management.

2. Another concerns dialogue between outside experts and local communities.

3. Yet another refers to outside experts doing research in local communities, sometimes as part of development planning.

The latter instance represents a particular disagreement with modernization theory, a disagreement concerning the epistemological and ontological assumptions underlying research methods and theory construction. Modernization theory embodied an approach to research that placed a barrier between researchers and local communities. This barrier allowed researchers to observe but never identify with communities. Research was an endeavor requiring university training in objectivity, and this training could only be compromised by emotional involvement in development. The second wave of interest in participation therefore not only redefined participation, but also redefined the proper relationship between researchers and those being researched (Jacobson, 1993). This redefinition has held that outside researchers might be useful to local communities, but the knowledge, experience, and goals of local communities themselves must occupy a central role in development planning, execution, and evaluation. In many instances, development research itself can become a community process, as participatory research (PR). Outside researchers can be valuable resources in such instances, but cannot be the prime movers.

This second wave has represented the concerns of field workers for a couple of decades, and this more participatory approach to participation has earned growing interest from academicians, development agencies, and nongovernmental organizations involved in development work (Casmir, 1991; Melkote, 1991; Servaes, Jacobson, & White, 1996). Nevertheless, this definition has never earned the widespread credence once held by modernization theory among academic theorists.

The reasons for this are complex, involving as they do a general shift in the relation between northern and southern countries. Signposts for this shift include the diminishing of U.S. support for United Nations (UN) development initiatives during the 1980s and the more recent preoccupation of the United States and most of Europe with the fate of post-Soviet states.

Another reason for its lack of credence concerns trends in philosophy and social theory. The notion of dialogue alluded to here has been substantially elaborated in schools of thought ranging from postmodernism to hermeneutics to cultural studies to postanalytic language philosophy. If Beltran's horizontal notion of communication argued that development communication patterns are invested with power, then Foucault's studies of power and knowledge have powerfully deepened the understanding of disciplinarity and its effects on development thinking. If Freire argued that possession of language is the foundation of emancipation, then hermeneutics has shown the reliance of the construction of the self on language, and deconstructionism has articulated the complexity of processes by which the self can be fragmented.

The combination of geopolitical and intellectual trends, as well as other factors, has left the study of participation itself decentered, along with the study of development generally. This is not all to the bad, but it would seem that applications of the new thinking to directed social change have lagged somewhat behind applications to critique of global trends and past theoretical approaches.

This book addresses the latter question (i.e., of what relevance are current theories to the study of participatory communication?). It would seem that most of contemporary theory has little to say about directed social change, aside from critique, or at least it has been applied primarily in critical efforts. This goes for Said's (1979) important work *Orientalism*, as well for writings on postcolonialism (Ashcroft, Griffiths, & Tiffin, 1995; Chambers & Curti, 1996) and the increasingly common applications of deconstructionism to global flows of cultural products (Wilson & Dissanayake, 1996). What we might loosely call *postmodernism* here does not support a separation between research and social change, between what epistemology traditionally refers to as fact and value, as modernization theory did. Nevertheless, more can be done to bridge the gap between critical theorizing and constructive national development efforts, especially efforts at the level of local and regional planning.

It can also be said that more can be done by way of exploring contemporary forms of praxis. Therefore, in Servaes (1989), a research design was advocated that starts from a more dialectic and multicentered perception of power. Factors in three general problem areas can be discerned: (a) the mutual dependency between the macro-level of the society or a given structure and the micro-level of the social actions involved; (b) the position and autonomy of organized subjects; and (c) the relation of domination, dependency, and subordination versus liberation, selective participation, and emancipation of power and interest contrapositions.

Whatever the reasons for the current situation, the third wave of interest in participation is rich in possibilities for theoretical analysis. Servaes (1989) referred to a range of contemporary theorists in arguing that a more culturally sensitive approach to participation must be taken in another sort of development theory, in place of the sort offered by modernization theory. But such references warrant more extended treatment. Many of the major social theorists writing in the 1990s have produced work that is directly applicable to development studies and to participatory communication, even though most of it has been produced in studies of social conditions in the developed north.

This volume identifies and explores the relevance of such theory. The contributors do not all agree on a single definition of participation, or of PR. But they do share a common interest in advancing a theoretical, as well as practical, understanding of participatory communication. The vast majority of works on participatory communication to date have brought together arguments advocating participatory communication based on practical, field-based experience. This volume considers the relevance of these pleas to theoretical concerns. Together, the chapters address community participation, communication, and culture from a number of specific contemporary theoretical perspectives. They raise for discussion a number of associated methodological and metatheoretical issues.

The chapters addressing these matters are organized into three parts. Part I identifies contexts in which participation should be treated. The aim here is not to specify participatory communication fully, but to raise for discussion matters overlooked in much previous writing.

In chapter 1, K. White introduces the terrain of participation by addressing the discourse of development generally, using concepts from deconstructionism, Foucault, Gramsci, and others. Focusing on Oxfam's work in Africa, White explores continuing evidence of paternalism in nongovernmental organizations (NGOs) that ostensibly endeavor to facilitate participation. She addresses the fact that participation assumes a number of forms, and she takes care in particular to differentiate more authentic forms of participation from those forms that use participation as a rubric under which to continue traditional, top–down development work.

Continuing the emphasis on how the terms of a discourse define its terrain, Mato (chap. 2) argues that analysis of local issues requires contextualization of local participation within a framework of regional, national, and even global processes. He notes the historical origins of what is now called Latin America, portraying the region as a geographical entity whose meaning and identity are contested among indigenous people, descendants of slaves imported from Africa, and descendants from European immigrants. He therefore employs the term Latin America (in quotes) for its name.

He points out that Latin America has a considerable record of experience with grassroots movements. He recounts a number of projects initiated by national governments, NGOs, regional entities, and local governments. From these he draws a number of observations, including overuse of out-of-the-box participation models, problems with project schedules and time lines required by large agencies, conflicts between participation, and other sometimes simultaneous national strategies associated with structural adjustment programs, and other problems. He concludes with a list of questions highlighting both the opportunities and problems associated with participatory communication work.

As it has often been treated in the past, participation is a local process focusing on community level efforts. However, the nature of locality as an experience can be affected by mass media. As Kivikuru argues in chapter 3, the relation between local, national, and global communication patterns is close and complex. Globalization in general has changed the experience of locality. Meyerowitz (1985) argued that mass communication is diminishing sense of place toward the vanishing point. Kivikuru disagrees and argues that especially in periphery countries locality remains an important element of identity. She claims that one of the major manifestations of a popular sense of identity—national as well as cultural—in mass communication is locality. She feels that communication theorists have not given the attention appropriate for such a complex dimension of social and communicative experience. In her treatment of this relation between locality, identity, and globalizing media she analyzes a number of "dimensions" of locality including space, place, power, status, change, and others.

Part II focuses on assumptions underlying methods and theories employed in the study of development. Beginning this discussion, Servaes and Arnst (chap. 4) ask "Why have the poor always been researched, described and interpreted by the rich and educated, never by themselves?" "Why shouldn't the researched do their own research?"

Servaes and Arnst advocate an approach to research that embodies social purpose and is devoted to social change. Contrasting positivist and interpretive approaches, they identify PR as interpretive. It is dialogical, deriving knowledge from concrete situations through collaborative reflection among local community members. In the course of this discussion, they address methodological issues such as validity, and they differentiate PR from neighboring approaches such as action research.

They also discuss obstacles. One such obstacle is a lack of interest in PR among influential and political figures due to the low visibility of nonquantitative approaches. Another obstacle is organizational imperatives of funding agencies that require programs with highly specified time frames, clearly articulated outcomes, and easily summarized evaluations. Opportunism among local volunteers can sometimes become a problem when successful participation projects provide platforms for individual professional advancement. Learned dependency among the poor, and ingrained obsequiousness to hierarchical modes of group work is another, all too common, problem.

Despite such challenges, Servaes and Arnst advocate PR as an approach that can be essential for building trust, identifying and supporting local culture, and building indigenous capacity for collective planning. Such a research design builds on participatory approaches that call for upward, transactive, open, and radical forms of planning that encompass both grassroots collective actions (i.e., planning in the small), and large-scale processes (i.e., planning in the large). This kind of planning and research is centrally conceived with human growth, that is, learning processes through mobilization, and the basic aim is to involve people cooperatively in the planning and research process, with the planner or researcher as a facilitator and participant. Servaes and Arnst argue that PR may be essential for development communication processes.

In chapter 5, Deetz expands this argument, making it relevant to all communication research, at all levels of analysis. He proposes a conception of participation as a normative standard against which all acts of communication can be judged employing elements of Rorty, Foucault, Habermas, Apel, Gadamer, and others.

Without overlooking the tension between these theorists, Deetz attempts to use elements of the work of contemporary theorists in a complementary fashion. With Rorty (1989), he advocates a pragmatist position in which different approaches to research are evaluated with regard not to whether they are right or wrong, but rather with regard to what they allow us to do. With Foucault, he acknowledges the power relations in which all research practices and knowledge claims are embedded The point here is not to find a way to settle conflicting knowledge claims, not to degrade truth, but to recall the disciplinary power necessary for any knowledge claims. With Habermas he sees dialogue as a means for coordinating action in a participatory, rather than merely a strategic or instrumental, manner.

Social engagement, responsible acknowledgment of political interests, and dialogue oriented toward understanding are all essential parts of the intellectual's role today. At base, Deetz's concern is to suggest that participatory forms of communication are central in daily life, in theorizing, and in democratically oriented political discourse.

In chapter 6, Dervin and Huesca focus on assumptions that underlie most previous work on participation. They focus on the considerable literature on participatory communication literature that has emerged from Latin America. And they extract six meta-theoretic aspects of this literature for extended treatment. These concern authority, naturalism, cultural relativism, constructivism, postmodernism, and communitarianism,

With the authors of preceding chapters they advocate research that is emancipatory, and orientated toward social change. The authors are sensitive to dual concerns of structure and process, and emphasize the importance of developing more knowledge about, and tools for, facilitating the latter. They find much to commend in communitarian writings as an embodiment of an approach that is socially constructivist and also oriented toward process.

Wildemeersch's development-related work focuses on adult education. In chapter 7, he addresses assumptions underlying both communication theory and adult education theory, particularly with regard to the frames within which the meaning of participation in development are viewed. He believes the potential for participation has been underestimated in both modernization and dependency theory, due in large part to their mechanistic traditions of theory and methodology. He contrasts with these the multiplicity paradigm and provides an illustrative analysis from a grassroots project in Belgium.

In the final chapter of Part II, R. White (chap. 8) visits some of the points made by others in this volume, and expands on the importance of considering the larger social and political contexts that confine local efforts. In contrast to the small, isolated community change projects that are the subject of most participatory communication projects, White focuses on peasant agrarian and national liberation movements as forces whose success can be essential to creating national political cultures respectful of local autonomy and self-reliance. Arguing that the major barriers to meaningful participation result from social structural inequalities, R. White says research should focus on how participatory communication emerges within a historical process of social change and how this process is affected by structural constraints at different stages of its development.

Specifically, he proposes four central analytic questions to be asked within the framework of a four-stage natural history of popular movements. These concern: (a) How dissident social organizations emerge in a way that permits autonomous communication channels, (b) How institutions of participatory communication emerge within social movements, (c) the political-economic conditions necessary for the survival and growth of democratic institutions, and (d) the type of research and policy strategies that can contribute to the development of democratic communications.

White also considers the kind of research required to support such social change, and criticizes both administrative and critical research approaches. Administrative researchers often fail to see participation as part of a long-term process of structural change. On the other hand, critical theory has been much better at diagnosing oppression than analyzing factors leading toward redistribution of social power and democratization. The rationalistic idealism and fascination with ideological control typical of some critical theorists lead to attempts to short-circuit the process of democratization of communication.

Parts I and II address empirical and metatheoretical issues associated with participatory communication. Part III assumes many of the arguments presented in these earlier sections and explores the relevance to participatory communication of specific theories. Each chapter addresses a major theorist's work insofar as it can be used to advance the study of participatory communication. These theorists include Jurgen Habermas, Anthony Giddens, Michele Foucault, Mikhail Bahktin, and also Barney Glaser and Anselm Strauss.

The relevance of Habermas' work to participation is raised a number of times throughout the volume, most notably by Deetz (chap 5). However, given the scope of Habermas' theory, it would be difficult to exhaust this theme, for the points of connection are many. For one example, the subject of *Between Facts and Norms: Contributions to a Discourse Theory of Law and Democracy* (Habermas, 1996) addresses the legal foundations of democratic institutions. The volume's analysis focuses particularly on the contemporary conditions inhibiting meaningful citizen participation in democratic will formation. This is a work that focuses on a macro sociological-level concern for communication and participation.

Another substantive contribution to participation theory can be found at a micro-, intra-, and interpersonal scale, in his treatment of the ideal speech situation. Habermas' proposition of a fictive ideal speech situation is usually discussed as the basis for a theory of rationality. But it can be treated on its own terms as a theory of communication, and applied to specific real-life contexts. This is the subject of chapter 9. Jacobson and Kolluri review Habermas' ideal speech situation with regard to its relevance for community participation processes. Then an agricultural program evaluation conducted in rural India is presented to illustrate the use of the ideal speech situation's validity claims in evaluating participatory processes.

Although Habermas' and Foucault's relevance to development studies is often noted in the research literature, Giddens' otherwise influential work has been less often discussed in this connection. Nevertheless, a number of touch points exist between participatory communication and PR on the one hand, and Giddens' system of structuration theory on the other. Gildart explores these in chapter 10. She notes that "both PAR [participatory action research] and structuration theory reject the objectivist, value-free tenets of positivist social science. Both are also concerned with praxis, or the relationship between knowledge, agency and action. Finally, both are interested in the ability of social research to facilitate change." In her treatment of these connections, Gildart explores such central structurationist ideas as the "double hermeneutic," and the "dialogical model."

One striking characteristic of global intellectual trends since the 1970s has been a move toward increasing centrality in many fields of communication. The linguistic turn in analytic philosophy gave epistemology a focus on language, and the subsequent influence of Austin's and Searle's common language philosophy gave this language analysis a decidedly behavioral turn. The centrality of discourse as a concern in postmodern and poststructuralist thought shows these trends to be communicative in their fundamental categories, thus influencing subjects ranging from literary criticism to architecture to philosophy. Sociologists as different as Giddens and Habermas, as noted, treat communication as being of central importance.

For Escobar, prospects for participation, or indeed anything else in the Third World, depend in large part on the power–knowledge discourse that comprises development. In chapter 11, he illustrates the relevance of Foucault's work to development studies.

> Michele Foucault's fundamental insights into the nature and dynamics of discourse, power and knowledge in Western societies invite similar inquires regarding the present situation of the Third World, in at least two important respects: 1) the extension to the Third World of Western disciplinary and normalizing mechanisms in a variety of fields, and 2) the production of discourses by Western countries about the Third World as a means effecting domination over it.

Escobar sketches the general relevance of a discourse critique. He describes specific ways in which normalizing tendencies contribute to the domination of the Third World, and he explores implications of Foucault's view of power for strategies of resistance. On this latter subject, he focuses on the insurrection of subjugated knowledges, and the development of counter discourses. It is through the development of such counter discourses that subjugated peoples can rely on their own indigenous knowledge to create discursive forms of participatory practice.

Another example of this communicative turn is the work of Russian literary theorist Bahktin. Bahktin argues that the essentially polysemic nature of language is an important characteristic of writing, and of the author–audience relationship. His work on the theory of the novel has been applied by cultural theorists in analyses of media systems, media texts, and audiences. In chapter 12 Storey employs Bahktin's work to argue that popular culture comprises an important element of social participation that can be used in service of public welfare in developing countries.

Storey focuses on Third World entertainment-education projects, suggesting that their popularity is due in part to the manner in which they use local aesthetic codes, or local discourses. Treated as discourses, such projects can be seen not only as interventions, but also as processes that are part of a larger political, cultural and historical context of communication. In this way, "development communication becomes a partnership of media institutions, development agencies, donor organizations, and the audience. . . ." His treatment of entertainment-education programs is illustrated with two cases studies from Pakistan and Indonesia.

The final chapter in Part III diverges from the others because it returns to an approach to theory that still keeps one foot in the more traditional empiricist camp. Einsiedel (chap 13) proposes that community-based participatory communication projects are suitably studied used Glaser and Strauss' (1967) grounded theory approach.

Glaser and Strauss argued that empirical theory construction is too often conducted in a hasty manner, employing conceptual frameworks drawn inappropriately from outside the relevant concrete social contexts. They advocate a more thorough and painstaking examination of social conditions that resembles the long-term involvement exhibited by field workers involved in participatory projects. They emphasize building theoretical categories from the ground up, using dialogue among researchers as well as local participants. Together, the commitments to careful observation and to dialogue move research toward a process in which researchers themselves are involved in local change-oriented praxis.

Although the grounded theory approach violates certain tenets of naturalistic methodology, it nevertheless remains oriented toward generating theories to explain the functions and change processes of social systems. The final difference is on theory generation rather than theory testing. This chapter argues for the continuing relevance of data-driven research in the participatory communication context.

The chapters presented here by no means comprise a thorough review of theoretical concerns relevant to participatory communication research. The empirical questions raised in Part I are not exhaustive of those begging attention. The metatheoretical points raised in Part II are intended to stimulate consideration of assumptions in development communication research, not answer philosophical questions. And the theorists treated in Part III by no means complete the list of those whose work may be relevant to participatory communication. Nevertheless, these chapters are intended to suggest in a compelling manner the fact that participatory communication is suitable for theoretical analysis. Not only is it suitable by virtue of need, it is also suitable due to the existence of relevant theory among major social theorists. Hopefully, this compilation of chapters will help stimulate systematic treatment of participatory communication in the context of contemporary social theory.

These chapters primarily represent efforts of the Participatory Communication Research Working Group, now a section of the International Association of Media and Communication Research (IAMCR). We acknowledge the support of IAMCR in providing a venue for the deliberations of communication researchers and field workers devoted to participation. Thanks also go to the Catholic University of Brussels and the State University of New York at Buffalo for supporting the activities of the Participatory Communication Research Network and IAMCR.

REFERENCES:

Almond, G., & Coleman, J. (Eds.). (1960). *The politics of the developing areas.* Princeton, NJ: Princeton University Press.

Apter, D. (1965). *The politics of modernization.* Chicago: University of Chicago Press.

Ashcroft, B., Griffiths, G., & Tiffin, H. (Eds.). (1995). *The post-colonial studies reader.* London: Routledge.

Beltran, L. (1980). Farewell to Aristotle: Horizontal communication. *Communication, 5*(1), 5-41.

Casmir, F. L. (Ed.). (1991). *Communication in development.* Norwood, NJ: Ablex.

Chambers, L., & Curti, L. (Eds.). (1996) *The post-colonial question: Common skies, divided horizons.* London: Routledge.

Eisenstadt, S. (1966). *Modernization: protest and change.* Englewood-Cliffs, NJ: Prentice-Hall.

Freire, P. (1970). *Pedagogy of the oppressed.* New York: Seabury Press.

Glaser, B., & Strauss, A. (1967). *The discovery of grounded theory.* Chicago: Aldine Atherton.

Habermas, J. (1996). *Between facts and norms: Contributions to a discourse theory of law and democracy.* Cambridge: The MIT Press.

Hoselitz, B. F. (1960). *Sociological factors in economic development.* Glencoe, IL: The Free Press.

Jacobson, T. (1993). A pragmatist account of participatory communication for national development. *Communication Theory, 3*(3), 214-230.

Lerner, D. (1958). *The passing of traditional society.* New York: The Free Press.

Melkote, S. R. (1991). *Communication for development in the Third World: Theory and practice.* New Delhi: Sage.

Meyerowitz, J. (1985). *No sense of place: The impact of electronic media on social behavior.* New York: Oxford University Press.

Parsons, T (1960). *Structure and process in modern societies.* Chicago: The Free Press.

Pye, L., & Verba, S. (Eds.). (1965). *Political culture and political development.* Princeton, NJ: Princeton University Press.

Rorty, R. (1989). *Contingency, irony and solidarity.* New York: Cambridge University Press.

Riano, P. (Ed.). (1994). *Women in grassroots communication: Furthering social change.* London: Sage.

Rostow, W. W. (1960). *Stages of economic growth, a non-communist manifesto.* Cambridge: Cambridge University Press.

Said, E. S. (1979). *Orientalism.* New York: Vintage Books.

Salmen, L. F. (1987). *Listen to the people : Participant-observer evaluation development projects.* New York: Oxford University Press.

Servaes, J. (1989). *One world, multiple cultures: A new paradigm on communication for development.* Leuven, Belgium: Acco.

Servaes, J., Jacobson, T., & White, S. (1996). *Participatory communication for social change.* New Delhi: Sage.

Wilson, R., & Dissanayake, W. (1996). *Global/local: Cultural production and the transnational image.* London: Duke University Press.

1

Participatory Communication Processes

1

The Importance of Sensitivity to Culture in Development Work

Kate White

In the summer of 1987, I traveled with a group of students to Africa to construct houses and latrines for a homeless population at the request of a local district government in southern Botswana. Lethlakeng, the village in which we worked, was small and situated in a valley between two low, sloping ridges. I collected local life histories for research on oral tradition and on one particular occasion, interviewed the village chief. On the appointed morning, I carried my work clothes and shoes with me and made my way through the village to meet a translator who would help me with the interview. It was winter there and the wind blew sand so hard that often huts 20 feet away could not be seen. A woman appeared and stopped me. She said nothing, her face incredibly sad, gesturing first to my shoes, then to her bare, cracked, bloody feet, then back to my shoes. I felt rooted in the sand. The shoes, I knew, would not fit her. In addition, the toes were torn and the leather on the right shoe was separating from the sole. I could not give them to her because I needed them for work yet I felt compelled to hand them to her. Why? Was it because I

17

had others pairs at home? Was it because she did not have a pair and I
could buy another? Then, was I feeling guilty because I was wealthier
than she? I tried to explain that I could not give her my shoes and
walked away.

Of the experiences I have had in Africa, this one stays riveted in
my mind because of the issues raised for me by the encounter with the
woman. Although my interest in so-called "development"[1] work began
several years earlier, it was this moment that keenly reminded me of my
identity: a Western, relatively wealthy, outsider working in a poor rural
village in a foreign land. The two of us, the woman and I, alone, facing
each other on that spot in the sandy village represented, for me, a micro-
cosm of the greater encounter of the Western world's presence within
Africa. I was there to build homes for destitute persons living in the area,
yet what this woman needed was shoes . . . and I would not give her
mine.

Many incidents like this encounter line the path I have taken to
explore the relation between the West and Africa. I have been tracking
development as a keyword (Williams, 1983), a word that has historically
linked Western and African countries. This chapter explores this term, yet I
do not seek its definition so much as I seek to define its perimeter as an
institution, one that constructs a certain reality whose main characteristics
include relations of dominance and power. Moreover, I examine the *discourse* of this institution—those language practices that reveal how statements have the capacity to create value in human relationships (Shapiro,
1988). Development studies, as an academic discipline, seeks to examine
the meaning of development, its history and practice, yet over the span of
the nearly four decades of its existence, little effort has been dedicated to
examine the power relations implicitly included as part of its rhetoric.
Language has the power to create, define, categorize, label, legalize, and
in any other way, bind groups of people. Language represents knowledge,
linking what can be known to "reality," constructing life in its shadow. The
politics of this kind of representation cannot be ignored.

The historical relation between the West and Africa shapes the
context for this study. Texts produced during the era of colonization represented Africa as it was interpreted through the eyes of the colonizer,
dominating what was known about the continent and its inhabitants.
Indigenous African knowledge and ideology did not circulate in dominant
societies; Africans were not in the habit of writing about themselves and
then presenting their texts to other cultures. Therefore, African knowledge was subjugated to a low if not unobserved place in a global hierar-

---

[1]*Development* is a complex concept. Although this chapter seeks to problematize its definitions and discourses constructed in its name, it is very limited.

chy.[2] Indeed, Africa was presented as the "dark" continent, or "the heart of darkness" (Said, 1993).[3] The literature of Western organizations that present ways to develop Africa necessarily begs interrogation: What ideology lies behind the now huge body of literature written by "developed" countries about "undeveloped" ones?

The answer to this question can be explored by presenting development literature as text, then clarifying what is absent or marginal with the use of deconstruction. In literary critical theory, postmodernism deconstructs reality, pointing to power structures, especially what has been called *standard* (read: true), has revealed how the voices of many cultures have been covered up by the predominantly Western, White, and male; it has created a space for expression from the marginalized voices. The rise of cultural studies as a discipline within the academy is linked to the application of deconstruction of academic canons. For hooks (1990), cultural studies provide a space for the marginalized to speak, a place hooks identifies as a space of resistance. As an activist for critical pedagogy within the academy, she employs "strategies that will be enable colonized folks to decolonize their minds and actions thereby promoting the insurrection of subjugated knowledge" (p. 8). With regard to development, this statement can translate into an acknowledgment of indigenous thinking, the "subjugated knowledge" of masses of people who live in Africa where often as much as one third of a country's income can be from international (foreign) aid. If challenges like hooks' (decolonization for insurrection of subjugated knowledge) are applied to international relations, the world hierarchy might be redefined to allow for "an alternative social order" (Esteva, 1991, p. 78). Then, the interpretation of Africa would include an Africa witnessed by African eyes, not a Western gaze. International development strategies might then seek to achieve goals set by African peoples. This begs the question: Can this honestly be an agenda in a donor–recipient relationship? Can foreign investors and aid organizations let African peoples set their own goals and realize their own limitations? Laying bare the bones of the attitudes beneath development discourse illuminate possible answers to these questions.

---

[2]Mudimbe wrote exclusively about this phenomenon, especially how "scientific" discourses have subjugated African Knowledge and its discourses. See Mudimbe (1988, 1994).

[3]See especially *Culture and Imperialism* (Said, 1993), where he discussed Joseph Conrad and *The Heart of Darkness*. Mudime and Said analyzed different texts for basically the same purpose: to reveal how indigenous, non-Western cultures have been subjuaged, romanticized, or made into fetish by Western institutions. Mudimbe analyzed "historical" or "scientific" texts, whereas Said deconstructed the novel.

For Foucault, the subjugated are those whose voices have been marginalized by dominating institutions such as medical and penal establishments (e.g., the clinic and the prison system). His employment of discourse analysis, especially the "archeology" of discourse, or, as one can imagine, digging through the layers of meaning buried within (or around) a text, reveals the ways the discourses of dominant institutions have been denied discursive space and therefore power to groups of people. Such analysis also uncovers the possibility of resistance to these dominant discourses. The discourse of subjugated knowledge is actually, the "reappearance of . . . these local popular knowledges, these disqualified knowledges," that is "a whole set of knowledges that has been disqualified as inadequate to their task or insufficiently elaborated: naive knowledges, located low down on the hierarchy, beneath the required level of cognition or scientificity" (Foucault, 1980, p. 84).

The only way to avoid subjugation is to disavow power, to refuse what Shapiro (1988) described as "the self that has been scripted for the individual." "What this involves," he states, "is not improving conversations but constructing counter discourses, modes of writing which oppose the terms of power and authority circulated and recirculated in prevailing modes of discourse" (p. 19). Language, then, becomes a place of struggle, a site for contestation. By writing "against the grain" of dominant ideology, one can bring implicit meanings to the surface. Although not a negation of what the dominant has produced, these counter discourses are an examination of power structures that ask us to consume them uncritically, often at great cost (Kuhn, 1985).

This chapter endeavors to create a counterdiscourse that will necessarily pique the consciousness of the development agent as a means for causing a "crisis in authority" (Gramsci, 1971), one that will necessarily disrupt the hold of development as a dominant institution. In addition, it creates a forum for local communities, a space in which they can act and speak in order to influence development practices. Redefining international relations is a question of a struggle between who has historically been in the center, and who has been located in the margins. By defining the space of development discourse, I design a discourse that allows local voices to speak and be heard. Moreover, I create a space within the field of social change by identifying the proponents of development as progenitors of a hegemonic cultural practice. This identification will frame the power of the dominant and provide a place for marginal groups to strengthen a discourse of their own.

In this postmodern era, scholars must provoke change, thus, this is an intervention. Discourse produced in the name of development masks issues of power by presenting a certain set of values as natural and necessary; as an institution, "development . . . tries to *frame* all competing definitions of the world within *its* range" (Clark, 1981, p. 59).

DEVELOPMENT, DISCOURSE, AND IDEOLOGY

One of the dominant Western metaphors in human understanding is often actively described in terms of *vision*. This concept, expressed primarily with the verb "to see," is key to our understanding of how Westerners view other cultures, cluing an aware reader in to the distance between viewer and viewed implied by the metaphor. Ethnographic and anthropological practices rely on participant-observation methodology that has come under recent criticism as being more observation than participant. The act of representing others in writing practices bears ethical considerations (cf. Clifford & Marcus, 1986). These writing practices, often depicted as "fact" or "truth," are no more than "partial truths" (Clifford, 1986) because they are the interpretations of culture by individuals, often Westerners. Who can project what they did not "see"?

This section concerns how the written word can inscribe a culture and thus the individual into a certain "reality" than affects gaze and hence experience. Language practices influence lived experience by constructing institutional creeds and, by extension, rules that society follows. These creeds become the stories of our lives. In *The Practice of Everyday Life*, de Certeau (1984) argued that the "*credibility* of a discourse is what first makes believers act in accord with it. It produces practitioners. To make people believe is to make them act" (p. 148). Written words not only reflect reality but become reality, thus by analyzing discourse, especially the stories that are told, which metaphors are chosen, we analyze systems of control and their values.

In her analysis of discourse on gender, technology and power in Africa, Stamp (1989) wrote of the way Western scholars have interpreted the lives of women in Africa, especially how their discourse has shaped relationships and development practices on the continent, creating power structures. Stamp explicitly called for an engagement with the discourse theory, for "researchers can no longer avoid the task of investigating the relationship between dominant power structures, past and present, and the nature of knowledge about Africa" (p. 129). Scholars themselves must examine their own roles in the hierarchy of knowledge, as representatives of one world writing about another. Stamp wrote, "Our ignorance leads us to universalize our own Western categories and concepts. The concrete realities as constructed and lived by Third World people thus disappear from our view (and often, as a result, from their own)" (p. 20). There is no one discourse about development, but a "multiplicity of discursive elements" (Foucault, 1990, p. 100). These elements reveal ideologies that in turn expose values.

Writing about other people, other cultures, embodied by science, simply, by the word "Other," subjugated what they (often the marginalized, those unable to compete in the sophisticated arena of the dominant) thought and felt. For writers such as hooks, who identified herself as "in the margins," this act of representing "Other," of telling the stories of the marginalized, is an act of oppression. She stated:

> Often this speech about the "Other" annihilates, erases: "No need to hear your voice when I can talk about you better than you can speak about yourself. No need to hear your voice. Only tell me about your pain. I want to know your story. And then I will tell it back to you in a new way. Tell it back to you in such a way that it has become mine, my own. I am still the colonizer, the speaking subject, and you are the center of my talk." (hooks, 1990, p. 152)

In his book, *Keywords*, Williams (1983) stated, "The most interesting usage of a group of words centered on *develop* relates to certain ideas of the nature of economic change" (pp. 102–103). It would seem that the birth of development ideology came with the notion of economic growth, as Tordoff observed, that development is a Western concept that grew out of industrialization. He stated, "[I]n the 1950's [development] spelt industrialism, which was seen as an essential and inevitable stage of economic growth" (p. 262). Williams (1983) noted the assumption that industrialism was "essential" and became "normal" in the 20th century, and along with it came notions of "progress" and "backwardness" that are still related to the term *develop* and its opposite, *undeveloped* (p. 103). What Williams and others explored is the relation of the so-called developed countries to the undeveloped, or more commonly, underdeveloped. Williams observed that the patronizing characteristic within the definitions of development is parallel with growth in the concept of *growing up*. The concept of time also plays an important role in this conversation: that *underdeveloped* countries are backward and need to be *developed*, and, with the *progress* of industrialization and economic growth, they will become like the *developed* countries. These words are italicized because they are Western constructions in that they are labels with Western definitions. In fact, the definitions become a cultural practice because they seek to define self—Western countries as *developed*—and other—poorer regions of the world—as *underdeveloped*, or the current common usage, *developing*. Williams (1983) summed up the relationship nicely:

> It is clear that, through these verbal tangles, an often generous idea of "*aid* to the *developing* countries" is confused with wholly ungenerous practices of cancellation of the identities of the others, by their definition as *underdeveloped* or *less developed*, and of imposed processes of *development* for a world market controlled by others. (p. 104)

The terminology that differentiates the two worlds arose out of post-World War II, Western foreign policy. In the spirit of reconstruction, the powerful victorious nations constructed policies that centered around "helping" world wide regions to become like them. Development policy dates back to 1949 when President Harry S. Truman aired his famous Point Four:

> Four, we must embark on a bold new program for making the bene-fits of our scientific advances and industrial progress available for the improvement and growth of underdeveloped areas . . . I believe that we should make available to peace-loving people the benefits of our store of technical knowledge in order to help them realise [sic] their aspirations for a better life. (cited in Gifondorwa, 1981, p. 30)

With a word, Truman changed the destiny of many people. As Esteva (1991) stated, "Never before has a word received universal acceptance the very day of its political coinage.[4] But it happened to this one. From one day to the next, 2 billion people became underdeveloped" (p. 75).

The play of words defined worlds, created policies, connected governments around the globe, and delineated the futures of billions of people. Contrasting constructions like developed/developing, first world/third world, and rich/poor are used as tools of development, especially in defining Africa or Asia in terms of the Western regions' living habits. Another language for this relation does not exist.[5] Although some development organizations seek to problematize these terms,[6] there remains an inconsistency in labeling that "carries the implication that Third World countries are not yet mature enough to join one of the more select clubs" of the "more mature" countries in North America and Europe (Horesh, 1985, p. 509).

The discourse has an historical base. Looking back, we can view how similar Western missionary impulses defined Africa. In his seminal work, *The Invention of Africa*, Mudimbe (1988) described Christian missionary text as one of the main discourses that influenced perceptions of Africa, both Western and African. The aims of Christian theology were to convert "pagan" culture, to bring "the Light of God and Civilization" to "primitive" Africa (p. 53). Mudimbe stated:

---

[4]According to Esteva, the word was invented by Wilfred Benson in 1942, but did not become popular, nor even seen in literature until 1949.

[5]Hettne (1990) and O'Neil (1984) listed possible terminology as alternatives to developed and less developed.

[6]For discussion of documents that problematize language see Horesh (1985).

In its standard form, the process of conversion which is the path to a "civilized life" is presented as a gradual one: at the lowest level one finds primitives or pagans; these, infected by the "will to become Westernized" become catechumens; the zenith of their development is achieved when they become Christians or "evolues," that is, Westernized individuals. (p. 52)

Next to development discourse, missionary statements described by Mudimbe are similar. Both project Africans as pathological or in some dysfunctional state that, through Western intervention, will become "civilized." Like missionary impulses from the 19th century to the end of the 20th, development discourse has "invented" an "Africa" through various representations of the region (documentaries, photographs, case studies, policy) and in need of Western expertise.

Foucault (1972) argued that a theory of knowledge must precede the subject because persons constitute their worlds based on some knowledgeable authority. He stated that "power is incorporated into our identities such that power functions through what is 'known' about us," then asks a crucial question: "[A]t what price can subjects speak the truth about themselves?" (cited in Raulet, 1983, p. 202).

In *Orientalism*, Said (1979) described the price non-Westerners pay for not speaking made all the more potent by his identity as a Palestinian. He portrayed ways in which Western academics construct Orientalism as a discipline and how it becomes a means for control, a way of constructing power and authority over another population. Said described how different powers produced the Orient by "making statements about it, authorizing views of it, describing it, by teaching it, settling it, ruling over it: in short, Orientalism [is] a Western style for restructuring, and having authority over the Orient" (p. 3).

Said's (1993) subsequent work, *Culture and Imperialism*, is a more focused testimony to the hegemony of Western cultural discourse. He used the novel as a discursive text, specifically novels written by Westerners about other cultures (e.g., Charles Dickens, Joseph Conrad). Deconstructed, he revealed how the West views a certain culture that he defined as aesthetic practices and a source of identity. These novels (stories) defined the "foreign" world. Ultimately, he revealed the imperialistic and paternalistic sentiments in these representations. Many of the characters in the novel have the same notions I have seen among Westerners doing development work in Africa. That is, as Said said, "There they imbue themselves with an idea of service, that they are there to help the people. But of course, they are there in process of enriching themselves" (Said & Barsamian, 1994, p. 70). Development work can be described by this explicit statement: "We are here for the sake of others" with an implicit meaning: "We are really here for ourselves."

This is why I draw a parallel between the deconstruction of the imperialist novel and development literature. In development discourse, not only do outside organizations describe the communities they seek to "improve" as different, but they also categorize and judge them in order to set priorities for intervention. Therefore, development activities include finding faults or problems within a community by comparing it to the apparent "success" of wealthier countries. In this light, development can be seen as a metaphor for the relationship between the "strong and the weak" (Horesh, 1985, p. 513).

In the following pages, I present analyses of the discourses of the World Bank as representative of the hierarchical voice within development discourse, and Oxfam as representative of the grassroots voice as further negations of African peoples. My presentation of two voices within development discourse, the hierarchical and the grassroots (top–down and bottom–up, respectively), shows how they interact within a larger discursive space, representing the "field of practice" (Ashley, 1987) of development discourse. In this sense, there is no "right" discourse, or "correct" practice, but a conglomeration of practices of Western ideologies, whether hierarchical or grassroots, subsumed under the rubric of development. Apthorpe (1984) described the situation succinctly: "If there is an incontrovertible lesson in the corpus of development literature it is that there is no single institutionalist posture about interventionalist or non-interventionalist doctrine of which certain schools or disciplines are guilty, others innocent" (p. 129).

Development policy proposed by Western organizations involves ideological questions of power by representing dominant cultures' intention to help to "solve" problems not their own. This intention becomes a mask or "the guise of caring, curing, educating, evaluating, motivating, and resolving disputes" (Shapiro, 1988, p. 18). Although agents who work with populations in rural Africa claim an altruistic ideological base, they often do not recognize that they are outsiders who privilege their knowledge over those who live within the countries they seek to aid. What they need to recognize is how they create a dominant role over the people they seek to help based on their own experiences, and by doing so, recognize the "misrecognized"; ideology is a practice as well (Bourdieu, 1977; Lovell, 1980). What needs to be asked is: Who is speaking? To whom and for whom are they speaking? And, what are they saying?

REPRESENTATION, HIERARCHY AND GRASSROOTS

Development policy is a mode of representation because it portrays a certain reality, one that assumes that its boundaries are the boundaries of others. Analysis of this mode captures the representation within a framework. The perimeter of the "development" institution can be defined by examining two distinct voices within its discourse: hierarchical and grassroots, represented here by two organizations, the World Bank and Oxfam UK respectively. Although often considered opposing points of view by scholars and practitioners, these voices form a dialectic that produce one product: *development*. My analysis of hierarchy and grassroots is an attempt to frame the development apparatus, but it certainly is not the whole picture. Although they are opposing development models, each partakes of the other's discourse resulting in a clashing of political wills in the effort to represent their discourse as "the way" to develop. Their opposition is implicit in their texts: The hierarchical voice claims that its strength lies in working from the top down, and the grassroots voice likewise claims that to work from the bottom up is best. Underlying both discourses, however, is the same premise that development is needed for social change. They form a larger development community that creates a discursive space that seeks to act on and within another culture, creating and recreating, shaping and dominating.

Hierarchy

Dominant discursive practices create the identity of impoverished populations with scientific objectifying language, and construct policy as the great enabler, the conduit to success, growth, and happiness. The deconstruction of hierarchical development discourse reveals how its power and authority scripts agencies and their agents. A Foucauldian application reverses the statement, *persons make statements* to, *statements make persons* (Shapiro, 1981). If applied to development policy discourse, this translates as: "rather than policy capturing a developmental initiative or intervention, policy is made the captive of a discursive intervention" (Apthorpe, 1986). Tens of thousands of development "experts" construct their professional identities from this discourse. Describing its boundaries is one way of defining dominant identity and a way to shed light on its power strategies.

The language of the hierarchical voice is codified to be understandable to those agents within its field. Its practices include labeling through which it directs and controls populations, and positivism, the Western, scientific, rational ideology: If it can't be measured, it isn't development (cf. Ferguson, 1990; Hettne, 1990, Tordoff, 1984) This positivism drives the gathering of measurable data as evidence of absolute truth, includes such indicators as gross national product, literacy rates, life expectancy at birth, and per capita income. Positivism is an "ends–means approach" that has a specific agenda in development practice (Kalyalya , Mhlanga, Seidman, & Semboja, 1988). Kalyalya et al. described it as the following:

> It identifies ends with values, about which people may debate, but which publicly available data cannot serve to validate. At the end of the day, this approach tends to take values and even institutional structures as reflecting "society's" goals. . . . It must leave intact the basic institutional behaviors and attitudes of society, although these are often interwoven into and sustain the fabric of underdevelopment. (p. 29)

Terry Lovell (1980) subsumed positivism under "empiricism," which seeks to process knowledge as a "matter of careful, objective recording of empirical regularities" (p. 11). To positivists, what *is* is what can be known; it is a language of observation. This obsession with so-called facts objectifies and depersonalizes the populations of developing countries. Thus, "people are treated as objects to be studied rather than as subjects of their own development; there is therefore a separation between the research and the object of research, and between understanding and action" (Edwards, 1989, p. 118). In this light, development discourse can be seen as a kind of imperialism, a gathering of information to define an institution in order to maintain power.

The World Bank annually publishes *The World Development Report* (*WDR*), which is known as a handbook for development work (or "The Bible") in nonformal circles. It advertises "comprehensive, up-to-date data on social and economic development in more than 180 countries and territories" (World Bank, 1990). The discourse published in the *WDR* is indicative of a development policy that objectifies populations and personifies policy, and ultimately constructs an identity of the nations it works within. Supporters of this discourse will argue that hierarchical structures are efficient ways of distributing wealth, but at what price? Language practices reveal ways in which this voice imposes Western values on and thus controls the populations it seeks to "aid." The use of this codified language negates the people in impoverished regions, the "beneficiaries" of development, by not including them in conversation.

Hierarchical discourse creates policies that will only apply to certain created identities such as "small farmer," "landless," "refugee" (cf. Horesh, 1985; Mueller, 1987; von Fremd, 1990; Wood, 1985). Thus, if a farmer needs a loan or other aid, he or she will have to fit into specifically defined categories. These labels reveal more about development planners, their "authoritative designation, agenda-setting and so on," than about the labeled themselves (Wood, 1985, p. 353). In order to counteract such hegemonic processes, we must ask who is doing the labeling and for what purpose. By bringing in the "realities" and desires of the local people, an effective de-labeling can occur.

Southall (1988) cited the World Bank as "the standard bearer of development organizations" (p. 2). "[T]hey are *quite honest*," he claimed, examining their charter, discovering that they explicitly state they wish to encourage "an adequate volume of capital flow, and to give those abroad reasonable assurance of the safety of their funds" (p. 2). In other words, the World Bank seeks to keep developing countries healthy to secure their investment, for, as Bank President Robert MacNamara pointed out, "economic backwardness breeds violence . . . without development there is no security" (Southall, 1988, p. 3). Poverty, then, is the illness or interloper the World Bank seeks to cure or eliminate. Indeed, MacNamara constructs poverty as an enemy, one that "breeds violence" threatening development "security." Thus, the Bank's discourse is a mode of representation that not only constructs outside presence as instructional and paternalistic but heroic, and in the process constructs identities of both "domestic selves and exotic others" (Shapiro, 1988, p. 90). The poor are now the students/children and victims to outside teachers/parents or saviors.

The 1990 *WDR* issue, dedicated explicitly to poverty, is a discursive document, constructing in great detail a Western image of poverty in developing countries. It constructs the Bank as container of knowledge that will enable it to attend to poor people's production capacity, describing them as "rarely self-sufficient" (World Bank, 1990, p. 33). By way of offering support to the poor, the World Bank personifies its policy: It will "lift" the poor out of poverty, and "strive" to raise productivity levels, "spur" growth, and "enable the poor to participate in growth". Poverty is described as a place that people "move in and out of" with distinct lines and absolutes (p. 35). Thus, Bank policy disguises intention with euphemism and masks of caring, and at the same time distances impoverished populations through objectification.

In his discussion of policy labeling, Wood (1985) called the process of constructing case studies, "de-linking" or "the separation of people from their 'story' . . ." (p. 355). He stated, "Government programmes [sic] transform *people* into objects—as recipients, applicants, claimants, clients, or even participants" (p. 355). A person's identity is manipulated to represent the "poor." Time, in effect, is abolished as identities enlarge to "fit" a mythical emblem. Labeling once again becomes integral to the dominant's attempt to *remain* dominant, the story of the marginalized, once told, is told back to them. Wood summed up the de-linking process, how it is used by development policy and its relation to the poor with the following statements:

The process of de-linking represents poverty as a series of degraded labels, involving pathologies and deviance which can be isolated and responded to without the huge political and ideological costs of changing relationships and deeper structures. In the "Western". . . social policy field, this is the ideological or "explanatory" context for programmes of positive discrimination. (Wood, 1985, p. 358)

The World Bank introduces its construction of the poor in Chapter 2 of the 1990 *WDR*: "What Do We Know About the Poor?" Three "case studies"—"poor families"—are selected as representations based on 10 years of household surveys. The following story is an example of these case studies:

A Poor Subsistence Farmer's Household in Ghana

In Ghana's Savannah region a typical family of seven lives in three one-room huts made from mud bricks, with earthen floors. They have little furniture and no toilet, electricity, or running water. Water is obtained from a stream a fifteen-minute walk away. The family has few possessions, apart from three acres of unirrigated land and one cow, and virtually no savings. The family raises sorghum, vegetables, and groundnuts on its land. At peak periods of tilling, sowing, and harvesting, all family members are involved, including the husband's parents, who are sixty and seventy years old. The soil is very low in quality, but the family lacks access to fertilizer and other modern inputs. Moreover, the region is susceptible to drought; the rains fail two years out of every five. The market town where the husband sells their meager cash crop and buys essentials is five miles away and is reached by dirt tracks and an unsealed road that is washed away every time the rains come. None of the older family members ever attended school, but the eight-year-old son is now in the first grade. The family hopes that he will be able to stay in school, although there is pressure to keep him at home to help with the farm in the busy periods. He and his two younger sisters have never seen a doctor. (World Bank, 1990, p. 24)

This short story reveals the values of the World Bank and its power as storyteller. The values represented are primarily Western: material goods, indoor plumbing, technology, "modern inputs," infrastructure, education, and medicine. These values are indicative of the experiences of possession and convenience of human life in a country (and culture) like the United States. A Ghanian might describe life differently through concepts of well-being or wealth on a local scale. In addition, life in Ghana is different depending on region. The Bank's lack of attention to historical, local, and relative detail is an example of how discourse of a dominant group can define the identity of a marginalized one.

Said (1993) also made this point when discussing imperialistic attitudes and the reactions of those in the recipient, exploited cultures. This most often manifests in foreign (and internal) criticism of countries that cannot seem to manage after all that was given to them during decolonization. A prevailing attitude is: "Why don't they appreciate us, after what we did for them!" (Said, 1993, p. 22). I have heard this echoed in the voices of Westerners who question my interest in living and working in Africa. One man went so far as to tell me that the new found country of Zimbabwe was "ruined" by African rule. He told me something like, "We gave it to them and look at what they've done with it . . . ruined it! It used to be a beautiful country." Said (1993) stated, "Dismissed or forgotten were the ravaged colonial peoples who for centuries endured summary justice, unending economic oppression, distortion of their social intimate lives, and a recourseless submission that was the function of the unchanging European superiority" (p. 23). One only has to look so far as the slave trade to think of one, single, monstrous atrocity visited on the continent of Africa, as well as the exploitive acts of colonization.

In a greater storytelling act, the Bank confines the history of the poor to the last 25 years, stating: "If history is to guide future policy toward poverty, it is important to be as accurate as possible about *what actually happened*" (World Bank, 1990, p. 39). The *WDR* then describes the "progress" of the impoverished since 1960 based on "indicators such as consumption per capita, life expectancy, and educational attainment" (World Bank, 1990, p. 39). What is not included are the political, social, and cultural histories of new nations like those within Africa, thereby ignoring critical historical events like colonization. The history of these nations reveals the toll taken by outside influence and domination when African countries like Ghana, having been colonized, were developed by exploitation. Infrastructure was intertwined with colonial need for export product. Thus, the economy was not geared to support the indigenous population. Consequently, the economy suffers in the postcolonial period. The Bank, by describing conditions of life in Ghana as natural—"an unsealed road" or "unirrigated land"—and not a product of certain experiences much of it caused by outsiders is denying history.

There is no question that there is much suffering in countries that do not have adequate resources to support its population. This is not a critique to halt aid to those who need it. Contact between aid giver and receiver is the site of the transfer of power. Where is the locus of control? This is where the rhetoric of "participation" enters the discourse, a domain much talked about by progenitors of grassroots development activities.

Grassroots

Grassroots discourse constructs a dialect around intervention in the name of development that asks the question: Who is development for? Any national or international intervention may fall short of its goals; often aid "does not help the hungry as it is supposed to, it only strengthens the powerful" (Ferguson, 1990, pp. 11–12). Grassroots interventions are often done so by and for "the people." When included in Western discourse, this kind of intervention is often called a *participatory approach* because it seeks to involve the local populations in the planning and implementing of programs for social change. This is not always the case, however. First, I present one position of grassroots-level discourse that centers on the participatory approach known as participatory research, then describe how it often fails to achieve its goals.[7] Second, I describe the discourse of one grassroots-level organization, Oxfam U.K., and present discursive evidence from its primary document, *The Field Director's Handbook* (1985) (Pratt & Boyden, 1985). Oxfam takes an oppositional stance to hierarchical development organizations, criticizing them for their topdown interventions that, we have seen, are imperialist in nature. Even though Oxfam's programs advocate social change by challenging oppression they remain within the boundaries of development discourse by advocating this change through "development." Finally, I present a case study of an Oxfam pilot program. Although less explicit about domination through development than the hierarchical voice, the grassroots voice (from a Western perspective) is perhaps the more dangerous of the two because it couches its discourse in the rhetoric of struggles for freedom and liberation.

People's participation in development is the discursive banner of grassroots development organizations. Nyerere (1973), former president of Tanzania and a major proponent of its social programs after independence, is perhaps the most famous advocate for people's involvement. He stated, "People cannot be developed, they can only develop themselves" (p. 60) Korten (1983), one of the well-known Western advocates of grassroots-level interventions idealizes the participatory approach, as in the following quote:

> Go to the people
> Live among the people
> Learn from the people
> Plan with the people

---

[7]This presentation is necessarily a narrow singular one. There are many views of grassroots development discourse including communist, feminist, socialist, nonpartisan, Gandhian, ecologically oriented, politically oriented discourses just to name a few.

Work with the people
Start with what the people know
Build on what the people have
Teach by showing; learn by doing
Not a showcase but a pattern
Not odds and ends but a system
Not piecemeal but integrated approach
Not to conform but to transform
Not relief but release. (p. 210)[8]

By stressing a participatory ideology, grassroots discourse seeks to oppose hierarchical forms of development (Korten & Klauss, 1984). In the mid-1970s, development specialists began to realize that their development programs were not working, and alternative methods were explored such as popular participation in the self-development planning and execution of development activities at the village level (Rogers, 1976). The participatory approach has the aim of bridging the gap between the research/extension worker and the indigenous people involved in a project. The ideal is to form a cooperative of inquiry between the two. Theoretically, the participatory approach adopts a political position that assumes a dissatisfaction with the current existing social order. Grassroots organizations have a history of being politically critical of local power structures, hence the notion of being "for the people" instead of "for the system" within a power struggle. Participatory ideology focuses on the needs of "the people," and how to bring about social change at their level instead of being manipulated by a central organization.

The principles of participatory ideology are seen in the body of research known as participatory research (PR). In a personal reflection, B. Hall (1981) described PR as "an integrated activity that combines social investigation, educational work, and action" (p. 7). One of its central premises is to strengthen the indigenous people's awareness of their own abilities, allowing them to delineate which cultural elements are their own and which have been imposed on them (Vio Grossi, 1981, p. 5). The production of knowledge is considered the core issue of PR because it sees knowledge as power, asserting that the "common people" must have control over the process of knowing—thereby inserting a political agenda that calls for a democratic process of bringing people together as a collective allied by the researcher. As a methodology, PR utilizes a qualitative and phenomenological approach. This approach assumes the following: (a) the process of knowing is linked to action, (b) this process is initiated in the context of those not in power with a focus

[8]Korten cited Yen, the founder of the Rural Reconstruction Movement in China, as the originator of this creed.

on what *they* want to change, (c) local people participate equally in the activities of knowing and acting, and (d) the control of the process must be in local hands. It is interpersonal; collective in nature, especially the analysis of any research done; and educatively experiential for all involved (Tandon, 1981).

The rhetoric that surrounds a participatory ideology includes the idea of *empowerment*. In *Approaches to Participation in Rural Development*, Oakley and Marsden (1984) defined *empowerment* as "the sharing of power and of scarce resources; deliberate efforts by social groups to control their own destinies and improve their living conditions; opening up opportunities from below" (p. 26). By definition, the process of empowering people would threaten controlling groups. Therefore, empowering the poorest class, or simply, those with the fewest resources is a dramatic idea, one that would turn the tables of local power. As a result, actual participation of local poor in social change rarely happens because it would mean political change as well.

Participation as a methodology is problematic if programs still focus on development. In fact, principles of participation break down at the moment of inclusion within development discourse because participants are participating in a dominant modality. Participation then becomes an insidious domination tactic. Although participatory ideology within development discourse seeks to define development in terms of social change and community empowerment, placing value on nontangible ideals like equality and freedom, it becomes a way to "lubricate" outside involvement (McCall, 1987). In his working paper on indigenous technology, McCall stated that: "Concepts like Local Level Development (LLD) and People's participation (PP) or bottom-up planning are becoming as much rhetoric as democracy or development. As with those words, governments can use them as a legitimizing smokescreen in the political arena with no intention of putting any but the most self-serving into effect" (p. 1).

Frequently, the role of participation in development often means that projects are designed outside the local area by *outsiders* (a classification for individuals not from the local community), and implemented through local power structures. McCall noted "participation" in the past has meant that the poorest of the poor were relegated to labor tasks and given little or no opportunity for input, neither in planning nor in implementation of a project. Current trends in participation include the local poor people's assessment of their needs.

In a recent document, Paul (1989) wrote of the World Bank experience with community participation. Within the Bank's conceptual framework, Paul stressed the role of "beneficiaries," which implies a passive role for local populations. To make matters worse, however, he described how these populations can be "made" to participate. He stated that: "In the context of a development project, beneficiaries, as individuals, can be made to participate in many ways. Their needs and preferences can be made to share in the project costs individually through a government order" (p. 2).

Furthermore, he described the standard participatory style of the World Bank, or community participation (CP) as occurring in different stages: reconnaissance, the stage during which outsiders gather information on the community; identification, where the beneficiaries needs are assessed; preparation, when the community is consulted on its role in the project; and implementation of the project. Decision-making power is never offered to "the people" except to decide what their role might be in an already designed program. Unfortunately, many projects that are described as participatory by both hierarchical and grassroots organizations follow this same pattern.

In contrast, there are organizations that identify the power structures within local communities and are aware of how their presence serves to create new power struggles in the name of development. I suggest that these organizations are problematic because they still cling to the notion of development as a driving force for intervention. Oxfam is one such organization. It operates on the belief that development will not occur if imposed from "the top" but must move from the "bottom upward."

Oxfam is remarkably different from the bulk of nongovernmental organizations (NGOs). It is decentralized, with offices located all over the globe, and it is primarily volunteer staffed, covering expenses with private donations instead of existing off government contracts. Unlike some NGOs, Oxfam designs its programs with local input, maintaining specific objectives. These include "raising people's consciousness, increasing solidarity and creating organizations through which the impoverished and marginalized groups within society can build a more secure, less oppressed base from which to challenge established privilege" (Pratt & Boyden, 1985, p. 16). If Oxfam truly achieved these objectives, its own presence would be challenged, yet it maintains its role in the "development" process as one of "partner" (Pratt & Boyden, 1985, p. 15).

Although grassroots discourse as represented by Oxfam may appear at first like the answer to problems of objectification posed by the hierarchical voice, it disguises oppression with this partnership. In Oxfam's words, it "exists to serve the people, not to promote an ideology or development model" (Pratt & Boyden, 1985, p. 14). Yet, to simply utilize the word *development* in discursive practice is ideologically grounded. "Seeing" development as part of the solution to oppression is not the answer.

Oxfam's discursive practices are elusive, however. Authors of documents almost always claim autonomy. Disclaimers appear at the bottom of articles by Oxfam staff stating that the ideas within are solely of the author and not representative of Oxfam. The only document I was able to find that represented Oxfam's policy statements was the *Field Director's Handbook: An Oxfam Manual for Development Workers.*[9] In its self-interpretation, Oxfam states that it "believes in the essential dignity of people and their capacity to overcome the problems and pressures which can crush or exploit them" (Pratt & Boyden, 1985, p. 11). Would this then include development as explored here? Oxfam sees itself as the "provider" for people all over the world with "the opportunity of playing a small part in the struggle to eliminate poverty and to help humankind develop in a spirit of partnership" (Pratt & Boyden, 1985, p. 11). Although Oxfam states it does not promote models of development, is not promoting itself as "provider" a model? In addition, Oxfam's policy is to fund local people as the "experts," seeking "to influence the process of development in such a way that the poorest are able to take charge of their lives" (Pratt & Boyden, 1985, p. 13). Oxfam is also a proponent of the participatory approach, stating that it "places strong emphasis on the need for social awareness, the identification of people and their common problems and goals" (Pratt & Boyden, 1985, p. 16).

Yet, Oxfam operates as if *development* is a universal concept. The discourse centers on development as a valid practice, setting up power relationships between field agents and local populations. It delineates between different kinds of development with the term social development through which it seeks validation. Oxfam's discourse contrasts with World Bank discourse through this delineation. Under the section marked, "Strategies of Social Development," the handbook reads:

> To have any real impact on the development process the funding agency should not confine itself to supporting programmes with narrow economic objectives. The main aim must be the development of people, enabling them to lead fuller and more satisfying lives, rather than simply the delivery of material benefits. (Pratt & Boyden, 1985, p. 140)

Oxfam's discourse objectifies and distances through this description by implying how development can enable better lives, not the people themselves. This is an example of how local voices are left out of development discourse. True, Oxfam works within the community and does not impose project design on local populations similar to, for example, World Bank-funded hydroelectric dams. Its discourse is subtly controlling, however; it seeks to describe a population without its representation. Although it shies away from jargon like *target groups* or other codelike discourse as identified in the hierarchical mode, it still maintains distance

---

[9]Citations in this section refer to this text unless otherwise marked.

that will need to be collapsed. For example, Oxfam views itself as "part-ner" in the development of local communities yet nowhere in its hand-book is there a local voice or suggestion as to how to "develop." Giving local people discursive representation will collapse the distance and lessen the position of the dominant.

In my search for actual fieldwork done by Oxfam I found few examples of project design procedures. One document, *Aid and Development in Southern Africa* edited by Kalyalya, et al. (1988), pre-sents a study of an Oxfam-funded pilot project in southern Africa. The project stressed a procedure, Learning Process, designed by Korten (1980). The Learning Process aimed "to create the necessary framework within which the project members [local populations] step-by-step, could enhance their self-reliant capacity to assess and improve their own skills and resources to fit their needs" (Kalyalya et al., 1988, p. 19). It is con-trasted with what Korten called the "blueprint" approach to development, the planning of programs for communities without their involvement that is indicative of hierarchical practices. In his article "Community Organization and Rural Development: A Learning Process Approach," Korten (1980) defined the Learning Process:

> The key was not preplanning, but an organization with a capacity for embracing error, learning with people, and building new knowledge and institutional capacity through action. A model of the learning process approach to building program strategies and appropriate organizational competence suggests a new program should progress through developmental stages in which the focal concern is successively learning to be *effective*, learning to be *efficient*, and learning to *expand*. (p. 481)

Korten described relationships with marginalized populations from a Western perspective. Much of his presentation is problematic because it continues the paternalistic tone of development discourse, that is, "Given this interest [the learning process approach] we might expect the difficult problems of *how* to involve the rural poor in their own development . . ." (Korten, 1980, p. 481). Rural populations are already involved in their own growth patterns, but what Korten truly meant is how to involve rural populations in a Western plan for social change. Particularly reflective of Western rational thought are the key words Korten used to describe the learning approach: *effective*, *efficient*, and *expand*.

The pilot project goes into detail about how this model works on the ground. It describes the learning process as a "problem-solving" methodology with a range of steps that are too lengthy to describe and analyze here. Basically, the model is designed to bring outsiders and local populations together to analyze the current status of local efforts for social change. By bringing national researchers, donor representatives, and local project members together, the processes within the project are evaluated from three different perspectives. The authors stated:

> Viewed in this way, the Learning Process constitutes more than an insightful "window" on the project for the donor agency. It contributes to the creation of new decision-making structures which empower project members to deal more effectively with their environment. *That, after all, is what aid is all about.* (Kalyalya et al., 1988, pp. 36-37, italics added).

The text describes locally designed projects, not impositions from outside, and thus has a few saving graces. Projects to be included for the pilot project were picked by southern Africans, not Westerners. This process is described in detail with attention to Oxfam's role as facilitator, not as organizer. In addition, the results of this project were not entirely flattering to outside involvement in southern Africa. With the recording of these results, Oxfam prints a self-critique.

Western grassroots discourse is written as a counter discourse to hierarchical discourse, but this is not entirely the case. Although it touts a participatory approach, it utilizes participation as a subtle means of control. Many grassroots organizations attempt to break away from standard development models they call the "blueprint" model and project themselves onto the side of "the people," fighting "the system" of dominant control. Nevertheless, their continuing representation of development discourse binds them to a dominant group. Oxfam is an example of such an organization that represents itself as a partner of marginalized populations while simultaneously denying them discursive space. This co-habitation of partnership and domination is characteristic of some grassroots discourse.

In her provocative essay, "An Open Letter to a Young Researcher," Adrian Adams (1979) included all the elements I presented here regarding the ways Western development interacts with a particular African culture. Adams' rhetorical strategy is to write a letter to a young development researcher who wants to come visit her while she is living in Jamaane, a rural village in Senegal. It is the story of outside involvement with the village containing historical information in brackets as factual evidence interspersed with interviews with Jamaane villagers so that readers will interpret the events as "real."

The story begins with one villager, Amara, who goes to Paris to buy a motorpump. There he meets representatives of development organizations who offer to help him. He happily agrees, and arrangements are made for Francois, an agricultural technician, to move with him to his village, Jamaane. The village accepts him and with great ceremony, makes a place for him among themselves. In time, however, the technician is lured away by an organization that offers him more money and a house in the city. Insulted, the villagers recover only to be approached by increasingly more organizations with the words, "We want to help." The villagers try to work with them but find they are not listened to. Instead, they watch with mounting horror as they are not involved in the changes instigated by outsiders in their village. Adams ends her story with blatant disgust for the development process. Of development, she says:

> [F]or development to take place, Jamaane must be destroyed (March 1975). As Amara put it: "They don't know that there are live people here." . . . The idea of "development" incarnate in the policies mediated by experts or dormant in the dreams of would-be counter experts, generates career opportunities for Europeans; but it means a negation of Jamaane. It is an idea which cannot be useful, since it has no adequate basis in reality: for Jamaane exists. (Adams, 1979, pp. 476–477)

Adams also leveled her critique at the critics of development, the proponents of the argument that Europeans have caused all the problems within Africa because they have created a dependency. The way in which development agents and development critics are alike, she said, "is that neither is able to acknowledge the existence of Jamaane here and now, having a past and a future because it is alive today" (p. 477). Neither do academic disciplines escape her critical eye, for they, too deny the presence of Jamaane. And of herself, Adams stated that her critique (although justifiable) has done nothing but "create, alongside the activities of development experts a body of ideas which cannot embody themselves in action, and so proliferate in helpless symbiosis with that which they criticize" (Adam, 1979, p. 475). Her conclusion is that still, "Jamaane exists."

Adams' ending is where we must begin—with what exists. Writing texts about Africa from the comfort of a Western lifestyle, whether an office in some Western country, or expatriate home in an African capital city with a guard, chauffeur, and cook, reinscribes the subjugation process. In the field, African realities are different.

In Senegal where, ironically, I was posted as a communications officer for a private research organization from 1992 to 1994, Adams' voice lingers, especially the refrain from the villagers of Jamaane: "They don't know that people live here." In my experience, African interpretation of development differs from those development texts I read in preparation for my work. The Senegalese are very aware of their history, and the roles they play not only within their family and local community, but in Africa and the world. I habitually ask Senegalese what they think of development. In one recent encounter, a young man eloquently recounted several dimensions of development's role in Africa. He explained that there is the dimension where development is beneficial to both the "developed" and the "underdeveloped" (*sous developé*), implying that both sides gain assets whether income or other. Yet another dimension as he interpreted it is never mentioned in text books: Simply, Western nations "develop" Africa so that Africans will not come to their countries. "They want us to stay here," he explained.

Still other Africans have explained to me that certain individuals, and therefore the groups that are connected to them (ethnic and familial) benefit directly from development projects by using Western money for their own purposes. They suggest that Western corporations are aware of this, and even budget it in to their investments. One of my colleagues was openly courted by an Italian construction company to covertly offer powerful individuals in African nations money to influence them in support of the company's capitalistic intentions. "This," he said to me, emphatically, "is 'development.'"

When I meet other Westerners working in Africa, or in "development," I sometimes question them about their motivation. It has become a way for me to interrogate myself, essentially. One critical thinker in the field justifies his continuing work by saying, "We need to change from within." A good friend, now a policy advisor at the U.S. Agency for International Development, is also critical of "development," and falls back on the idiom that change needs to occur from within. She defines herself as having "ambition with integrity." Another colleague flatly tells me that it is his "love with difference" that motivates him to do development work, like so many Westerners (both real and fictional) who have gone to Africa.

Like Adams, I feel frustrated that theory is difficult to apply in practice. These African voices are all to easily relegated to those discontented groups who did not receive the aid they wanted, or some such argument. Could development change from its current, dominant presentation as a benevolent force that, in some cases (not all), has become a cloak over otherwise shady or discriminatory actions? And what of the needy, the dying, the starving, the sick that are a part of everyday life, but most evident in places where there are not enough resources to go around? They cry out for "development." "We are the underdeveloped here," the Senegalese explain to me when something goes wrong. Time and again, I come back to the voice of a South African who appealed to me to continue my work: "Please," she said, "we need all the help we can get," and the Senegalese filmmaker who, when I told him that Africans need to help Africans, responded, "One drowning man cannot help another."

I have become aware of my own conditioning, of how I "see" the world. It is difficult to break those habits that culture inscribes in the individual. A comparison of African and U.S. values is beyond the scope of this chapter, but it is equally important for "development agents" to be aware of the sets of rules each society scripts for itself and its citizens; actions have a social, historical context for each individual. "Development," as a Western institution, can be interpreted as an attempt to deny the identity of an impoverished other. It encourages a kind of fetishism—"the means by which otherness is acknowledged and simultaneously negated" (Modelski, in press, p. 274). Development policy—hierarchical and grassroots—constructs a certain image of populations in regions like Africa. So long as there is "development" there needs to be "undevelopment," or "underdevelopment," thus perpetuating a never ending cycle. There are many villages around the world like Jamaane containing populations caught in development's discursive practices.

Identity, Knowledge and Power

There is an emerging body of literature on indigenous knowledge systems that describe the expertise of local peoples with and without Western intervention (cf. Brokensha, 1980; McCall, 1987; Richards, 1987; Sharland, 1989; Warren, Brokemsha, & Slikkerveer, 1991; Warren, Slikkerveer, & Titilola, 1989). This final section describes this body of literature. I will then use this analysis as a springboard to shape the space for local voices within the field of social change. Like Adams, I argue that these local practices exist, despite development, and are proving to work in fields such as agriculture not only as successes, but often to counteract damage done to local lands in development's name. Many of these discursive texts available are often written by Westerners about indigenous practice, however, reinscribing the domination of the West in development discourse in this "new" kind of literature. Ideally, local knowledge should stand on its own with a distinctive space in the field of social change. The question remains how to create that space. Warren, director of the Center for Indigenous Knowledge and Research on Development, offers a definition for indigenous knowledge (IK):

> Indigenous knowledge (IK) is "local knowledge"—knowledge that is unique to a given culture or society. This knowledge is the information base for a society. Codified in the language of the society, it facilitates communication and decision making. Indigenous knowledge is dynamic; it changes through indigenous creativity and innovativeness as well through contact with other knowledge systems. (Richards, 1987, p. 1)

Within the discourse on social change, IK systems center around adaptations for survival such as agriculture and health. Examples of IK systems include technical and aesthetic knowledge with regard to such activities as agriculture, medicine, and education. For example, a well-known indigenous technique helped Indonesia during the aftermath of an outside agricultural intervention failure ("Local Heroes," 1991). An agricultural program concerning rice hybrids developed through outside intervention required a lot of fertilizer. It turned out that this fertilizer was expensive and engendered the breeding of a new pest that summarily destroyed the rice crop. Indonesia's economy was devastated. With the help of local farmers, the cash crop was replanted and is maintained by pest management, an indigenous system that depends on pest's natural feeding systems to control damaging pest invasion. The national university now offers a course in pest management and encourages local villagers to participate.

My research in IK focuses on communication. Briefly, I explored how popular theater can engender a dialogue between agents of social change and the public in rural areas of impoverished regions. The technique involves outside agents and local people in a dialogic inquiry into problems within the community. It draws from the pedagogy of Freire and his colleague, Boal (1974), contending the need for recognition of oppression. Freire's (1970) notions of "liberation through education" lead to a kind of consciousness raising called "conscientization" to stimulate social change. Oral and interactive communication methods are familiar to the cultures of many rural populations in regions populated by development programs. Often, these programs depend on printed materials or one-way communication techniques to get a point across. In principle, the dialogical method of theatre allows outside facilitators with material resources and local villagers with needs to meet and discuss problems and their solutions. Unfortunately, this is not always the case (cf. Desai, 1990). This form is often co-opted by dominate agencies as rhetorical tools. The point is that the two-way nature of this process has the potential for dialogue between outside and local agents of social change rather than the one-way imposition of projects of development organizations.

In their essay, "Applied Ethnoscience and Dialogical Communication in Rural Development," Warren and Meehan (1980) draw on Freire's experiments in literacy to present a dialogical approach to rural development. For Warren and Meehan, local knowledge becomes "ethnoscience, the formal description of knowledge systems from the indigenous—as opposed to the outsider's—perspective" (p. 321). Furthermore, they stated that the "ethnoscientific understanding can be used in rural development programming to increase agents' sensitivity to local needs, facilitate meaningful dialogue, and, in this way, provide a mechanism by which small scale agriculturalists can become involved in the development process" (p. 322).

Utilization of local knowledge is one of the first steps in a participatory approach that seeks to build the self-confidence of local people. McCall (1987) stressed that local knowledge, like pest management described earlier is the first resource needed for social change because it engenders self-confidence. He stated, "The argument behind [indigenous knowledge systems] is that the active processes of indigenous research, and release of the active processes of inherent knowledge, themselves provide the initial self-belief and 'confidence' needed to counter the culture of poverty and lead to some form of self-development" (McCall, 1987, p. 12). In his dissertation on the Kpelle of Liberia, Thomasson (1987) presented an outline for "reconceptualizing" development based on Kpelle way of life. He contended that the Kpelle were:

> Both a developed and a developing people up until the time that forces beyond their control (rule by men with relatively more "modern" armaments, and the "invisible hand" of the world economic system) denied them self-control over their own socio-cultural change. From that moment of conquest, alienation, exploitation and expropriation of labor, land and other resources by outsiders began a process which, to redefine a term, I shall call "undevelopment" among the Kpelle. (Thomasson, 1987, p. 23)

Such a view turns development discourse on its head by suggesting that local people were already "developed" and then were subsequently "undeveloped" by outsider intervention. What the Kpelle, and other indigenous peoples within impoverished areas lack is money and the respect of the powerful within the global milieux. Scientists have been known to be grateful that indigenous people do not have access to resources such as writing and Western analytic skills. For example, one agricultural technician, thinking he had made a break through in cassava research, arrived in Nigeria where the plant had been introduced to discover that local farmers were way ahead of him. He reportedly said, "Thank God these farmers don't write scientific papers" (Howes & Chambers, 1980, p. 331). This example suggests that it is in "modern" scientific interest to keep local knowledge out of discursive circles. McCall (1987) reiterated this theme:

> The concept of "local knowledge" is not new to outsiders; but despite the collection of local knowledge on farming systems, very little of it is taken up into development interventions. The reasons for the deliberate neglect need deeper examination—in brief, they are part racist, part gender-biased, partly the ideology of superior western science, partly the dominance of positivism in science, partly social ideologies of submission to mandarins and gurus. (p. 6)

IK systems are formal ways that the West classifies local knowledge. It has the potential of becoming a bridge between outsiders who wish to encourage social change in impoverished areas because it utilizes local resources and mobilizes local populations. The use of such knowledge boosts the confidences of local people and contributes to planning programs for change. Inclusion of local knowledge within planning programs by outsiders involves a forfeit of power that does not always occur. Sadly, the development institution is discovering the importance of IK four decades after its incipience during the Truman era. What does this reveal about the Western point of view? Could we not turn our gaze inward to observe ourselves and conclude that one of our cultural practices is to dominate others?

In an effort to bring this analysis to conclusion, I present a possible process that includes local voices in the needs assessment and process for social change. It has four parts: (a) desire for change must come from within; (b) if outsiders are involved, they must privilege local knowledge; (c) planning and implementation of social change must be done by local populations supported by donor organizations; and (d) discursive texts that describe these activities are written by local people, or at least in their voice. Creating space that will counter dominant ideology demands an alternative discursive practice.

Local populations must initiate social change processes. Outsiders cannot go into communities and tell them what they need. Local people know their own needs, they just need the opportunity to express them and be heard, not glanced over. This becomes problematic when local power structures are vying for power. Those who supply material resources need to be aware of how local organizations communicate, and how outside intervention often strengthens the local elite and further weakens the marginalized.

If approached by impoverished populations for aid, outsiders must look within the community for resources and privilege local knowledge as the first source. Local knowledge biases might prevent certain aspects of change, however. For example, in many African countries (mainly those that are influenced by the Muslim religion), women are often not included in the planning of changes in labor intensive areas like agriculture even though they may do up to 80% of the work. Outsiders and sympathetic local people will have to do consciousness-raising efforts to change these biases but do so slowly with tangible examples. More than likely there are already local groups lobbying for such change.

Planning should always be a dialogue between local communities and funders. There is a fundamental problem with how development policy portrays itself as the enabler when local people are the major factor for change. Focusing on this third function will increase the self-confidence of local populations, especially the confidence in their own identity. Their knowledge is deeply imbedded in cultural practices that reflect their experiences.

Finally, local voices need to be made a part of the discursive practices for social change. I have presented the varying voices within a discourse on development and how each purports to represent methods of social change for the impoverished. Each discourse, however, is a Western voice in a Western concept. Written texts by representatives from Africa, Latin America, Asia, and other marginal populations need to be supported and circulated. Techniques that will include local voices involve an ethnographic methodology, if the participants be nonliterate. Recording devices and direct translation are necessary but problematic. Power structures are easily built between outsiders and local populations that can influence discursive constructions.

Continuing study of ways to create discursive space for marginal audiences is necessary. The rise in cultural studies as a discipline is representative of such a need. The key point to the importance of supporting local knowledge as a discursive practice is that, for once, it acts as an educating tool for dominant cultures; it raises their consciousness. A program that supports this effort will be like the social programs outsiders instigate within local communities to inform them about social change only in the reverse.

CONCLUSION

Writing counter discourses is a political act, one that reveals how human realities are constructed by writing practices. With his writings on sexuality, insanity, and the prison system, Foucault showed that this process of "referring not to things but how they have been made, has a demystifying effect on our current understanding" (Shapiro, 1988, p. 4). This level of understanding cannot be reached unless we seek to identify linguistic practices, particularly the policy statements of governing or dominant institutions, and reveal the ideologies behind them. If we accept the given reality, we fall into the trap of "misreading" thereby blinding ourselves to the powers that bind us. Shapiro (1988) stated, "In general, the misreading involved in one's succumbing to ideological thought is a failure to discern the power and authority effects which are part of the scripting of seemingly politically innocent objects, forms of subjectivity, actions, and events" (p. 21). He further stated that not recognizing the politicization of "ingrained forms of power and authority" is to not recognize its boundaries (p. 49). By presenting two of the discourses within development discourse that are dialectically but not ideologically opposed, I have sought to describe its boundaries with the hope that this knowledge will politicize readers and activate them to cross over their borders.

I think back to the woman I spoke of at the beginning of this chapter and wonder where she is now. Could she know that my encounter with her would turn my gaze inward? Since that time, I have had many encounters that would cause me to interrogate my motives, which have, in turn, led me to question others about what "development" is. Sometimes I would find myself in heated discussions. One such time has stayed with me, and I have incorporated remarks said—perhaps the most critical and judgmental of all—into the collection of voices inside of me. A young philosophy teacher in Senegal, deeply nationalistic and defensive, once told me that my work in family planning was essentially oppression of his people. I responded by saying that I saw my role as helping women make choices about their lives and that really the society itself promoted oppression. His response rings in my ears; he said, "Our youth (*notre jeunesse*) is what is important. We have our own ways (*nos propres méthods*) of planning families, and we need to teach them that, not some outsider. You (*vous, les Occidentales*) are the problem."

As I walk through the halls of my current employment, still working as a development agent, the words, *notre jeunesse*, often repeat. As I look inside, I have mixed feelings about my own role in "development." This chapter is the product of such a gaze. Now back in my own country, I am receiving training to do local health work. After more than a decade of being dedicated to improving quality of life in Africa, the transition has not been easy. Potential new employers look at me askance and question whether or not I can really make the change. I have learned, however, that Westerners can change their roles vis-a-vis other cultures by accepting the challenge to carry within a relentless self-critique and the courage to act against, or better yet, to write against the grain of dominant discourses.

REFERENCES

Adams, A. (1979). An open letter to a young researcher. *African Affairs* *78*(313), 453–479.

Apthorpe, R. (1984). Agriculture and strategies: The language of development policy. In E. J. Clay & B. B. Schaffer (Eds.), *Room for manoeuvre: An exploring of public policy planning in agriculture and rural development* (pp. 127-141). Rutherford, NJ: Fairleigh Dickinson University Press.

Apthorpe, R. (1986). Development policy discourse. *Public Administration and Development, 6*, 377-389.

Ashley, R. (1987). The geopolitics of geopolitical space: Toward a critical social theory of international politics, *Alternatives, 12*(4), 403-434.

Boal, A. (1974). *Theatre of the oppressed*. New York: Urizen.

Bourdieu, P. (1977). *Outline of a theory of practice* (R. Nice, trans.). Cambridge: Cambridge University Press.

Brokensha, D., Warren, D.M., & Warren, O. (Eds.). (1980). *Indigenous knowledge systems and development*. Lanham: University Press of America.

Certeau, M. de. (1984). *The practice of everyday life*. Berkeley: University of California Press.

Clarke, J. et al. (1981). Subcultures, cultures and class. In T. Bennett et al. (Eds.), *Culture, ideology and social process: A reader* (pp. 53-80). London: Billing.

Clifford, J. (1986). Introduction: Partial truths. In J. Clifford & G. E. Marcus (Eds.), *Writing culture: The poetics and politics of ethnography* (pp. 1-26). Berkeley: University of California Press.

Clifford, J., & Marcus, G. E. (Eds.). (1986). *Writing culture: The poetics and politics of ethnography*. Berkeley: University of California Press.

Desai, G. (1990). Theatre as praxis: Discursive strategies in African popular theatre. *African Studies Review, 33*(1), 65-92.

Edwards, M. (1989). The irrelevance of development studies. *Third World Quarterly, 11*(1), 116-35.

Escobar, A. (1985). Discourse and power in development: Michel Foucault and the relevance of his work to the Third World. *Alternatives, 10*, 377-400.

Escobar, A. (1987). *Power and visibility: The invention and management of development in the Third World*. Unpublished doctoral dissertation, University of California, Berkeley.

Esteva, G. (1991) Preventing green redevelopment. *Development, 2*, 74-78.

Ferguson, J. (1990). *The anti-politics machine: "Development," depoliticization, and bureaucratic power in Lesotho*. Cambridge: Cambridge University Press.

Foucault, M. (1972). *The archeology of knowledge and the discourse on language* (A. M. Sheridan Smith, trans.). New York: Pantheon.

Foucault, M. (1980) *Power/knowledge: Selected interviews and other writings 1972–1977* (C. Gordon, ed.; Colin Gordon et al., trans.). Brighton, Sussex: The Harvester.

Foucault, M. (1990). *The history of sexuality* (R. Hurley, trans.). New York: Vintage.

Freire, P. (1970) *Pedagogy of the oppressed*. New York: Continuum.

Gifondorwa, D. S. (1981). *Adult education and rural development: A study of participatory planning as an alternative approach to adult education and rural development in less developed countries*. Unpublished doctoral dissertation, Syracuse University, Syracuse, NY.

Gramsci, A. (1971). *Selection from the prison notebooks*. New York: Internationalist.

Hall, B. L. (1981). Participatory research, popular knowledge and power: A personal reflection. *Convergence, 14*(3),16-17.

Hettne, B. (1990) *Development theory and the three worlds*. Harlow, Essex: Longman Scientific and Technical.

hooks, b. (1990) *Yearning: Race, gender, and cultural politics*. Boston: South End.

Horesh, E. (1985) Labelling and the language of international development. *Development and Change, 16*(3), 503-514.

Kalyalya, D., Mhlanga, K., Seidman, A., & Semboja, J. (Eds.). (1988). *Aid and development in southern Africa: Evaluating a participatory learning process*. Trenton, NJ: Africa World.

Korten, D. (1980). Community organization and rural development: A learning process approach. *Public Administration Review, 40*, 480-504.

Korten, D. (1983). Social development: Putting people first. In D. C. Korten & F. B. Alfonso (Eds.), *Bureaucracy and the poor*. West Hartford, CT: Kumarian.

Korten, D., & Klauss, R. (Eds.). (1984). *People-centered development: Contributions toward theory and planning frameworks*. West Hartford, CT: Kumarian.

Kuhn, A. (1985). *The power of the image: Essays on representation and sexuality*. New York: Routledge.

Local Heroes, Global Change. (1991). (film) World Development Productions.

Lovell, T. (1980). *Pictures of reality: Aesthetics, politics and pleasure*. London: British Film Institute.

McCall, M. (1987). *Indigenous knowledge systems as the basis for participation: East African potentials*. Enschede, Netherlands: University of Twente.

Mudimbe, V. Y. (1988). *The invention of Africa: Gnosis, philosophy, and the order of knowledge*. Bloomington: Indiana University Press.

Mudimbe, V. Y. (1994). *The idea of Africa*. Bloomington & Indianapolis: Indiana University Press.

Mueller, A. (1987). *The "Discovery" of women in development: The case of women in Peru*. Paper presented at the annual Meeting of Comparative and International Education Society, Washington, DC.

Nyerere, J. (1973). *Freedom and development*. Oxford: Oxford University Press.

Oakely, P., & Marsden, D. (1984). *Approaches to participation in rural development*. Geneva: ILO for ACC Task Force on Rural Development.

O'Neil, H. (1984). HICs, MICs, NICs, and LICs: Some elements in the political economy of graduation and differentiation. *World Development, 12*(7), 693-712.

Paul, S. (1989). *Community participation in development projects: The World Bank Experience* (World Bank Discussion Paper No. 6). Washington, DC: The World Bank.

Pratt, B., & Boyden, J. (Eds.). (1985). *The field directors' handbook: An Oxfam manual for development workers.* Oxford: Oxford University Press.

Raulet, G. (1983). Structuralism and post-structuralism: An interview with Michel Foucault. *Telos, 55*, 195-211.

Richards, P. (1987). *Indigenous knowledge systems for agriculture and rural development: The CIKARD inaugural lectures.* Ames: Iowa State University, Technology and Social Change Program.

Rogers, E. M. (1976). Communication and development: The passing of the dominant paradigm. *Communication Research, 3*(2), 213-240.

Said, E. W. (1979). *Orientalism.* New York: Vintage.

Said, E. W. (1993) *Culture and imperialism.* New York: Knopf.

Said, E. W., & Barsamian, D. (1994). *The pen and the sword: Conversations with David Barsamian.* Monroe: Common Courage.

Shapiro, M. J. (1981). *Language and political understanding: The politics of discursive practices.* New Haven: Yale University Press.

Shapiro. M. J. (1988). *The politics of representation: Writing practices in biography, photography, and policy analysis.* Madison: University of Wisconsin Press.

Sharland, R.W. (1989). *Indigenous knowledge and technological change in subsistence society: Lessons from the Moru of Sudan.* London: ODI, Agricultural Adminstration Unit.

Southall, A. (1988). "The rain fell on its own:" The Alur theory of development and its western counterparts. *African Studies Review, 31*(2), 1-15.

Stamp, P. (1989). *Technology, gender, and power in Africa.* Ottawa: International Development Research Centre.

Tandon, R. (1981). Participatory research in the empowerment of people. *Convergence, 14*(3), 20-29.

Thomasson, G. (1987). *Indigenous knowledge systems, sciences, and technologies: Ethnographic and ethnohistorical perspectives on the educational foundation for development in Kpelle culture.* Unpublished doctoral dissertation, Cornell University, Ithaca, NY.

Tordoff, W. (1984). *Government and politics in Africa.* Bloomington: Indiana University.

Vio Grossi, F. (1981). Socio-political implications of participatory research. *Convergence, 14*(3),43-50.

Von Fremd, Sarah E. (1990). Interpreting refugees' lives: The power and performance of labeling. In *A cultural lexicon: Words in the social* (Working Paper Series No. 2). Evanston, IL: Northwestern University, Center for Interdisciplinary Research in the Arts.

Warren, D. M., Brokensha, D., &Slikkerveer, L. J. (1991). *Indigenous knowledge systems: The cultural dimension of development.* London: Kegan Paul.

Warren, D. M., & Meehan, P. (1980). Applied ethnoscience and a dialogical approach to rural development. In D. Brokensha, D. M. Warren, & O. Warren (Eds.), *Indigenous knowledge systems and development.* Lanham, MD: University Press of America.

Warren, D. M., Slikkerveer, L. J., & Titilola, S. O. (Eds.). (1989). *Indigenous knowledge systems: Implications for agriculture and international development.* Ames: Iowa State University & the Academy for Educational Development, Technology and Social Change Program.

Williams, R. (1983). *Keywords: A vocabulary of culture and society.* New York: Oxford University Press.

Wood, G. (1985). The politics of development policy labelling. *Development and Change, 16*(3), 347-373.

World Bank. (1990). *World Development Report 1990: Poverty.* Oxford: Oxford University.

2

Problems of Social Participation in "Latin" America in the Age of Globalization: Theoretical and Case-Based Considerations for Practitioners and Researchers

Daniel Mato
Universidad Central de Venezuela

In this chapter I present a discussion on current problems and perspectives of social participation in "Latin" America. To evaluate those problems and perspectives requires placing them in the context of the ongoing globalization process, otherwise any conclusion would be built on the unrealistic assumption that contemporary societies or communities constitute bounded isolated units. It also requires an exploration of the relations between social participation and the social processes of identity-making and agenda-setting, because—to say it in a very reductive way—only those collectivities who exist as social actors and have their own social or political agendas can really participate. Those other collectivities who do not constitute themselves as social actors can only contribute to or resist the implementation of socially constituted and recognized actors' proposals.

The discussion of some theoretical, historical, and contextual elements as well as of some reports of local participation experiences and indigenous peoples leaders' statements serve as a basis for drawing some conclusions I hope will awaken researchers' and practitioners' interest. Although discussing the name of the region is not my objective here, a reflection on its historical and current implications is a fruitful way to begin this analysis. But first a few preliminary matters must be clearly set up.

Currently, research in the field is affected by two complementary problems. On the one hand there is the unreflected stretching of old categories to include new phenomena and/or old phenomena that have recently acquired more salience from the perspectives of new theoretical developments. On the other, it is saturated by the introduction of too many new categories whose meanings remain loose. Therefore, I begin by making clear the meanings that a few key categories have in this chapter. I use the expression *global agents* as a general and heterogeneous category that includes a wide variety of agents who develop worldwide, or at least potentially worldwide practices, practices that regularly involve the developing of international or transnational relations. If *international relations* is the name usually given to those relations maintained between governments (or their agencies), invoking the nation-states they are supposed to represent in the so-called international system, then *transnational* must be the name given to those relations deployed across nation-state borders among two or more social subjects when at least one subject is not an agent of a government or intergovernmental organization.[1]

The importance of this distinction is that it will aid in being able to more properly discuss particular cases. For example, according to these definitions, certain global agents are only capable of maintaining transnational relations (because they themselves are nongovernmental), whereas others can maintain either transnational or international relations (because they are governmental, the inter- or transcharacter of these relations would depend on the character of other involved agents). Intergovernmental agencies (like those of the United Nations and similar regional systems), foreign governmental cooperation agencies (like those of the United States, Japan, and western Europe), and multilateral banking, are global agents who maintain both international and transnational relations. Thus, as a general denomination they must be called global agents; one may use the more particular expression *international* or *transnational agent* only when referring to a particular situation in

---

[1]This is not only my criterion, but one that has already gained other supporters (e.g., Keohane & Nye, 1971; Stack, 1981). I have more extensively discussed these denominations in other writings (Mato, 1993, 1995, 1996a, 1996b, 1998a).

which the agency in question is engaged in one of the two possible kinds of relations, which depends on the character of the other agents with which it is involved. On the other hand, large non-govermental organizations (NGOs) and private foundations that usually act beyond the borders of the nation-states where they have been originated only can maintain transnational relations, thus they might be called either *global agents* or, more specifically, *transnational agents*, but never international agents. The Ford Foundation, as an example, is not an international foundation but a transnational one. Finally, transnational corporations (it does not matter whether they are dedicated to mass communications or to any other kind of business) are also transnational agents, and thus, for example, when a government negotiates with any of them the kind of relation established is transnational, not international. There is nothing particularly wrong or right in being a transnational or an international actor, but these differentiated denominations may help identify significant differences on a case-by-case basis, particularly when trying to analyze actors' balances of power, and how and by whom their agendas and behaviors are shaped.[2]

This chapter attempts to offer to both researchers and practitioners some perspectives on social participation. Most governments and some global agents often assume that they, or the "experts" they hire, should teach communities and local leadership how to participate, or that their "ready-to-use" models for participation incorporated in their projects must be followed by the "beneficiaries" of their practices. I argue, however, that experience demonstrates that they themselves need to improve their participatory capabilities, and particularly to be open to learning from those they attempt to teach. This, of course, does not mean that local communities and leadership do not need to learn certain skills that may help them participate in more advantageous ways. Nor, of course, does this imply that researchers do not need to learn lots of things from both sides. I return to these questions at the end of this chapter.

"LATIN" AMERICA?

The term *Latin America* is loaded. The word *Latin* in this name recalls a long-term process of social construction of identities and differences and still serves as a subtle legitimating device in the present system of exclusion of large groups in this geopolitical region. So-called *Latinoamericanismo* has been seen as a nationalism building a quasi-continental "nation," and its roots—not the expression itself—date to the

---

[2]I have discussed a research-based typology of global and local agents in a recent article (see Mato, 1997).

period of the anticolonial movements.[3] At that time, White and mestizo elites began building new nation-states on the system of exclusions of the colonial period. Those elites assumed that they, not the so-called indios, nor the imported African slaves and their descendants, were "the people." The alliances developed during the quasi-continental anticolonial war were the origin of the interdependent making of official national identities and the interstate-crafted representations of what began to be called Latin American culture.

Those historical processes of identity or difference making have set up the broad coordinates of the regional system of inclusions and exclusions within which more recent and more specific processes of identity-difference making and social participation have taken place, and are still going on. Today, this interdependent system of representations still legitimizes social inequity, cultural discrimination, and economic disadvantage to certain peoples and social groups throughout the region, preventing democratic participation and stimulating social conflicts. This hegemonic system particularly—but not only—affects those indigenous peoples who still try to maintain relatively independent socioeconomic systems. It also affects different social groups originating in the peasantization, proletarization, and more recent "economic informalization" of social groups constituted by mestizos and by the descendants of freed African slaves, of "integrated" indigenous peoples, and of lower class European migrants.

In constructing a "Latin" American identity, states' policies and practices regarding those excluded peoples and social groups have not been totally homogeneous. They have varied with countries' peculiarities and with historical circumstances. Even in the same country and period they have differed according to different constructions of ethnic, racial, and class identities of both these populations and the ruling groups of the larger societies of which they form part. Nevertheless, in one way or another, the participation of these peoples and social groups has been completely cut off or at least severely hindered not only in national public spheres and political systems, but also in regional (subnational) and local ones as well as in the decision making, planning, and managing of activities related to their most elemental concerns (e.g., production, environment, health, housing, and education). Since the origin of the "modern" states, the political and functional organizations of these peoples and social groups have been openly repressed, ignored, or targeted by the respective states with the aim of controlling them, or at least of

---

[3]The expression *Latin America* did not exist in the lexicon of those anticolonial movements. The idea of Latinness and its application as an adjective to this region was first crafted by the French intellectual Michel Chevalier in 1836. "Latin America" as a composed name first appeared in writing in a book by the Colombian intellectual José María Torres Caicedo in 1865 (Ardao, 1980).

developing clientelistic relations with them. There have unfortunately been too few exceptions to these state practices to take them into account in making this generalizing statement.

In response to both those long-term issues and the problems and opportunities that the present period of the globalization process entails for them, functional and political organizations of these excluded peoples and social groups are increasingly engaging not only in building translocal and transnational networks for mutual support among themselves but also in developing transnational relations with "global" agents. These different kinds of transnational relations affect, in diverse ways, the social processes through which identity-difference representations and associated agendas are continuously made. These processes are part of the current "age of globalization," are meaningfully interconnected with other ongoing transnational phenomena, and therefore must be analyzed in the context of these interconnections, and not as if they were isolated phenomena.

THE GLOBAL CONTEXT

I present two contextualizing statements that help when discussing some current problems and perspectives on social participation in "Latin" America, particularly insofar as problems are considered to be isolated at the local level.

My first contextualizing statement is as follows: In the present age of globalization it does not make much sense to analyze so-called local issues without taking into account the complex web of relations that nowadays interlink the local, regional (subnational), national, and global levels.

The former statement should not need epistemological justification because these levels exist only as analytical categories; that is, they do not exist by themselves. This is not the opportunity to develop an epistemological discussion about these analytical levels and the relationship between their existence and the territorial and nation-state constraints of our imagination, an issue that is at the center of some ongoing debates in anthropology (e.g., Ferguson & Gupta, 1992). It seems, however, necessary to discuss some characteristics of the ongoing age of globalization that are particularly relevant to understanding why developing such an interconnected approach is imperative and how to do so. The globalization process is longstanding phenomena, but it has greatly accelerated and become increasingly complex in recent years. I use the expression *age of globalization* to emphasize the growing cultural and political relevance of the worldwide interplays among peoples, their cultures, and institutions; the growing political salience of transnational networking activities among diverse social agencies; and the relatively recent and unequally developed worldwide consciousness of the process of globalization.

The globalization process is not merely the transnational organization of production and markets and related political and economic agreements and institutions, as economists and corporate managers usually assume, although these are very important elements of this process. Neither is this process merely a communicative phenomenon, as some communication specialists often assume, although the enlargement and densifying of mass and data communication flows are also very important features of this process. It is a process through which the whole planet is increasingly becoming a space of multidimensional crisscrossed relations among a variety of social agents. This process not only involves those major economic and communicational phenomena that affect human activities at any analytical level and also in dimensions that are not just economic or communicational. It also involves other phenomena that are particularly relevant to analyzing so-called local issues. For example, apart from those broad economic aspects directly related to the practices of states apparatuses and transnational corporations, the present age of globalization involves other "economic" phenomena that are less visible (but highly significant for "local" communities, and sometimes even for regional and national societies and economies), like so-called eco- and cultural- tourism, ethno-music production and trade, and the production of handicrafts, and organic coffee, cacao, and other environmentally and socially sound products that are usually promoted and traded by so-called alternative trade organizations. In addition, the globalization process also involves the enlargement and diversification of migration movements (for economic as well as political reasons, if one can separate them); new transnational networks (not just electronic) of diverse kinds of social agents; the global politicization of ethnicity, race, human rights, gender, and ecological concerns; and the conscious management of all these phenomena for sociopolitical purposes.[4]

In relation to these global phenomena, significant changes are taking place in the making of identities, related social movements, and associated social, economic, and political agendas at local, national, regional, and global levels, as well as in the interrelations among these (analytical) levels. Such changes should cause no surprise if we assume that cultures and identities are not frozen products. They are continuously produced in the social life and are the subject of confrontations and negotiations among social agents. We must also be aware that these cultural processes take place not in imaginary closed and isolated societies but in actual social spaces that are internationally and transnationally interconnected. Previously, I illustrated through some case studies (Mato, 1993, 1994, 1995, 1996a, 1998a, 1998b) that current social

---

[4]I have discussed these issues in a more detailed way in other publications (see Mato, 1995, 1996b).

processes of making of identities and associated social, economic and political agendas are shaped by the practices of a variety of social agents and related translocal and transnational networks, such as local, ethnic, and other kinds of grassroots organizations, intermediary NGOs, state agencies, and what I call *global agents.*

The present age of globalization also involves the consolidation of a worldwide political system organized in so-called nation-states. As we already know, this system is not free from conflicts and contradictions. It fosters ethnic and racial conflicts everywhere by uniformly imposing so-called national identities and repressing internal differentiation. Besides, national governments open national territories to the activities of corporations and a variety of global agents, and to the regulations and influence of international agreements and institutions. Nevertheless, for all its limits and contradictions, and whatever we may speculate about its ongoing transformation, the system of so-called nation-states is the way the world is politically organized at present. This organizing principle gives "national" ruling groups the exclusive right to control the populations within their state borders, although that right is conditional on the actual game of international relations. This organizing principle, jointly with the nationalist ideologies, creates and reproduces the illusion of extended homogeneous communities that supposedly share common national interests. It is, however, significant that in the age of globalization the processes of constructing these communities and the associated systems of representation of peoplehood take place not in imaginary closed and isolated societies, but—as I said before—in actual social spaces internationally and transnationally interconnected. As a result of this, local, regional, and national governments, and a large variety of global agents, constantly cooperate, dispute, and negotiate in the name of—and for the political and economic allegiances—"local" communities, and particularly of those presented as poor or ethnically differentiated.

My second contextualizing statement is as follows. If in the present age of globalization it is not very meaningful to study "local" issues without taking into account the complex web of relations that interlink the local, regional, national, and global levels, then the study of so-called "popular," "social," or "community" participation experiences at "local" levels is even less meaningful, unless we place these experiences within the framework of this complex web of relations among social agents.

The reason that studying "local" participation requires, more than any other local issue, a translevel analysis is that "participation" has become a critical keyword in the discourses of NGOs, national governments, and global agents everywhere, and—although usually in controversial ways—even in their practices. Moreover, numerous studies of local participation experiences, as well as current discussions within specialized organizations, allow us to realize that these participatory experiences are the site of conflicts and negotiations involving not only the practices of local, regional, and national agents, but also of global ones. Most prominent among those agents are local/ethnic leadership and local NGOs (which, of course, should not be simplistically taken for homogeneously imagined local communities); state/provincial, regional, and/or national level NGOs, ruling groups, state bureaucracies, political parties, and global agents. In any case, the point is that it seems naive to discuss problems and perspectives of local participation as if they were just local phenomena, or even local phenomena within national boundaries, when we are aware of the existence and importance of these transnational relations as well as of the international linkages held by local and national state agencies.

A SHORT CONCEPTUAL COMMENT

There is no single, generally accepted definition of participation. Rather, this notion is the subject of diverse and contested meanings. Part of the problem here could be of course attributed to the fact that I have not yet specified the kind of participation experiences about which I am discussing. I have said that I am interested in "local" participation, but this does not seem to be a sufficient delimitation of the question. Am I talking about so-called citizen participation, understood as the participation of the citizens in the political system? And, if this is the case, am I talking about local participation in the local political system, or in the state or national ones? Or am I talking about participation in development programs? Or about participation in rural development, or in health programs, or in educational programs? But we must be careful, because to define limits in those ways could be problematic. By placing those kinds of limits, we would be taking as a foundational reference of our analysis the very vocabulary that the institutional discourses of diverse agencies have coined; and, therefore, we risk the danger of being trapped in the ideological web that informs that vocabulary. As some of the testimonies and case examples reported in the final pages of this chapter illustrate, it is frequently difficult, if not frustrating, and sometimes even risky, to exercise participation in just one sector or functionally isolated compartment of a given society.

Nevertheless, and as a way to make more manageable the communication of these reflections, we can arbitrarily reduce their scope to certain fields of participation experiences, like those currently denominated "participation in development programs" (usually assumed as merely "economic") and "participation in social development." These are still two large connected fields about which we can find abundant literature and current experiences everywhere. But even limiting in this way the subject of our interest, we will have no more success in finding a clear and uncontested definition of participation. On the contrary, the notion is the subject of diverse and contested meanings (e.g., Bhatnagar & Williams, 1992; Green, 1986; Stiefel & Wolfe, 1994), and that important debate about how participatory are our own research methodologies is going on, as Servaes (1989) has clearly pointed out.

Some authors have used various adjectives to establish differentiations. Some talk about *community participation*, whereas others use the expression *social participation*, and still others prefer to talk about *popular participation*, or about *grassroots participation*. Nevertheless, depending on the authors compared, these different terms sometimes have very similar meanings, and, on the other hand, it is also possible to show how the same term has different meanings for different authors. Although advancing in the analysis of competitive definitions could be important, it is not the purpose of this chapter. Instead, I assume the current disputes as an indicator of the profound disagreements that are characteristic of this matter, which in turn I assume to be a consequence of its conflictual character.

In any case, and at least within the limits of our arbitrarily reduced universe of development and social development, it would seem possible to present a minimal proposition that might be acceptable to most specialists. It would seem acceptable to state that social participation involves people taking part in social experiences; but still the meaning and scope of this participation would remain a matter of debate.

It is necessary to avoid superficial consensus and to differentiate between two basic kinds of participation. One would be constituted by those experiences in which the individuals or social agents who take the initiative to participate are at the same time those who constitute what in the vocabulary of governments, NGOs, and global agents, is called a *beneficiary group*, and in which only they and not any other kind of social agent participate in the experience. These kinds of experiences are also named *self-management* (in Spanish we use the word *autogestión*). The second kind of participation would correspond to those cases in which not all the individuals or social agents involved belong to the beneficiary group. Within this second category we can still differentiate between two subcases. The first would be the subcase in which the initiative for and the control of the program come from within the beneficiary group. This kind of participation is called bottom–up participation. The second would be the subcase in which the program is promoted by a participant who does not belong to the "beneficiary" group, a kind of program that usually is not controlled by the "beneficiary" group. This sub-case is called top-down participation. In these examples, the external agent could be an agency of the local, provincial/state, or national government, a local, regional, national, or international NGO, a foreign-government development agency, a church or religious agency, and so on. Reality is, of course, always more complicated than any classification, and complex, or combined, or shifting, situations abound; for example, there are many experiences that begin as bottom–up and shift to top–down, or vice versa, or that begin as self-managed and shift to top–down, and so forth.

CURRENT PROBLEMS AND PERSPECTIVES IN "LATIN" AMERICA

In "Latin" America, and even within the limits of our arbitrarily reduced universe of development and social development programs, there is a long history of experiences of the kind that could be conceptualized as *self-management*, although not incidentally they are not very much taken into account when experts debate participation. Diverse forms of cooperative work are part of the cultural practices that contemporary lower class "Latin" Americans have elaborated through the traditionalization of older American, African, and European forms—which, of course, does not mean their unchanged preservation, but their continuous transformation over centuries (e.g., the *minga*, etc). I illustrate the case of self-management with two general "urban-modern" cases, without discussing to what extent they may or may not incorporate those so-called old traditional practices.

I first call attention to the existence of the diverse kinds of grass-roots organizational forms that make possible the functioning of the so-called informal economy. Second, I highlight that the founding, defense, and development of the thousands of slums throughout "Latin" America are also products of self-managed participatory processes. These participatory experiences include at least the selection of and often planned invasion of terrains and the housing construction process. These actions are carried out not only without the participation of government agencies, but even against the will of some of these agencies, and usually without any assistance from any external agent. Once the first step is taken (invasion and housing construction), new opportunities for participation become available in the struggles for the legal recognition of the slum as a neighborhood, the provision of water, electricity, health, and education services. The poor quality of these services does not matter at this point. What is significant is that people must organize themselves and participate in decision making, the elaboration of proposals, political lobbying, and direct action to achieve their goals. Another significant outcome of these experiences is that they provide renewed opportunities for people acquiring experience in social participation and political struggle.

I do not like to romanticize these kinds of experiences, which I do not think are satisfactory solutions, but remedial ones. Nevertheless, anyone who doubts the capacity of the so-called poor of Latin America to organize by themselves in response to their problems, even in the most unfavorable conditions, must look at this eloquent reality. Yet most of these experiences remain largely ignored by specialists in the field, and when approaching "local" communities to "offer" their assistance, most external agents do not take into account this kind of local knowledge, or local cultural capital. And what is even worse, most of them even assume that they have to teach "local" communities how to participate. As the history of experiences in which one or more external agents participate tends to demonstrate, those who more often need to learn how to participate are not the so-called beneficiary groups, but governments and, NGOs, technical cooperation and donor agencies, and, of course, researchers and practitioners.

In "Latin" America, the history of experiences in which one or more external agents participate is relatively more limited and recent than the self-managed ones. The rest of this chapter, however, focuses on this kind of participation experiences because of both their growing relevance in present times and my purpose of pointing out what those external agents should learn. My primary interest here is to highlight some problems associated with the roles played by states; and the roles played by other external agents are only a secondary interest. In order to present a broader picture of these problems, I choose not to present a detailed discussion of one case, but a brief panorama of diverse recent experiences in "Latin" America.

SOME EXAMPLES AT THE REGIONAL LEVEL

A Regional Workshop on Community Participation, Sanitary Education and Personal Hygiene was held in Lima in 1990 under the sponsorship of the German technical cooperation agency (GTZ) and the Pan American Health Organization. Representatives of governmental agencies, NGOs, health professionals, community leaders, and other concerned people from six South American countries and the Dominican Republic participated in the workshop. The final report of the workshop contains some remarks useful to reproduce here. Among the main obstacles to community participation, the report points out the following two: (a) the political, institutional, technical, and organizational manipulation that obstructs the involvement of the population in planning processes; and (b) the absence of institutionalized participation in Latin American countries that have been subjugated by authoritarian governments and dictatorships characterized by strong centralization of power, and in which public participation and social organization forms and practices are not respected (*Primer Taller Regional sobre Participación Comunitaria, Educación Sanitaria e Higiene Personal*, 1990). The report also makes some recommendations. It emphasizes that for social participation to be effective it must be conceived and institutionalized at nationally integrated levels and not solely as sectoral programs, and that social participation programs should involve not only the poorest sectors of society but all the social agents that are responsible for the development of public services: politicians, technicians, communicators, entrepreneurs, universities, users, and so on. (*Primer Taller Regional sobre Participación Comunitaria, Educación Sanitaria e Higiene Personal*, 1990).

A recent discussion of community participation in malaria, dengue, and Chagas' disease vector control experiences in eight Latin American countries concludes that

> "participation" should be optimized in the government, the private sector and among community residents simultaneously. . . . Government participation cannot be assumed. . . . Vector control programmes in ministries of health will . . . need to develop the use of different channels of communication and methods for decentralizing planning, decision-making and programme evaluation. Perhaps of more importance, governments must learn how to respond quickly and appropriately to legitimate community concerns. If this is not done, people may conclude that there is no point in their participation. (Winch, Kendall, & Gubler, 1992, p. 349)

SOME EXAMPLES AT THE INDIVIDUAL COUNTRY LEVEL

Chile

A recent publication offers the results of research carried out by a Chilean NGO with the sponsorship of the Pan American Health Organization, the Ford Foundation, and the Inter-American Foundation. The authors pointed out that although social participation is one of the main elements of the governmental democratization strategy, there is still a significant gap between theory and practice, and that legal regulations and organizational mechanisms must be developed to ensure social participation in health. They emphasized that the good international reputation of social participation and the technical consensus regarding its value have not been positively echoed by the political will, which seems to be afraid of technical knowledge, the role of uneducated people, and the government's inability to satisfy health service demands (CORSAPS, 1991).

Peru

A report based on the study of community participation in health experiences in 34 locations (many of them sponsored by transnational agencies) states "Community health committees that in many cases have been organized on Ministry of Health insistence, as a way of stimulating community participation, have been superimposed on existing community leadership organizations that subsequently refuse to cooperate with them," and concludes that "effective community participation simply cannot be imposed from above; it must arise from within the community" (Davidson & Stein, 1988, p. 68).

Nicaragua

In the name of the strengthening of the democratization process, the post-Sandinista Nicaraguan government is demanding that the whole society participate. To that end, it proposes that social participation in the local integrated health care systems (SILAIS) must be institutionalized, and that communities, NGOs, and other sectors of the society must share responsibilities in planning, management, and control of health services (Malo, 1992). NGOs also assume they must play an important role in the process of democratization, participating and promoting organization and participation of the civil society. Nevertheless, well-informed observers state that most SILAIS officers have maintained a vertical and strictly utilitarian relationship with other social actors, calling on them only for special campaigns, but impeding their participation in processes of negotiated planning. It is also pointed out that the economic contributions of the communities and NGOs to primary health care activities are often under recorded (Malo, 1992).

Honduras

Among other important difficulties for maintaining community participation in health programs, a recent field research report points out the following: local governments' opposition to the participation of community organizations in the management of local systems, government agencies' incapacity to satisfy the increasing social demands, political inter-

ference, and communities' fear of having their organizational efforts mis-
interpreted by the authorities (Reyes, 1993).

Panama

Community participation through organized health committees was
implemented in Panama in 1969 by the military government as an
attempt to gain mass support. By 1984, 15 years after its implementation, the majority of health committees were inoperative. Among other
relevant reasons for difficulties an extensive report pointed out that the
ministry

> receives little information from the field in terms of community health
> problems and institutional operations. In contrast to the early years
> of the program, health officials infrequently visit communities,
> inspect facilities or attend health committee meetings. . . . There are
> ongoing conflicts between doctors and medical directors on one
> side, and public health officials and the health committees on the
> other. (La Forgia, 1985, p. 61)

Political interference has also hindered the functioning of health committees: "Such interference generally takes the form of gaining control of a
committee's directorship or denying the right to carry out activities"
(1985, p. 61).

Mexico

Mexican democracy's shortcomings and lack of legitimacy have recently
become internationally notorious, but these are old problems in this
country. In 1988, President Salinas de Gortari's administration launched
a program that an analyst suggestively termed a "neopopulist solution to
neoliberal problems" (Dresser, 1991). The program, called PRONASOL,
National Solidarity Program, is an umbrella organization aimed at developing health, education, nutrition, housing, and other projects for 17 mil-
lion Mexicans living in so-called extreme poverty (Dresser, 1991).
PRONASOL is a so-called compensatory program to the International
Monetary Found-advised structural economic adjustment program.
According to specialists on the matter, "PRONASOL has awakened
great expectations about improved living standards, popular involvement
in decision making, and a truly participatory form of development"
(Dresser, 1991, p. 3). Salinas' PRONASOL staff recorded the popular
demands made during the president's weekly tours of the countryside,

then local PRONASOL committees design projects, in collaboration with government staff, to address these demands (Dresser, 1991). PRONA-SOL authorities state that "Salinas efforts are popular, not populist, because citizens participate in constructing public works, supervise their execution, and assure transparency in the use of resources" (cited in Dresser, 1991, p. 10). According to the same analyst of the program,

> instead of establishing top-down bureaucratic structures, the program aims to build on representative local organizations. . . . This emphasis on community participation can be explained in part by the government's drive to enhance PRONASOL's accountability and effectiveness. However, popular participation in solving community problems also functions to generate political support for government-sponsored development programs, and consequently for the political system itself. (Dresser, 1991, p. 9)

The same analyst states that there exist about 50,000 solidarity committees and that "through their emphasis on concertation, participatory frameworks . . . and community-based leadership, PRONASOL programs create a sense of inclusion and serve as agencies through which popular groups can express their demands" (Dresser, 1991, p. 26). "PRONASOL emphasizes identifying 'natural leaders' in popular communities, but frequently those leaders turn out to be *priistas* [supporters of the government party] . . . who use their influence to create solidarity committees . . ." (Dresser, 1991, p. 33).

PRONASOL has various sectoral subprograms through which it mobilizes its own budget, and also works with other government agencies. The Mexican Institute of Social Security runs a health program called IMSS–Solidaridad. More than 12,000 solidarity and health committees and almost 90,000 volunteer health promoters are involved in this program. The program publishes a series of books called *Testimonios de Solidaridad*, which are specially prepared for community volunteers and members of the health teams. It is useful to quote a few statements from these testimonies to understand the way in which the Mexican government manipulated social participation for its own agenda.

The president of a health and solidarity committee in Chiapas claims to speak in the name of the communities when giving thanks for the support of "our President of the Republic, through the participation of the state government" in solving the health problems of the communities (IMSS-Solidaridad, 1993, p. 27). It is necessary to take into account that Chiapas is the Mexican state in which a world-renowned Indian uprising began on January 1, 1994, and that among the main reasons given by those who rebelled were national and state government authoritarianism, corruption, and neglect of indigenous peoples' and poor peasants' concerns. The president of another committee, also in Chiapas (and more exactly in the same Sierra Madre that has been the center of the uprising), expresses his gratitude to "our governor," and interestingly adds: "I want to make a petition, not to the authorities, who are doing their work, but to my companions. I want to ask them not to wait for the authorities to visit our homes to do what we must do ourselves" (IMSS-Solidaridad, 1993, p. 28, my translation). Also from Chiapas, a rural midwife expressed her thanks to the president and the governor for the new hospital (IMSS-Solidaridad, 1993). Testimonies of this same sort can be multiplied. They constitute examples of political manipulation of peoples' needs and of blaming the victim.

Guatemala

A private voluntary agency initiated a health program in the department of Chimaltenango. The program focused on the selection, training, and use of village health workers who worked in their own communities of Cachikel Indians. The program was controlled by a board of Indians, and the health workers were chosen by their neighbors themselves. The philosophy of the program was holistic and it also promoted agricultural development activities, child health services, and the like. Many of the village health workers, as well as other local leaders, began to develop other agricultural development projects (Heggenhougen, 1984).

> At the end of the 1970s and during the first of the 1980s certain factions within Guatemala became increasingly concerned and threatened by these activities which seemed to improve the lot of the Indians . . . . Those villagers attempting to make changes were called unpatriotic, traitors and communists by those who benefited from maintaining a suppressed and dependent Indian population . . . . Paramilitary gangs from the towns invaded the countryside. Houses were destroyed. The incidence of torture and murder increased. The village health workers were some of those particularly sought out in their villages for reprisals. Many were killed . . . . They were far from being revolutionaries . . . they were not involved in aggressive actions . . . . But in attempting to make changes in their villages and become more independent and self-reliant they were seen as threatening the existing power structure. (Heggenhougen, 1984, p. 219)

A FEW EXAMPLES FROM THE INDIGENOUS PEOPLES

Most indigenous people's leaders usually present their problems in ways that illustrate both how governments and diverse external agents prevent them from having a protagonistic participation in projects and programs involving issues of their major concern, and how conscious they are of the significance of developing transnational relations. Let us consider some examples.

To begin with, Marcial Fabricano, the president of CIDOB, a federation in which 17 Indigenous Peoples from eastern Bolivia are represented, explained to me during a recent interview:

> . . . it is already time for us to live in true democracies in our countries, and for every human being to feel free, and to enjoy the rights that every human being is entitled to as a person. . . . . [The indigenous peoples] have always experienced a lack of opportunities. Because it is not acceptable that some people have more rights than others. . . . In Bolivia, for example, they pretend that the national constitution does not acknowledge us, and it does not entitle us to have a territory . . . . [But] this is a legitimate right. I am a Bolivian and I have the right to make use of my space, my territory . . . my natural resources . . . . We need a space because if we do not have such a space, where are we going to develop what we are as a people, with our own identity, with our own culture? Where are we going to develop it? (Fabricano, personal communication, July 1, 1994; author's translation)

But, as Fabricano pointed out, their participation not only confronts problems at the national level but also at the smaller development project level. In connection with this, he said that it is important for "genuine" organizations to create direct channels of communication with concerned organizations and governments abroad in order to provide guidance about the kind of cooperation needed, because of the existence of different kinds of intermediaries who often talk and receive money on behalf of indigenous peoples whom they do not represent. He said that this is not only the case of some NGOs, but also of some indigenous individuals who have lived in Europe and the United States for many years and have lost any connection with their communities of origin (Fabricano, personal communication, July 1, 1994).

Another example may be provided by the statements of Felipe Tsenkush, the general secretary of the Shuar-Achuar Federation from Ecuador, when I asked him about the reasons that the Federation had to send a delegation to participate in an event held in Washington, DC, He said, "to express to the people of the United States that we the indigenous peoples also have rights that must be acknowledged. We are struggling to make the United Nations recognize our rights, and the United States has power in this organization that may help us to gain this approval. The Latin American states do not respect our rights."

He explained to me that there is discrimination in Ecuador and that although the Constitution consecrates equality, it does not exist in practice, and added that in being in Washington, DC:

> we have the opportunity to present our problems to the governmental agencies and nongovernmental organizations in the United States, in order somehow to make our government aware of our claims. It is a way to press politically our national government. I say this because the only way that we have had to gain respect at home has been going to international agencies and organizations which, generally speaking, are controlled by the United States. We appeal to those international entities and they exert certain pressure on the government, which may lead it to solve some situations that infringe the indigenous peoples' rights. . . . This way of doing things has been very useful for us in the past. (Tsenkush, personal communication, July 3, 1994; author's translation)

In a way very similar to that of Fabricano, during a different interview, Tsenkush also stated that his organization was interested in maintaining direct relations with donor and technical cooperation agencies because the indigenous peoples of Latin America, were confronting serious problems with the activities of diverse intermediary agencies. He even said,

> We have sometimes called them [the intermediary agents] Indian traffickers, please excuse me if I have to talk in these terms. We have said it in this way in several occasions because they pretend to speak on behalf of the Indians, but this intermediation must disappear. We cannot continue accepting the existence of intermediaries. To have intermediation means that one depends on others, it implies that others perhaps consider us incapable. This [intermediation] must disappear. Because I think that we—many organizations— have already demonstrated managing capability, and the ability to carry out programs, and we think that they [donor and technical cooperation agencies] must work directly with us. . . . Because if these [intermediaries] exist they cannot forget their own interests . . . they must work for their own interests. (Tsenkush, personal communication, July 10, 1994; author's translation)

Due to space constraints, I cannot include more testimonies here, but I want to stress that the two cited here are not exceptional cases, but examples representative of many others I have collected in recent years.

These two examples, like many of the others, reflect problems regarding participation at both national and local levels, and some of them also provide clues about a relatively hidden but significant issue, the setting of agendas. The problems of agenda-setting in the relations between governments and global agents on the one hand and indigenous people's organizations or other grassroots organizations on the other are strikingly important in the present age of globalization. I do not have space to discuss these problems here, but they have been addressed in already published articles by some indigenous leaders from "Latin" America (e.g., Coc, 1989; Flores, 1989; Nugkuag, 1989). I have more extensively discussed the issue elsewhere (Mato, 1995, 1996a, 1998a). Of course, these problems are not exclusively "Latin" American and have been also been revealingly addressed for other world regions (e.g., Louw, 1993).

A FEW INCONCLUSIVE CONCLUSIONS AND MANY OPEN QUESTIONS

I know that it is possible to make a list of counterargumentative examples from positive experiences. Nevertheless, it seems that most people with practical experience in this field would agree that the panorama I present very much illustrates the most typical kinds of situations, and that in any case it is representative of the kinds of problems that more frequently affect participatory experiences. I hope my brief panorama can at least help increase understanding that external agents should learn how to participate themselves instead of "helping" poor or indigenous peoples either by teaching them how to participate, or by promoting "ready-to-use" participatory development programs conceived by outside "experts."

The most general conclusion can be drawn from reviewing the case reports and testimonies is that the roles of "Latin" American states regarding "local" and indigenous people's participation, even in those programs that states have recognized as legitimate or have even promoted, have been problematic. These cases clearly illustrate the ways in which "Latin" American governments have assumed social participation, or at least the gaps between their rhetoric and their practices. But governments are not the only problematic partner; local and national NGOs, diverse global agents, and researchers and practitioners also seem to be playing their roles in unsatisfactory ways.

As almost everybody involved in this field knows, "Latin" American governments have received abundant financial and technical support for participatory projects from foreign donor and technical cooperation agencies. Although part of this money has been used to pay international consultants and national bureaucracies, another part has served to finance the legitimation of inefficient political systems and of the ruling parties, and still another part has even been misused, or openly stolen by corrupt officers and politicians. As some of the examples presented here show, communities have received only what is left, and have paid a very high price for it, in terms of their own work and their own money and material resources, and even in terms of the lives of not a few of their members.

Facing this reality one must question what happens to the foreign donor and technical cooperation agency mandatory rules and project evaluations. Do their evaluations not show these problems? Who makes those evaluations, and how? And, in those cases in which these evaluations uncover these problems, why do they keep lending or giving in the same ways, through the same agencies, imposing the same project cycles and participation models designed by experts, even when there is evidence that these cycles and models prevent or constrain real participation? Why do they not find alternative mechanisms of lending/giving and evaluating? Are they exempt from responsibility for these problems? How far are they taking into account grassroots local/ethnic knowledge and agendas? How far are beneficiaries involved in programs' design, implementation, and evaluation? Do global agents know how to give beneficiaries a protagonistic role and take their knowledge and agendas into account? Do global agents really want to do so? Whose opinions have they consulted when they attempted to learn how to do so? Are there not certain vicious circles here?

What is the future of "local" participation in Latin America? Some analysts suggest that it would be better for the communities if we do not insist on implementing participatory programs (e.g., Ugalde, 1985). Nevertheless, many others state that social participation helps to improve the quality of life and the political power of relatively powerless groups in Latin America. What in any case seems to be more significant in practical terms is that the World Bank, the Inter-American Development Bank, the International Fund for Agricultural Development, the Pan-American Health Organization, several private large foundations, and many other significant global agencies do promote social participation in at least two ways: financing training and publications on the matter, and financing projects that require a participatory component. Most of this financial support is mainly conducted through governmental agencies at national, state, or municipal levels, a smaller part is conducted through local NGOs, and only an even smaller portion is directly handed to the so-called beneficiaries of the projects.

Many ongoing circumstances suggest that the time of "local" participation has not ended, and, furthermore, that it has a long future ahead. Among other circumstances, I mention:

1. The policies and programs of those global agencies.
2. The constant willingness of Latin American governments to use this money and capture its material and symbolic benefits.
3. The close association of participation with two other ideas of great symbolic power, democratization, and decentralization.
4. The application of the structural economic adjustment programs and two associated pressures they create: (a) the so-called shrinking of the states and the economic pressure for the decentralizing of state functions, and (b) the economic pressures that local communities and NGOs experience, which make them seek transnational economic relations and support.

Given these current trends, researchers and practitioners need to interrogate themselves and very particularly interrogate those who usually are assumed and proclaimed as beneficiaries of their practices: What could be done in these circumstances and in the context of the globalization process? What kinds of changes in practices as researchers and practitioners would be appropriate? I know these questions are too general, and that the need exists not only for specific ones, but also for some answers and practical suggestions, because there are compelling needs that do not allow us to paralyze ourselves by an over-questioning attitude. Elsewhere (Cerqueira & Mato, 1995), I proposed some practical guidelines for action and I dealt with some specific questions that have partially contributed to the preparation of those guidelines and that presently guide my own practice. Some of these may interest others.

Do the indigenous peoples and the so-called poor of "Latin" America (and other regions) benefit from our current orientation to producing knowledge about them from which not they themselves but only global agents, governments, university students, and other researchers and practitioners can benefit?

How could research and practitioner practices contribute to the valorization and promotion of every form of indigenous knowledge in projects' design and implementation? How could our practices contribute to the accomplishment of grassroots communities' and indigenous peoples' own agendas?

How could our research and project reports promote changes in the practices and agendas of diverse global agencies involved in participatory experiences? Are the behaviors of all these agencies alike? What kind of differences are relevant? Are their bureaucracies homogeneous bodies? What do we know about their organizational cultures? And more important, what do grassroots communities' and indigenous peoples' leaders know about these matters? How could our researcher and practitioner practices help them to learn about these agencies' behaviors, and about the systems of relations and interdependencies of the globalization process?

What kind of problems do communities experience in their relations with governments, NGOs, and transnational agencies? What kind of problems are NGOs experiencing in their particular intermediary role?

How could our research and applied practices be useful to grassroots communities and indigenous peoples in their struggles for empowering themselves and reaching better participatory positions?

How could our practices help them to evaluate the actual risks of involving themselves in participatory experiences that are not protected by legal and political institutions rooted in democratic political cultures, and to carefully work out solutions to this delicate and crucial problem?

How could our practices help societies at the national and local levels to understand the pressing necessity and mutual usefulness of enhancing the participatory opportunities of socially excluded peoples and social groups?

ACKNOWLEDGEMENTS

An earlier version of this chapter was presented in lectures I gave at the Institute for Development Anthropology (IDA) and the Pan-American Health Organization (PAHO) in 1994. Parts of this chapter were also included in presentations at the Foro Participación Comunitaria en Salud (El Colegio de Sonora, Mexico) in 1995.

I am thankful to those who contributed to my thinking on the matter through their comments on those occasions. I am particularly grateful to María Teresa Cerqueira (at PAHO) and Pía Córdova, with whom I have intensively discussed some of the matters treated in this chapter for more than a year; to Jan Servaes (co-editor of this book) who made thought-provoking questions and suggestions for the preparation of this chapter; and to the following indigenous people's organizations' leaders and practitioner professionals who helped me to deepen my understanding of some problems of social participation in the region: Evelyn Barrón (Centro de Capacitación Integral de la Mujer Campesina, Bolivia), Mónica Cheuquián (Casa de la Mujer Mapuche, Chile), Marcial Fabricano (Central de Pueblos Indígenas del Oriente Boliviano, Bolivia), Manuel Fernández (México), Ana Victoria García (Cooperación para el Desarrollo Rural de Occidente, Guatemala), Gabriel Martínez (Antropólogos del Sur Andino, Bolivia), Carlos Moreno (Sistemas de Investigación y Desarrollo Comunitario, Ecuador), Miguel Tankamash and Felipe Tsenkush (Federación de Centros Shuar-Achuar, Ecuador), Pilar Ramírez (Bolivia), Víctor Toledo Llancaqueo (Coordinadora de Instituciones Mapuches, Chile), Antonio Ugarte (Servicios Múltiples de Desarrollo, Bolivia), *cacique* Leonidas Cantule Váldez and Nicanor

González (Congreso Kuna, Panama), Néstor Vega (Sistemas de Consulta y Servicios, Guatemala), and Félix S. Zambrana (Confederación Sindical Unica de Trabajadores Campesinos de Bolivia). I am also thankful to the following people who very generously contributed hints, comments, bibliography, and documents: Sonia Arellano-López, John Burstein, Olivia Cadaval, Ernesto Castagnino, Shelton Davis, Vicky Denman, Henry Dietz, Anne Deruyttere, Carmen Ferradás, Jessamyn Jackson, Charles Kleymeyer, Chris Krueger, Emile MacAnany, Michael Painter, Charles Reilly, Lynn Renner, Marion Ritchey Vance, Bryan Roberts, Peter Seitel, Michael Shuman, Antonio Ugalde, Jorge Uquillas, Peter Ward, Armstrong Wiggins, Patricia Wilson, and Robert Wilson. Finally, I thank Jessamyn Jackson also for her editorial assistance with the English of this piece. In any case, I alone am responsible for the opinions expressed in this chapter.

REFERENCES

Ardao, A. (1980). *Génesis de la Idea y el Nombre de América Latina*. Caracas: Centro de Estudios Latinoamericanos Rómulo Gallegos.

Bhatnagar, B., & Williams, A. (1992). *Participatory development and the World Bank* (World Bank discussion papers No. 183). Washington, DC: World Bank.

Cerqueira, M. T., & Mato, D. (1995). Evaluación participativa de la participacíon social en programas de promoción y desarrollo de la salud. In B. de Kjeizer & J. A. Haro (Eds.), *Participación comunitaria en salud: Evaluación de experiencias y tareas para el futuro*. Hermosillo, Mexico: El Colegio de Sonora-Organización Panamericana de la Salud.

Coc, P. (1989). Development aid—An indigenous perspective. In *IWGIA Document 63: Indigenous self-Development in the Americas* (pp. 67–72). Copenhagen: IWGIA.

CORSAPS (Corporación de Salud y Políticas Sociales). (1991). Participación en salud: *Lecciones y Desafíos*. Santiago, Chile: CORSAPS.

Davidson, J., & Stein, S. (1988). Economic crisis, social polarization, and community participation in health care. In D. K. Zschock (Ed.), *Health care in Peru: Resources and policy* (pp. 53–77). Boulder, CO: Westview.

Dresser, D. (1991). *Neopopulist solutions to neoliberal problems: Mexico's national solidarity program*. San Diego: University of California, Center for U.S.–Mexican Studies.

Ferguson, J., & Gupta, A. (1992). Beyond "culture": Space, identity and the politics of difference. *Cultural Anthropology, 7*(1),6-23.

Flores, S. P. (1989). Communal self-management: Considerations for better external aid. In *IWGIA Document 63: Indigenous self-development in the Americas* (pp. 93–104). Copenhagen: IWGIA.

Heggenhougen, H. K. (1984). Will primary health care efforts be allowed to succeed? *Social Science and Medicine, 19*(3), 217-224

Green, L. W. (1986). The theory of participation: A qualitative analysis of its expression in national and international health policies. *Advances in Health Education and Promotion, 1*, 211-236.

IMSS-Solidaridad. (1993). *Testimonios de Solidaridad.* México DF: Author.

Keohane, R. O., & Nye, J. S. (Eds.). (1971). *Transnational relations and world politics.* Cambridge, MA: Harvard University Press.

La Forgia, G. M. (1985). Fifteen years of community organization for health in Panama. *Social Scince and Medicine, 21*(1), 55-65

Louw, E. (1993). Participative media: Whose agendas? *PCR-Newsletter, 1*(2), 1-3.

Malo, M. (1992). *Informe de Viaje a Nicaragua.* Unpublished manuscript.

Mato, D. (1993). Construcción de identidades pannacionales y transnacionales en tiempos de globalización. In D. Mato (Ed.), *Diversidad cultural y construcción de identidades* (pp. 211-231). Caracas: Tropikos.

Mato, D. (1994). Procesos de construcción de identidades en América "Latina" en tiempos de globalización. In D. Mato (Ed). *Teoría y política de la construcción de identidades y diferencias en America Latina y el Caribe* (pp. 251-261). Caracas: UNESCO-Nueva Sociedad.

Mato, D. (1995). *Crítica de la modernidad, globalización y construcción de identidades en América Latina y el Caribe.* Caracas: Universidad Central de Venezuela.

Mato, D. (1996a). International and transnational relations and the struggles for the rights of indigenous peoples in "Latin" America. *Sociotam, 6*(2), 45-79.

Mato, D. (1996b). Globalizacíón, procesos culturales y cambios sociopolíticos en América Latina. In D. Mato, M. Montero, & E. Amodio (Eds.), *América Latina en tiempos de globalización* (pp. 11-37). Caracas: Unesco-Asociación Latinoamericana de Sociolegia-UCV.

Mato, D. (1997). A research based framework for analyzing processes of (re)construction of civil societies in the age of globalization. In J. Servaes & R. Lie (Eds.), *Media and politics in transition* (pp. 127-140). Louvain: Acco Publishers.

Mato, D. (1998a). On global agents, transnational relations, and the social making of transnational identities and related agendas in "Latin" America. *Identities, 4*(2), 167-212.

Mato, D. (1998b). The transnational making of representations of gender, ethnicity and culture: Indigenous peoples' organizations at the Smithsonian Institute's festival. *Cultural Studies, 12*(2), 193-209.

Nugkuag, E. (1989). Analysis and proposals concerning development assistance and ethno-development. In *IWGIA Document 63: Indigenous self-development in the Americas* (pp. 151-158). Copenhagen: IWGIA.

Primer Taller Regional sobre Participación Comunitaria, Educación Sanitaria e Higiene Personal. (1990). *Participación comunitaria, educación sanitaria e higiene personal: Memorias del primer taller regional, realizado en Lima, Perú 19-23 de marzo de 1990.* Lima: CEPIS.

Reyes, G. (1993). *Investigación sobre Experiencias de participación comunitaria en proyectos de salud ambiental.* Unpublished manuscript.

Servaes, J. (1989). *One world, multiple cultures: A new paradigm on community for development.* Leuven, Belgium: Acco.

Stack, J. F., Jr. (Ed.). (1981). *Ethnic identities in a transnational world.* Westport, CT: Greenwood.

Stiefel, M., & Wolfe, M. (1994). *A voice for the excluded: Popular participation in development, utopia or necessity?* London: Zed.

Ugalde, A. (1985). Ideological dimensions of community participation in Latin American health programs. *Social Science and Medicine, 21*(1), 41-53.

Winch, P., Kendall, C., & Gubler, D. (1992). Effectiveness of community participation. *Health Policy and Planning, 7*(4), 342-351.

3

Locality in Mass Communication: An Irreplaceable Quality or a Relic From the Past?

Ullamaija Kivikuru
University of Helsinki

So far, mass communication research has viewed locality in a fairly mechanistic manner, predominantly as a question of proportions: proportions of homemade and foreign, national and international, genuine and transnational. The key assumption behind this practice is that there is a strong and distinct linkage between national culture and cultural identity, on the one hand; and locality, on the other. I do not challenge the key assumption as such, although the reality has recently shown in various forms in Eastern and Southern Europe, how bitter and complicated this linkage might turn even in the 1990s. However, I do advocate a somewhat more elaborated perception of locality and its components. Hence, spatiality or territorial consciousness is predominantly discussed on very general terms, without focusing on mass communication particularities.

This chapter concludes with some more specific notions on expressions of locality in mass communication, but rather than documentation, these should be treated as tidbits deserving further research.

DIMENSIONS OF LOCALITY

From the early days of bourgeois revolution, the concept of *nation* has been attached to geographic locality and interests developed in order to defend this locality: a combination of ideology, culture, language, and ethnicity. Inconsistencies and contradictions in the concept of *nation* in classic liberalism have paved the way also to societal movements characterized by assumed superiority, domination, and lack of democracy. Hence, the whole concept has lost its popularity considerably. It is not a "placeless culture" (Meyrowitz, 1986, p. 71) exactly that we are talking about now, but the locality dimension seems to have split into two, into a globally oriented space and a geographically oriented place, whereas the territorially based layer of nation-state seems to have weakened culturally, although not ideologically. The fashionable slogan of integrated "Europe of regions" reflects the very same thinking, though it could be interpreted to be on defense against the rest of the world also.

The idea here is not to write a reappraisal of nationhood and nationalism, although the dialectics of the concept are discussed here almost entirely in relation to dimensions of culture only, and, accordingly, quite simple cohesion-making elements are stressed, whereas such vital aspects as the dimension of power are not given due attention.

However, the power axis is essential for any formation of a metropolis-periphery set-up that is especially intriguing when locality is discussed. A periphery does not need to exist within the framework of a nation-state, but a periphery position indicates always a form of felt or real underdog status: economic, political, cultural, racial, or linguistic inferiority. Researchers of power and economy simply define *peripheries* as powerless societies, above all lacking what is called "structural" or "position" power, although they might have what is referred to as "resource" power.

Identical interaction involving the same societal sectors, aiming at processing the same societal goods, causes diversified effects in "have" and "have-not" societies (Galtung, 1980). Cultural domination, however, is in general far less vertical than economic domination. Furthermore, culturally, each upperdog and each underdog culture should be seen as an American sandwich with numerous layers, frequently contradictory by substance and under continuous change. What is essential from the standpoint of cultural research is the fact that an underdog society is characterized by a sense of boundary and a sense of unity with others living in the same society, however few the actual unifying components might be. Due to the peripheral status and the internal fragility that characterize peripheries, a sense of boundary tends to be deliberately exaggerated by the power structure. In short, spatiality or locality is an innate quality of peripheries, much more distinct there than in metropolises. Consequently, locality is given much more attention in cultural peripheries than in core or metropolis cultures. A metropolis can afford a more "liberal" interpretation of its own culture, because it is strong and persistent, whereas for a peripheral culture, the sense of boundary is a precondition for its sheer existence.

Identification Mechanisms

Another vital distinction should be made clear: the difference between national and cultural identity, quite rarely done in communication research so far. Both concepts have joint roots and they presuppose each other's existence to flourish, but their societal functions are, in fact, opposite to each other. National identity stands for uniformity and subordination, whereas cultural identity advocates diversification and cultural spontaneity.

The distinction deserves elaboration in order to be understood properly. National culture is in layman's language most often seen as "the culture of a nation," idealistically interpreted as an expression of spontaneous and genuine national property. However, one could look at it from a much more pragmatic perspective: In fact, *national culture* as a concept has been developed in most cases simply for purposes of cultural or communication policymaking. It is not a petrified collection of characteristics, but rather a process, molding itself in continuous interaction with other cultures and elements, creating an ideological atmosphere. In short, it could be seen as an ideology of integration (Siippainen, 1987), and it acquires its final definition from identification, that is, identity.

Definitions of *collective identity* are almost as numerous as those on culture and nationalism. Here, the concept is understood as simply as possible: It is the individual societal or popular consciousness we discuss here, under gradual change rather than a static state of affairs. The popular aspect is essential because an identity does not survive without acceptance. Identity operates with symbols, and, hence, processes affecting meanings of societal symbols also affect the identity. Collective identities are compilations of multiple, partly contradictory elements. In short, the term *collective identity*, according to Oriol and Igonet-Fastiger, can be viewed as "the sign of the most pressing invitation to a dialectic: that of always situating 'us' in relation to 'them,' the lived experience in relation to the institutionalized one, the present in relation to history, all of these prescriptions immediately calling forth a reciprocal effort" (cited in Schlesinger, 1991, pp. 152–153).

Thus, the layman's idea of national identity as a collection of the greatest common denominators is not misleading, although quite general. First, the strength of identification indicates the significance of national culture to its members. The culture is national only if the citizenry feels so. National identity is a gatekeeper, a selection mechanism exercising critical control over cultural influences and the interaction of societies. Compared with national identity, cultural identity is a mixture of cultural similarities and contrasts, disorganized, and often almost chaotic.

National symbols—or, more often, local or regional, that is, the more concrete components of cohesion and boundary—also have a part in cultural identity. Cultural identity means automatically the existence of a multitude of cultural "layers": rising, dominant, and declining cultures, countercultures, subcultures, and their various combinations. Cultural identity means a social potential for cultural self-expression, and it is, in principle, a source for activation while national identity gives a base for self-understanding.

Culture as an aspect of identity dates back to Montaigne and Montesquieu. They identified culture with tradition transmitted from one generation to the next. Only gradually did the concept acquire a political dimension (Desaulniers, 1987). During the 19th century, culture became associated with the strong nationalist movements, and cultural identity and national identity merged. In his analysis on Ernest Renan's theories on nationalism, Gellner (1987) gave two basic characteristics of a nation: a shared past—or, as Gellner elegantly turned it around, a shared amnesia, a collective forgetfulness—and the anonymity of membership.

The elements of shared past assist in composing a collectivity with which a community's members identify themselves, without being acquainted with all its members or subgroups of members. All subgroups are fluid, and not comparable with the national community. Nations are made by human will, and a modern nationalist consciously wills his or her identification with a culture. The consciousness element is included in most definitions of nationalism, although, in general, it has been seen as a very complex concept. Edwards sees ethnicity as a state of prenationalism and nationalism as self-aware ethnicity, or "organized ethnocultural solidarity." It is important to realize that both notions rest on a sense of community that can have many different manifestations, none of which is indispensable for the continuation of the sense itself. If the feeling of groupness disappears, then boundaries disappear (Edwards, 1985).

Gellner also sees that the overt consciousness of one's own culture is, in a historical perspective, an interesting oddity. A traditional man always had mediators between himself and the culture. Culture was like the air he breathed, without being able to name it. He knew the gods of his culture, but not the culture itself.

Only in the age of nationalism has this mediation been abolished. The shared culture is offered directly, that "a veil of forgetfulness should discretely cover obscure internal differences," which, of course, have not ceased to exist (Gellner, 1987, p. 10). National symbols may unify, but they also discriminate, divide, and place social groups in hierarchies of power or evaluation. Principles of cohesion and of boundary became distinct in the modern nation-state, and this is why the equation of national identity with cultural identity has been so difficult to break, although their contradictory elements have been recognized repeatedly especially by anthropologists (e.g., Desaulniers, 1987; Geertz, 1973; Gellner, 1987). National identity calls for homogeneity, or at least continuity, by emphasizing the collective "greatest common denominators," the shared past and the shared amnesia, however one wants to call them, and all this is made in the name of societal cohesion.

A Ladder of Identification Poles

Among the main means for reaching the level of superconsciousness—or, in Gellner's formulation, a mobile, continuous society with a merely fluid "atomized" inequality—literacy and education are often mentioned (Gellner, 1987), but one factor could be added in the list: mass communication. It has potential for the establishment of a popular sense of national identity. This consolidation power has also been widely recognized by new elites in developing countries—actually more frequently than the media's potential for more specific economic or educational objectives.

My claim is that one of the major manifestations of a popular sense of identity—national as well as cultural—in mass communication is locality, its expressions varying greatly depending on the society and the culture as a whole, but also the media mode and the professional culture in particular. Furthermore, I claim that mass communication in this respect indicates distinctly peripheral qualities, tending to exaggerate the significance of sense of boundary, illusionary or real.

In principle, mass communication carries potential for profound and essential expressions of locality, but in practice, crude, sloganized, and vulgar forms of locality frequent in mass communication content. Their function could be considered to be biased toward cohesion-promotion rather than activation and cultural variety. Hence, a reinforcement apparatus of locality is easily developed: Mass communication content carrying locality-specific particularities form an identification mechanism where people are "branded" with an easily adopted overt "spatial identity."

This identity, in turn, does have particular geographic dimensions, but also other somewhat more complex "poles of identification"(Desaulniers, 1985, p. 122). They vary according to social status, occupation, gender, and age group. We are Finns because we live in or near a given city, and personalities such as politicians, academicians, entertainers, and artists form a frequently repeated body of identification poles, as do particular sociopolitical processes typical to this spatial entity. Through a process that mass communication research has traditionally called *agenda setting*, people are given the spatial frames of identification in their symbolic universe, a history-bound composition of values and norms. Other and more systematic "value harbors" provide the essence of the symbolic universe, but mass communication could be considered to bring into it one significant element: situation-specificity and, with it, a potential of change.

Language: A Bygone Bastion of Cohesion-Building?

The instrument of cohesion and groupness that is mentioned so often in popular discussion that it has almost become a clichè is *language*. Most often, maturity of language is linked with the formation of a nation-state (Geertz, 1973; Klinge, 1975). Language is even equated with ethnicity or nationhood, and the idea of cultural identity being based on national language appears, for example, in most recent communication research (e.g., Gifrey, 1986). However, most linguistic literature has for a long time seen the relation between language and identity as an extremely complex one.

The strong German research tradition of Fichte and Herder perceived language as an almost sacred concomitant of nationality, but they also demonstrated how this could lead to a denigration of other groups and languages. Antedating, but supporting, linguistic nationalism was the idea of keeping languages "pure." This flourished above all in the French Academy, as explained by Edwards (1985).

In his almost clinically nonideological discussion on language and identity, Edwards described both identity and language as evolving concepts impossible to halt or reverse without artificial or undemocratic methods. Language decline cannot be understood if it is treated in isolation from the more general social fabric. For Edwards, the communicative and symbolic aspects of language are separable during periods of change. Hence, the latter might continue to exercise a role in group identity in the absence of the former: A language might emerge as a manifestation of identity due to its history, although nobody uses it as a means of communication any more (Edwards, 1985). Quite naturally, minority group members, whose identity appears at risk, tend to stress their groupness more than dominant groups that rarely define themselves as ethnic.

So, linguistic research seems to suggest that there does not exist a particularly strong relation between language and national culture or cultural identity. Furthermore, the significance of that relation varies in different parts of the world. The marriage between language and nation has been historically strongest in Europe and the Middle East, whereas the tie has been especially weak in the new nations of Africa (Smith, 1971). As Geertz (1973) pointed out, a linguistic standpoint might even be misleading here: The choice of language is a politically important, pragmatic issue for a nation.

On the other hand, it seems natural that language does have significance as a "natural" factor tracing cultural demarcation lines, especially for minorities and peripheries having a more limited storage of means available for emphasizing their uniqueness and cohesion. Still, this linkage can be found as a variable affecting, say, the composition of simple statistical data. For example, when problems of television program trade in Europe were discussed recently, language barriers were frequently seen as the "last borders existing in the European continent." In these discussions, language differences were also perceived as indicators of both cultural diversity and spatial specifity: Finnish television humor is not necessarily found humorous even in Sweden, not to mention more distant language realms (Hellman, 1989).

If the argumentation is brought back to the relation between cultural and national identity, the role of language seems definitely more decisive for the progress of national identity; but it does have significance also as a "frame" component of cultural identity, at least in most cultures. The mode in which it manifests itself in a culture varies depending on situational and historical reasons. Hence, mass communication content using the national language or the national languages has definitely a specific function, as an extensive and continuously operating reinforcer of this cohesion-making apparatus.

It is even justified to pose a question, whether mass communication could be considered a partial replacement or at least an "amplifier" of the function that has been so eagerly given to national language: Is not mass communication a far more efficient manifestation of territorial consciousness and togetherness in a "written" culture like ours than the orality-biased "plain" interpersonal use of language could ever be? The distinction does not carry any significance as long as dominant mass communication uses the national language or the national languages, but the picture becomes more complex, for example, in the age of direct satellites using one to two world languages and focusing global markets.

My documentation is admittedly scarce (Kivikuru, 1990), but it suggests that the role of language used in mass communication depends on the format (pattern of expression) or rather genre (mode of expression) that can be viewed as a nonannounced agreement of expression rules and practices between the sender and the receiver (e.g., Reunanen, 1991). In news, the significance of language as such seems to be modest, whereas in other genres ("non-news") the role of language is greater. Instead, genre of news is powerful in its ability for

reality-framing and updatedness, being in a particular place at a particular moment, thus increasing togetherness by other means. Mass communication using local language seems to increase cultural variety and
intimacy even in stereotyped products, whereas a world language often
operates as a promoter of standardization and conformity.

Spatiality: The Real Thing?

Besides language, the relation between cultural identity and territorial consciousness approaches cliché interpretation. Quite often, research combines the two claiming that they comprise what has been called a *cultural
heritage* (Gifrey, 1986). Of course, territorial consciousness does have a
clear and direct relation with nation-state and nationalism. From the cultural point of view, the situation is not quite as obvious: As in language use,
the symbolic aspect of territory could be separated from the concrete situation, and, still, it could offer a territorial element to cultural processes. The
"land of dreams" manifests in cultural products of emigrants, however well
they have assimilated into their present sociocultural surroundings.

On the other hand, territorial consciousness also has an effect
on cultural activities on a quite simple and concrete level: Without much
argumentation or rationalization, we, both in research and in popular
opinion, assume that what is geographically closer is also culturally closer to us. In a deeper analysis, this might or might not be the case, due to
historic and situation-based reasons. Cultures and people living in cultural group formations place themselves territorially with simplistic terms
like "north," or "south," or "east," or "west." This, again, is a connection
based on selection and will—we place ourselves where we want to
belong. Other options are also available.

Yet, dependence research has shown that physical proximity to
a core country definitely transforms cultural links. Seers (1979) discussed spatial patterns in Europe, stressing the fact that in the cultural
sphere proximity matters considerably. "Softer" elements affecting the
character of core-periphery relation, such as tourism and migration, similarities in professional skills, traditions, and language use, as well as the
availability of mass communication produced by the core. The shorter
the distance between the core and the periphery, the more these tend to
accumulate in the periphery (Seers, 1979).

This, in turn, affects the mode of cultural dependence, increasing the acceptability of dependence in the periphery. This is why the
locality factor could also be strengthened artificially, by establishing and
developing, most often with the support of local elite groups, cultural
"subcenters" that actually carry the basics of the metropolitan culture,
but adopt also cultural characteristics of their surroundings in the satel-

lite society (Hamelink, 1983). If Johan Galtung's (1980, p. 119) vocabulary is used, this means that a chain of core-culture "bridgeheads" is established deliberately in the periphery in order to strengthen the linkage to the core, while making the domination more fluid. Spatiality operates as a means to get "under the skin" of the cultural periphery: The local elite bridgeheads can develop a climate of closeness and familiarity. The core emerges as a natural choice for source of influences.

Conceptions of locality as a social phenomenon do vary—some advocates even claim that with increased mobility, changed lifestyle and such societal developments as the economic integration in Europe, the concept of locality in the meaning of "home territory" might be losing its significance gradually, and this is going to be reflected in the cultural mediations accordingly (e.g., Heiskanen, 1988b). For example, western European integration could be seen simply as a definite defeat to nationalism but, on the other hand, as a chance for European community-based "provincialism" on the one hand, and individual-based cosmopolitanism on the other (Heiskanen, 1988a). Definitely, all such social phenomena as locality reflect socioeconomic changes and, due to the quite close link with technology, the reflections are probably stronger in mass communication than in other cultural mediations, but also in mass communication the link is rarely straight, due to the fact that the symbolic aspect of territory can be separated from that of the actual situation.

If we accept that mass communication, due to its time-boundedness and semi-industrial character, tends to bias toward stereotyped practices, it could be claimed that the present situation concerning spatiality is extremely interesting. Locality as a concept seems to deserve redefinition due to more distinct abstract forms of locality emerging in the society as a whole. How, then, is the vibration between the general and the particular, traditionally so common in mass communication, going to express itself in the new circumstances?

The complexity of paradoxes involved in the concept of locality is reflected in discussions concerning mass media: for example, the role of national and regional identities in mass communication is persistently emphasized by the very same bodies that promote increased integration in economic and political relations. Activities of the European Union on the defense of European television broadcasting in the form of quotas offer an example on this. Simultaneously, contradictory developments also occur more spontaneously. Europe has recently experienced a sprouting of different regional and minority cultures, and throughout the industrialized world an interest in "ethnomusic" has emerged. These phenomena are definitely much weaker than developments of cultural homogenization taking place in the same areas. Similarly, most European countries have experienced a renaissance of various forms of local mass communication, in broadcasting as well as on the print side.

The interest in national or subcultural identity could be interpreted as a "counteragent" for attempts to increase universalism. The existence of this type of ability in peripheries has been acknowledged in many occasions (e.g., Boyd-Barrett, 1977, Salinas & Paldan, 1979). Whatever the explanation, these phenomena as such are manifestations of the contradictory character of locality.

There is another territory-related dimension here as well, although it is not "purely" territorial: the size of the society or social entity involved in the cultural processes. As Senghaas (1985) said, populous territorial states are protected by their very size, whereas small countries are from the very beginning especially exposed to the competence differential between more and less highly developed societies. Senghaas views the latter as extremely interesting cases from the angle of peripheralization.

Concerning culture, this seems to be an even more significant factor than the general socioeconomic development to which Senghaas referred. With the aid of different forms of industrialism, dominant cultures have always emerged among the strong and "big" societies throughout history, although not all strong societies have had a culture liable to dominate others (Innis, 1951). There seems to be a tendency among large societies to gain "naturally" more cultural self-esteem than the small ones. In a small society with a low-esteem culture, a quest for over emphasis on the genuiness and uniqueness of its own culture tends to appear more frequently than in an upperdog society with a high-esteem—but much more heterogenous—culture, thus paying little attention to the dangers of cultural mixture.

The conclusion concerning size tends to be dialectic again: a strong upperdog society is apt to develop a stronger but heterogenous culture, whereas the degree of cultural dynamics and sense of boundary is stronger in a small underdog society, which is able to maintain a "purer," more homogeneous cultural identity.

If these considerations are now applied to a periphery, its culture takes predominantly the mode of a small society. A peripheral culture entails intensity, but also a quest for cultural purity—that is, conformity. Thus, an innate contradiction is embedded in it. By definition, this means that a peripheral culture is prone to enthnocentric and isolationist tendencies. It is predominantly through culture that a periphery is able, on a continuous basis, to "implement" the foundation of the peripheral existence, namely a sense of boundary. There is cultural potential for multiple interaction with others.

There is, simultaneously, a societal urgency to isolation. And parallel to these contradictory tendencies the bitter, history-conditioned reality reinforces dependence on a particular direction. My claim is that these cultural developments tend to amplify in mass communication due to its semi-industrial, time-bound character, and, further, the changes taking place in mass communication receive an "overdose" of societal attention as well, due to a "balloon" function of mass communication. The role of mass communication in the creation and reinforcement of the symbolic universe tends to be exaggerated.

On the side of senders as well as receivers, mass communication is frequently understood as carrying qualities strongly affecting the symbolic universe, while, actually its role is modest compared with other value harbors, such as educational, economic, or political institutions. Furthermore, some modes and formats of mass communication—such as news—are overrated, whereas others—such as entertainment—do not receive much appreciation by the partners of the publicity mechanism.

The Dialectics of Origin

It is also easy to trace a territorial background for the often made equation of domestic with national plus, as an extension to it, the concern about domestic cultural production as a base of national culture. These concerns have recently grown, especially with the increased international orientation in production and distribution of cultural products. Similarly, exposure to extensive foreign-origin, exogenous cultural production has easily been judged as dangerous to cultural identity. Fairly often, these concerns are naively phrased.

Simultaneously, they are quite understandable due to the existence of stereotyped conceptions of nationalism, patriotism, language, and culture and also patterns established in the study of economics for example.

In the study of economic dependencies, peripherialization has most often been deduced from clearly quantitative factors like trade, migration, or professional structures (e.g., Seers, 1979). Certain parameters indicate the depth of dependence. This analogy is easily available, and tends to lead research on culture to the analysis of ownership structures in cultural industries, and measurement of volumes of imported cultural products only.

However, the relation between national and international is not that simplistic in culture, although quantitative proportions should not be ignored by any means. If there is no base for domestic cultural activity in a particular field of culture, there must be domination, and the domination is straight and simple. There is no other option. But homemade, domestic per se does not automatically mean anything more deeply national or endogenous than a foreign-origin, exogenous cultural product. The divesting of national culture of its mythic elements is necessary. It is also necessary to accept value judgments concerning cultural production. It is the substance, not the origin as such that determines whether a cultural product is relevant.

Furthermore, the relation is complex due to culture-specific factors. The concept of *culture* covers a much wider range of "nonmeasurable" components: The policy component and the professional culture have quite a considerable role. The border line between endogenous and exogenous is far from clear-cut. What this indicates is that even in the quantitative sectors, nonmeasurable components are intertwined with measurable factors.

It is a pity that discussions on nationality and internationalism have been divided into so many disciplines. For example, sophisticated and relaxed discussions on the relation between general and national literature (e.g., Wellek-Warren, 1963) or universal and national liberal arts indicate that in the humanities, both researchers and artists and authors alike have quite a natural—and less dramatic—view on this particular issue. Universal or cosmopolitan and national are seen as qualities implicating and supplementing each other, not as antitheses of each other. National qualities combine and generate international and universal trends reflected in cultural products.

There is an interesting contradiction hidden here: Literature, liberal arts, and the study of both are mostly placed under the national sciences and considered as supporting pillars of national culture. However, their relation to exogeny differs distinctly from that of mass communication research, for example. For the creative arts and the disciplines studying them, impact on other national cultures and the general "pool" of achievements of human culture are considered a source for enriching one's own culture and creativity, whereas in the social sciences and economics this relation is quite often understood as basically negative, as a stronger person's or entity's attempt to exercise power over weaker ones. If put into simple language, the humanities tend to look at exogenous influences as a chance to share the best genuine achievements of human culture, whereas social science tends to favor an interpretation that, due to exogenous influences, we are automatically condemned to exposure to the worst products of the human race.

Of course, the existence of stronger and weaker cultures is not denied in the humanities. In fact, literary research quite often sees literature composed of different, history-conditioned layers of international trends, that is, as a "memorial" of dominating cultures refined into unique expressions of modern time and current phenomena. With a slight exaggeration, it could be said that without the common cultural inheritance from the past, a relevant artistic work of our time and a particular culture could not be created: But it must also have a living contact with our time, not only the past. Perhaps the decisive factor for these opposite views lies in a distinction between the particular and the general. Literature and the liberal arts tend to consider general cultural trends as being predominantly composed of individual expressions of genuine, spontaneous creativity (e.g., books, paintings, and sculptures), whereas social science looks at the very same books and pictures more as products of cultural industries, involving creativity but simultaneously more general economic and political interests as well. This difference obliges the humanities to base argumentation on optimism on intelligent selection. Social science, instead, easily falls into cynical scepticism and anticipation of coercive domination.

The least that counterargumentation of the type just described should lead social scientists to is encouragement to sharpen vocabulary and concepts. Instead of a dichotomy into domestic and foreign, good and bad, more elaborate and "airy" categories should be established— starting maybe from closed indigeny, running through endogeny, to exogeny, regionalism, internationalism, transnationalism, and, finally, to cosmopolitanism and universalism. Furthermore, the different shades of spatiality within each of such categories should be studied, as well as different conditions given to the implementation of creativity in them.

These qualities could, furthermore, be understood more as a state of mind than anything specific. They are general qualities impossible to be measured straight—but they do exist. This is how, for example, a quality called *Europeanism* could be explained. On the one hand, and in our days to an increasing extent, Europeanism is a politico-economic ideology, and, on the other hand, a state of mind. If scrutinized properly, not too many common cultural qualities can be distinguished to be truly European. Maybe Heller (1988) is right in her argumentation that Europeanism, in fact, is only a post- and reinterpretation of history, and that modernity is the only quality to be attached to all shades of this intellectual construction. According to Heller, "European identity" is simply based on abstract and general assessments on the arts and culture, and the assessment norms have been established by the very same Europeans who do the assessment. Still, Europeanism does exist as a state of mind, and it plays a role in the creation of cultural products that simultaneously reinforce this abstract construction named Europeanism.

Perhaps one reason for the categorical attitude found in the study of international communication is related to the specific nature of mass communication. Its production and distribution is tightly time-bound and demands a considerable degree of standardization. There is not space enough for creativity and, through it, cultural refinement. Exogenous-origin products are transferred to another culture in a crude form, without necessary cultural adjustments. The characteristic affects the sources of influence: the easier at hand, the better, for an industrial production branch.

Furthermore, the demand for topicality reduces the potential for using fewer time-bound elements of the common cultural inheritance. Finally, in areas like mass communication, the contradiction between the strong and the weak on the technology axis also easily leads to favoring of quite crude modes of domination without reciprocity.

If combined with the elaboration on territorial size, it is consistent that in the field of mass communication, the strong tend to grow stronger and the weak weaker. This, again, has substance-bound consequences that mass communication research has often viewed as agenda-setting: Mass communication imports tend to accumulate to very few large territorial entities, and, due to the repetitive character of mass communication, spatial notions in the imported media contents easily lead to a restricted view of the world. Both media professionals and receivers accept that the strong and the close territorial entities—states, nations, regions—deserve much attention. Simultaneously, "out-of-focus" territories develop a stereotype of exotism.

Although mass communication, in principle, is projected to wide, unidentified audiences, there is always a certain amount of spatiality involved in projection and, respectively, in reception. Indigenous and endogenous mass communication is strictly projection-specific, but this is also the case in the majority of exogenous material: Mass communication is projected to a particular spatiality, but this spatiality-specificity can be transferred to another specific audience locality. In certain traits of international mass communication aimed at universalism, the spatiality axis does exist, but it is quite indefinite, attempting to cover practically the whole world. In some other modes of international mass communication, however, deliberate action has been carried out to reduce and even abolish existing spatiality artificially. This concerns above all transnational and quasi-transnational mass communication aimed at global audiences. Hence, it could be claimed that a basic distinction lies between exogenous and transnational-oriented mass communication—maybe domestically produced, but "modeled" according to transnational patterns—rather than endogenous and exogenous, which both fall into the category of projection-specific production. Instead, transnational or transnationally inclined material deliberately lacks this quality: Locality-specific aspects are rarely emphasized in transnational material.

The mass communication mainstream takes here two distinctly different routes. In news transmission, exaggerated projection-specificity is preferred: Datelines are distinct, sources identified, personalized and placed in the spatial social strata. Particularity of individual news events is emphasized, and locality serves as an ideal means to promote particularity. In mainstream entertainment, personification is used also, but rarely in a spatial mode. The individuals described in entertainment modes are actually merely reflectors of general, "universally relevant" human affections: love, hate, longing, despair.

In any event, a reformulation of categories is necessary. First, neither endogenous nor even indigenous equate with "national" automatically: nationalism might be imported to a large extent, and still relevant for the society in which it is implanted, whereas indigenous material might as well not meet even the slightest relevance requirements of national culture. Furthermore, a simple dichotomy of national/endogenous and international/exogenous is neither fruitful nor relevant. In cultural spheres, it is better to look at the issue as a continuum starting from indigeny and ending up in several categories of international, each category having ambiguous border lines. None of these concepts is exclusive: Each also carries in its substance elements of the others, although one component is dominating.

However, at least a weak sociospatial dimension is needed in a cultural product in order to ensure a living relation with the society for which the cultural product is meant. The basic distinction between a cultural stereotype and a spontaneous cultural product—again, spontaneity understood as a continuum, and in many cultural products the proportion of spontaneity being quite limited—lies in this relation. An increase in stereotyped qualities means a reduced quantity of spontaneity and creativity. Furthermore, stereotypes are fixed: They lack flexibility and might lead to strong biases in relation to the societal reality.

A type of cultural activity favoring stereotyping in cultural products is transnational culture, organized predominantly through transnational corporations directing their messages to worldwide audiences and, hence, investing in reduced sociospatial qualities and increased redundancy, "playing it safe" with cards that are assumed to be known by anybody. So, transnational cultural substance emerges in this continuum as a special case, representing an extreme case of cultural "industrialization." Transnational substance is not limited to products of transnational corporations only, and products of transnational corporations do not automatically fall into the category of transnational substance. Instead, it could be said that their products have set the pattern for quasi-transnational cultural substance, which could, in principle, solicit quite crude and vulgar endogenous imitations as well.

Not even all stereotypes can be listed in the same category: Few are absolutely artificial, most do have qualities originating from the common cultural heritage, but reformulated into homogeneous, pseudoharmonious compositions.

This discussion brings up the innate contradiction of the concept *tradition*: Most often, the proportions of the universal cultural property used by transnational culture originate from the most "outworn" elements of culture. If we see culture in any society as a composition of rising, dominant, and declining cultural elements, the most industrialized forms of cultural production tend to select values representing the declining culture for material of new products, whereas the experimental, most creativity-laden rising culture is underrepresented. For market-oriented production, compositions of new cultural elements mean increased inexpectancy and uncertainty, which "assemblyline" production inherently tends to avoid.

The sometimes irrational and unwise "resistance movement" against exogenous domination becomes more understandable first against this background: When, in fact, the resistance is directed against the domination of outdated context in cultural industries, the criticism is turned to a phenomenon related to it, but distinctly different from it, namely foreign domination. It is easier to recognize, because it is exogenous, whereas elements of the declining culture are, to a larger extent at least, integral parts of the domestic culture.

In fact, however, the problem is homemade as well as of foreign-origin—cultural production tends to favor elements of the declining culture, the stronger and the more extensive the production and distribution systems are. Hence, transnational corporations with worldwide markets tend to be more conservative in this aspect than, for example, national broadcasting companies. But, again, there is a contradiction embedded: Big corporations have great resources and the competence for production, whereas a small company might lack both.

Locality Mediation in Action

In terms of nationality, one is either Finnish or not, but culturally one might be Finnish to varying degrees. In his redefinition of cultural identity after "washing out" nationalist and patriotic elements, Desaulniers (1987) brought in one addition component, mentioned often by anthropologists as well: the fact that the basic "aim" of cultural identity is antagonistic to the goal of national identity, because its purpose is to bring out differences between people, to encourage cultural diversity. Culture serves as an instrument of differentiation within a community; it creates social meanings engaged in maintaining differences, disparities, and dissimilarities.

Perhaps due to the enthusiasm to distinguish from the previous research on cultural identity—and popular opinion as well—the recent study of cultural identity has not paid much attention to the links and joint mediations common to both of these concepts. The concepts are interlinked, and it is sometimes even difficult to determine the causal relation. Judging from the orientation of research authorities today, one could say that cultural indentity is the more "innate," more ethnic, whereas man-made elements dominate the concepts of national identity and national culture. If the spatiality is elaborated, it could be claimed that cultural identity is linked more to such general and fairly abstract expressions of spatiality as language and style, values, and tradition, whereas national identity rather takes more concrete and territorially defined modes. Consequently, mass communication as a form of semi-industrial cultural production naturally emphasizes more national identity.

The borderline between the two concepts is far from distinct, however. For example, both anthropologists and communication researchers have quite frequently misused the concept of *cultural identity* for what could be named more precisely as "cultural archetypes" or "cultural stereotypes." It seems to be so that although theoretically quite clear and solid, cultural identity is difficult to be recognized and operationalized in "real life."

In mass communication practice, the mediations promoting the two identities are even more mixed. It is not very complicated to draft the basic tasks for national and cultural identity mediations, but in practice, these tasks are frequently intertwined. The agenda-setting function of mass communication operates predominantly for national identity via legitimation of the power structure: Mass communication is an important factor in the creation of cultural publicity or, as it is fashionable to say nowadays, of the public sphere, which is, on the one hand, an outcome of the dominant value harbors existing in the society but, on the other, also composes a potential for change, and, thus, cultural diversity. An individual always finds him or herself in a discursive position with mass communication and other cultural networks: cultural mediations are interpreted both socially and individually. Concerning locality, elements of "real" and surrogate spatiality meet during this process, affecting each other. Furthermore, news and non-news mass communication operate differently in this particular question.

In the following, an attempt is made to present some more specific examples of locality expressed in mass communication.

News: Localization Via Professional Particularization

It is not difficult to find documentation in news transmission for the general tendencies discussed earlier. Even a crude quantitative content analysis is able to indicate various trends of news particularity (Kivikuru, 1990). The geographic set-up of the news world is well established, even rigid—it is misleading to claim that it is the individual pieces of news that create the map. Rather, it is more justified to say that the news attention is, on a continuous basis, directed to areas that have been assessed newsworthy previously; occasional "flash" news breaks the rule, but it also disappears from the news arena quite soon (Chaney, 1986). The spatial view of news is kept stable, but the view as such is highly conditioned by history and geography: the news arenas of Finland and Tanzania for example, vary considerably.

At the first look, the Tanzanian news scenery looks more bound to concrete geography than does the Finnish, but the picture changes, if it is studied more carefully. Naturally, locality can never be defined solely with components of geography, but the "big issue" on the Tanzanian news arena has been for more than 20 years the racial situation in South Africa—an issue related to politics and race rather than geography. In Finland, instead, the issue of the decade seems to be European integration, which is not purely tied to concrete spatialism, but is definitely more related to it than the apartheid in South Africa (Kivikuru, 1990).

In Finland, however, it is obvious that an attempt is made to abolish peripheralism appearing in news reporting. The news apparatus has volunteered to the function of accommodator in bringing Finland into partnership in the emerging European "superstate" (Galtung, 1980); no options are given to this development in dominant journalism. Because of this mission, the proximity axis is given less attention. The interest to the rest of Scandinavia—an interest explained by proximity and joint historical roots—seems to be on a permanent downslide, and Russia/Soviet Union is given increased attention rather because of its superpower status than of geography as such (Kivikuru, 1990).

An interesting trait of news localization is the distinct ethnocentrism that labels news reporting both in Finland and in Tanzania. Although interest in foreign developments is in general high, if quantitative proportions are studied, both news systems view the rest of the world from a clearly ethnocentric angle (Bürki, 1977). The dominant news criteria in Finland increasingly emphasize the role of Finland in world issues (Kivikuru, 1990), whereas in Tanzania, the form of ethnocentrism is somewhat different, and deliberate policymaking interchange with occasionalism. Quite interestingly, the news "vehicle" in both countries is capable of creating ethnocentric journalism, watching the world through an endogenous window. In Tanzania, this is carried out via exclusion only: The refocusing is implemented through "dropping out" large parts of the world from the news arena. In Finland, the process is much more sophisticated, but the outcome quite similar. For example, the high appreciation given to nonaligned industrial countries in world issues indirectly promotes "positive" ethnocentrism because this is the political group with which Finland identifies herself. The Tanzanian news system emphasizes phenomena and developments that are essential to Black Africa, not Tanzania alone. Obviously, tendencies to integrate the periphery with the metropolis are not as strong as in the Finnish news vehicle (Kivikuru, 1990). In fact, at the moment the Tanzanian news system seems to identify with a loose compilation mixing elements of both periphery and core but still under domination: the Black African superstate block. If only journalism is studied, it could be claimed that the high concentration to Black Africa and issues relevant to it, could be interpreted to represent isolative tendencies.

Another characteristic of Tanzanian mass communication increases the sentiment of isolation: Besides conventional mass media, different forms of *oramedia* are essential in Tanzania. Village meetings, women's gatherings at the well, age rites are a vital part of rural life and of urban squatters, strengthening partly nation-level mass communication via face-to-face communication, but above all refocusing the main news attention to local and regional issues (Ugboajah, 1985). Oramedia are much more significant in non-news communication, but have a role also in the news sector as a balancing factor in the built-in contradiction. Nation-level conventional mass communication remain remote to the ordinary person's life, whereas the oramedia bring in intimacy and concrete locality. In a postcolonial society such as Tanzania, the contradiction is very sharp: the legacy of colonial one-way *gazeti* journalism is easily traced in the authority orientation of present nation-level news journalism.

Obviously, the channels to express sense of boundary and territorialism in news journalism are conditioned by journalistic practices and professional prerequisites such as timeliness and semi-industrial character, but the determining factors are still the basic societal developments in a periphery, disregarding, to a large extent, such factors as media ownership and control.

One means to handle the tension between the general and the particular—in both countries, but especially in Finland using visual mass communication much more in journalism—is the visual component. Visual expression has only rarely any independent role in news journalism, most often it primarily stereotypes and reinforces stereotypes via particularization and personification. Individuals are exhibited to represent systems and organizations, particular individuals are placed to label even activities that they have hardly anything to do with. A picture of Yasser Arafat is automatically attached to any piece of news on Palestinians. Certain buildings and activities are repeatedly linked, via pictures and news films, with prosperity and well-being, others with poverty and war. But in the most popular news pictures of hunger, it is easy to recognize familiar elements of Christianity and European culture; a dying mother with a baby (the madonna effect) has been the most popular image of hunger in Finnish papers (Tanner, 1994). In short, pictures compose an essential element of both real and quasi-spatiality in news reporting.

Expansion Brings Conformity

In the field of entertainment there is no use paying much attention to origin—the complex marketing mechanisms of mass communication non-news may create a full chain of domestication bridgeheads, although the substance and format still follow the original patterns on broad lines. And the original patterns are easily defined: Popular entertainment tends to favor the immediate, the tangible, and the specific, its style matters more than the substance, and transience breeds tension and despair, thus catalysing cult-making, especially about the youth (Fishwick, 1985). Popular entertainment in strongly biased toward generalization, but it requires seeds of particularization as spices.

The non-news content is much more tightly linked with multinational and transnational marketing than the substance of the news realm, which is finally determined by domestic politics. Global markets as an ideal mean that generalization instead of particularization is emphasized as a content quality; hence, the domestication concerns only insignificant aspects. Furthermore, the primary non-news market is strongly dominated by a few producers with a transnational orientation, concerning film, television, as well as print media content—the mainstream is easily available at a reasonable price. Particularities of a concrete, geographic territory are useful for "spice" use, offering identification poles: names, buildings, symbols of a particular social status or age group operate as an artificially localized frame for a plot underlining "universal" human sentiments such as love, hate, or despair. These overt poles of identification could be called *surrogate localizations*, "diluted" spatiality that only occasionally touches deeper levels of meanings than mere denotation. Especially a medium such as television is considered committed to mobility and boundless space: "any territorial boundary, including national frontiers, appears as a relic of a bygone past" (Desaulniers, 1985, p. 121).

However, the picture is hardly as simple in actual reality as Desaulniers wants to believe. For example, language-based barriers are still quite hard to exceed in program trade.

In principle, a mixture of the general and the particular offers potential for creativity-laden modes, for combining the domestic and the foreign, the endogenous and the exogenous in mass communication. This kind of enrichening "cultural borrowing" belongs predominantly to the realm of high culture (Kivikuru, 1990). However, in certain entertainment modes, such as *feulleton, telenovela*, or *fotonovela*, domestication of the "international quest for melodrama" (Eliot, 1934, p. 422) has taken place also, leading to a variety of artifacts carrying also societal relevance (de Souza, 1988). In simple language, this means that the international melodrama scheme has been adjusted to local circumstances, concerning both the format and the substance. In Tanzania, stereotyped moralities, earlier transferred via oral narration in poetry and rite formats, emerge presently also in bookstand literature, cartoons and *fotonovela* melodrama (Kivikuru, 1990).

Unfortunately, quite crude and "unnecessary" factors frequently ruin these endeavors, changing them into simple mainstream stereotyping. Thus, it is interesting to see what happens in the near future in Tanzania, because television started in mainland Tanzania first in 1994, with multiple private efforts, on a mini scale but in a highly commercial mode.

The realm of non-news indicates rapid growth in any form of mass communication vehicle in any country. This, in turn, leads not only to high dependence on imports (Kivikuru, 1990), but especially imports provided by the transnational production and marketing mechanisms. Smooth operation and reasonable costs are the basic principles that kill the use of experimental non-news products. These are also available on markets, but not easily at hands and rarely in bulks: the non-news sector devours rapidly growing quantities of material on a daily basis. This is one major reason leading to the domination of the few in non-news markets, and, for example, previous colonial ties live longer on the non-news side than in news transmission. Entertainment is not an appreciated sector of mass communication; hence, it does not matter very much, what kind of material is used, as long as it is easily available and its transmission is smooth (Kivikuru, 1990).

Logistics promote strongly the Anglicization of the non-news world, and these logistic factors also affect the professional culture: through frequent repetition of, say, Anglo-American material, legitimation is gained for a professional policy tolerating the domination of this particular type of material. Consequently, soft and hard structural factors are interlinked. The selective processes of interpretation might also lead to "collective forgetfulness" of distinct biases of the cultural publicity. As Constantino (1978) pointed out, in the Philippines, liberation from the Spanish is glorified, whereas the rapid Americanization of the culture remains unnoticed.

Thus, it seems justified to say that spatial elements in mass communication are "treated" and twisted also on the level of whole societies, and this is one dimension that frequently achieves legitimation via mass communication. Cultural mainstreaming is born—but also its "counter force." Especially in wealthy and mature societies, peripheral autonomy exists especially in societally appreciated sectors of mass communication, such as news and high culture segments of non-news.

In an ideal case, exogenous modes, formata, and contents are adjusted, domesticated to meet the particular requirements of the society concerned. In practice, this means an increase of elements expressing concrete forms of spatiality. But the "resistance movement" requires operational space and time.

In the most industrialized segments of non-news mass communication, catalysts for adjustment transformation are overwhelmed by novelties appearing in the arena on a continuous basis. The media vehicle indicates disproportional growth and, this, subsequently, leads to increased time-boundness, stereotyping, and mainstreaming.

Non-news locality is, however, still far more intriguing than could be judged considering only the mainstream, doomed to a battle between stereotyping with a bias to diluted spatiality and expressions of spontaneous creativity and more flexible forms of locality. The boundless "base of leisure society" (Desaulniers, 1985, p. 114) is also a bastion of ethnocentrism, manifested in oramedia content. This form of locality is biased toward the declining sentiments of the culture, because orality in general has, throughout centuries, operated as a means for "freezing the information," linking the present to the past via memorizing the tradition in modes of poetry, drama, or recitation (Havelock, 1986). It is vital for the society, either as a cultural relic or part of the daily practice, but its significance is still "landlocked" to limited sectors of life, even in a Tanzanian village: oramedia rarely operate as catalysts of change. Their role is predominantly in reinforcement of the value system of the present or past power structure (Vansina, 1985). The spatial base for identification is given, but in a fairly one-sided form.

In short, a strong oramedia sector in mass communication seems to be temporary by character, forced to yield gradually to conventional mass communication. However, for the time being, the existence of oramedia "softens" the abrupt change of locality from static village scope to nation-level horizons that is underway in such societies as Tanzania, experiencing drastic sociopolitical changes: for example, the media behavior of a recently urbanized squatter population follows more the media use of the rural areas where the population comes from. The rural cultural identification poles last, although the living mode becomes urbanized (Ugboajah, 1985). As such, the existence of locality is not in danger, but both the mode of expressing locality and the spatiality focus change. The media vehicle follows societal change, but does not give up the sense of border and spatiality as a whole. However, the mass communication culture in transition societies, in its search for a new locality focus, tends to "overdo" it by exaggerating the significance of the nation level and the urban components and ignoring the rural and local elements in conventional mass communication.

This forms a built-in contradiction in media content. However, the orality sentiment does not disappear. In Finland, the "traditional" oramedia are almost nonexisting, but traits characteristic to orality emerge in new, admittedly vulgar and often highly commercialized versions. Togetherness and lack of distinction into senders and receivers are found today in rock concerts and other gatherings of the youth, in activist movements mainly operating outside the conventional media. In general, it seems that diluted or surrogate locality is sufficient for reinforcement identification, but if a society is experiencing changes, more concrete forms of spatiality are necessary in any society; recent developments in eastern European mass communication give support to this reasoning. The greatest common denominators are searched also via mass communication content that makes the border line between "us and the others" distinct.

Corpus: An Excursion to Mobilization and Self-Understanding

In summary, according to the arguments presented here, spatiality is an integral part of mass communication, but its expressions vary considerably depending on the society, media mode, and content formats. It is not possible to judge the character of media locality based on an analysis of only one dimension. Due to its semi-industrial nature, mass communication is liable to stereotyping and, hence, vulgarized spatiality. Only its high culture-oriented sectors seem able to develop spontaneously into "meeting places" of multiorigin but still locality-specific contents: Literature, music, and film are able to exhibit also rich genuine and spontaneous spatiality of various forms.

The dominant trend, in news as well as in non-news, seems to lead from concrete locality to more abstract or even surrogate forms of spatiality; still, the function of these components in media content is to create territorial consciousness and, through it, security and togetherness. Simultaneously, quests for togetherness and mobilization seem to search for communication modes outside the conventional media vehicle. This suggests support to the idea that locality as such is merely a relic from the past, gradually dissolving and maybe disappearing totally from mass communication mainstream, in metropolises and peripheries alike; again, the semi-industrial character of conventional mass communication ties core and periphery cultures fairly much to the same mainstream, although situation-specific variation appears continuously. The mainstream is the same, but the small whirls do definitely not occur simultaneously and in the same form everywhere.

In disintegrated "new" peripheries, however, the population itself obviously forms one resistance force. If the majority of people has a strongly horizontal and localized lifestyle, it is impossible to imagine them as heavy users of transnational mass communication with dissolved locality. They simply drop out, because the media content does not make any sense to them. In "old" peripheries with sophisticated al traditions and tendencies to integrate to metropolises, instead, the sense of locality in general is weaker, and no strong people's resistance against large volumes of irrelevant exogenous mass communication will arise.

In fact, dissolved locality seems to be more a problem of core societies and old peripheries, eagerly adopting any professional novelties and subsequently binding mass communication both structurally and professionally to continuous growth and intensified time-consciousness. Furthermore, if domestic production is once totally given up, it is extremely difficult to set it up again (Kivikuru, 1990), however strong political will may push it. On the other hand, endogenous production as such does not ensure self-reliance to select the most relevant modes of locality; it is just a prerequisite. The second major factor lies in the professional culture. Owing to direct and indirect exogenous "bombardment," mass communication professionals tend easily to favor imitation and patternized modeling. Endogenous modes of mass communication are easily turned down as unprofessional or old fashioned.

It is intriguing to think about the kind of role the built-in quest for topicality and time consciousness has in the hunt for novelties and subsequent tendency to vulgarization that so distinctly characterize the various professional cultures in the realm of mass communication.

Perhaps, however, the whole problem setting requires further elaboration. It is perhaps justified to rename the umbrella under which the manyfold phenomena linked with locality or spatiality have been placed in the argumentation just presented. Perhaps it is more adequate to talk about an indispensable corpus function than locality as such. A corpus means that a collective operates jointly as a pool of information, no distinction into senders and receivers is done, or the tasks keep varying (Vansina, 1985). Via corpus, a collective is able to exercise simultaneously mobilization and express security of anonymous membership.

"Pure" territorial consciousness does not necessarily give impulses to mobilization and participation. However, it is difficult to imagine that a corpus collective could develop without experienced sense of border. This, again, requires poles of locality identification for the individuals forming the collective. Consequently, the key question remains unchanged even when the umbrella concept is redefined and locality allowed a position only as a branch of corpus: Does the dilution of corpus factors in mass communication content indicate that there can be innate vicious circles promoting uniformity and mainstreaming also on the "soft" side of mass communication, not only on the side of structures and technology?

This, again, could be interpreted so that the "change agent" function of mass communication is due to weaken. It is easy to accept that exaggerated underlining of sense of boundary leads to assumed superiority and lack of democracy; documentation is easily found in mass communication with strong nationalist components. But is it true that exaggeration of the opposite extreme in mass communication does not lead to a global village but, rather, to promotion of values characteristic to a stagnant society, eagerly cherishing an illusion of a world without boundaries, because this illusion gives that society a justification to exist?

In fact, an analyst is inclined to view the corpus component as the essence of true popular culture, genuinely representative of the community in question. In principle, it could be found in the heavy international flow of transnational cultural industries as well as genuine endogenous mass communication. As Schiller (1989) justifiedly argued, the transnational flow may in certain cases constitute an improvement of availability of material "offering some pleasure to a good many people in most societies—despite the grave social disabilities that accompany it" (p. 36). National cultures have frequently been compromise cultures and quite nondemocratic by nature. But the demystification of locality with all its components should not lead to the mystification of another concept; instead, the corpus function deserves serious and unprejudiced analysis.

REFERENCES

Boyd-Barrett, O. (1977). Media imperialism: Towards an international framework for the analysis of media systems. In J. Curran, M. Gurewitch, & J. Woollacott (Eds.), *Mass communication and society* (pp. 116-135). London: Arnold & Open University Press.

Bürki, J-F. (1977). *Der Ethnozentrismus und das Schwarzafrikabild. Eine Begriffsstimmung, gefolgt von einer Analyse des Schwarzafrikabildes in drei grossen europäischen Tageszeitungen: Neue Zürcher Zeitung, Die Welt, Le Monde.* Universite de Geneve Institut Universitaire de Hautes Etudes Internationales, These No. 290/Peter Lang.

Chaney, D. (1986). The symbolic form of ritual in mass communication. In P. Golding, G. Murdock, & P. Schlesinger (Eds.), *Communicating politics. Mass communications and the political process* (pp. 115-132). New York: Holmes & Meier.

Constantino, R. (1978). *Neocolonial identity and counter consciousness. Essays on cultural decolonization.* London: Merlin.

Desaulniers, J-P. (1985). Television and nationalism: From culture to communication In P. Drummond & R. Paterson (Eds.), *Television in transition. Papers from the First International Television Studies Conference* (pp. 112-122). London: British Film Institute Books.

Desaulniers, J-P. (1987). What does Canada want? or L' histoire sans lecon. *Media, Culture and Society, 9,* 149-57.

Edwards, J. (1985). *Language, society and identity.* New York/London: Basil Blackwell in association with Andre Deutsch.

Eliot, T. S. (1934) *Selected essays.* London: Faber & Faber.

Fishwick, M. (1985). *Seven pillars of popular culture.* Westport, CT & London: Greenwood Press.

Galtung, J. (1980). *The true worlds. A transnational perspective.* New York: The Free Press.

Geertz, C. (1973). *The interpretation of cultures.* New York: Basic Books.

Gellner, E. (1987). *Culture, identity, and politics.* Cambridge, UK: Cambridge University Press.

Gifrey, J. (1986). From communication policy to reconstruction of cultural identity: Prospects for Catalonia. *European Journal of Communication, 1*(4), 463-446.

Hamelink, C. (1983). *Cultural autonomy in global communications. Planning national information policy.* New York/London: Longman.

Havelock, E. A. (1986). *The muse learns to write. Reflections on orality and literacy from antiquity to the present.* New Haven, CT: Yale University Press.

Heiskanen, I. (1988a). *Europeanism and Finnish culture.* In *Yearbook of Finnish Foreign Policy* (pp. 3-7). Helsinki: Finnish Institute of Foreign Affairs.

Heiskanen, I. (1988b, July). *Local media, regionalism and international economic integration.* Paper presented at the IAMCR Conference, Barcelona.

Heller, A. (1988). L' Europe, un epilogue? *Lettre Internationale.*

Hellman, H. (1989, November 23) Unohda realismi [Forget realism]. *Helsingin Sanomat,* B8.

Innis, H. A. (1951). *Empire and communications.* Oxford, UK: Clarendon.

Kivikuru, U. (1990). *Tinned novelties or creative culture? A study on the role of mass communication in peripheral nations* (Publication No. 1F/10/90). Helsinki: University of Helsinki, Department of Communication.

Klinge, M. (1975). *Bernadotten ja Leninin välissä* [Between Bernadotte and Lenin]. Porvoo: WSOY.

Meyrowitz, J. (1986). *No sense of place: The impact of electronic media on social behavior.* New York: Oxford University Press.

Reunanen, E. (1991). *Merkitysympäristö ja uutisgenren säännät* [Meaning environment and rules of the news genre] (Publication A76). Tampere: University of Tampere, Department of Journalism and Mass Communication.

Salinas, R., & Paldan, L. (1979). Culture in the process of dependent development: Theoretical perspectives. In K. Nordenstreng & H. Schiller (Eds.), *National sovereignty and international communication: A reader* (pp. 82-98). Norwood, NJ: Ablex.

Schiller, H. (1989, April). *Farewell to cultural sovereignty.* Paper presented at the conference Television, Entertainment and National Culture—The Canada–U.S. Dilemma in a Broader Perspective, Quebec.

Schlesinger, P. (1991). *Media, state and nation: Political violence and collective identities.* London: Sage.

Seers, D. (1979). The periphery of Europe. In D. Seers, B. Schaffer, & M. Kiljunen (Eds.), *Underdeveloped Europe: Studies in core-periphery relations* (pp. 3-34). Hassocks: Harvester.

Senghaas, D. (1985). *The European experience. A historical critique of development theory.* Leamington & Spa, NH: Berg.

Siippainen, M. (1987). *Kansakunnan kulttuuri. Kansallisen kulttuurin käsitteen tarkastelua* [The culture of the nation. An examination on the concept of national culture]. Unpublished master's thesis, University of Tampere.

Smith, A. (1971). *Theories of nationalism.* London: Duckworth.

de Souza, M. W. (1988, July). *The soap opera and its mediations in the urban centers*. Paper presented at the IAMCR Conference, Barcelona.

Tanner, S. (1994). *Image of hunger. The visual representations of hunger in two Finnish newspapers 1983-1992*. Unpublished master's thesis, University of Tampere.

Ugboajah, F. O. (1985). Media habits of rural and semi-rural (slum) Kenya. *Gazette, 36*, 155-174.

Vansina, J. (1985). *Oral tradition as history*. London: James Currey & Heinemann Kenya.

Wellek, R-W., & Warren, A. (1963). *Theory of literature*. London: Penguin.

//

Metatheoretical Considerations

4

Principles of Participatory Communication Research: Its Strengths (!) and Weaknesses (?)

Jan Servaes
Katholieke Universiteit Brussels

Randy Arnst
Project Director of World Education
Vientiane, Laos

All research begins with some set of assumptions that are untested but believed. Positivistic research, which comprises the mass of modern communication and development research, proceeds from the presupposition that all knowledge is based on an observable reality and that social phenomena can be studied on the basis of methodologies and techniques adopted from the natural sciences. In other words, "reality" exists apart from our interpretation of it, we can objectively perceive, understand, predict, and control it. Social scientists, enamored by the notion of a predictable universe, therefore conclude that, by applying the methods of positivistic science to study human affairs, it would be possible to predict, and ultimately to control human social behavior. Furthermore, its methodological premises and epistemological assumptions are based almost exclusively on the Western experience and worldview; a view that holds the world as a phenomenon to be controlled, manipulated, and exploited.

If we subscribe to the notion that social research should have a beneficial impact on society, it is imperative that we pay more attention to research philosophies that can profitably handle, and indeed stimulate, social change. Therefore, participatory research, (PR), in our opinion, borrows the concept of the interpretive, intersubjective, and human nature of social reality from qualitative research, and the inherent basis of an ideological stance from critical research, combines them, and goes one step further. Rather than erecting elaborate methodological facades to mask the ideological slant and purpose of inquiry, the question becomes, "Why shouldn't research have a direct, articulated social purpose?" Instead of relying on participant observation or complex techniques to gain the subjective, "insider's" perspective, it is asked, "Why shouldn't the 'researched' do their own research?" Why is it "The poor have always been researched, described, and interpreted by the rich and educated, never by themselves"?

Regarding the topic at hand, why is it that so much research has been conducted about participation in a nonparticipatory fashion? As in the case of participatory communication, the major obstacles to PR are antiparticipatory, often inflexible structures and ideologies. We cannot be reductionistic about holism, static about dynamism, value-free about systematic oppression, nor detached about participation. Participatory research may not be good social science in positivist terms, but it may be better than positivist social science for many development purposes.

PRINCIPLES OF PARTICIPATORY COMMUNICATION RESEARCH

That the mass of social research is largely guided by the social context in which it operates, and largely does not function to serve those studied, has been argued at length. Participatory research was conceived in reaction to this elitist research bias. It is ideological by intent; it is the research of involvement. It is not only research with the people—it is people's research. As such it largely rejects both the development policies of states and the "objectivity" and "universal validity claims" of many methodologies in the social sciences. Even if we momentarily assume that contemporary research practices are free of ideology and do not constitute a means of oppression, the fact remains they are of little utility to the poor:

> We have moved beyond the whole notion of some of us leading the struggles of others. This shift . . . in the control over knowledge, production of knowledge, and the tools of production of knowledge is equally legitimate in our continued struggles towards local control and overcoming dependency. It is here that PR can be an important contribution . . . PR is quite the opposite of what social science research has been meant to be. It is partisan, ideologically biased and explicitly non-neutral. (Tandon, 1985, p. 21)

It is the realization that most of the present professional approach to research is in fact a reproduction of our unjust society in which a few decision makers control the rest of the population that has led many to move away from the classical methods and experiment with alternative approaches. In urging PR, we are not speaking of the involvement of groups or classes already aligned with power. These groups already have at their disposal all the mechanisms necessary to shape and inform our explanation of the world.

Therefore, a basic tenet of PR is that whoever does the research, the results must be shared. They must be available to the people among whom research is conducted and on whose lives it is based. Data is not kept under lock and key or behind computer access codes, results are not cloaked in obfuscating jargon and statistical symbols.

Furthermore, and perhaps most importantly, the inquiry must be of immediate and direct benefit to the community, and not just a means to an end set by the researcher. This direct benefit is contrasted to the circuitous theory–research design–data–analysis–policy–government service route that neutralizes, standardizes, dehumanizes, and ultimately functions as a means of social control: "People's voices undergo a metamorphosis into useful data, and instrument of power in the hands of another. Rather than assembling collectively for themselves, political constituencies are assembled by pollsters, collecting fragmentary data into 'public opinion'" (Ewen, 1983, p. 222).

Again, PR challenges the notion that only professional researchers can generate knowledge for meaningful social reform. Like authentic participation, PR believes in the knowledge and ability of ordinary people to reflect on their oppressive situation and change it. To the contrary, in many cases at the local community level, participants have proved to be more capable than "experts" because they best know their situation and have a perspective on problems and needs that outsiders cannot fully share. This perspective is quite divergent from the abstract concepts, hypothetical scenarios, and macro-level strategies that occupy the minds and consume the budgets of development "experts" and planners.

Differences Between PR and Action Research

Because of this nature of involvement, PR is often known under the rubric of social action or action research (Argyris, Putnam, & Smith, 1985; Fals Borda, 1988; Kassam & Mustafa, 1982; Whyte, 1991). In numerous respects they are similar, and PR is not really new. It is a novel concept only to the extent that it questions the domains of the research as well as the economic and political elites.

However, there are fundamental differences between action and participatory research. Chantana and Wun Gaeo (1985) wrote that action research "can be non-participatory and related to top down development . . . whereas participatory research must involve the people throughout the process. Action research can be intended to preserve and strengthen the status quo, whereas participatory research . . . is intended to contribute to the enhancement of social power for the hitherto excluded people" (p. 37).

By way of example, in the realm of media production, Varma, Ghosal, and Hulls (1973) defined action research as a "systematic study, incorporated into the production of media, the results of which are fed back directly and immediately to the production staff to help them to improve the effectiveness of their communication" (p. 4).

Conversely, PR assumes a bias toward the poor rather than the professional. Participatory research is related to the processes of conscientization and empowerment. It was probably Freire himself who introduced the first version of this approach in his philosophy of conscientization. Rather than agendas being defined by an academic elite and programs enacted by a bureaucratic elite for the benefit of an economic or political elite, PR involves people gaining an understanding of their situation, confidence, and an ability to change that situation. White (1984) wrote this is quite divergent from "the functionalist approach which starts with the scientist's own model of social and psychological behavior and gathers data for the purpose of prediction and control of audience behavior. The emphasis is on the awareness of the subjective meaning and organization of reality for purposes of self-determination" (p. 28).

Participatory research is egalitarian. Thematic investigation thus becomes a common striving toward awareness of reality and toward self-awareness. It is an educational process in which the roles of the educator and the educated are constantly reversed and the common search unites all those engaged in the endeavor. It immerses the exogenous "researcher" in the setting on an equal basis. Considering the necessary trust and attitudes as well as cultural differences, the task is not easy, and makes unfamiliar demands on researchers/educators.

A Definition of PR

The recent popularity of PR, the act of labeling it as such, may have implied that it is something special that requires a particular expertise, a particular strategy, or a specific methodology. Similar to participation, there has been great effort toward definitions and models of PR to lend an air of "respectability." Also similar to participation, perhaps this is no more than an attempt to claim title or credit for an approach that, by its very nature, belongs to the people involved. As one is dealing with people within changing social relations and cultural patterns, one cannot afford to be dogmatic about methods but should keep oneself open to people. This openness comes out of a trust in people and a realization that the oppressed are capable of understanding their situation, searching for alternatives, and taking their own decisions.

Because there is no reality "out there" separate from human perception and, as put forth in the multiplicity paradigm (Servaes, 1989, 1999), there is no universal path to development, it is maintained that each community or grouping must proceed from its own plan in consideration of its own situation. In other words, to the extent the methodology is rigidly structured by the requisites of academia, PR is denied.

By its nature, this type of research does not incorporate the rigid controls of the physical scientist or the traditional models of social science researchers. Chantana and Wun Gaeo (1985) stated:

> There is no magic formula for the methodology of such PR projects. . . . However, there are common features taking place in the process: (1) It consists of continuous dialogue and discussion among research participants in all stages; [and] (2) Knowledge must be derived from concrete situations of the people and through collaborative reflection . . . return to the people, continuously and dialectically. (p. 39)

Therefore, we delineate PR as an educational process involving three interrelated parts:

1. Collective definition and investigation of a problem by a group of people struggling to deal with it. This involves the social investigation that determines the concrete condition existing within the community under study, by those embedded in the social context.
2. Group analysis of the underlying causes of their problems, which is similar to the conscientization and pedagogical processes previously addressed.
3. Group action to attempt to solve the problem.

Therefore, the process of PR is cyclical, continuous, local, and accessible. Study–reflection–action is the integrating process in this type of research. Kronenburg (1986) gave the following characteristics of participatory research:

> [It] rests on the assumption that human beings have an innate ability to create knowledge. It rejects the notion that knowledge production is a monopoly of "professionals"; [It] is seen as an educational process for the participants . . . as well as the researcher; it involves the identification of community needs, augmented awareness about obstacles to need fulfillment, an analysis of the causes of the problems and the formulation and implementation of relevant solutions; The researcher is consciously committed to the cause of the community involved in the research. This challenges the traditional principle of scientific neutrality and rejects the position of the scientist as a social engineer. Dialogue provides for a framework which guards against manipulative scientific interference and serves as a means of control by the community. (p. 255)

Evaluation and Validity in PR

Given a continuous cycle of study-reflection-action, PR inherently involves formative evaluation. Indeed, the terms *participatory research* and *participatory evaluation* are often used synonymously. Actors are exercising themselves in participatory evaluation by the whole group of the situation of underdevelopment and oppression.

Congruent with the objectives of PR, the purpose of evaluation is to benefit the participants themselves. It does not function to test the efficiency of an exogenous program, formulate diffusion tactics or marketing strategies for expansion to a broader level, gather hard data for publication, justify the implementing body, or collect dust on a ministry shelf. In brief, it is an ongoing process as opposed to an end product of a report for funding structures.

Whether PR "succeeds" or "fails" is secondary to the interaction and communication processes of participating groups. The success of the research is seen no more in publications in "reputed" journals but in what happens during the process of research. Bogaert Bhagat, and Bam (1981) added that "participatory evaluation generates a lot of qualitative data which is rich in experiences of the participants. It may be . . . quantitative data is sacrificed in the process. However, what is lost in statistics is more than made up by the enhanced richness of data" (p. 181).

The implication is not that other methods or exogenous collaboration in evaluation are forbidden. Writing about research participants,

D'Abreo (1981) stated, "While they, as agents of their own programme, can understand it better and be more involved in it, the outside evaluator may bring greater objectivity and insights from other programmes that might be of great use to them. However, the main agents of evaluation, even when conducted with the help of an outside agency or individual, are they themselves" (p. 108).

Turning to the question of validity, Tandon (1981) suggested, on a methodological level, "getting into a debate about reliability and validity of PR is irrelevant because it is quite the opposite shift in understanding what this research is" (p. 22). Its focus is on authenticity as opposed to validity. However, referring to generalizability and validity addressed in relation to qualitative research, it can be argued that validity in its less esoteric sense is PR's hallmark. "If ordinary people define the problem of research themselves, they will ensure its relevance" (Tandon, 1981, p. 24), and their involvement "will provide the 'demand-pull' necessary to ensure accuracy of focus" (Farrington, 1988, p. 271).

Finally, the basis of PR, indigenous knowledge, is inherently valid. This is not to say conditions are not changing or that this knowledge cannot benefit from adaptation. The argument is that, in most cases, this knowledge is the most valid place from which to begin.

A Word of Caution

Participatory research can all too easily be utilized as yet another tool of manipulation by vested interests. Charges are correctly made that it is often a means of political indoctrination by both the right and the left. Often, organizers have been attacked for manipulating people's minds and managing their actions toward their own ends.

Although the approach strives toward empowerment, challenges existing structures, and is consequently ideological, rigidly prescribed ideologies must be avoided. In addition, knowledge and perspective gained may well empower exploitative economic and authoritarian interests instead of local groups. Far from helping the process of liberation, if the researcher is not careful, he or she may only enable the traditional policymakers and vested interests to present their goods in a more attractive package without changing their substance. Even the best intentioned researcher or activist can inadvertently enhance dependency rather than empowerment. If he or she enters communities with ready-made tools for analyzing reality and solving problems, the result will likely be that as far as those tools are successful, dependency will simply be moved from one tyrant to another.

In other words, overzealous researchers can easily attempt to compensate for an initial apathy by assuming the role of an advocate rather than a facilitator. "What looks like progress is all too often a return to the dependent client relationship" (Kennedy, 1984, p. 86). This approach is no better than more traditional researchers with hypotheses and constructs to validate, or the diffusionist with an innovation for every ill.

OBSTACLES TO PR

Participation is currently popular, and one can hardly argue against the concept, broadly conceived. However, even though it is widely shared theoretically, it is difficult to promote in practice, as most scholars admit, in fact, that participation in communication hardly exists, except, in a very limited way, in a number of small localized experiments. In translating broad policies to specific practices, obstacles arise: "The danger for development practice is that we will mistake the consensus of academics for the prevailing situation of the real world and the existing obstacles to social change. It is clear that proclaiming development to be a widely participatory process of social change . . . to bring about both social and material advancement . . . for the majority of the people through gaining greater control over their environment" (see Rogers, 1976, p.133) would be readily accepted by many academics. Yet when such efforts are implemented they are complicated by real-world realities and sharp political conflicts.

The inherent nature of conflict, and the propensity to avoid it, is but one example of barriers to participation. Another is that participative endeavors are not in the interest of those seeking high visibility. Their demands for detailed, up-front planning, coupled with rigorous adherence to fast-paced implementation schedules and preplanned specifications ensure that the real decisions will remain with professional technicians and government bureaucrats.

In organizational excitement and zeal to demonstrate quantitative results from new projects, the tendency is to promote rapid expansion of highly structured program models that emphasize quantitative targets and quick evaluation, reflecting a "compulsion for measurement." The thrust is results over process, ends over means. Efficiency is their watchword, and participation is not likely to be efficient.

Change and Agencies

Frustrated with the participatory approach, McKee (1989), a social marketing specialist stated that "participation was just not consistent with the organizational realities of development where you have fairly narrow time frames, you've got to get projects off the ground" (p. 26). McKee also stated that funding agencies introduce their own bias in this respect. Their concerns are budgets and reports on progress. "They are rewarded according to the size of their portfolios and are often looking for a 'blueprint' to follow, not a complicated community process that may take years to be realized" (McKee, 1989, p. 40).

Hence, even though when people authentically participate and are thus committed to an idea, they can often mobilize an astonishing variety of resources to realize it, it is certainly not the most expedient or easily assessable route from this "quick-and-visible-results" perspective because it takes time, money, and effort to consult the people. Therefore, it could be said that building roads and dams and breeding high-yielding crops is "child's play" compared with the difficulties of working with people.

Such highly publicized, tightly structured, and deeply institutionalized projects also serve to "give the appearance that social development is underway, thereby throwing a smoke-screen over the deeper causes of poverty" (Fuglesang, 1982, p. 46). Nyoni (1987) added:

> most development agencies are centers of power which try to help others change. But they do not themselves change. They aim at creating awareness among the people yet they are not themselves aware of their negative impact on those they claim to serve. They claim to help people change their situation through participation, democracy and self-help and yet they themselves are non-participatory, non-democratic and dependent on outside help for their survival. (p. 53)

Participation and Power

Neither is genuine participation congruent with the concerns of those who would maintain a facade of social harmony, order, bureaucratic and economic efficiency, or political continuity. Participation can lead to developments that are of an unpredictable nature. However, to embark on a conscious policy of participative or democratic decision making is consciously to sacrifice the ability to make fast and stable decisions. Conversely, policies implemented in the name of order and efficiency are often more akin to repression.

Authentic participation directly addresses power and its distribution in society. It touches the very core of power relationships. Consequently, it may not sit well with those who favor the status quo and thus they may be expected to resist such efforts of reallocating more power to the people. In other words, it is not in the interest of dominant classes, both at national and international levels, to implement policies and plans that would substantially improve the conditions of the lower classes or masses. In a certain way, every center needs its periphery!

Just as "another development" or "multiplicity" argues for structural change, it also asserts that the route to individual and social development is seen as precisely as being the route to increased participation. Development and participation are inextricably linked. Participation involves the more equitable sharing of both political and economic power, which often decreases the advantage of certain groups. On the political front, when participation is likely to encourage such changes, it is probable that it will be viewed as a potential threat to those who stand to lose some of their power. For instance, Bordenave (1989) wrote:

> it is difficult to imagine a participative society in which the means of production are owned by a few persons who have the capital and who reserve important decisions exclusively for themselves. The organization of the economy, then, is the crucial difference between a non-participative society and a participative one. However, the major resistance to participation is most often not such overt, cataclysmic actions. Rather, the main obstacle is the much less visible, yet insidious and continuous reluctance to organizational change. (p. 8)

Governments and Bureaucracies

Even though development advocates encourage change and discourage maintenance of the status quo, believing that only when change takes place will there be progress and improvements, criticism of people's traditionalism, under education, and recalcitrance are often lamented as major obstacles to change. However, far less attention is given to the reverse—institutional or bureaucratic intransigence. In describing efforts to promote participation at the local level, Blair (1981) related:

> The programs were seeking the benefits of structural change for the poor while trying to avoid substantial change for the status quo. For participatory institutions to make decisions that can improve the lives of the participants, they must have political power. "Empowerment" at the bottom, however, was the one thing that those in charge were unwilling to give. (p. 80)

Governments have historically been timid toward direct or participatory democracy. In framing the U.S. constitution, for instance, many of

America's founders feared the political influence of undereducated people, and participation was therefore deliberately restricted through the establishment of a representative system and an electoral college, in order to establish government by those thought best able to contribute. This representative democracy is not to be confused with direct democracy or popular participation, which more directly realizes the conditions of self-management and participation in decision making by all those affected by it. The premise here is that control over an action should rest with the people who will bear the major force of its consequences, not with their mouthpieces, nor their representatives. Granting this direct participation is often not feasible, efficient or, at broader levels, even possible, logistical constraints are not foremost among reasons political and cultural structures do not include a more direct mode of participation. Silberman (1979) stated "bureaucrats and planners tend to look with disfavor on participation, particularly when it involves their own domain . . . participation could reduce their own social status" (p. 100). Furthermore, change may be resisted even in institutions that publicly acknowledge the need for alternative communication for development and take pride in their progressive stance.

Participation and Hierarchies

The elites go to great lengths to maintain their positions of power and what those positions bring to them. What those positions of power often bring is more power and material wealth. The purpose is not only maintenance, but expansion. For some, it is advantageous to conserve a particular social arrangement that allows for their own development as a group or, in a stricter sociological sense, as a class. During the British occupation of India, Lord Macaulay portrayed that one of the goals was to create "a class of persons, Indian in blood and color, but English in taste, in opinions, in morals, and in intellect [who would] be interpreters between us and the millions we govern" (Narula & Pearce, 1986, p. 65). Terms such as *morals, intellect* and *govern* are open to interpretation, of course, but an argument could be made this class continues not as interpreters, but as governors.

It is argued that the primary objective of any bureaucracy or organization, much like all living organisms, is its own sustenance, perpetuation, and possible expansion. The Peace Corps/Vista adage, "to work oneself out of a job" is contrary to the individual and collective aspirations of government personnel. Describing efforts in "streamlining" the government sector of the Comillia project, Khan (1976) stated that "the prospect of fewer government 'workers' did not at all please the departments. Instinctively they hated decentralization, delegation, and autonomy" (p. 73).

The overriding interest of bureaucratic personnel in the country side, as that of most people, is to perform well enough so that they will be transferred back to the metropolis as soon as possible. They tend to practice upward orientation, they care mainly to please their superiors. And rightfully so, they are rarely rewarded for being responsive to local conditions nor contributing toward the development of local institutional capacity. This is antagonistic to the requirements of participation, which mandates a focus toward the poor rather than promotion.

Change, especially structural change, involving the redistribution of power is inherently antagonistic to the need for continuity. An organization's need for self-perpetuation necessarily requires the continued existence of the larger system of which it is a part, which it serves, and from which it benefits. Consequently, even minor change is a sensitive issue in discussion, and often a revolutionary one in advocacy. But it is quite simple, convenient, and popular to place all fault with existing structures, with much "wringing of the hands," which, in turn, blames the intransigence of the people, who, in turn, blame the government, and so on. These patterns of reciprocated blame wreck the kind of coordination necessary to achieve development objectives.

Again, structural change alone will accomplish little. As it is not enough to provide participation in the system, even if this can be made less formal and more substantial; the aim is to create a more just society. Participation is necessary but not sufficient for this to happen. What is needed is self-government, a decentralized order through which the masses are empowered. The "chicken and egg" paradox is that, while existing structures are a substantial impediment to participatory processes, valid, applicable restructuring can occur only through some degree of authentic participation. Therefore, unless policymaking and the social process are themselves participatory, it is unlikely that the result will be a democratic pattern of communication.

Participation and Vested Interests

There is no magic formula for injecting participation into projects, it must come from within. Furthermore, barriers to participation are most certainly not limited to government–populace or powerful–powerless relationships. There is little substantive interaction among various governmental and private units, and that which does occur is often continuous infighting over budgets, prestige, and power. Therefore, sectarianism and propaganda interests of specific government departments often enmesh and destroy projects. Heim, Rabibhadana, and Pinthong (1983) explained, "The budget is divided centrally, various departments vying for larger amounts of the limited fund by presenting and showing off their plans and schemes . . . such departmental jealousy and competition, cooperation and team work among officials of various departments at the local level are very weak or almost non-existent" (p. 20).

Nor do problems stop at the gates of the rural community. Each charge cited here is applicable to the local context. Communities are seldom unified groups of people. To be avoided is "the romantic image of a community as one big happy family. . . . Each of the sub-communities or factions has its own self-interest to protect—and endeavor which may or may not serve the needs of the community at large" (Kennedy, 1984, p. 85).

We see that elitist attitudes are not limited to exogenous leaders, and neither are elitist aspirations. Khan (1976) related, in the Comillia project, "wolves quickly volunteered to herd the sheep" (p. 70), and Nanavatty (1988) wrote as a result of democratic decentralization within development programs, "the dominant caste and class got a free hand to usurp the resources of development in its own interests" (p. 97). In other words, the local elites often hijack the struggles of the poor in order to meet their individual needs. More powerful community members take advantage of any available opportunity for influence, thus corrupting the purpose of the participatory approach and destroying the spirit of cooperative effort. In particular reference to the Indian context, Narula and Pearce (1986) wrote that within communities "partisan relationships, caste memberships, resentments . . . and the traditional power structure can preclude the cooperation necessary for popular participation" (p. 43). Furthermore, even though village "Panchayats" were established through egalitarian ideals and "are elected by the community . . . decisions are often governed by vested interests . . . panchayats no longer remain a democratic forum for village participation" (p. 131).

Self-Depreciation

Finally, from international to local contexts, the long-term existence of hierarchical structures have often conditioned rural people to see "themselves as 'consumers' rather than 'participants' in development" (Narula & Pearce, 1986, p. 21), and as a consequence, people often have lost the power to make decisions affecting their communities, and expect solutions to come from above. Self-depreciation is another characteristic of the oppressed. So often do they hear they are good for nothing, know nothing, and are incapable of learning anything—that they are sick, lazy, and unproductive—that in the end they become convinced of their own unfitness. Because people are not stupid about how others regard them, the communication that operates according to these principles puts peoples backs up. It may be much more effective at creating resentment than change (Freire, 1983).

Narula and Pearce (1986) defined this as *learned dependency*. In Indian democratic socialism there are "two mutually exclusive forms of action: providing for the masses' material welfare and eliciting active participation" (p. 149). The paradox is often the development agents who intend to foster increased social welfare, participation, and self-reliance, and seeing themselves as the participation "experts," interject themselves into the local context and simply transfer dependency from local elites to government elites. "The pattern is such that the actions taken by various agents to change it themselves become the forces that perpetuate it" (p. 183).

Development, participation, and such become, from the perspective of the poor, notions that are conceived, initiated, and controlled by the government. Why shouldn't it be the government's responsibility to carry them out?

Culture

What exactly constitutes a culture, or different cultures? Culture is the collective equivalent of personality, and consequently is not amenable to simplistic classification or "pigeonholing." Cultures have indistinct peripheries; and they shade off into one another in a quite indefinite way. We do not always recognize a culture when we see one. Cultures can overlap, absorb, encompass, and blend. They can be differentiated according to environment, custom, social class, worldview or *Weltanschauung*. The tendency is to think of another culture as somewhat foreign or exotic, as existing outside of one's national borders. However, some international communications can be far more cross-cultural than international communications. Often, for instance, there exists an easily discernible cultural gap between the ruling elite and the masses in many developing nations. In other words, culture varies with the parameters through which we choose to look at it. Culture can be taken as the way we perceive and interact with the world, and those with whom we share similar perceptions. It is precisely such shared, often unarticulated and sometimes inarticulable patterns of perception, communication, and behavior that are referred to as a *culture*. Culture is subjective, and it is personal. Aider (1985) believes the core "of cultural identity is an image of the self and culture intertwined in the individual's total conception of reality. This image, a patchwork of internalized roles, rules, and norms, functions as the coordinating mechanism in personal and interpersonal situations" (p. 413).

Hence, the nexus of intercultural communication is that any two individuals or groups can communicate effectively in so far as they share past experience and worldviews, but they differ culturally to the extent they do not share these same phenomena. As cultural variance increases, so does the difficulty of communication.

In summary, one could conceive culture as the manifestations of man's and woman's attempt to relate meaningfully to his or her environment. An excellent conceptual, although very poorly labeled, delineation of the differences between agrarian and bureaucratic cultures in their orientation is discussed by Howard (1986), who divides worldviews into "primitive" and "civilized" (p. 241).

> The primitive world view is essentially a personal view of the universe in which humans are seen as united with nature. . . . [It] reflects the close social relationships that members of small-scale societies maintain with each other and the close relationship with nature that their technology and adaptive strategies entail. The civilized world view . . . reflects the impersonal nature of social relationships in large-scale societies . . . and a technology that allows people to become distant from nature. . . . [It] stresses our separation from nature and our role of conqueror of nature. (Howard, 1986, p. 241)

An association can be drawn between these worldviews and Hall's (1976) "high-context" and "low-context" cultures. Operating from their worldview and a low-context culture, officials ("developers") analyze a situation as a discrete entity, existing "out there," something to be overcome with technology, "know-how," or sheer numbers. "He [or she] perceives and evaluates the promises and performances of development from his [or her] concrete, here and now, location in the factual order" (Ramashray & Srivastava, 1986, p. 77). Khan (1976) painted a picture of those with such an orientation: "Their proposals were precise; more assistants, more demonstration plots, more teaching of improved methods, more supplies. . . . The system seized them like a boa constrictor. They rushed from one time-consuming meeting to another, and, in between, read heaps of files and received numberless visitors and telephone calls. Always busy counting the trees, they never saw the woods" (pp. 69–74). The richness, complexity, and diversity of local life and self-help action often blend into highly aggregated statistics or are reduced to the abstractions of theoretical models, and once removed from consciousness, cease to exist in practical reality.

On the other hand, if the rural farmer, the "developee," subscribing primarily to the another worldview and living in a high-context culture, sees the same situation as a problem at all, he or she may approach it as something to be tolerated, or addressed in consideration of the total physical and social environment. He or she sees the situation in its social context. He or she is "guided more by intuitive understanding than by organized and systemized knowledge" (Ariyaratne, 1986, p. 32). It is important to recognize that this social intelligence of the farmer is often a more necessary possession than abstract intelligence of the "expert."

For example, the "expert" sees the social orientation, the time spent on the maintenance of relations with other community members, as laziness, as whiling away the hours in gibberish. The "expert" does not often realize that in the community, the production system is communal, that in many rural, agrarian contexts "sitting" is not a "waste of time" nor is it a manifestation of laziness. Sitting is having time together, time to cultivate social relations. Quite possibly ensuring good social relations is as important as producing food. In other words, different people see the same phenomena and, based on different cultural perspectives, indeed different realities, they arrive at different conclusions.

Logic and Language

To assert that logic is culturally relative may approach blasphemy to the "scientific" mind, but the fact remains that foreign systems of reason are usually deemed illogical using the accuser's system of logic. Logic "is a cultural product, and not universal. Logic . . . is the basis of rhetoric. . . . Rhetoric, then, is not universal either, but varies from culture to culture and from time to time within a given culture" (Ishii, 1985, p. 98).

Considering Suzuki's study of Zen logic, Ishii continued: "Being is Being because Being is not Being; i.e., A is A because A is not A. Suzuki's logic is in absolute contrast with Aristotelian dichotomous antimony" (p. 99). It follows that the logical and rhetorical framework of a culture influences the manner in which that culture perceives and employs language and communication, as well as what constitutes knowledge. This, in turn, relates back to the question of "expert" and "indigenous" knowledge. Perhaps Fuglesang (1982) put it best in saying "there cannot be a formal logic which is universal. . . . So, how can there be a knowledge which is universally valid?" (p. 71). As such, each culture has to be analyzed on the basis of its own "logical" structure.

The reverse, that communication, language, and knowledge also impact logical frameworks and worldviews follows. Logic and language are linked. "We overlook the simple circumstance that the universality is not a fact in reality, but only a feature in the linguistic picture we are using" (Fuglesang, 1982, p. 21). Rockhill (1982) further stated, "The symbolic interpretation of gestures and words is of primary concern as they mediate human interaction and provide the lenses through which the inner experience is viewed" (p. 15). In brief, this is symbolic interactionism. It is mistaken to imagine that one adjusts to reality essentially without the use of language and that language is merely an incidental means of solving specific problems of communication or reflection. The fact of the matter is that the real world is to a large extent unconsciously built up on the language habits of the group.

To carry linguistic relativity to its extreme, it can be held that even our most "certain" presuppositions, those of time, space, and matter, are not "real" at all. Fuglesang (1982) attested that "Newton did not find these concepts in reality but in language" (p. 41). And Kozol (1975) wrote that words can be a major factor "in determination of our ideologies and our desires. . . . Words that seem the most accessible, or those we have been trained to find most pleasing, are powerful forms of limitation on the kinds of things we can experience, or advocate, or even learn to long for" (p. 116).

Perhaps no one understood these ideas of culture and language better than Gandhi. He adamantly used the local language and lived by, and in, the indigenous culture. He sought to propagate new ideals, values, and thought patterns consonant with modern times, but in terms of the traditional cultural symbolic systems.

In comparing "Eastern and Western" orientations to the use of language, Kim (1985) postulated that the Western (taken here as broadly representative of the bureaucratic, low-context) mode is largely a "direct, explicit, verbal realm, relying heavily on logical and rational perception, thinking, and articulation" (p. 405). Thunberg, Nowak, Rosengren, and Sigurd (1982) applied this concept to the development professional's style, whose "manner of expression or style often seems unnecessarily complicated and abstract, and particularly bureaucratic prose tends to follow formal codes far removed from daily usage" (p. 145). This contrasts with the orientation of the East (loosely associated here with agrarian, high-context cultures) where "the primary source of interpersonal understanding is the unwritten and often unspoken norms, values and ritualized mannerisms relevant to a particular interpersonal context" (Kim, 1985, p. 405). To relate this to India as well as alternate views of communication:

> According to the Indian view, the realization of truth is facilitated neither by language nor by logic and rationality. It is only intuition that will ensure the achievement of this objective. To know is to be; to know is to become aware of the artificial categorization imposed on the world by language and logic. It is only through an intuitive process that man [and woman] will be able to lift himself [or herself] out of the illusory world which, indeed, according to the Indian viewpoint, is the aim of communication. Therefore, if the Western models of communication are ratiocination-oriented models, the Indian one is intuition-oriented. (Dissanayake, 1986, p. 30)

Halloran (1981) illustrated this variance in relating that scholars from different cultures "had difficulty in finding a level for mutual understanding, not only because their national languages differed, but because they classified reality in different ways" (p. 42). The cross-cultural communication effort par excellence is the technical expert in the rural village; the man (or woman) whose thinking and acting are shaped in the concepts of the written language, trying to communicate with the people whose minds and behavior are molded by an oral tradition—or conversely.

These incongruencies have profound implications for both communication and participation between exogenous development personnel and rural populations, as well as instances where models, methods, and strategies formulated in the West are applied, largely intact, in other cultures. "The exchange between government officials and their constituencies is conducted in a bureaucratic sub-language which has one meaning to the official and an entirely different meaning to the average citizen. . . . In this situation, communication has not 'broken down'; it has never even begun" (Kennedy, 1984, p. 87).

To reiterate, we see that culture is a function of collective worldview, perception, logic, and language rather than geographical location or nationality. There is an inverse relation between cultural differences and communication ease. Whereas communication between national development institutions and rural populations is often assumed to be intracultural in nature, this is not often the case. Culture, when not understood, or seen as antagonistic as in the modernization paradigm, constitutes a substantial barrier in development communications and participatory endeavors both inter- and intranationally.

"Insiders" and "Outsiders"

Interaction fosters a pedagogical environment for all participants. The researcher, as a newcomer, contributes in that he or she requires the membership to give an account of how things are done, which fosters an atmosphere where participants may better know themselves, question themselves, and consciously reflect on the reality of their lives and their sociocultural milieu. Through such interaction, a fresh understanding, new knowledge, and self-confidence may be gained. Furthermore, awareness, confidence, and cohesiveness are enhanced not only for group members, but also among and between those members and outsiders who may participate, thereby increasing their understanding of the context and obstacles under which the people strive. Education goes both ways. This learning process can instill confidence and ultimately empowerment. The intent of PR is not latent awareness. Relevant knowledge increases self-respect and confidence, and leads to exploration of alternatives toward the attainment of goals, and to action. Through this process, the givenness of the group is revealed on which one can build up a superior, higher vision.

Trust, Attitudes, and Listening

Trust can foster or inhibit communication and participation between and among all groups regardless of education, culture, social, or economic status. It is "an a priori requirement for dialogue . . . without this faith . . . dialogue is a farce which inevitably degenerates into paternalistic manipulation" (Freire, 1983, p. 79). It may be more important to know about trust than about educational standards, pedagogical methods, media technology, or communication benchmarks.

Trust is egalitarian. We may succumb to superiors, and condescend to subordinates, but these are not manifestations of genuine trust. In Pakistan, Khan (1976) felt people "valued my human worth, not my office or patronage. Trust, not cleverness, was the medium of communication" (p. 70). Freire (1983) contended those who do not trust others "will fail to initiate (or will abandon) dialogue, reflection and communication, and will fall into using slogans, communiques, monologues, and instructions" (p. 53). Trust is not manifest in positions or labels, but in persons. In contrasting the "professional" and rural world, Fuglesang (1982) wrote "a judgment of reality made by a technical expert is more trusted than a judgment by the village farmer. We disrespect the ideas and opinions of people who happen to have their knowledge from sources other than books" (p. 20).

If we do not trust, we deem others untrustworthy. But is that quality within them, or in our own attitudes of insecurity and aspirations of superiority? More often than not, it may be the latter. Again, to the extent we trust, we are equals. We often do not trust those we want, and are socialized, to feel above, those "lower on the ladder."

We erect elaborate status symbols, orate eloquent speeches, and conduct village meetings with much pomp and formality, all in the name of credibility and integrity. Yet it often seems more akin to an injudicious pageant of unbridled egos. In promoting "expertise," trust is destroyed. A fundamental distrust, therefore, often exists on the part of the officials that is manifested in their opinions and actions.

Hence, PR and planning requires first of all changes in the thinking of development workers themselves. The needles, targets, and audiences of communication and development models, combined with self-righteousness, titles, and insecurities, perhaps sprinkled with a dash of misdirected benevolence, often renders "experts" a bit too verbose and pushy. Perhaps this is because it requires much more imagination, preparation, and hard work to have dialogical learning. It is far easier to prepare and give lectures. However, there is possibly a valid reason why we have two ears, but only one mouth. Communication between people thrives not on the ability to talk fast, but the ability to listen well. People are voiceless not because they have nothing to say, but because nobody cares to listen to them. In this perspective, it is legitimate to say that development begins with listening. It is so simple and yet we fail often because of an egocentric attitude. Fuglesang and Chandler (1987) maintained that in the oral culture of the Massaii "no one dare talk before learning the art of listening. Perhaps the best advice to the modern development communicators is to shut up for awhile" (p. 3). Authentic listening fosters trust much more than incessant talking. Participation, which necessitates listening, and more-over, trust, will "help reduce the social distance between government leaders and villagers as well as facilitate a more equitable exchange of knowledge and articulation of group interests" (Awa, 1987a, p. 24). However, the need to listen is not limited to the poor. It must involve the governments as well as the citizens, the poor as well as the rich, the planners and administrators as well as their targets. This is not to imply that lack of trust is limited to the "experts." Trust, or the lack thereof, is reciprocal. A condescending and paternalistic attitude "tends to build resistance among local peoples to . . . 'foreign' ideas" (Awa, 1987b, p. 9).

BY WAY OF CONCLUSION

Like all research, PR is ideological. It is biased in the sense that it holds that research should be guided by, available to, and of direct benefit to the "researched," rather than privileged information for a manipulative elite. It further believes research is not, nor should it be, the domain of a powerful few with the "proper" tools.

Participatory research is similar, but not equal, to social action research. It is research of involvement, not of detachment. It includes all parties in a process of mutual and increasing awareness and confidence. It is research of conscientization and of empowerment.

There can be no strict methodology for participatory research. However, it must actively and authentically involve participants throughout a cyclical process and the general flow is from study to reflection to action.

Evaluation is inherent in PR. However, it is formative rather than summary evaluation. Its purpose is not for journals, ego-boosting, or to solicit further funding, but rather to monitor and reflect on the process as it unfolds. Furthermore, people's involvement in the research assures validity of the inquiry, their validity.

Even though participation and social development are mammoth, complex issues, we believe that complexity too overwhelming for one person to handle can be figured out by all of us together. We will need a new kind of "school"; not a school for teaching writing and arithmetic, but a school for problems. This type of school necessitates the latitude for participation, for the appropriate attitudes and structures on the part of exogenous personnel and institutions. A school that gives people the opportunity to identify their problems, deal with their problems, and learn from their problems. "Analysis should begin at the level of the people within their own experience and their own level of understanding. This ensures people's collective initiative and participation in the direct development process" (Xavier Institute, 1980, p. 11).

REFERENCES

Aider, P. S. (1985). Beyond cultural identity: Reflections on cultural and intercultural man. In L. A. Samovar & R. E. Porter (Eds.), *Intercultural communication: A reader.* Belmont, CA: Wadsworth.

Albert, M., Cagan, L., Chomsky, N. et al. (1986). *Liberating theory.* Boston: South End Press.

Anyanwu, C. N. (1988). The technique of participatory research in community development. *Communitv Development Journal, 23*(1), 11–15.

Ariyaratne, A. T. (1986). Asian values as a basis for Asian development. In D. C. Korten (Ed.), *Communitv manaqement: Asian experience and perspectives.* West Hartford, CT: Kumarian Press.

Argyris, C., Putnam, R., & Smith D. (1985). *Action science.* San Francisco: Jossey-Bass.

Awa, N. (1987a). Bringing indigenous knowledge into planning. *Media Development, 34*(1).

Awa, N. (1987b, November). *Taking indigenous knowledge seriously in rural development programs.* Paper presented at the 73rd annual meeting of the Speech Communication Association, Boston.

Blair, H. W. (1981). *The political economy of participation in local development programs: Short term impasse and long term change in South Asia and the United States for the 1950's to the 1970's.* Ithaca: Cornell University, Center for International Studies, Rural Development Committee.

Bogaert, MVD., Bhagat S., & Bam., N. B. (1981). Participatory evaluation of an adult education programme. In W. Fernandes & R. Tandon (Eds.), *Participatory research and evaluation: Experiments in research as a process of liberation.* New Delhi: Indian Social Institute.

Bordenave, J. D. (1989, February). *Participative communication as a part of the building of a participative society.* Paper presented at the conference "Participation: A Key Concept in Communication for Change and Development", University of Poona, Pune, India.

Chantana, P., & Wun Gaeo, S. (1985). Participatory research and rural development in Thailand. In Farmer's Assistance Board (Ed.), *Participatory research: Response to Asian people's struggle for social transformation.* Manila: Farmer's Assistance Board.

D'Abreo, D. A. (1981). Training for participatory evaluation. In W. Fernandes & R. Tandon (Eds.), *Participatory research and evaluation: Experiments in research as a process of liberation*. New Delhi: Indian Social Institute.

Dissanayake, W. (1986). The need for the study of Asian approaches to communication. *Media Asia, 13*(1).

Ewen, S. (1983). The implications of empiricism. *Journal of Communication, 33*(3), 219-225.

Fals Borda, 0. (1988). *Knowledge and people's power lessons with peasants in Nicaragua, Mexico and Colombia*. New Delhi: Indian Social Institute.

Farrington, J. (1988). Farmer participatory research: Editorial introduction. *Experimental Agriculture, 24*.

Fernandes, W., & Tandon, R. (Eds.). (1981). *Participatory research and research and evaluation: Experiment in research as a process of liberation*. New Delhi: Indian Social Institute.

Freire, P. (1983). *Pedagogy of the oppressed*. New York: Continuum.

Fuglesang, A. (1982). The myth of people's ignorance. *Development Dialogue, 1*(2).

Fuglesang, A., & Chandler, D. (1987). *The paradigm of communication in development: From knowledge transfer to community participation—lessons from the Grameen Bank* Bangaladesh. Rome: Food and Agriculture Organization (FAO).

Hall, E. (1976). *Beyond culture*. New York: Doubleday.

Halloran, J. D. (1981). The context of mass communication research. In E. G. McAnany, J. Schnitman, & N. Janus (Eds.), *Communication and social structure: Critical studies in mass media research*. New York: Praeger.

Heim, F. G., Rabibhadana, A., & Pinthong, C. (1983). *How to work with farmers: A manual for field workers*. Khon Kaen, Thailand: Khon Kaen University, Research and Development Institute.

Howard, M. C. (1986). *Contemporare cultural anthropology*. Boston: Little, Brown.

Ishii, S. (1985). Thought patterns as modes of rhetoric: The United States and Japan. In L. A. Samovar & R. E. Porter (Eds.), *Intercultural communication: A reader*. Belmont, CA: Wadsworth.

Jacobson, T. (1993). A pragmatist account of participatory communication research for national development. *Communication Theory, 3*(3), 214-230.

Kassam, Y., & Mustafa, K. (Eds.). (1982). *Participatory research. An emerging alternative methodology in social science research*. New Delhi: Society for Participatory Research in Asia.

Kennedy, T. W. (1984). *Beyond advocacy: An animative approach to public participation*. Unpublished doctoral dissertation, Cornell University, Ithaca, NY.

Khan, A. H. (1976). The Comillia experience in Bangladesh—My lessons in communication. In W. Schramm & D. Lerner (Eds.),

Communication and change: The last ten years—and the next. Honolulu: East–West Center.

Kim, Y. Y. (1985). Communication and acculturation. In L. A. Samovar & R. E. Porter (Eds.), *Intercultural communication: A reader.* Belmont, CA: Wadsworth.

Kronenburg, J. (1986). *Empowerment of the poor: A comparative analysis of two development endeavors in Kenya.* Nijmegen: Third World Center.

Kozol, J. (1975). *The night is dark and I am far from home.* Boston: Houghton Mifflin.

Le Boterf, G. (1983). Reformulating participatory research. *Assignment Children, 63*(64), 167-192.

McAnany, E. G. (1983, April). From modernization and diffusion to dependency and beyond: Theory and practice in communication for social change in the 1980s. In *Development Communications in the Third World*, Proceedings of a Midwest Symposium, University of Illinois.

McKee, N. (1989, February). *Beyond social marketing: A community-based learning model.* Paper presented at the conference "Participation: A Key Concept in Communication for Change and Development". University of Poona, Pune, India.

Nanavatty, M. C. (1988). The community development movement in south east Asian Countries: An Asian perspective. *Community Development Journal, 23*(2), 194-199.

Narula, U., & Pearce, W. B. (1986). *Development as communication: A perspective on India.* Carbondale: Southern Illinois University Press.

Nyoni, S. (1987). Indigenous NGOs: Liberation, self-reliance, and development. *World Development, 15*, 51-56.

Ramashray, R., & Srivastava, R.K. (1986). *Dialogues on development: The individual, society, and political order.* New Delhi: Sage.

Rockhill, K. (1982). Researching participation in adult education: The potential of the qualitative perspective. *Adult Education, 33*(1), 3-19.

Rogers, E. (1976). The passing of the dominant paradigm—Reflections on diffusion research. In W. Schramm & D. Lerner (Eds.), *Communication and change: The last ten years—and the next.* Honolulu: East–West Center.

Salmen, L.F. (1987). *Listen to the people: Participant-observer evaluation of development projects.* New York: Oxford University Press.

Servaes, J. (1989). *One world. Multiple cultures. Toward a new paradigm on communication for development.* Louvain: Acco.

Servaes, J. (1992). *Advocacy strategies for health and development: Development communication in action.* Geneva: WHO, Division of Health Education.

Servaes, J. (1994, October). *Communication for development in a global perspective of the role of governmental and non-governmental agencies.* Paper presented at ACCE Conference, Accra.

Servaes, J. (1999). *Communication for development. One world, multiple cultures.* Cresskill, NJ: Hampton Press.

Silberman, M. (1979). Popular participation through communications. *Media Asia, 6*(2).

Tandon, R. (1981). Participatory evaluation and research: Main concepts and issues. In W. Fernandes & R. Tandon (Eds.), *Participatory research and evaluation: Experiments in research as a process of liberation.* New Delhi: Indian Social Institute.

Tandon, R. (1985). Participatory research: Issues and prospects. In Farmer's Assistance Board (Ed.), *Participatory research: Response to Asian people's struggle for social transformation.* Manila: Farmer's Assistance Board.

Thunberg, A-M., Nowak, K., Rosengren, K. E., & Sigurd, B. (1982). *Communication and equality: A Swedish perspective.* Stockholm: Almqvist & Wiksell International.

Varma, R., Ghosal, J., & Hulls, R. (1973, September). *Action research and the production of communication media.* Paper All India Field Workshop, Udaipur.

White, R. (1984, May). *The need for new strategies of research on the democratization of communication.* Paper presented at the Annual Conference of the International Communication Association, San Francisco.

Whyte, W. F. (Ed.). (1991). *Participatory action research.* Newbury Park, CA: Sage.

Xavier Institute. (1980). *Development from below: Notes for workers engaged in rural development and adult education.* Ranchi, India:Author.

5

Participatory Democracy as A Normative Foundation for Communication Studies

Stanley Deetz
University of Colorado

> Democracy is not an alternative to other principles of associated life.
> It is the idea of community life itself . . . a name for a life of free and
> enriching communion.
> —John Dewey (1916)

With the restriction of super powers and the general decline of central planning, increasing numbers of communities and societies are struggling with self-determination. With this, the interlinking of concerns with democracy and communication have become increasingly salient especially in development and planning. From the time of the Greeks and forward, communities have had to rethink how communication processes can advance democratic participation in their time. The modern age is no exception. In the "Western" world, for the past 200 years a belief in "natural rights" has provided a foundation for conceptions of democratic institutions and conceptions of "free speech," "the informed public," and "the marketplace of ideas." Most conceptions of effectiveness, decision making, ethics, responsibilities of the mass media, and access to information, technologies, and media are elaborations of these conceptions. Together, these make up the concept of *liberal democracy*. Largely these same conceptions have been imported with democracy into societies throughout the world. But, certainly since the 1960s, a growing number of political scientists, social philosophers, and communication scholars have questioned the adequacy of such concept for grounding a meaningful democracy or advancing the development of democratic institutions (e.g., Barber, 1984; Deetz, 1992; Hall, 1989; Schiller, 1989).

Several difficulties with liberal democracy are reflected in these works. Speaker rights have been emphasized over information acquisition and listener rights. Expressions of self-interest are emphasized over the development of collective good. The state institution and episodic "political" process are emphasized over daily processes in other institutions. Private choice has been emphasized over the public development of choices. But most significantly, these works have argued that 18th-century conceptions of language, experience, communication, and the human individual as chooser were flawed. Democratic processes have to consider the social production of knowledge, experience, and identity, not merely their expression. In this argument, the focus on the politics of expression rather than on the politics of experience and understanding has been based on inadequate and politically motivated concepts of communication and democracy (see Deetz, 1995b).

Neither the inadequacies nor political motivation can be described as based on clear foresight or conscious design. More appropriately, practical historical solutions to the issues of one time have stretched over into new contexts and situations and need reassessment. Such a reassessment cannot arise from a new philosophical foundation based in natural rights nor from simply making more empirical observations. As a society, we must choose the nature of our democracy. Neither nature nor causal or evolutionary models of transformation can redeem us from the inevitability of continued practical and theoretical choices and our moral responsibility to good choices. To be meaningful, such examination must be theoretically guided. Saying this does not mean to suggest that we can or should implement simple theoretical solutions to our complex life situation. The failure of utopian and even less grand attempts at the "great society" are too obvious and too numerous to need recounting here. Rather, I believe that we share in the community ascertainable principles and methods for productive discussion and development that exceed our current practices and that these cannot be simply discovered in empirical observations. Our pretheoretical understandings and prejudices provide important guidance to our theory and judgments. But not all are equally valid.

Communication researchers can provide the important insights for good social choices. This requires, however, examining the democratic political foundations of research as well as the practices of other communities. Generally, I support a "stakeholder" model of representation in community decision making (see Deetz, 1995b, 1995c). Such a model specifies the need for both forums for stakeholder involvement and the development of stakeholder voice. The liberal democracy model based on individualism and advocacy accomplished neither very well. In contrast, this chapter will develop a general theoretical perspective for the analysis of communication processes guided by a model of *participatory democracy*. In order to accomplish this, a conception of theory and research as intrinsically linked to a historical social setting and the development of social good are proposed. Furthermore, the chapter develops the value of communication as a mode of analysis as well as a phenomenon for analysis. From this initial base, a conception of participation is developed out of the critical hermeneutic tradition as a pretheoretical normative foundation for acting in and evaluating communication systems. The chapter ends with a discussion of the role of the intellectual in using participative democratic theory to guide the ongoing practices of understanding, critique, and education in teaching and research.

A SOCIAL CONCEPTION OF THEORY

Theory is one of many modern contested terms. The attempt by many to give it a definition, to reduce it to a dead, neutral entity, can be readily grasped as a political maneuver. Theory in the popular parlance is treated as abstract and separated from the real world. The development of "positivist" science and elaboration of the hypothetical deductive model institutionalizes theory as representational of experience. Against this background I wish to claim theory as an intrinsic part of experience itself. To examine theory is to examine experience and vice versa.

A theory is a way of seeing and thinking about the world rather than an abstract representation of it. As such, it is better seen as the "lens" one uses in observation than a "mirror" of nature (Rorty, 1979). Lest the lens metaphor suggest the possible transparency of theory, as if it disappears if it is a good clean lens, recall that the clearest microscope gives us radically different observation from the telescope. Furthermore, if the metaphor suggests the stability of a world only shown differently through different lens, where is the world not seen through some lens? The lens metaphor helps us think productively about theory choice: What do we want to pay attention to? What will help us attend to that? What are the consequences of attending to that? The treatment of observation as if it preceded and could be compared to theoretical accounts, hides the theoretical choice (whether through concept or instrumentation or both) implicit in the observation itself. Hanson (1965) captured well for the natural sciences what seems so hard for social scientist and everyday people to accept. All observations are theory-laden. In his metaphor, theory and the external world are like the warp and woof in the fabric called observation. Although the woof may typically be the more visible, the observation cannot exist without the warp. The attempt to talk about one in the absence of the other unravels the total observation leaving neither the theory nor world as of any interest.

The problem with most theories is not that they are wrong nor lacking in confirming experiences but that they are often irrelevant, misdirect observation, or function to aid only dominant groups. They do not help us make the observations that are important to meeting critical goals and needs of the full variety of community stakeholders. Despite popular mythologies, social science theories, whether by everyday people or scholars, are rarely accepted or dismissed because of the data. As Gergen (1982) showed, the major theories that have shaped everyday thinking and definition of social science problems have had very little data. Rather, they offered compelling conceptions of core life issues challenging both existing assumptions and the supporting dominant values. This should be no surprise as Kuhn demonstrated much the same in the natural sciences. There are reasons why certain theories are accepted and not others, but not simply facts. Furthermore, the use of certain theories and even the findings from them are often best explained by popularity cycles, boredom, career needs, and social and economic conditions (Wagner & Gooding, 1987). Theory and research are deeply value-laden (Hamnett, Porter, Singh, & Kumar, 1984).

Gergen (1978, 1982) and Rorty (1979), among many, showed the inadequacy of theories as representational and the hypothetical deductive model as a way of thinking about theory choice. The various assumptions of the preeminence of objective facts, the demand for verification, the goal of universal atemporarily findings, and the presumption of a dispassionate bystander all hide the nature and evaluation of theories (Gergen, 1978, 1982). "Facts" imply either a completion or suppression of a conflictual negotiation process involving different interest and stakeholders. "Scientific procedures" often suppress negotiation or lead us away from examining its character. Hypothesis testing is largely self-fulfilling over time because the theory shapes what will be attended to and people respond interactively in testing situations. All findings are a historical artifact both because of theory and because people change over time in part in response to social science reports. The question is only whether we accept the conditions and practices necessary to produce the scientific artifact. Every theory carries the values of a research community that often substitutes its terms and interpretations for those lived by the subject community (Deetz, 1973). Modern philosophy of science, particularly as practiced in the social sciences, overcompensated for the fear of the medieval authority of the church, rhetoric over reason, and the ideological bases of knowledge and in doing so became an arbitrary and at time capricious authority producing an ideology itself with its own rhetorical appeal (Schaffer, 1989). The greatest problem with a theory is not being wrong (for that will be discovered) but with misdirecting our collective attention and hindering our assessment of where it takes us. Rather than assuming simplistic conceptions of science as a fixed answer, the relation of knowledge to the human community is the task to be worked out. Such a relation is acknowledged by every good researcher. Most often, however, it merely gets an "of course" or smile and nod before the return to hypothesis testing. If we take this obvious point seriously, how would we change our theorizing, research, and teaching?

The point here is not to reject hypothesis testing or finding careful methodical ways to distinguish reality-based from imaginary relations. Such activities, whether in the field or in the lab, however, need to be complemented by a more basic understanding of the relation of theories and the world, relations of power and knowledge, and the relation of theories to real human communities. To do so we best understand theory as a way of being in the world. Theories are developed and are accepted in human communities based on their ability to provide interesting and useful ways of conceptualizing, thinking, and talking about life events. The social science community differs from life world community primary in regard to what is interesting and useful because of both community standards and the events that are significant (Deetz, 1995a). Most often, a philosophy of science attempts to reconstruct the practices of researchers as if they could be freed from the events of their time, as if we wished that they were freed, and as if everyday people's theories in natural languages had more difficulties than social science theories in technical languages. More realistically, both everyday life and social science conceptions are needed. Everyday people respond to many mythologies and we have yet to see a life or a society run well based on a social science theory. This partially explains the double feeling of researchers that no one listens to them and the fear that someone might. Rather than beginning with an elitist view of theory, let us start with a reconstruction of everyday life.

The Functions of Theory

All creatures develop ways of dealing with practical tasks and problems in their worlds. In that sense they all have theories. They have plans, they make observations, they have an idea of how these observations fit together, and a set of activities that follow. This is all we would expect of any theory. Some of them work, others fail. When they work, it is always within certain parameters or domains. Few theories are failures in regard to specific situations. All theories ultimately fail if applied far enough outside of the specific conditions for which they were developed. Theories thus differ more in the size of their domain and the realistic nature of the parameters than in correctness. We all operate day in and out with flat earth assumptions. It is only on the occasions when we wish to do things that require another model that we increase the complexity of our thought. In this sense, all theories will fail in time, not because of falsity, but because human purposes and environments change.

Abstracting theory from this life context is essential for testing and critical reflection, but we can lose this essential connection. In this sense, critical reflection and testing are moments in human theorizing but scientific research and theorizing can not be reduced to these processes. This may be clearer in an example from Austin (1961) in his analysis of the "representation" problem in language analysis. As he reasoned, the question "What is a rat?" differs greatly from the question "What is the meaning of the word 'rat'?" The former treats conception as part of the human act of seeing the world in a specific interest, from a point of view. The latter question removes us from the life context and poses an abstract and universalizing question stripped of the specific domain and practical parameters. Whether the question, "What is a rat?" arises as a child's question or as part of a dispute as to whether the creature standing there is one, the focus is to the world, to the subject matter. The conception raises new looks, new considerations, further observations, and a relation to the other. The latter question poses the issue of correctness, cleaning up the word, nomenclature committees, and operational definitions. As an analog, the latter question is about theory, the former about the world with a theory as the point of view. When thinking about theory these are important complementary questions. Unfortunately, we often contextualize the former in regard to the later rather than vice versa. When this happens, theory is abstracted from the world rather than intrinsic to our being directed to it. The variable analytic tradition of sequential hypothesis testing, with its strings of research reports disconnected from their conditions of production, resulted in "textbook" style knowledge. All those have this odd quality of being concrete and specific yet only referring back to themselves in their logical interdependence rather than leading to understanding the world. Mills aptly referred to this as *abstracted empiricism.* Ironically, the more applied and specific such knowledge is made, the further it gets from directing attention to significant features of the outside world and the more self-referential it is to its own imaginary world produced out of itself.

By investigating the function of theory in life, we can arrive at more fruitful ways of thinking about testing theory abstracted from life. Allow me to suggest three basic functions, directing attention, organizing experience, and enabling useful responses. Can we see differences that make a difference? Can we form and recognize patterns that specify what things are and how they relate? Can we make choices that not only enable us to survive and fulfill needs but also to create the future we want?

Directing Attention. Attention is largely a trained capacity. While our sense equipment is nature's or more properly our ancient forbearers' theory of what we should be able to detect, our conceptual schemes and sense extensions become the manner of our more immediate history. At the most basic level, theories direct our attention, that is, they guide us to see details of importance. Plato was certainly right (but for the wrong reasons) that if you didn't know what you were looking for, you wouldn't know when you had found it. Perceptually, this is easy to see. I can recall the first time I looked into a microscope in biology class. What was gray mass to me were clear cells to the instructor. The eye needed to be trained not so much in seeing but in seeing the differences that mattered, setting the apparatus to be able to make those differences visible. The matter organizable as a "cell" had to be out there, but it also needed to be in here in both setting the right power and noting the key features. Changing theories is like making a gestalt shift. The issue is what is figure and what is ground. Like changing a microscope's power of magnification, you lose the ability to see certain structures for the sake of seeing others. It is not as if one or the other is the better representation of the "real" thing. Each draws attention to and displays a different structure of potential interest, a different real thing.

Perceptual examples show the basic relation but can be misleading. The following first-grade example keeps the perceptional experience "constant," but works with the conceptual relation. The teacher presents four boxes. In each box is a picture—a tree, a cat, a dog, and a squirrel, respectively. The child is asked which picture is different. A child ready for advancement to second grade immediately picks the tree. The child knows not only how to divide plants from animals, but also that the plant–animal distinction is the preferred one to apply. The perception is valuational. We know from the outside, however, that the choice is arbitrary and hardly a very interesting way to think about the problem; the choice is made more from the power of the teacher in evaluation embedded in routine classroom choices than from the nature of "reality." The squirrel as easily could have been picked if the child had distinguished on the bases of domesticity or things that can be bought at the store. The dog could have been picked because the cat, squirrel, and tree relate in a playful, interactive way. The child could have picked the cat because he or she has seen the other three in the yard. Or any one of them could have been picked based on having or not having, liking or not liking bases.

The issue is not one of the linguistic or conceptual determination of perception (e.g., how many kinds of snow Eskimos have). Rather the issue is the choice of the distinctions to be used, the differences that matter. There is little problem working through the reconception of the dog, cat, squirrel, and tree and finding a way to see each of them as the different one. Nature is indifferent to the choice. The question is knowing which is the better frame to use to view the world, rather than the issue of accuracy or truth. Once the system of distinction is "chosen," then questions arise such as: "Should this be classified as an animal?" "What features distinguish plants and animals?" "How should individuals be classified" (e.g., which is a virus?)? And finally, abstract theories and "empirical" questions and hypothesis can be raised and tested. For example, "How many animals are there?" "Since this is an animal, what behaviors should we expect? The problem with starting with an hypothesis tested against the "real" world is that the reason for the quotation marks around "chosen," "empirical," and "real" is lost. The child who chooses the tree rarely raises the alternative conceptual distinctions to make the choice, nor do we typically when presented with the same problem. The issues do not become empirical after we have "decided" to utilize the plant–animal rather domestic–wild point of view, it already was. We would smile at the child who when challenged, said that "Yeah, we could divide them into categories of domestic and wild, but they're really plants and animals." The child's complaint that we are relativists totally misses the point. The presumed real, empirical, and unchosen often misses the value-laden, theory-based observation. Human choices, even if unwittingly made, are key, not the assumed nature of the things themselves. Quoting Rorty (1981):

> If we fail to discern the same virtues in Skinner as in Bohr, it is not because Skinner does not understand his pigeons or his people as well as Bohr understands his particles, but because we are, reasonably enough, suspicious of people who make a business of predicting and controlling other people. We think that these virtues are not appropriate for the situation. We think that there are more important things to find out about people than how to predict and control them, even though there be nothing more important to find out about rocks, and perhaps even pigeons. But once we say that what human beings are *in themselves* suits them to be described in terms which as less apt for prediction and control than Skinner's, we are off down the same garden path as when we say that what atoms are *in themselves* suits

them to be described in terms which *are* apt for predication and control. In neither case do we have the slightest idea what "in themselves" means. We are simply expressing a preference for predicting rocks over doing anything else with them, and a preference for doing other things with people over predicting their behavior. (p. 5)

Unfortunately we have acquired a number of bad habits from the old philosophy of science that lead us away from understanding the importance of theory in directing attention. The metaphysical position that theory provides words to name characteristics of objects in themselves and mirror fixed relations among objects, underestimates the inexhaustible number of things and relations our attention might be directed to see in things and hides the important issues in theory selection. Our simple practices of defining terms operationally or attributionally hide the construct's function in providing or collecting a stable object with presumed fixed attributes. Rather than seeking definitions and moving to categorize, we should ask: "What am I able to see or think about if I talk about it in this way rather than that?"

Organizing Experience. Theory not only directs our attention, it also presents our observation as being part of meaningful patterns. The perception of an individual already pulls together past experience with similar people (the lines of relation following the distinctions being utilized) and reaches to anticipate possible actions. Everyday people, like social scientists, are constantly engaged in the process of trying to explain the past and present and trying to predict the future and possible responses to our own actions. But prediction and control, like spiritual and teleological models, account for only part of the available structurings and human interests displayed in patterning. The nature and types of patterns experienced is potentially very rich. The observation of continuity rather than discontinuity, pattern simplification rather than pattern complexification are not simply given in nature but arise out of human orientation to the world (Foucault, 1970). Predication and control should properly be seen as one human motive that is at times privileged over competing motives and organizing schemes.

One of the facets of modern social science is the projection of its own motive to enhance control onto the subjects that it studies. This is perhaps clearest in interpersonal interaction studies. In everyday life, interpersonal relationships often show the greatest degree of open negotiation and mutual decision making. Ironically, the usual research emphasis on uncertainty reduction, compliance-gaining, and persuasion mirror more the philosophy of science used by the researchers than people to whom I relate. The recent focus on uncertainty-reduction theory in intercultural communication research appears to be based on an assumed fear of difference and the otherness of others. Researchers could be focusing on the difference of the other enjoying curiosity, excitement of novelty, and self-change (one wonders whether objectifying the other is the cause or result of the fear that seems to fill the research).

Clearly, all research is historically situated. People and societies concerned with individualism and control organize experience different from those interested in the community and fate. Each orientation can produce empirically confirmable structures and orders, but all can be one-sided. Cognitive theorists have been most sensitive to the relation of social science community orders and everyday orders and tell us much about the various types of ordering relations people have developed and use. Unfortunately, they tend to glorify rule following reasoning as a metatext for examining and discussing alternatives. Although the orders produced may be quite different, the twin themes of differentiation and organization appear central to theorizing.

Enabling Useful Responses. Theories in everyday life as well as in social science have a pragmatic motive. Although this may often be covered up with a claim of truth or demonstration of what is, the choice is always of this truth versus that one, this "what" versus that one. Kelly (1955) demonstrated this clearly from the individual standpoint in his development of the pragmatic basis of personal constructs. Constructs are developed and elaborated in directions that help people accomplish life goals. Institutionalized social science merely extends this individual process. There appears to be little disagreement with this basic motivational frame, although it can be quite complex in practice.

Theoretical conceptions that are useful to one individual or group can be quite detrimental to others. The social choice of theories thus always has to consider questions such as whose goals will count for how much. Consequently, looked at from the perspective of the society, useful responses have to be considered in terms of some conception of social good as viewed from multiple stakeholders. Unfortunately, the issue of pragmatics is often read too narrowly both in everyday life and in the social sciences. Pragmatics as a simple instrumental motive overlooks the competing human desires to overcome their initial subjective motives, to make their own histories toward a richer collective life (Habermas, 1971). When theories are considered instrumentally, efficient and effective goal accomplishment would appear to be easily agreed on social goods. But not only do such goals have be be assessed from the standpoint of whose goals are accomplished, but efficiency and effectiveness are not themselves goods (Carter & Jackson, 1987).

Dewey presented a better lead on making choices regarding alternative theories. Rorty (1982) phrased his basic questions as: "What would it be like to believe that? What would happen if I did? What would I be committing myself to?" (p. 163). Such a position does not so much give us an answer to the questions of social good, but poses the locus and nature of responsibility. Theories about human beings are different from theories about chemicals, they ultimately influence what people as the subjects of the research will become. How we conceptualize and talk about ourselves and others influences what we become. Theories function to produce responses that produce ourselves, our social interaction, our institutions, and our collective future. Theories must be assessed in light of the kind of society we wish to produce. We are concerned with meeting our needs and with doing so in a way that makes us better people. In Rorty's (1979) words:

> To say that we become different people, that we ("remake") our-selves as we read more, talk more, and write more, is simply a dramatic way of saying that sentences which become true of us by virtue of such activities are often more important to us than sentences which become true of us when we drink more, earn more, and so on . . . getting the facts right . . . is merely propaedeutic to finding new and more interesting ways of expressing ourselves, and thus of coping with the world. (p. 359)

All current theories will pass in time. It is not as if they are in error, at least little more or less so than those in the past. Older theories were useful in handling different kinds of human problems, problems we might find ill-formed and even silly, as others will find ours. What remains is the human attempt to produce theories that are useful in responding to our own issues. We are struggling to find interesting and useful ways of thinking and talking about our current situation and helping us build the future we want. Such hope is intrinsic to theorizing rather than external to it.

Power and Knowledge

At least since Bacon most Westerners have believed that knowledge is power, that having or possessing knowledge gives its holder choices and influence. Contemporary thinking has of course totally rearranged such an equation. Foucault (1970, 1980b) in particular, focused attention on the power in, rather than to the power of, knowledge. There is a politics within the production of knowledge. As Hoy (1986) expressed it, "the relation is such that knowledge is not gained prior to and independent of the use to which it will be put in order to achieve power (whether over nature or over people), but is already a function of human interests and power relations" (p. 129). In this sense, in each society in each age there is a regime of truth generated out of a network of power relations. Certain discourses are accepted and made true and mechanisms are developed that enable the distinction between true and false statements. Experts are produced out of the same system to affirm the knowledge claims (Knights, 1992; Townley, 1992). Again, this does not suggest that "truth" is relative in any simple way, for within the constraint of interests and values, competing claims can be compared. But the choice of research questions and the choice of constraints and values are historical and are politically charged. For example, the frequent tension between religious and scientific truth exists at the point each tries to extend itself into the other's discourse. When science describes what is and religion describes what one should do, they coexist. In contemporary society, science gets into trouble when it tries to empirically derive thoughts, and religion when it tries to explain empirical reality. The conditions for making a claim to truth differ in each. Knowledge is not so much to be accepted, then, as to be explained. The concern is to explain the conditions constitutive of leading forms of knowledge in particular communities.

The point is not to find a way to settle conflicting knowledge claims, not to degrade truth, but to recall the disciplinary power necessary for any knowledge claim (Foucault, 1980b). The knowledge claimed in everyday life—in its institutions of science, commerce, and religion—as well as knowledge about knowledge claims in everyday life are politically loaded. Laying out their driving interests and mechanisms of knowledge production and defense is central to understanding how they work. The central problem in most community-based decisions in not in the lack of adequately distributed information (although that can be a problem), but in processes of information production. Open participation can be advanced at each point in information production through examination of choice of questions, conception, and research practices (Harding, 1992; Whyte, 1991) through publication (Deetz, 1995a), and interpretation. Issues of power are involved at each point, issues that are often obscured by claims of truth and expertise.

THE VALUE OF A COMMUNICATION PERSPECTIVE

A leading goal of intellectual work is to provide theoretical perspectives that lead us to perceive differences that make a difference and organizes our perceptions toward making useful social responses. To be successful, such perspectives should be grounded in the present social historical context aimed at enhancing useful social responses to contemporary social issues that are themselves partially theoretically constructed. Such perspectives are ultimately answerable to real communities of actors rather than to universal standards of truth. They also must grow out of that community's struggle to understand and respond to its actual historical context, although it cannot simply end there. In this sense, neither a formal reconstructed normative science nor ethnography of everyday life will do. A necessary interactivity of social science, researched subjects, and audience community is necessarily assumed (Apel, 1979; Bernstein, 1984). I have conceptualized this as dialogic research (Deetz, 1994, 1996).

Contemporary issues of democracy and communication are clearly complex. Portions of these issues have been usefully described using economic, sociological, historical, psychological, and technological descriptions. Everyday actors like social scientists have tended to be either monist or pluralists in their theorizing; either reducing alternative conceptions to a central driving one (the various ". . .ists"), or oscillating between different and often incommensurable perspectives without a conception of how the "elephant" fits together (Albert et al., 1986). Part of the reason for this is the representational theory of knowledge that treats different means of explanation as if they represented a particular domain of experience, as if there were "actual" economic events, psychological events, and so forth. More appropriately, modes of explanation are simply different perspectives on and ways of talking about and constituting events. Albert et al. (1986) referred to this as enabling the development of a complementary holist perspective whereby different perspectives are seen as different ways of articulating the same complex moment of interconnectedness that gains constancy as an event only as described. In this sense, a holist perspective draws attention to the complex that can be unpacked along different horizons; the same "stuff" collected as different "objects" rather than one "object" composed of distinctly different parts or seen in different ways. For example, money can be seen as a resource in economic theory, a commodification of value in sociological theory, or information in a communication theory. Personality can be abstracted from a set of communicative behaviors (including test-taking) or treated as a cause of communication behaviors (such as giving answers). Voting can be a political act or a communicative one. The question then is not what is this thing really or which came first, but which way of conceptualizing it and its relations to other events enable the most interesting and socially useful conception. The existence of a reductionist thesis tends to privilege more atomistic explanations over holistic ones, but there is no evidence that such preference is any more than a power move in relation to sciences' struggle for legitimacy in the 19th century (Schaffer, 1989). Any such preference should be open to examination.

Different social science disciplines arise at the point when certain social conditions posed a problem or set of issues to which current approaches could not provide a useful conception (Foucault, 1970). Psychology could not exist without a concern with nonspiritual hidden causes and could not be sustained without the development of an individualistic point of view and the desire to predict and control individual behavior. Modern economics required an exchange theory of value, sociology required urbanization and the breakdown of community structures.

Modern social conditions have led both scholars and everyday people to pose communication questions. This does not so much foster an academic discipline (for the institutionalized study of communication primarily engages in psychological explanations) nor a new domain of phenomena (although some technologies are somewhat new), but a way of thinking about and conceptualizing social issues—a discipline (see Deetz, 1994). Such a change can be readily evidenced in several academic disciplines. For example, literary studies have gradually come to be understood in communication terms. This contrasts with understanding mass communication in literary terms as was done at the turn of the century. Such changes arose from the so-called linguistic turn in philosophy that produced the community of natural language users as more central than consciousness as the site of knowledge and understanding. Communication explanations growing out of this stretch widely into critical theory, ordinary language philosophy, structuralist, and postmodern thought. The alignment of new technologies, organizational structures, linguistic and symbolic forms, rapid individual life changes, new interactional places and constraints, and the need for constant social negotiation of the premises for collective decisions enable and call for a new way of thinking. Development can be explained in economic, technological, and psychological terms, but we can initiate a productive discussion by conceptualizing each of these from a communication perspective. A communication perspective allows a better accounting of different groups and their possible contribution to understanding and decision making.

But what does it mean to discuss psychology, economics, and sociology in communication terms rather than to explain communication in psychological, economic, or sociological terms? Certainly, communication as meaning transmission or self-expression offers little. A communication perspective denotes here the primacy of the system of interaction as "textual" in several areas: the production of personal identity, the meaning of individual behavior, the formation of social structure, and the determination of value (Deetz, 1995b; for a similar development, see Pearce, 1989). Such a position is consistent with Baudrillard's (1981) more fully developed argument that every commodity signifies. This includes material texts, objects, behaviors, and technologies. This is not to claim that everything is communication (a domain problem of nonexclusion). Such a problem does not arise if communication is understood as one of the several perspectives through which everything can be viewed, that among other ways everything can be seen in its communicative constitution and communicative function. Each has costs and advantages. A communication perspective gives unique and interesting insights into today's issues.

A communication explanation is structural and multidimensional, producing unity and discontinuity. Watzlawick, Beavin, and Jackson (1967) clearly demonstrated such a position in their treatment of the family interaction system. More recently, Gergen and Davis (1985) collected works that focus more clearly on the communicative production of the human subject. The individual personality is not fixed but is produced in the family systems and fulfills functions unique to that system. Although a produced personality may influence the formation and function of a new system, the assumed casual direction of the relation between personality and interaction system is a choice. More properly, the individual is seen as one of many sites of agency each having limited but real effects and all effects being interactive. Weedon (1987), from a very different theoretical perspective, concluded much the same about the production of identity and subjectivity. She showed, however, that the decision to position a unified subject as first cause of experience performs a political function to hide power relations in the construction of identity and experience. Reproblematizing this political relation ultimately leads to a preference for a structural communication explanation over competing ones. Space here does not permit the similar consideration of the communication account of social structure or the discursive quality of economic resources (see Deetz, 1995b).

The justification for a communication perspective, however, cannot exist in demonstrating its possibility or its historical presence, rather theories developed with a communication perspective can be developed that pose and give insight into significant social issues. This position does not promise an ultimate cause and delineation of causal forces but descriptions of the various forms of interactivities, the processes by which the elements produce, are produced by, and reproduce structural configurations. To work this through, I return to the issue of community-based social good only now in the context of a communication perspective.

PARTICIPATORY THEORIES OF COMMUNICATION

Clearly, an historical tension has existed between between effectiveness and participation as the basic communication goal (see Deetz, 1992). Development literature often focuses on communication as a means of control, diffusion, colonization, and integration. Good communication is considered that which effectively organizes, diffuses, controls, or informs. But many theorists and practitioners have also focused on processes of codetermination and negotiation (see Forester, 1989; Friedman, 1973; Golembiewski, 1989). Recently, participation has been recovered as an issue in the everyday social construction of meaning and identity (Hall, 1989). The choice of participation over effectiveness as an evaluative principle is not based simply on a preference any of us might have but can be shown to be an anticipated, but unfulfilled, normative condition of every act of communication. Current social conditions, however, make it difficult to clearly understand and articulate these assumed norms in everyday life situations. Habermas (1979, 1984) has done much to thematize this everyday life condition in his analysis of communicative action. Although I wish to add to and depart from his analysis at places, I believe he provided a good point of departure.

Much has been written on Habermas' theory of communicative action, so I am brief here. Most commonly used theories of communication focus on effective transmission and persuasive effectiveness (Axley, 1984). The communication goals and difficulties commonly identified by these theories have to do with the distribution of appropriate, high-fidelity information or with processes of influence and control. Communication effectiveness is based primarily on reproductive fidelity. Process models may break the linear conception of this reproduction but still set as an ideal the speaker's ability to lead the listener to a predefined thought or action. Many works have shown the several liabilities of such conceptions through reconceptions of "process," "dialectics," and more recently through the politics of representation (Hall, 1989). Despite the commonsense character of the effective transmission view, Gadamer (1975) and Habermas (1984, 1987) showed this strategic use of communication to depend on a more basic communicative attempt to reach mutual understanding. Although their conceptions differ on the nature of the process, they both emphasize the continual social formation of consensus in interaction beyond the intentions and opinions of the participants. Mutual understanding focuses attention on reaching openly formed agreement regarding the subject matter under discussion rather than on the agreement of the perspective of the participants. As Habermas (1984) presented his position:

> Processes of reaching understanding aim at an agreement that meets the conditions of rationally motivated assent [*Zustimmung*] to the content of an utterance. A communicatively achieved agreement has a rational basis; it cannot be imposed by either party, whether instrumentally through intervention in the situation directly or strategically. . . . This is not a question of the predicates an observer uses when describing processes of reaching understanding, but of the

> pretheoretical knowledge of competent speakers, who can them-
> selves distinguish situations in which they are causally exerting an
> influence *upon* others from those where they are coming to an
> understanding *with* them. . . . [T]he use of language with an orienta-
> tion to reaching understanding is the *original mode* of language use,
> upon which indirect understanding, giving something to understand
> or letting something be understood, and the instrumental use of lan-
> guage in general, are parasitic. (pp. 286–288)

Such an analysis depends on a careful description of the attempt to reach mutual understanding, a socially based description of morally guided dispute resolution, and a description of communicative difficulties (i.e., communicative processes that preclude mutual understanding). The effectiveness–ineffectiveness issues become recontextualized by a concern with participation. From a participation perspective, communication difficulties arise from communication practices that preclude value debate and conflict, that substitute images and imaginary relations for self-presentation and negotiable truth claims, that arbitrarily limit access to communication channels and forums, and that lead to decisions based on arbitrary authority relations. Let me start by developing a conception of participation as a normative standard against which all acts of communication can be judged, consider objections to the primacy of this standard, and provide an initial development of models of participation.

Participation as a Shared Ideal

Trying to identify a normative standard for any human enterprise is filled with pitfalls. Most scholars have given up on the attempt to privilege certain forms of communication or social organization on philosophical grounds, although many in the society still argue for certain basic human rights. Although most today refuse to articulate normative principles at all, I have not yet seen a work on communication that does not implicitly advance some good–bad, better–worse, healthy–pathological position. In most cases, the standard is implicit and not open to debate, although certainly present and operant. A few, however, reject the possibility of any norms not based in opinion and power relations. Foucault (1980b) in particular, has most adamantly rejected the possibility of nonethnocentric, ahistorical normative principles. Nonetheless, even in Foucault, one can discern a desire for a type of domination-free "dialogue" where common concerns and conflicting interpretations could be articulated. Even without proclaiming a universal foundation, looking at the attempts to do so can be instructive and useful toward making the more fluid and momentary normative choices we must make. German philosophical writings in general and critical theory in particular have contributed much.

Following Apel (1979), a twofold foundation for regulative communication principles can be advanced:

> First, in all actions and omissions, it should be a matter of ensuring the *survival* of the human species *qua real* communication community. Second, it should be a matter of realizing the *ideal* communication community in the real one. The first goal is the necessary condition for the second; and the second goal provides the first with meaning. . . . [T]he task of realizing the ideal communication community [aims at] the elimination of all socially determined asymmetries of interpersonal dialogue. (pp. 282–283)

The key issues here rest in the relation of the real and ideal communication community and the nature of socially determined asymmetries. The significance of the ideal communication community rests in its preacceptance (although usually unaware) by each interactant when engaging in communication. The argument here is not simply that we should believe in and try to create the ideal but that each and every interactant presents an acceptance of the ideal as a background for each communicative act performed. Even the most strategic act of self-interested expression takes place in a language community where presumptions of reciprocity and symmetry exist. For example, lying can only work to one's advantage in a community where honesty is assumed. The act of lying has to present an anticipation of truthfulness. The lie's social violation from a participation standpoint does not come in the deception per se, for the speaker is as much removing him or herself from representation in the distortion of decision making. The lie, however, functions to undermine the social consensus necessary for the act of communication to function at all. It is not only false, but anticipates and at once denies the social possibility of communication.

The support for participation as a normative ground is thus based on the presumption or anticipation of some ideal communication situation by each real communication community. The anticipation of the ideal community has been demonstrated in two ways. First, Gadamer (1975), in developing an ontology of understanding, demonstrated the social character of the formation of experience that precedes each and every expression of it—the hermeneutic situation. Second, Habermas (1979, 1984) and Apel (1979) showed that the illocutionary structures in discourse demonstrate the types of claims that can be made in a society and anticipate the forms of support and dispute in contested claims—the ideal speech situation. In both cases, the "hermeneutic" and "ideal speech" situation are counterfactual—that is, rarely fully realized—but each is a necessary anticipation.

The counterfactual nature of this ideal is frequently bothersome to "empirical" investigators primarily interested in generalization from physical artifacts. They might well ask what the empirical evidence is for such anticipations. Many researchers would only accept a concept of anticipation if it were a testable psychological state such as a goal or attitude. The idea of a structural or implicative relation appropriate to a communication analysis may seem inadequate. There are a number of ways in which most already unproblematically accept such anticipations. The clearest nonempirical communal assumption is grammar. As Chomsky (1959) clearly demonstrated, no set of probability models could ever give us grammar. They could only give the likelihood of any word following another in the sentence. No person has to be able to articulate the rules of grammar to speak grammatically. An ungrammatical sentence does not disclaim grammar but is judged ungrammatical or anticipates another grammar that is simply not yet described. In Wittgenstien's sense, to speak a language already anticipates a community of language users. The empirical demonstration of the anticipated ideal requires a careful analysis of empirical events, not a simple empirical generalization.

Furthermore, the claim is not only for the interstructure anticipation, but also for the preferability of participation over effectiveness as a normative ground. Neither effectiveness nor participation are fully present in any communication event. Even the best strategies sometimes fail, understanding is rarely complete, and participation is always only partial. Effectiveness and participation are goals that guide the improvement of communicative interaction. Their empirical absence in real situations is in fact what guides conceptions and writings about them. The goal of effectiveness, like participation, is socially developed in communication communities, the concern with social good asks to which goals or goals we wish to commit ourselves. Shall effectiveness be seen within the context of the promotion of participation or participation out of the context of effectiveness; the dialectic or marketplace conceptions of democracy?

The argument to be advanced is that the participative goal is essential for the social development of community good. The continued direction of effectiveness-based communication analysis will lead to progressively more systems of privatized interest control and consequently, more need for internal and external systems of monitoring and control, and, finally, less explicit exploration of social choice (Habermas, 1987). The preferred hope, I believe, is for more open participation and the evolution of more representative and responsive institutions. This is a change from seeing the individual as more or less effective to seeing the interaction as more or less productive—that is, in the service of further understanding and agreement on the subject matter being determined by the open nature of the subject matter itself. The change is from seeing the individual's point of view and how it is presented to determining whether the interaction includes all relevant positions and interests. Whenever the results of science or the "objects" of one's experience are held as natural and self-evident, the subject's relation to the world (open to negotiation with others) is transformed to a limited subjective domination of the world with objectification blocking productive interaction with the world or the other. Interaction cannot be participatory without representing the various interests within a context of world openness.

Conversation and Mutual Understanding

Gadamer (1975) offered much to the development of the concept of participative meaning and interaction as productive in his ontological analysis of understanding. The full significance of his position requires a careful development of a hermeneutic description of language, a development that is beyond the scope of this work and can be found elsewhere (see Deetz, 1978). Central to his theory of language and implicit normative ideal is his description of the genuine conversation. The genuine conversation is hermeneutically shown to be a special interaction among two persons and the subject matter before them. Although most communication studies turn to consider what each person has to say about the subject matter, Gadamer focused on what the subject matter "says" to each. The relationship may be clearer if we look at the experience of a great work of art.

In Gadamer's analysis, the significance of a great work of art rests more in what it demands of us than in what we say about it or judge it to be. In fact, a great work of art demands from us thoughts, feelings, the formation of concepts and evaluative criteria that do not precede its presence—it questions the adequacy of what we think and say. If the person with such an experience wishes to bring it to another, it is not one's own feelings and concepts that are at issue for they are inevitably less than the work has to offer. The attempt is rather to help the other remove limitations to his or her own seeing so that the work may more thoroughly draw on them. Ideally, the other will help reveal aspects of the work that enriches one's own experience. The conversation has the character of progressively opening the prejudicial certainty of each individual to question. A truly great work might call one's very way of life into question.

Although the subject matter of most conversations does not have the significance and power of the great work of art, a productive rather than reproductive conception of communication shows the fundamental process by which mutual understanding arises in regard to the subject matter rather than the sharing of opinion. Gadamer (1975) argued that the ideal is not "self-expression and the successful assertion of one's point of view, but a transformation into communion, in which we do not remain what we were" (p. 341). Although the dialectic of the genuine conversation requires a certain commonality of prior understanding, it works more to create and recreate a common language and experience. More than sharing one's experience or point of view, it is the "art of seeing things in the unity of an aspect, i.e., it is the art of the formation of concepts as the working out of common meaning" (Gadamer, 1975, p. 331). It is not the insides of the other or the self that is to be understood for either would be covering up the objective demand of the subject matter with one's subjective reaction.

In this brief description, it becomes clear why " successful" presentation of one's own meaning can limit rather than aid productive communication. For to the extent that the external world or other person is silenced by the success of placing one's position in place of conflict with alternatives, the capacity to engage in conceptual expansion and reach open consensus on the subject matter is limited. The "otherness" of the other and of the subject matter before us draws one's concepts to the limit and forces a surrender of them to the development of consenual thought. Levinas (1969) presented the understanding poetically: "The presence of the Other is equivalent to calling into question my joyous possession of the world" (p. 75). The loss and the growth are critical to human social conduct.

As an ontology of understanding, Gadamer claimed the genuine conversation as the fundamental way all understanding happens. All reproductions rest on this fundamental production (see Deetz, 1978). Conversation is the ongoing process of creating mutual understanding through the open formation of experience. On the basis of Gadamer's description of the genuine conversation, we can establish a basic guiding principle for interaction; a normative principle based on the very conditions for communicative understanding. This principle can be expressed as follows: Every communicative act should have as its ethical condition the attempt to keep the conversation—the open development of experience—going (for development, see Apel, 1979; Deetz, 1990; Rorty 1979). That is, the communicative act should be responsive to the subject matter of the conversation and at the same time should help to establish the conditions for future unrestrained formation of experience.

Normatively based interaction is not willed or chosen by the individual nor does it conform to some routine social practice. Rather, in its natural state the will is produced out of the demand of the subject matter in interaction. But, the "conversation" can be blocked or distorted in a variety of ways. The presence of stoppages maintained in an interaction system is what is meant by an unethical communication system (for development, see Deetz, 1992). The maintenance of a blockage provides an arbitrary restraint on the interaction and prohibits the undistorted expression of human interest and the formation of consensus on the subject matter.

Even if we wholeheartedly endorse Gadamer's description of the social development of human understanding and even if we raise his characterization of genuine conversation to a normative ideal for all communicative interaction, we come up short of an adequate view of communication. Although it is possible to participate in genuine conversations, such opportunities are relatively rare because of the limitations daily life imposes both on ourselves and others. Rarely is an experience so powerful that the disciplines, routines of life, and ordinary ways of seeing are spontaneously overcome. And from where are the experiences to come that escape routinization and normalcy? There are real power relations, manifested as institutional arrangements and structures of permissible discourse that preclude otherness and block conversation. Our shared history carries unexamined beliefs and attitudes that maintain preference for the expression of certain views of reality and of certain social groups. Under such conditions, genuine conversation cannot take place because there is no "other," because there is no means or forum for "otherness" to be expressed. We gain much from Gadamer's analysis of how new understanding is possible and how we can open to the claims of the subject matter, but how is this to happen in practical contexts? Although Gadamer recovered dialectics and understanding from modern epistemological domination, his politics was left unclear. Such a politics requires a more complete analysis of actual communication processes.

Discourse and Dispute Resolution

Habermas, in what has been aptly described as a *hermeneutics of suspicion*, took head on the issues Gadamer left aside. Systems of domination usually preclude the genuine conversation. What is the nature of interaction where a new consensus does not arise organically out of the interaction? What is the nature of the interaction by which competing claims can be resolved? How can one distinguish consensus reached regarding the subject matter from those knowingly or unknowingly produced by authority or relations of power? Since Habermas' position is well known, I am brief here.

Basically, Habermas argued that every speech act can function in communication by virtue of common presumptions made by speaker and listener. Even when these presumptions are not fulfilled in an actual situation, they serve as a base of appeal as failed conversation turns to argumentation regarding the disputed validity claims. The basic presumptions and validity claims arise out of four shared domains of reality: the external world, human relations, the individual's internal world, and language. The claims raised in each are respectively, truth, correctness, sincerity, and intelligibility. Thus, we can claim that each competent, communicative act represents facts, establishes legitimate social relations, discloses the speaker's point of view, and is understandable. Any claim that cannot be brought to open dispute serves as the basis for systematically distorted communication. The ideal speech situation must be recovered to avoid or overcome such distortions. It should be clear that this conception applies not only to the everyday and ordinary acts of communication but also models the ideal process by which collective decisions can be made as to what our society will be and what kind of people we will become—our moral responsibility. Four basic guiding conditions are necessary for free and open participation in the resolution of claims.

First, the attempt to reach understanding presupposes a symmetrical distribution of the chances to choose and apply speech acts. This would specify the minimal conditions of skills and opportunities for expression including access to meaningful forums and channels of communication. When we extend these through a consideration of communication technologies, initial focus needs to be on equal access, distribution of training opportunities, and development of technologies that can be used to express a full variety of human experiences.

Second, the understanding and representation of the external world needs to be freed from privileged preconceptions in the social development of "truth." Ideally, participants have the opportunity to express interpretations and explanations with conflicts resolved in reciprocal claims and counter claims without privileging particular epistemologies or forms of data. The freedom from preconception implies an examination of ideologies that would privilege one form of discourse, disqualify certain possible participants, and universalize any particular sectional interest. Communication technologies need to be examined with regard to how they function ideologically to privilege certain perceptions and forms of data and obscure historical processes.

Third, participants need to have the opportunity to establish legitimate social relationships and norms for conduct and interaction. The rights and responsibilities of people are not given in advance by nature or by a privileged, universal value structure, but are negotiated through interaction. Acceptance of views because of an individual's privilege or authority or because of the nature of the medium represents a possible illegitimate relation. Authority itself is legitimate only if redeemable by appeal to an open interactional formation of relations freed from the appeal to authority. Values and norms legitimately exist in society by the achievement of rational consensus subject to appeals to warrants supporting the assumed social relations. To the extent that particular technologies embody values, hide authority relations, or reify social relations, they participate in domination.

Finally, interactants need to be able to express their own authentic interests, needs, and feelings. This would require freedom from various coercive and hegemonic processes by which the individual is unable to form experience openly, to understand the self, and to form expressions presenting them. Technology can aid in the formation of self or other as images and establish distance that denies the formation of "otherness" and the interrogation of self. The examination of technology in its structuring of the interior would be important to understanding its effect on the accomplishment of such an ideal.

The most frequent objections to Habermas is that he has overemphasized reason, particularly self-reflection, and has only a negative view of power that hampers both the conception of social change and seeing the possible positivity of power. What Habermas does well is to give an arguable standard for normative guidance to communication as a critique of domination, even if his position is distinctly Western and intellectual. Habermas' description can be transformed from a faith in rational consensus to partial guidance on how conflicting knowledge claims can be expressed to recover conflict from closure. The ideal communication situation is a fiction, but perhaps Habermas is correct that "on this unavoidable fiction rests the humanity of relations among" people.

DISCURSIVE CLOSURE AND SYSTEMATICALLY DISTORTED COMMUNICATION

Gadamer and Habermas each offered much to developing communication research grounded in a normative ideal of participation. The participatory democratic conception of communication describes the possibility and conditions for the mutual production of meaning, but also provides a description of potential communication problems and inadequacies. In general, most strategic or instrumental communicative acts have the potential of asserting the speaker's opinion over the attempt to reach mutual understanding regarding the subject matter, the flaw generally seen in liberal democratic conceptions. In such cases, an apparent agreement precludes the conflict that could lead to a new position of open mutual assent. In cases where the one-sidedness is apparent, usually the processes of assertion-counter-assertion and questions–answers reclaim a situation approximating participation. And, certainly conditions of mutuality are unproblematically temporarily suspended in authority relations such as parent–child, doctor–patient, or teacher–student where we can at least imagine an equable discussion where the asymmetry could be openly affirmed. Asymmetry and subordination are not themselves the problem. Yet even here we are mindful of the possible arbitrariness of these relations, the power relations that produced as well as are reproduced by them, the need to constantly reassess the possible excessive normalizing and routinizing effects of these relations, and the desire to foster the conflictual as well as consensual aspects of these relations.

In general, we understand the issues of domination when raised by strategy, manipulation, and instrumental uses of communication, even though such issues are not always taken seriously and the effort to overcome them might be great. The more serious issues posed by modern analyses are the invisible constraints that are disguised as neutral and self-evident. In a general way, these can be described as discursive closures and systematically distorted communication. Both concepts become central when we turn to look at the processes of domination in development decisions and consider alternative communicative practices. Forester (1989) was very helpful in the planning literature in describing the various common forms of domination and closure. Some limitations are inevitable, but there are clear differences between those that are random versus those that are systematic and those that are particularistic versus those that are global and structural.

Discursive closure exists whenever potential conflict is suppressed. This might derive from several processes, many of which were previously described (see Deetz, 1992). One of the most common is the disqualification of certain groups or participants (Bavelas & Chovil, 1986). Disqualification can occur through the denial of the right of expression; denial of access to speaking forums, assertion of the need for certain expertise in order to speak; or through rendering the other unable to speak adequately, including processes of deskilling. Closure is also possible through the privileging of certain discourses and the marginalization of others. For example, Habermas and other critical theorists extensively detailed the domination of technical-instrumental reasoning over other forms in the Western world. Foucault, in his many works, showed how certain discourses historically arise as normal and preferred. Organizational studies clearly show how managerial groups and technical reasoning become privileged (Mumby, 1987, 1988). Furthermore, closure is present in each move to determine origins and demonstrate unity. In each case, the multiple-motived and conflict-filled nature of experience becomes suppressed by a dominant aspect. This has most clearly been developed in narrative theory (e.g., Jameson, 1981). With unity, the continued production of experience is constrained because the tension of difference is lost. Habermas' work itself can be said to produce this type of closure to the extent that his consensus is fixed rather than a moment to be deconstructed and reformed in continued movement.

Systematically distorted communication is itself both evidence for and productive of discursive closure, but the concept provides a slightly different focus for the analysis. Habermas presented the concept based on a psychoanalytic analog as descriptive of those times when an interactant is self-deceived. The most obvious case of this is the repression of a certain experience, which consequently causes the psychological experience and the expression of it to become displaced or projected. In this sense, an individual is out of touch with self-interests, needs, and feelings and may well substitute other socially derived experiences and expression for his or her own—an ideological expression or false consciousness. In the extreme model, only through a "talking cure" can the code be broken so that the disguised expression of the repressed state can be read and the individual can reconnect with self-experience. In this view, society and organizations can be seen as filled with "social neurosis." This particular version is not of much interest here. The role of social therapist is elitist and filled with contradictions. The searching for real motives, needs, and interests can certainly structure another privileged discourse (Clegg, 1989). The implicit assumption that linguistic expression should represent a fixed, knowable interior provides a weak understanding of language and experience. But we can learn from this analysis.

Intuitively, we know that we respond to unknown elements of experience. We see people unwittingly act in opposition to their own values and needs. We hear and participate in discourses that feel restrictive, such as trying to express a sunset on canvas without really knowing how to paint. These are significant to the communication process. Here, systematic distortion is not based on a simple mismatch of a fixed interest with a fixed expression but on an interactionally determined reduction of certain experiences to other ones.

I believe that Habermas (1984) is correct here. What is involved is a learning process rather than a therapy. We can participate in the development of distinctions and articulation. This involvement is certainly not neutral because our involvement partially determines the direction of development. But, we can determine when we participate with the other in development versus when we try to teach them how to think and express. And we can become aware of when even subtle authority relations change enabling power relations into disqualification and discursive privilege. Such a learning process, however, is not one of putting the person in touch with him or herself or learning to articulate his or her insides clearly (hidden effectiveness issues), but is one that reopens engagement in the development of differentiated feelings and discursive possibilities, to participate in the affective and expressive development of self and other.

Systematic distortion is a common property of human communication rather than of something that occasionally arises during periods of
transition. Human thought, feelings, actions, and expressions are often
skewed. Certain dominant forms of reasoning and articulations stand in
the stead of other valuational schemes. If career development exhausts
the expression of personal development, if control drives the forms of
human sociation, or if statements about the external world preclude
those about affective states, we have a certain one-sidedness or systematic distortion. Such expressions can and should be examined for
possible suppressions of alternative voices, not to implement alternative
values, but as part of ongoing community development.

Processes of discursive closure and systematically distorted communication can be said to be pathological to the extent that they (a)
endanger the survival of the human and other species, (b) violate normative standards already freely shared by members of a community, and (c)
pose arbitrary limits on the development of individualization and the realization of collective good. The latter two are of primary interest here. A fair
amount is already known about pathological interpersonal systems.

Interaction process analysis (Pearce & Cronen, 1980;
Watzlawick, Beavin, & Jackson, 1967) initiated careful research into the
way family systems can develop internal logics and rules that structure
frozen identities for the participants, which preclude the meeting of critical needs in their production of other needs, and finally strip participants
of responsibility and responsiveness (see Laing, 1971, for the most
extreme examples).

Such systems, through closure and fixed interpretive processes,
probably have no outside, no natural checks and balances, and few
moments of escape to see the system as it works, yet they grow,
become supported by external structures, and engulf others in their
peculiar logics. Although the theoretical base of these studies, particularly in regard to the social structure of identity and reality, is too weak to
show their political character, their descriptions are useful is showing
how pathological systems work. Studies of the mass media (Grossberg,
1987; Hall 1989; Schiller, 1989), communication technologies (Murdock
& Golding, 1989), and organizational communication (Alvesson, 1987;
Burrell, 1988; Mumby; 1988) have pushed further in displaying the
nature of "self-referential," closed, or distorted communication systems.
As more works in communication studies explicitly, although often
implicitly, develop with the motive of greater participation, the need
exists not only to relate them theoretically but also to continue to develop
concepts of theory adequate to them. Without such guidance, participation programs in development processes become new systems of control, equal access becomes an alibi for homogeneous programming, and
expressive individualism and self-interest advocacy becomes substituted

for autonomy and collective decision making. In short, having a say or having an affect can displace the possibility of participatory responsiveness to life situations.

THE ROLE OF THE INTELLECTUAL

This chapter focuses on the role of communication theory and analysis in the development of democracy within a politics of everyday life. In so doing I have juxtaposed conceptions from hermeneutics, critical theory, and poststructuralism. I hope I have shown a common movement within these works, gaining something of the power from each without totally losing the tensions among them, a set of tension I think we have to live with.

I see this as more complementary than integrative or pluralistic. The tension and the complementarity can be revealed one more time here. What is the appropriate role of the intellectual in development processes? I use the term *role of the intellectual* rather than role of theory or research because it is individuals alone and in concert who act and who are responsible. The terms *researcher* or *scholar* are too detached and appear neutral when they are implicitly privileged and highly political. *Intellectual* here is meant to simply mean anyone who systematically reflects on life's experiences, an attribute I believe should apply to communication theorists. The primary intellectual role is as a facilitator rather than a leader.

Critical theorists borrowed from the enlightenment a conception of the intellectual vanguard, believing that it could make possible the progress of the masses through conceptual and philosophical elaboration of ideas that could enlighten and lead revolutionary change. Habermas provided a more restricted conception of cultural criticism along the lines of the enlightenment ideal of self-understanding and reasoned discourse. The modern intellectual, however, lacks any basis for a "universal" role as the conscience of the collectivity and as a "specialist" often engages in privileging systems of expertise growing out of conceptions of universal or objective truth.

The intellectual role today is more appropriately one of enabling an open discourse among the various social stakeholders (see Deetz, 1995b). The research and facilitation activities should themselves should be openly participative. This is a role with three movements which I call *insight* (hermeneutic understanding in the critical tradition, archaeology to Foucault), *critique* (genealogy to Foucault, deconstruction to the poststructuralists), and *education* (in Dewey's sense, conscientization in the critical tradition).

Insight: Hermeneutic Understanding and the Archaeology of Knowledge

Most modern social science organizes itself around the production of cumulative knowledge. This knowledge about the world is held outside of and finally instead of contact with the world itself. A participatory view of theory leads instead to progressive development of distinctions and alternative conceptions—an opening of human dialogue in contact with the variety of the world. It is not the objectivity of objectified knowledge that creates limitations but its subjectivity and the power that supports one type of engaging with the world and object production over other equally plausible ones. Everyday knowledge and scientific research are produced out of a set of interrelated structures that are both present in them and extend in an implicative web. Most of the time, social members as well as traditional researchers take for granted this knowledge and the formed nature of objects and events. *Insight* denotes the process of seeing into the manners by which this knowledge and the objective character of objects and events are formed and sustained. The term recalls the hermeneutic understanding of language as disclosive and opening a field of consideration rather than the representational view of language that under grids knowledge as truth claims. Insight can properly be called the leading edge of human thought. It is structured along the line of the powerful exemplar rather than the mass of data. Insight is both the process of producing a unity of interest in the data—of knowing what data to collect and how it fits together—and understanding the conditions for such a unity.

Insight is a type of practical knowing, a seeing of what is important. Insight, as suggested in the more general look at communication, is not into individuals, situations, or their meanings but of the systems of relations that make such meaning possible (Deetz, 1973, 1982). As Foucault (1970) described his archaeology, "an inquiry whose aim is to rediscover on what basis knowledge and theory became possible; within what space of order knowledge was constituted; on the basis of what historical a priori, and in the element of what positivity, ideas could appear, sciences could be established, experience be reflected in philosophies, rationalities be formed, only, perhaps, to dissolve and vanish soon afterwards" (pp. xxi–xxii). In this sense, most ethnographies and cultural studies are at most a first step in a much larger analysis. Particular persons and situations are artifacts used to understand the system of meanings through which particular persons and situations are composed and connected to the larger sociocultural context. How are particular kinds of knowledge and members constructed and sustained in discourse?

Insight in both a hermeneutic and archaeological sense detaches knowledge from the ahistorical "truth" claim and reopens a consideration of its formation thereby reframing knowledge and giving choices that previously were hidden by the accepted knowledge, standard practices, and existing concepts. The production of insight establishes the possibility of competing discourses through the recovery of conflict and choice. Without such insight members remain in a sense victims of meaning structures that were developed in response to past situations and perpetuated in their talk and actions. Although as Giddens (1979) argued, all cultural members have some degree of "discursive penetration"—that is, some insight into the structural properties of knowledge production—they are unlikely to enlarge the penetration on their own due to practical restrictions and various mechanisms of discursive closure. The intellectual is free of some of these constraints, although not privileged, is capable of the distantiation of claiming counterdiscourses within particular sites of production.

Critique: Deconstruction and the Genealogy of Knowledge

Political, economic, and community forces are inscribed in organizational arrangements, social relations, and every perception. It is not sufficient to describe these as naturally occurring, they arise historically and they arbitrarily give advantage to certain groups. Participation as a normative foundation for communication draws attention to both describe and criticize such systems. The participative ideal does not so much give a norm or criteria for evaluation as it provides a set of interests and analytic foci for acting on them, a way of thinking about these systems. Grossberg (1984) described the task as one to "describe (and intervene in) the way messages are produced by, inserted into, and function within the everyday lives of concrete human beings so as to reproduce and transforms structures of power and domination" (p. 393).

Foucault, in recognizing the need to go beyond neutral descriptions, presented a "genealogy" to complement the archaeology. Orders are selected, controlled, and distributed within societies along lines of strategy and advantage. Foucault used the term *apparatus* to denote the heterogeneous forces that direct the presence of certain constitutive conditions. As Foucault (1980a) described:

> the apparatus is essentially of a *strategic* nature, which means assuming that it is a matter of a certain manipulation or relation of forces, either developing them in a particular direction, blocking them, stabilizing them, utilizing them, etc. The apparatus is thus always inscribed in the play of power, but it is also always linked to certain coordinates of knowledge which issue from it but, to an equal degree, condition it. (p. 196)

Insight into these strategies and understanding them to be deployments of power is itself a strategy toward recovering alternative practices and marginalized alternative meanings. Knowledge is an important part of this relation, for the apparatus both produces knowledge and is extended and sustained by it. Produced knowledge can guide participation or domination. The point is not to try to disconnect power relations from the production of truth as Gadamer or Habermas would do, but of "detaching the power of truth from the forms of hegemony, social, economic and cultural within which it operates at the present time" (Smart, 1986, p. 166; see also Knights, 1992). Thus the critique of everyday dominations must always include a critique of the social science, the communication science, which accompanies it.

The Derridian conception of *deconstruction* is also useful in filling out the concept of *critique*. The movement of science as production of knowledge and communication as the transmission of it share the privileging of the speaker and the known and producing what can be called a *centered text*, the dominance of a particular unity or point of view over others. The unity appears innocent as a consensus. Deconstruction shows the manner of historical privilege and recalls the equivocality, the many voices, the alternative texts that become the hidden background for the centered one. As Culler (1983) said, "deconstruction is not a theory that defines meaning in order to tell you how to find it. As a critical undoing of the hierarchical oppositions on which theories depend, it demonstrates the difficulty of any theory that would define meaning in a univocal way: as what the author intends, what conventions determine, what a reader experiences" (p. 131). In the broader terms of this work, deconstruction denies the univocal products of the intellectual, the result of methods and procedures, and common sense of the public and in its place opens the movements in and between them.

Critique, thus, is directed at the conventions and structures of social orders and the forms of knowledge and privileged understanding that are complicit with such orders. Critique itself operates as part of a participative communicative act, the act of reopening effective communication to productive conversation.

Education: Concept Formation, Resistance, and Conscientization

Education is the natural counterpart to insight and critique. It can easily be claimed that critical writings in both the enlightenment and postenlightenment traditions have placed too much attention on awareness and understanding and not enough on enabling alternative responses. The implicit faith—that if people knew what they wanted and the system of constraints limiting them, they would know how to act differently—has little basis. Those who hold out for revolutionary change miss the implications of modern forms of control and democracy. Meaningful change is in the micro-practices at the innumerable sites of power relations (Foucault, 1980b). Democracy cannot simply be found in some new form of social relations but in an ongoing task of struggle and decision as new forms of control evolve. Communication education must be involved in the production and distribution of a kind of political competence. Following Simonds (1989), political competence in modern society means, "not just access to information but access to the entire range of skills required to decode, encode, interpret, reflect upon, appraise, contextualize, integrate, and arrive at decisions respecting that information" (p. 198). Clearly, as we have seen around the world, increased literacy is more threatening to autocratic rule than an uncensored press. Literacy regarding complex communication systems and technologies is itself a complex phenomenon. The concern is not just that people get wrong or biased information (the propagation of false consciousness), but that they lack the resources to assess what they have. And more importantly, they do not understand the modern means by which control is exerted and participation undermined.

Freire (1970) provided the most stirring discussion of the role of education to open cultural development. Although much of his social theory was caught in the Marxism of his day and the immediate political realities of Brazil, his conception of conscientização locates a meaningful role for intellectuals in the construction of human agents—that is, subjects who chose to make their own history. Although many researchers today conceptualize and teach their subjects to be objects, known and acted on, objects can be taught to be subjects who know and act. The point is then not to produce a new theory of domination as knowledge, but to produce ways of seeing and thinking and contexts for action in which groups can express themselves and act.

Thus,the movement toward greater participation and democracy is not accomplished by rational arguments and the display of systems of domination alone, but also by helping to create responses to the current situation. Members of the everyday community have learned their concepts, practices, and skills over a lengthy period of time. Learning competing discourses, embracing conflict, and participating in decision making are necessary skills. But interaction skills are only part of the matrix. Developing technologies for participation and skills in using technologies and communication media are important parts of the democratizing effort.

Furthermore, the intellectual is not a teacher in any standard sense. We do not know a lot about participation and we certainly do not know the contours of the sites as well as everyday participants. The role Freire (1970) ascribed is more appropriate to the need to combine research with education:

> We must never merely discourse on the present situation, must
> never provide the people with program which have little or nothing to
> do with their own preoccupations, doubts, hopes, and fears. . . . It is
> not our role to speak to the people about our own view of the world,
> not to attempt to impose that view on them, but rather to dialogue
> with the people about their view and ours. (p. 85)

Unfortunately, it is not they who are not ready to talk with us, it is us who
are often not yet ready.

Despite the power in various social formations, there is always
resistance and opportunity for difference and change. Local resistance
often fails, owing to trained incapacities, inadequate concepts, and
unknown structural constraints. The final goal is the formation of new concepts and practices for social members and researchers in such a way as
to enhance understanding of social life. Living and working are practical
activities for members. The choices in the everyday context require a type
of *practical consciousness* or adequate knowledge as suggested by
Giddens (1979) or *phronesis* (practical wisdom) as suggested by
Gadamer (1975). Certainly, the modern intellectual can aid the production
of this. Concepts developed by the academic community need not be privileged to give voice to concerns and understanding that have not been
brought to discourse in everyday contexts and such concepts can be generative thus question and reconstitute social experience (see Gergen,
1982; Giddens, 1979). To fulfill this function, our concepts must be recovered from operational and textbook definitions and reconnected to ways of
seeing and thinking about the world. In the dialectics of the situation and
the talk of individuals with different perspectives, the emergence of new
ways of talking becomes possible. Such a process both enhances the natural language of social members and leads to the development of new
concepts to direct the attention of the research community. Such is important for the participation conception of communication as a foundation for
political democracy in the modern context.

REFERENCES

Albert, M., Cagan, L., Chomsky, N., Hahnel, R., King, M., Sargent, L., &
Sklar, H. (Eds.). (1986). *Liberating theory.* Boston: South End.
Alvesson, M. (1987). *Organization theory and technocratic conscious-
ness: Rationality, ideology and quality of work.* New York: de
Gruyter.
Apel, K.O. (1979). The a priori of the communication community and the
foundation of ethics: The problem of a rational foundation of ethics
in the scientific age. In G. Adey & D. Frisby (Trans.), *Towards a
transformation of philosophy* (pp. 225-300). London: Routledge &
Kegan Paul.

Austin, J. (1961). *Philosophical papers* (J. O. Urmson & G. J. Warnock, eds.). Oxford: Clarendon.

Axley, S. (1984). Managerial and organizational communication in terms of the conduit metaphor. *Academy of Management Review, 9*(3), 428-437.

Barber, B. (1984). *Strong democracy.* Berkeley: University of California Press.

Baudrillard, J. (1981). *For a critique of the political economy of the sign.* St. Louis, MO: Telos.

Bavelas, J., & Chovil, N. (1986). How people disqualify: Experimental studies of spontaneous written disqualification. *Communication Monographs, 53,* 70-74.

Bernstein, R. (1984). *Beyond objectivism and relativism.* Philadelphia: University of Pennsylvania Press.

Burrell, G. (1988). Modernism, postmodernism and organizational analysis 2: The contribution of Michel Foucault. *Organization Studies, 9*(2), 221-235.

Carter, P., & Jackson, N. (1987). Management, myth, and metatheory— From scarcity to post scarcity. *International Studies of Management and Organizations, 17,* 64-89.

Chomsky, N. (1959). A review of B. F. Skinner's *Verbal Behavior. Language, 35*(1), 26-57.

Clegg, S. (1989). *Frameworks of power.* Newbury Park, CA: Sage.

Culler, J. (1983). *On deconstruction.* London: Routledge & Kegan Paul.

Deetz, S. (1973). An understanding of science and a hermeneutic science of understanding. *Journal of Communication, 23*(2), 139-159.

Deetz, S. (1978). Conceptualizing human understanding: Gadamer"s hermeneutics and American communication research. *Communication Quarterly, 26*(2), 12-23.

Deetz, S. (1982). Critical-interpretive research in organizational communication. *Western Journal of Speech Communication, 46,* 131-149.

Deetz, S. (1990). Reclaiming the subject matter as a guide to mutual understanding: Effectiveness and ethics in interpersonal interaction. *Communication Quarterly, 38*(3), 226-243.

Deetz, S. (1992). *Democracy in the age of corporate colonization: Developments in communication and the politics of everyday life.* Albany: State University of New York Press.

Deetz, S. (1994). The future of the discipline: The challenges, the research, and the social contribution In S. Deetz (Ed.), *Communication yearbook 17* (pp. 565-600). Newbury Park, CA: Sage.

Deetz, S. (1995a). The social production of knowledge and the commercial artifact. In L.L. Cummings & P. Frost (Eds.), *Publishing in the organizational sciences* (pp. 44-63). Newbury Park, CA: Sage.

Deetz, S. (1995b) *Transforming communication, transforming business: Building responsive and responsible workplaces.* Cresskill, NJ: Hampton Press.

Deetz, S. (1995c) Transforming communication, transforming business: Stimulating value debate to build more responsive and responsible workplaces. *International Journal of Value-Based Management.*

Deetz, S. (1996). Describing differences in approaches to organizational science: Rethinking Burrell and Morgan and their legacy. *Organization Science.*

Dewey, J. (1916). *Democracy and education.* New York: Macmillian.

Forester, J. (1989). *Planning in the face of power.* Berkeley: University of California Press.

Foucault, M. (1970). *The order of things.* New York: Random House.

Foucault, M. (1980a). *The history of sexuality* (R. Hurley, trans.). New York: Vintage.

Foucault, M. (1980b). *Power knowledge: Selected interviews and other writings, 1972–1977* (C. Gordon, ed.). New York: Pantheon.

Freire, P. (1970). *Pedagogy of the oppressed.* New York: Herder & Herder.

Friedman, J. (1973). *Retracking America.* New York. Bantam.

Gadamer, H.G. (1975). *Truth and method* (G. Barden & J. Cumming, eds. and trans.). New York: Seabury.

Gergen, K. (1978). Toward generative theory. *Journal of Personality and Social Psychology, 31,* 1344-60.

Gergen, K. (1982). *Towards transformation in social knowledge.* New York: Springer-Verlag.

Gergen, K., & Davis, K. (Eds.). (1985). *The social construction of the person.* New York: Springer-Verlag.

Giddens, A. (1979). *Central problems in social theory.* Berkeley: University of California Press.

Golembiewski, R. (1989). Toward a positive and practical public management: Organizational research supporting a fourth critical citizenship. *Administration & Society, 21*(2), 200-227.

Grossberg, L. (1984). Strategies of Marxist cultural interpretation. *Critical Studies in Mass Communication, 1,* 391-421.

Grossberg, L. (1987). Critical theory and the politics of empirical research. In M. Gurevitch & M. Levy (Eds.), *Communication review yearbook* (Vol. 6, pp. 86-106). Newbury Park, CA: Sage.

Habermas, J. (1971). *Knowledge and human interests* (J. Shapiro, trans.). Boston: Beacon.

Habermas, J. (1979). *Communication and the evolution of society* (T. McCarthy, trans.). Boston: Beacon.

Habermas, J. (1984). *The theory of communicative action, Vol. 1: Reason and the rationalization of society* (T. McCarthy, trans.). Boston: Beacon.

Habermas, J. (1987). *The theory of communicative action, Vol. 2: Lifeworld and system* (T. McCarthy, trans.). Boston: Beacon.

Hall, S. (1989). Ideology and communication theory. In B. Dervin, L. Grossberg, B. O'Keefe, & E. Wartella (Eds.), *Rethinking communication* (Vol. 1, pp. 40-52). Newbury Park, CA: Sage.

Hamnett, M., Porter, D., Singh, A., & Kumar, K. (1984). *Ethics, politics, and international social science research*. Honolulu, HI: East–West Center and University of Hawaii Press.

Hanson, N. (1965). *Patterns of discovery*. Cambridge: Cambridge University Press.

Harding, S. (1992). *Whose science? Whose knowledge?* Ithaca, NY: Cornell University Press.

Hoy, D.C. (1986). Power, repression, progress: Foucault, Lukes, and the Frankfurt School. In D.C. Hoy (Ed.), *Foucault: A critical reader* (pp. 123-148). Oxford: Basil Blackwell.

Jameson, F. (1981). *The political unconscious: Narrative as a social symbolic act*. Ithaca, NY: Cornell University Press.

Kelly, G. (1955). *Psychology of personal constructs*. New York: Norton.

Knights, D. (1992). Changing spaces: The disruptive impact of a new epistemological location for the study of management. *Academy of Management Review, 17*(3), 514-536.

Laing, R. D. (1971). *The politics of the family*. New York: Vintage.

Levinas, E. (1969). *Totality and infinity* (A. Lingis, trans.). Pittsburgh, OH: Duquesne University Press.

Mumby, D.K. (1987). The political function of narrative in organizations. *Communication Monographs, 54*, 113-127.

Mumby, D.K. (1988). *Communication and power in organizations: Discourse, ideology, and domination*. Norwood, NJ: Ablex.

Murdock, G., & Golding, P. (1989). Information poverty and political inequality: Citizenship in the age of privatized communications. *Journal of Communication, 39*(3), 180-195.

Pearce, W. B. (1989). *Communication and the human condition*. Carbondale: Southern Illinois University Press.

Pearce, W. B., & Cronen, V. (1980). *Communication, action and meaning*. New York: Prather.

Rorty, R. (1979). *Philosophy and the mirror of nature*. Princeton, NJ: Princeton University Press.

Rorty, R. (1981, October). *Hermeneutics and the social sciences*. Paper presented at the annual conference of the Society for Phenomenology and Existential Philosophy, St. Louis.

Rorty, R. (1982). *Consequences of pragmatism*. Minneapolis: University of Minnesota Press.

Schaffer, S. (1989, November). *Realities in the eighteenth century: Nature's representatives and their cultural resources*. Paper presented at the Realism and Representation Conference, Rutgers University, New Brunswick, NJ.

Schiller, H. (1989). *Culture, Inc.: The corporate takeover of public expression*. Oxford: Oxford University Press.

Simonds, A. (1989). Ideological domination and the political information market. *Theory and Society, 18*(2), 181-211.

Smart, B. (1986). The politics of truth and the problem of hegemony. In D. Hoy (Ed.), *Foucault: A critical reader*. Oxford: Basil Blackwell.

Townley, B. (1992). Foucault, power/knowledge, and its relevance for human resource management. *Academy of Management Review, 18*(3), 518-545.

Wagner, J., III & Gooding, R. (1987). Effects of societal trends on participation research. *Administrative Science Quarterly, 32*, 241-262.

Watzlawick, P., Beavin, J., & Jackson, D. (1967). *Pragmatics of human communication.* New York: Norton.

Weedon, C. (1987). *Feminist practice and poststructuralist theory.* Oxford: Basil Blackwell.

Whyte, W. (Ed.). (1991). *Participatory action research.* Newbury Park, CA: Sage.

6

The Participatory Communication for Development Narrative: An Examination of Meta-Theoretic Assumptions and Their Impacts

Brenda Dervin
Ohio State University

Robert Huesca
Trinity University

Interest in participatory communication for development has gained increased scholarly attention since the 1970s and, in the late 1990s constitutes a rich and diverse body of theoretical and empirical research. Although this work is complex—even contradictory—in its nuances, it is bound together by a metanarrative that is embedded with particular assumptions about participation, communication, and development. The metanarrative—in an admittedly oversimplified portrayal—goes something like this: Communication is the road whereby consciousness and liberation are attained; ordinary human subjects—variously referred to as the grass roots, the oppressed, *el pueblo*—are the most solid vessels of wisdom and knowledge concerning their living conditions and must be involved in planning as well as implementation processes if development is to occur. Scholars entering the arena of participatory communication for development tacitly absorb this metanarrative regardless of the particular practical, empirical, or theoretical directions of their work.

Yet, the wide body of research comprised by this metanarrative is curiously filled with essentially unexamined contradictions. These contradictions are examined in more detail here but briefly, and far too simply, they involve differences in whether attention is focused on structure or on process. In good part, these contradictions remain unresolved in the participatory communication literatures. And, interestingly, the very same contradictions are permeating into the resurgence of debates regarding the public sphere as we move into the post-cold war rise in acceptance of entrepreneurship capitalism and global marketing.

It is our position that the contradictions laid out in the participatory communication literature are primarily surface manifestations and that the root of the contradictions lies more at meta-theoretical levels than at theoretical, empirical, or practical levels. In essence, we are suggesting that an examination of fundamental assumptions regarding reality (ontology) and knowing (epistemology) must be addressed if the research area known as *participatory communication for development* is to continue contributing to the improvement of the human condition as well as to the construction of a useful theory of participatory practice.[1]

It might be fairer to label this a call for re-examination for clearly the early participatory communication literatures attended vigorously to epistemological questions because one of the main thrusts of the arguments was that different peoples see reality differently. We suggest, however, that recent work has paid relatively little meta-theoretic attention to epistemological issues and, further, the ontological questions have been all but absent in this literature from the very beginning. It is a major premise of this chapter that scholars in this field have been skirting around the fundamental issues regarding the relations between epistemological and ontological assumptions for many years. Failing to identify these issues as such, however, has led to what appears to be conceptual disarray.

Our primary purpose here, then, is to examine the relations between basic ontological and epistemological assumptions and understandings of participation, communication, and development. The first part of this contribution explores the diversity of the participatory commu-

---

[1]For a related discussion of this same body of literature see Huesca and Dervin (1994).

nication literature by focusing on a particularly rich subset of research—that emerging from Latin America. The second part of this chapter describes six separate and distinct intellectual clusters in terms of their epistemological and ontological assumptions and the relations between these and assumptions regarding power and participation. A final section draws conclusions.

We acknowledge at the outset that we are imposing a framework on a body of literature that in many ways has few linkages to the explicit discourse in that literature. Our purpose, however, is not to place an inappropriate conceptual overlay on a literature that has been struggling for more just, equitable, and dignified societies. Rather, our belief is that by positioning this research within the context of a conscious and self-reflexive web of foundational assumptions we can begin to disentangle and respond to the tensions that are apparent in that literature.

LATIN AMERICAN CONTRIBUTIONS

Scholarship from Latin America constitutes an apt subset of research for examining the general topic of participatory communication for development. Its tradition can be seen as a part of the intentional struggle for the right to communicate growing out of the new world information and communication order debates. Many of the early suggested remedies for attaining more equitable communication relations struck a responsive chord within the oppressive, authoritarian political arrangements dominating Latin America and other developing countries of the world. Recently, however, researchers have begun to question these remedies in light of the transition from authoritarian governments to neoliberal, democratic regimes (López Vigil, 1993; O'Connor, 1990). Thus, participatory communication for development is undergoing a serious interrogation of its relevance, effectiveness, and appropriateness by theorists and practitioners because of the radically changing media environment in Latin America. The growing sense that participatory communication methods may have exhausted themselves is pertinent, as well, to African, Asian, and eastern European nations experiencing sweeping political changes that have led communication scholars to scramble for strategies that are responsive to this new social and political context.

A review of the literature from Latin America reveals that a dialectical tension has permeated this world. Teasing out this tension, which pits a worldview of constraints, structures, and certainty against a worldview of flux, negotiation, and mediation, is useful for revealing signposts pointing to areas of greatest theoretical and practical strength in conceptualizing participatory communication for development. These signposts will come into sharper focus when viewed through the foundational assumptions developed in the second part of this chapter. The review that follows sets the context for the meta-theoretical analysis presented here.

The review of the Latin American literature is organized into three general categories of communication, participation, and applications. The order of presentation moves from the most abstract to the most concrete, for it is in the practical arena of communication applications where the meta-theoretic tensions are most clearly pushed to their limits.

Ideas about Communication

In the Latin American alternative communication literature, the development of ideas about communication were both outgrowth of and reaction against diverse circumstances experienced in Latin America. First, after two development decades in which diffusion and modernization theories dominated communication projects, statistical indicators demonstrated that human well-being had not only not improved over the years, but that the gap between the wealthy and the impoverished had widened dramatically. Second, by the late 1950s and increasingly thereafter, Western dominance of developing nations in media products, such as news and entertainment, was so overwhelming that it constituted a state of "communication atrophy" for the vast majority of citizens (Pasquali, 1963). Many writers alluded to dependency relations prominent in economic theory at the time as a useful analogue for thinking about Latin America's communication environment. Third, the Catholic Church's tradition of hierarchical subordination of the indigenous population began to weaken under challenges of the movement that became known as liberation theology.

The convergence of these diverse circumstances constitutes the contextual conjuncture that helps us interpret the various ideas about communication that developed in Latin America. The earliest notions of communication are best captured in the metaphor of "horizontal" communication, which was proposed as a conceptual template to replace the top–down, one-way transmission of information that permeated the Latin American experience as noted earlier (Beltrán, 1975, 1980; Freire, 1970, 1973). The move from vertical to horizontal communication was seen as a structural solution to the problem of unegalitarian and immoral social, political, and economic relations. The move was seen as a remedy to communication domination evident in the one-way flows of information from the north to the south. Furthermore, it was a rejection of the "extension" model of communication used in development campaigns that effectively objectified social actors and promoted adaptation to imposed power in attitudes, behaviors, and values, all while cloaked in scientific detachment. Beltrán (1980) was participatory adamant in promoting a structural solution for rearranging communication flows and even warned of the dangers of focusing solely on the development of theories of "communication process" that did not attend to rearranging directions and flows of information. Focusing on the theoretical efforts of Berlo (1960), Beltrán suggested that emphasizing the process nature of communication alone "falls short of divesting the scheme from its authoritarian affiliation" (p. 20).

It is important to note that in effect what emerged was a direct challenge to the increasingly sophisticated communication models of top–down approaches with their emphasis on adapting both innovations and messages about them to local circumstances and involving locals in feedback (input after the fact) and feedforward (input before the fact) in attempts to entice adaptation to top–down mandates. Although these communication approaches involved something approximating participation in a variety of forms (e.g., citizen input, formative evaluations), it was decidedly not what the Latin Americans were defining as alternative or participatory communication, which focused not on adaptation but on empowerment. Empowerment was seen as made possible only in changed structural conditions.

The important place that communication structure played in Beltrán's work also is reflected in communication notions of other scholars. A number of scholars have suggested that peasants and the urban poor live in a psychological state of marginalization wherein oppression is internalized (Beltrán 1975; Fals Borda, 1988; Freire, 1970; O'Sullivan-Ryan & Kaplún, 1978). A focus on communication process alone, they claim, is insufficient to break out of this state of internalized oppression. This problem for communication is perhaps best illustrated in Kaplún's (1980) use of the concept of ideological resistance. He suggests that ideological resistance permeates communication processes whereby participants "reproduce and reinforce the values of the dominant ideology. In truth, both forms of communication—the conventional and the alternative—seem to be subject, although not in equal measure, to the cultural and ideological conditionings in which they are produced" (p. 71). Rather than receiving guidance from a process understanding of communication that focuses on its changing, dynamic nature, Kaplún and like-minded writers have suggested a more interventionist, structural approach capable of shedding light on the relationships between dominant social groups and ideas circulating among marginalized people (López Vigil, 1993; O'Connor, 1990; Valdeavellano, 1989).

Although these approaches to ideas about communication emphasize structure, they actually existed simultaneously (and often within the work of the same writer) with ideas about communication that

were more fluid and elastic. These more fluid conceptualizations of communication emphasized intersubjectivity, phenomenological "being in the
world," and praxis. For example, the early turn away from information
transfer and communication as extension suggested that human understanding was forged through intersubjective co-activity (Beltrán, 1980;
Pasquali, 1963). Communication was posited as a process whereby
humans entered into mental cooperation, not exchange, but an allitera-
tive interlocution marked by an openness and discovery of one's own
consciousness and a forging of a common conscience. The intersubjective process transformed both individual and common understanding, in
effect, resulting in "actively sharing experiences and jointly re-construct-
ing reality" (Beltrán, 1980, p. 26).

Reconstructing reality was a radical concept but one that was
never fully integrated nor problematized in terms of its ontological implications (which we explore later in this chapter). Rather, Latin American
scholars granted primacy to constructing reality through the lived experience, but, following assumptions from phenomenology, bracketing fundamental questions about the nature of that reality (Fals Borda, 1991;
Freire, 1973; Pasquali, 1963). In describing the nature of knowing, Freire
wrote:

> One's consciousness, "intentionality" toward the world, is always
> consciousness of, and in permanent movement toward reality. . . .
> This relationship constitutes, with this, a dialectical unity in which
> knowing-in-solidarity is generated in being and vice versa. For this
> reason, both objectivist and subjectivist explanations that break this
> dialectic, dichotomizing that which is not dichotomizable
> (subject–object), are not capable of understanding reality. Both
> approaches lack teleological sense. (p. 85)

Rather than taking on the issue of the nature of reality, writers displaying
a phenomenological influence privileged the human subject's experience
of it, privileging in essence epistemology over ontology. The emphasis
on both intersubjectivity and being-in-the-world was raised to a level of
reflexivity and identified as an ideal form of communication: dialogue as
praxis. Virtually all scholars from Latin America placed a claim on the
term *dialogue* at some point in their definition of communication. But
Freire (1970) pushed the notion to an explicit level of reflection and
action by distinguishing *verbalism* (reflection alone) and *activism* (action
alone) from *dialogue* (praxis-reflection and action). He offered the fullest
treatment of the notion of dialogue, which has been adopted widely by
scholars following in his wake.

Taken together, horizontality, intersubjectivity, knowing by
being-in-the-world, and dialogue as praxis-manifested constitute the

pieces of one perspective on communication drawn from the Latin American tradition. At the same time, another contradictory perspective existed, one focusing on the necessity of structural changes to eliminate dependencies and make participation possible. In one sense, these two avenues—structural versus process—in the development of ideas about alternative communication seem entirely complimentary—structural change, it is assumed, makes participatory processes possible. At a deeper level, however, we suggest they become contradictory because they imply different but undiscussed ontological and epistemological assumptions and emphases. The structural avenue, even when it starts off with epistemological assumptions (e.g., diversity in perspectives), ends up privileging ontology and often setting epistemology aside. In contrast, the process avenue usually takes ontology out of the question and focuses on epistemology.

It would be unfair to suggest that there has been no awareness in the Latin American literature of the dialectical tension between static, structural versus dynamic, process understandings of the interrelations between communication, participation, and development. However, as time went on and as these theories moved into practice, these tensions seem to be weighed more heavily toward static, structural understandings. This statement should not be interpreted as a negative judgment because in a related review, we (Huesca & Dervin, 1994) suggested that the Latin American literature has been steps ahead of other communication literatures in struggling with rather than merely reifying structure versus process and the related dualism of structure versus agency. Furthermore, in her reviews of related bodies of literature in the United States, Dervin (1989a, 1989b) likewise charged that process as a concept is reified but rarely examined.

Ideas About Participation

Notions of participation in the Latin American literature grew out of the same historical conditions that led to the ideas about communication just outlined. The grassroots of Latin American societies were conceptualized as occupying a marginal position in a dependency relation with national and transnational communication powers. Participation was posited as the way out of the dependency relation and the key to social transformation. In an often cited participatory communication monograph, O'Sullivan-Ryan and Kaplún (1978) explained this situation:

> In synthesis, marginality is basically a situation of non-participation
> for certain groups of the population that is produced by an economic
> system incapable of offering them permanent productive employ-

ment and which extends to the other spheres of social life. Marginality is a chronic and growing situation (and herein lies a critical consideration for participatory communication); it is not a question of a structure independent of the global system; rather it is an integral part of it to such an extent that it would appear to be, under certain perspectives, a prerequisite for maintaining the present system: capitalism, dependency, and underdevelopment. (p. 10)

Numerous scholars following the dependency logic just outlined adopted the call to participation as embodying egalitarian and pro-democratic tendencies (Barlow, 1990; Cornejo Portugal, 1993; Fals Borda, 1988, 1991; Kaplún, 1980; López Vigil, 1993). This adoption took on several forms with rare examinations of underlying assumptions. Sometimes, scholars adopted a general assumption that greater participation in communication would naturally lead to a participatory society (Barlow, 1990; López Vigil, 1993). Other times, researchers posited more specific results from participation, such as the strengthening of new social movements (Fals Borda, 1988, 1991), the enhancement of cohesion across isolated, indigenous communities (Cornejo Portugal, 1993), and the intensification of "collective consciousness" while weakening individualism (Kaplún, 1980).

Although there is a general assumption of greater participation leading to greater social and economic justice, these same scholars also acknowledged the complexity of participation by noting the many levels at which this concept can operate (Moemoka, 1994; Nair & White, 1993; Servaes, 1996). For example, scholars divided media practice into production and consumption moments, conceptualizing both as open to popular participation (Barlow, 1990; Santoro, 1992). Others pushed this notion further and identified more specific stages of participation, including the planning, production, and evaluation of communication projects (Aguirre Alvis & Abbott, 1991; Cornejo Portugal, 1993; Hein, 1984). The differentiated nature of participation seems to be tied to the elusive, symbolic nature of communication, as explained by Simpson Grinberg (1986a):

> In addition, if we understand communication—*all communication*—as a process of symbolic interaction in a given social and cultural context, we will see that the problem does not reside in the unidirectionality of a medium, but in the degrees of participation, in the diverse levels of communication, which can be direct or *indirect* in its potential mechanisms of access and the type of discourse. (p. 149)

The sense from these positions is that one begins to appreciate the diverse levels and degrees of participation in implementation of communication programs. Yet, although the complexity of participation is revealed in these discussions, the portrait of participation that emerges is both vague and static. At best, participation is a vague concept that one can place on a continuum of higher and lower intensities according to moments in a communication cycle: planning, producing, consuming, evaluating. At worst, participation is a fixed notion that can be turned off and on in binary fashion, controlled at different levels and in different intensities, depending on the communication task at hand. The traces of the dynamic, process aspects developed in the ideas of communication begin to fade as the discussion moves into notions of participation, Ironically, a concept that inherently implies process ends up being conceptualized in nonprocess ways. This contradiction becomes clearer as we examine the ways in which these models of participatory communication have been applied.

Ideas About Applications

The biggest challenges to participatory communication for development have come where theory meets practice—in communication applications. The pragmatic necessity to make practical decisions constitutes the greatest challenge and source of inspiration for scholars promoting the need for participation in development.

When it comes to applying ideas relating to communication and participation in development contexts, situations and behaviors must be treated momentarily as static states. If these situations and behaviors were conceptualized in a larger theory-for-practice that took time, space, and context into account this would not become problematic.[2] When, however, practice is conceptualized as momentary responses to temporarily frozen situations, applications often have been advanced as recipes for communicative action that transcend sense and moment. When this happens, the resulting communication applications often appear naive, simplistic, and overly optimistic.

---

[2]In making this statement, we are aware that it rests on an assumption that it is possible to develop theory-for-practice by incorporating time, space, and context to provide guidance across situations. It must be acknowledged that most scholars working in the Latin American participatory communication arena would not make this assumption. They might even charge that this assumption harkens back to a search for "universal" theories, a search that was, of course, the subject of vigorous attack because it implied the imperialistic imposition of northern-bred theorizing on southern experience. It is one of our major premises, however, that the universal theories rightly under attack have been static, nonprocess theories that have not taken time, space, or context into account in their theoretical structures, whereas the kind of theories-for-practice we have in mind would position this accounting as their primary focus.

Scholars have suggested, for example, a rejection of all top–down, "authoritarian" structures in communication practice in favor of grassroots, democratic control of media (Barlow, 1990; Hein, 1984; O'Connor, 1990; Simpson Grinberg, 1986b). Such a shift, "in its widest sense, implies the exercise of *direct communication democracy*, free from control and without any need for the gifted interpreters of the collective feeling" (Simpson Grinberg, 1986b, p. 178). Such proclamations bear an utopian enthusiasm but are troubling in their refusal to problematize "freedom" and their inability to be self-reflexive. The suggestion that "direct communication democracy" is readily attainable is dubious and quickly discarded when one considers research, for example, revealing the continual oppression of women by so-called progressive projects (Flores Bedregal, 1989; Riaño, 1994; Santa Cruz, 1983).

Even less ambitious applications run into the same difficulty. In fact, the bulk of recommendations for communication applications take the form of rather modest, specific actions such as linking up with popular organizations, unions, and civic groups; scheduling a high percentage of programming in indigenous languages; recruiting practitioners from surrounding communities; visiting popular gathering spots when constructing sociodramas and news; incorporating a variety of formats— humor, debate, games,and so on—into programming (Barlow, 1990; Fals Borda, 1988, 1991; Hein, 1984; Kaplún, 1980, 1985; López Vigil, 1993). All of these recommendations contain obvious contextual limitations, yet they have been advanced as theoretically broad and potentially applicable in cross-cultural situations. Such recommendations appear to have weak theoretical reach because they have conceptualized each frozen thought and situation as continuous across time and space rather than as temporarily fixed moments giving way to permutations and flux.

The ramifications of shifting one's perspective in this way will become clearer later. In essence, what happens is that a concept that inherently implies fluidity, dynamics, change over time and across space, gets conceptualized statically. Elsewhere this has been referred to as a consequence of conceptualizing the communication process in nonprocess or noncommunication ways. What should be a practice based on a theory for practice that incorporates understandings of contexts and contingencies becomes a set of static recipes.[3]

Perhaps in no place has the tension between fluid process and static recipe been better illustrated than in a recent development in the Latin American participatory communication literature. A recent concept posited as a refinement of participation is the split between communication as a process versus communication as a product (Decker, 1988;

---

[3]For discussions of the development of process theories of communication practice see Dervin (1991, 1993) and Dervin and Clark (1993).

Fontes, 1992; Kaplún, 1989; Rodríguez, 1994; Roncagliolo, 1989; Santoro, 1992). Media practices adopting a communication process approach focus on the experience of collectively planning, producing, and reading or viewing a mediated product. The emphasis is on the growth and learning experienced by the participants engaged in the communication activities. In contrast, media practices adopting a communication product approach attend to narrative and aesthetic qualities of a final videotape, newsletter, or photograph without much concern for participation in the production of mediated products. By constructing professional, engaging, high-quality materials, practitioners adopting this approach have the goal of drawing large numbers of participants as audiences.

Although it has not been identified as such, the process–product split is essentially a way of coping with the tension identified earlier in this chapter—a tension between static, structural and dynamic, process understandings. The communication process approach implements media practices as dynamic processes, whereas the communication product approach treats media constructions as static and structural. Because the two approaches have not been identified as a means for coping with foundationally different assumptions of thought and reality, they are deployed schizophrenically, as distinct, even oppositional, strategies. Placing them centrally within a perspective that is conscious of fundamental epistemological and ontological assumptions will demonstrate that these approaches are not oppositional but closely related.

In summary, we have pointed to three tensions in the Latin American alternative communication and development literature: structure versus process, process as recipe versus process as contingency, and product versus process. The connecting word, versus, more often than not has managed the tensions and seeming incommensurabilities in this literature, particularly when theorizing practice. We suggest, however, that this is symptom rather than root, of unexamined attentions to philosophical ontological and epistemological underpinnings.

SIX SETS OF UNDERLYING META-THEORETIC ASSUMPTIONS

The purpose of this section is to examine the foundational ontological and epistemological assumptions undergirding the different versions of the participatory communication for development narrative. Six alternative sets of assumptions are summarized in Table 6.1.[4] Each set of alternative

---

[4]Dervin (1994) applied the same six alternative sets of assumptions to a different body of literature, that pertaining to issues relating to information and democracy. The presentation here is an adaptation of the line of thinking developed there.

Table 6.1 Display of the Analysis of Six Stereotyped Sets of Meta-Theoretic Assumptions—Ontological, Epistemological, and Ideological—Underlying Different.

Stereotypic Label	Meta-Theoretic Assumptions			Application to Participation in Development	
	Ontology	Epistemology	Ideological Warrant	Why Participation	Development Models
Authority Dogma Positivism-accused	Fixed and continuous and orderly	Isomorphic to reality	Inheritance force	None required or assumed as inherent	Top-down
Naturalism Empiricism Positivism	Same	Prone to bias but centered and trainable	Expertise accuracy	To get accuracy To reify expertise	Two-step flow Development Support Communication
Cultural relativity	Same	Orderly but different between cultures	Inheritance Force Expertise Accuracy within cultures	To give cultural anchor, to reify cultural power	Networking Weak participatory models-

Table 6.1 Display of the Analysis of Six Stereotyped Sets of Meta-Theoretic Assumptions—Ontological, Epistemological, and Ideological—Underlying Different (cont'd).

Constructivism	Same	Orderly but different between persons	Within persons	To entice individual action	
Postmodernism Postparadigmatic	Bracketed or chaotic and changing	Decentered Chaotic	None possible or everywhere	None required (participation is imposition)	
Communication Dialogic Verbings	Fixed and continuous and chaotic and changing	Centered and Decentered	Bracketed or Exposed	Participation made in communication; participation designs processes and outcomes	Strong partici-patory models

assumptions is cast deliberately as a stereotype, for this chapter does not aim to fashion an extended discussion of different philosophical positions, but to delineate conceptual categories in the manner of Weber's (1963) ideal types. The categories, therefore, are not real in the sense that scholars regularly adopt any particular set wholesale, but they operate as a conceptual pastiche of approaches often reified in stereotypic ways in the participatory communication for development research.

The six sets of stereotypes have been ordered into the following labels: authority, naturalism, cultural relativity, constructivism, postmodernism, and communitarianism. Table 6.1 lays out each stereotype in its own row with its own set of ontological assumptions (about the nature of reality); epistemological assumptions (about the nature of knowing); and an ideological warrant (the rhetorical platform power must use for its exertion). The table also sets out two columns that attend to how we see each stereotype as having been applied in development approaches. One column focuses on teleology—the why of participation in development. The second identifies different development approaches that are seen as exemplifying each stereotype. Although it is not specified in Table 6.1, it is assumed that the six sets of assumptions are laid out in a rough chronological order from earliest presence in our episteme to those most recently emerging.

Our hope in presenting the six stereotypes is to extend our reach beyond the usual dualistic discussions of these issues that one finds in the literature (top–down vs. bottom–up, oppressive vs. liberating, etc.) and to suggest the range of complexities applicable to participatory communication in the development context. By marking our examination in terms of six major disjunctures, however, we can get a better picture of the variety of positions being brought to bear on these issues.

Order Versus Chaos—the Fault Line

The primary organizing concepts in the table rotate around a central dualism—order versus chaos. Recent discussions of communication and development are peppered with dualisms (e.g., structure vs. agency, individual vs. community, diversity vs. homogeneity, local vs. global, and contextual vs. universal.)[5] For the purposes of this chapter, it is assumed that one particular dualism is foundational to the others—order versus chaos. Furthermore, it is assumed that the ricocheting of our models between concepts of order and concepts of chaos poses the greatest challenge to our conceptions of communication and participation and,

---

[5]Overviews of some of the debates in the field of communication include Delia (1987), Dervin (1993), and Rosengren (1989).

thus, to the communication–participation–development relation. We can see this richochet in our overview of the Latin American literature previously presented in that two competing perspectives on participatory communication have emerged. One emphasizes structure, recipes, and products and can be seen as richocheting to the order end of the continuum. The other emphasizes process, flux, and mediation and can be seen as richocheting more to the chaos end of the continuum.

Because we are focusing on order versus chaos as a central organizing polarity, Table 6.1 is ordered primarily by focusing on issues of order versus chaos and how they are conceptualized in various ontological and epistemological positions. Furthermore, in line with Hayles' (1990) portrayal of both the sciences and humanities in the last half of this century, as destabilized by the order–chaos dichotomy,[6] Table 6.1 is developed on the assumption that this destabilization and the dialectical discourses surrounding it drives our movement from Row 1 assumptions to Row 6 assumptions, with each successive row, modifying and contesting those preceding.

The Ideological Warrant

Finally, before proceeding with the discussions of the six sets of assumptions, a note is in order on the column in Table 6.1 labeled, "Ideological Warrant." As used here, ideology refers to modes of thought that stem from, and conceal, social contradictions.[7] Most discussions of ideology, informed as they are by classical Marxist thought, anchor themselves primarily to examinations of economic structures and the forces they exert on the constitution of daily life. In contrast, the discussion here tries to ferret out how the spaces left by different ontological and epistemological assumptions allow the forces of power, however defined, to issue warrants—claims derived from whatever is rhetorically defined as evidence or reason and applied to generalizations.[8] Although usual discussions might

[6]Hayles (1990) encapsulated this view succinctly when she called the destabilization of the order–chaos dichotomy—a central dichotomy in Western thought—a "major fault line . . . in the episteme" (p. 16), one that has a magnet like attraction and therefore points to places of pervasive contradiction and contest in scholarly literatures.

[7]The definition comes from Bottomore (1983) who actually used the term *distortions* rather than *modes*. The latter term is used here in keeping with the premise that distortions anchor themselves on an ideal of an external standard. The communitarian position, which is where we end up after walking through all the sets of assumptions, requires in its most general frame a more general term. The procedure—anchoring to an external standard—would be an instance of the possibilities. Works particularly helpful in developing this section include Freire (1970), Gramsci (1988), Hall (1989), and Lukes (1974).

[8]Our discussion of ideological warrants is informed by Toulmin, Rieke, and Janik's (1979) use of warrants in the explication of argumentation strategies.

ask, for example, how an ideology focused on the reification of an uncontrolled capitalism might use a particular ontological or epistemological view to serve its end, this discussion asks how a particular ontological–epistemological view lays itself open to this co-optation.

In asking this question, we are concerned with two dimensions of ideology. One is the question of who gets to decide what reality is called: in Freire's (1970) terms, who names the world.

The second dimension is more subtle and elusive and focuses on the principles and criteria embedded in rules, procedures, and other institutional forms. Here, in the domain of taken-for-granted institutional forms, power more often runs silently and unrecognized (Shields, personal communication, September 23, 1993). When this discussion is applied to participatory development communication programs, it involves the naming and identifying of situations, the planning and strategizing of actions, the producing and implementing of programs, and the evaluating of outcomes related to whatever the specific context defines as "development."

It is important to note that in attending to power as we have here we are assuming that power in some way always exerts a force, either obvious or subtle, apparent or hidden, overt or covert. In the context of this discussion, a primary impact of power is assumed to be the homogenization and leveling out of chaos, manifested either ontologically (by homogenizing contradictory material conditions) or epistemologically (by homogenizing differing worldviews).[9] One of power's jobs in this conceptualization is, in essence, to make tidy difference, incompleteness, and disorderliness.

Authority[10]

Authority is defined, in *Webster's New World Dictionary*, as the power to command, enforce, decide. *Dogma*, traditionally defined as the formulation of belief based on the scriptures (Owen, 1967), is used in the more generally accepted meaning, again per *Webster's*, of any belief or opin-

---

What we wish to emphasize, however, is that which is absent in Toulmin's work: the exertion of power through warrants.

[9]Our position on the play of power in human affairs suggests we must consider the possibility that power works in pervasive ways—in the very ontological and epistemological worlds of our times, in the discourses by which we constitute and by which we are constituted, in the values we apply to judging appropriateness, in the design of our communication and information systems, and in the procedures we call participatory.

[10]The reader needs to read both this section and the next one on empiricism, in order to understand the distinction between *positivism-accused* and *positivism*.

ion. The use of positivism-accused is explained here. In this version of the narrative, ontologically, the sense-of-being implied is that there is a reality "out there" that is fixed and continuous—definite entities exist in definite places with definite patterns of relations that transcend moments in time and space. Epistemologically, it is assumed that knowing is isomorphic to that reality and produces truthful statements about that reality. In essence, epistemological issues as we know them are not relevant. There is no room in this conceptualization for a gap between the observer and the observed. The ideological warrant is inheritance and/or force. Those with the power given by inheritance and/or force claim the right to define reality although in actuality no such claim is necessary for the underlying foundational assumptions make stating a claim unnecessary.

In such a perspective, ironically, participation can be assumed to be either not required or universally inherent. Because reality is defined by those in power and is assumed to be the reality, those not falling in line must be assumed to be out of touch with reality whereas those falling into line are assumed to be in touch with reality, doing what is assumed to be inherently obvious given the assumptions of both ontological and epistemological order. With such a set of assumptions, participation should be guaranteed when information is made accessible to all. Given assumed-to-be truthful statements about reality from the top, those at the bottom should simply follow without question. This view of participation in development is, thus, essentially a noncommunicative view .

In such an ontologized arena, the ideological warrant—where power issues its claims—is determined in nonparticipatory arenas, through rarefied positions of institutional authority. There is no procedural or even philosophic role for compromise, negotiation, intersubjectivity, or dialogue. In this worldview, authority as the source of ontological truth is unquestioned. If the ontological truth is questioned, power must be brought to bear to eliminate difference. One of the difficulties of Row 1 assumptions is that it assumes that power is either nonexistent or is obvious but, in either case, irrelevant. Reality is as power says it is. In such a tautological net there is no way to question power whether obvious or hidden.

Clearly, row 1 assumptions are out of favor. It is important, however, not to cast aside attention to them too hastily as overly simplistic and something of the past because using them as an anchor helps us explore some issues. The use of the terms *dogma* and *positivism-accused* as secondary labels under *authority* in this row of Table 6.1 is purposive. Although the term *positivism* was first used to designate the scientific method, it came to designate a powerful philosophic movement in the Western world whose "characteristic theses . . . are that science is the only valid knowledge and facts the only possible objects of knowledge" (Abbagnano, 1967, p. 414). As a scientific philosophy, positivism has been outdated since the 1920s.[11] However, the term has come to stand as a stereotypic label for any practice of what might be called dogmatic science, based on an ontological realism with little or no philosophic or material intercourse with the environment beyond its confines.

In actuality, the larger enterprise called science cannot so easily be judged guilty on these counts.[12] However, when it comes to what might be called an ideology of science in the world of practice and policy, the philosophic arguments and even the elaborate corrective mechanisms of science within its own ontological–epistemological frame are often left behind. The evidence is seen in current contests between calls for tolerance and acceptance of diversity, on the one hand, and totalizing beliefs anchored in prejudice and dogma (including a modern version of dogma—the mindless application of uncontested "findings" generated by a brute or misused science), on the other. We see development efforts around the world—both top-down and horizontal—where rhetorics of diversity are heavily used but mandates are issued in the name of a brute science as to what is correct practice in a host of arenas (e.g., health care, education, crime control, and technology adoption).

The important point here is that Row 1 assumptions incorporate neither concepts of diversity nor error nor chaos. Participation is assumed to inherently produce singular and accurate understandings of reality. Participation that does not produce these understandings is judged ipso facto to be nonrelevant. Because the rhetorics of diversity make it fashionable for difference to have voice, difference will be given space to speak. The resulting voices can then be ignored, construed as babble, and, thus, cleverly marginalized.

Naturalism

Row 2 of Table 6.1 has the stereotypic labels of "naturalism" and "positivism."[13] *Naturalism* refers to an approach that assumes "whatever exists or happens is natural [sic] in the sense of being susceptible to explanation through methods which, although paradigmatically exempli-

---

[11]As Giddens (1989) emphasized, positivism has become "son of a scarce term" (p. 53) and few scientists exist that would now call themselves positivists.

[12]The issue of what comprises knowledge within science has been the subject of enormous and continuing philosophical and methodological debate. And, as Hayles (1990) demonstrated, it is possible to argue that science itself has as much of a stake in the move away from positivist theories as have the various branches of the humanities. In Hayles' terms, the move is part of the fracture in the episteme.

[13]Giddens was particularly helpful in developing this sections; the foregrounding of naturalism here follows his.

fied in the natural sciences, are continuous from domain to domain of objects and events" (Wollheim, 1967, p. 448). *Positivism*, defined in the preceding section, implies an extension of scientific ideas to the study of society and an emphasis in that context on facts as the only valid objects of knowledge (Abbagnano, 1967). Both naturalism and positivism are offshoots of empiricism—"the theory that experience rather than reason is the source of knowledge" (Hamlyn, 1967, p. 499).

The importance of presenting these definitions is not to anchor our discussions in any essential view of what naturalism is or is not but rather to provide a starting point for examining Row 2 assumption. The dominant approach to the sciences, including the social sciences, at least since the 1940s, has been a naturalistic empiricism based on beliefs that science should generate knowledge of the causal mechanisms operating in the physical and natural as well as social and psychological worlds.[14] Implementing these beliefs has typically involved an elaborate set of methods—for example, operationalization, reliability and validity checks, use of reproducibility standards—to identify and control sources of so-called errors, biases, and constraints. In line with their ontological assumptions, these beliefs have also incorporated narrow views of the potential relations that might be observed in reality, limiting the possibilities to what can be modeled by using causality statistics that are assumed to map reality in isomorphic ways.[15]

What is most definitive about Row 2 is that epistemology begins to take on a major role. The important change between Row 1 and 2 assumptions is that in Row 2 our human is conceptualized as being something less than a perfect observer. Knowing becomes potentially biased, constrained, and erroneous. Introduced is the idea, widely accepted in the social sciences and in common parlance, that not all humans see the same things when they observe and that some humans are "better" observers than others. For example, in this context, it is assumed that humans have physiological limitations, both as a species (e.g., humans cannot hear some sounds that dogs can) and as individuals (e.g., some people are nearsighted). It is also assumed that there are psychological limitations (e.g. the selectivity processes assumed by social psychology: selective attention, retention, and recall) and psychoanalytic limitations assumed by psychiatry (e.g., illusions and delusions).

Although Row 1 assumes an orderly observing human, Row 2 introduces an element of chaos: a human conceptualized with a propen-

[14]It is, of course, well accepted that this is a far too narrow view of science as practiced today. See, for example, Bronowski (1973), Hayles (1990), and Zukav (1979).

[15]The same has been true in the natural and physical sciences, as Hayles (1990) pointed out when she described chaos theories as moving science in general beyond linear, causal models.

sity toward disorderliness. The ideological warrant in Row 2 is similar to that in Row 1 but with a slight difference. Here, power must put forth credentials of accuracy and expertise. Theoretically, power is more open and available than it was in Row 1; in practice, however, subtle restrictions regulate the flow of candidates receiving the appropriate training and credentialing. In order for power to put forth credentials, the standards for judging expertise must be widely accepted. This is an important difference between Row 1 and Row 2. In Row 1, power—whether benign or brutal—is more likely to be materially derived from heritage or strength. In Row 2, power is as likely to be derived through interpretation, requiring wide acceptance of similar standards and values and commensurate investments by power in the development and maintenance of symbolically based hegemonies—a new credentialism.

This has implications for participatory communication programs for development. With historicized power, the authorial voice is sufficient; with expert power, the authorial voice must invoke procedures and structures that confer the right to speak based on expertise. With this turn, participation must necessarily reify specific individuals and modes of participating in the implementation of development goals. One can see the application of these ideas in modifications of top–down theories of development into various two-step models. In these approaches, ideas about reality assumed to be ontologically correct are seen as moving from experts to innovators and opinion leaders. The intermediaries are most often conceptualized as assisting development efforts in getting past the selectivity and other barriers that intended audiences erect. As in Row 1 assumptions, it is ultimately assumed that participation is inherent because what is being asked is assumed to be ontologically correct. The refinement in participation offered here is that specifically invited participation is assumed to both reify expertise and improve the accuracy of reception of development messages. In addition, in the context of Row 2 assumptions, a wide variety of various communication strategies are applied to increase accuracy of transmission.

Cultural Relativity

Although the introduction of the ideas of bias and constraint in knowing in the "naturalism" stereotype points toward at least a theoretic acceptance of diversity, the retention of assumptions of a complete ontology and the ideal of an orderly human required that the idea of accuracy—a new kind of authority—be introduced. In effect, this still privileges a single voice. Yet, perhaps the dominant characteristic of our experience over the last century has been the continuing rise in the variety and volume of voices of difference that refuse to accept externally imposed standards. In terms of the participatory communication for development narrative, there have been two different alterations introduced. One of these still essentially (and ironically) upholds the basic narrative; the second begins to topple it to the ground.

Upholding the narrative is the set of assumptions detailed in Row 3 of the table labeled Cultural Relativity. In essence, these assumptions duplicate Row 1 with one essential difference: Culture is privileged and order is seen as sensible only within or relative to cultures.[16] The majority of calls for participatory communication programs would fit most comfortably here. Our human observers are now embedded in cultural discourses and their observations constitute and are constituted by this embeddedness. Observations have only contextual, cultural generalizability, and the standard for judgment is still an external standard informed by that context. Reality is still seen as fixed and continuous, but bounded within its own context and time-place. This applies not just to making sense of the social world, but of the natural and physical worlds as well. The result is a mandate for pluralistic participation, with each constituent group in the plurality adhering to its own standard. This set of assumptions is a major impetus of the original call for a new world information and communication order and for the rebirth of that call in mid-1998.[17]

In this set of assumptions, we begin to see a fracture, a destabilization, of the tautological tidiness of the assumptions in Rows 1 and 2. On the surface, it appears as if the different viewpoints arising from different contexts have something to share with each other. But because each is anchored in an assumption that its version of fixed and continuous reality is the one reality, no amount of well-meaning acceptance of difference will allow the different constituent pluralities to travel anywhere together where differences require comprehension or amelioration. There is neither an agreed-on allegiance to an external standard nor a procedural capacity for compromise and negotiation; these flexibilities are not required by the ontological basis of the assumptions.

What is most interesting about Row 3 assumptions is that despite pluralistic intentions they revert to a nonepistemological view of participation. Cultural difference is assumed to be a sufficient explanation for differences in worldviews and within cultures, homogeneity is

---

[16]Particularly helpful in developing this section have been the following, none of whom should be held responsible for the stereotypes presented here: Clifford (1986), Geertz (1975), and Rorty (1991). It needs to be emphasized that there are numerous approaches to scholarship that call themselves *cultural*. Some would be clearly recognized if one applied as a map the cultural relativity stereotype used in this chapter. Others would be more readily recognized using the contructivist or postmodern stereotypes.

[17]See, in particular, Gerbner, Mowlana, and Nordenstreng (1993).

assumed. Differences that emerge within cultures must be homogenized. The ideological warrant is held by those occupying positions within the culture that are assumed to allow more complete and accurate interpretations of the culture's norms and cultures as well as the culture's needs. In some cases, these positions are assumed to be inherited; in others they are obtained by force; in others they are assumed to be occupied by more expert, more accurate observers. Views that do not conform to the renditions drawn out in this warrant are at best considered anomalies, and at worst labeled deviance. The narrative has no way philosophically, and therefore, theoretically, of dealing with diversity and incommensurability within cultures. In the context of such assumptions, we have seen highly contested anthropological description of cultures emerge: for example, emergent feminist voices in a culture challenging the authorial male voice.[18]

It is in this meta-theoretic terrain that we see top-down and alternative approaches to development both incorporating participation in similar practices based on very different intentions. Top-down efforts, for example, call for adapting the planned innovation to the cultural context. In implementation, there are attempts to incorporate advice from key informants and opinion leaders and to utilize cultural networks. And, messages promoting development are strategized to be maximally appealing to the particular cultural audience.

Despite their different intentions, the same kinds of communication strategies are utilized by those working in the Latin American alternative communication tradition: for example, linking up with local groups, using indigenous languages, recruiting communication specialists from the community. Although there is a clear difference between these two literatures in their philosophic and ideological intentions, it is especially ironic that some of the practices end up looking so much alike. In the context of this chapter, we suggest that this happens at least in part because alternative communication practice proceeds without a communication theory of communication practice. Because of this, in the long run it has no way of implementing a sustained focus on process and reverts to emphasis on recipes and products.

Constructivism

With Row 4—the constructivism perspective—the emphasis on order faces its most serious challenge. The move from cultural relativity to personal relativity assumes that each person constructs understandings of the world in interaction with an individual symbolic, social, natural, and

---

[18]For recent relevant works, see Gonzalez and Peterson (1993) and Rakow (1992).

physical world. Delia's (1977) description of constructivism captures the essence of the stereotype we are using here: "meanings are rooted in individual responses to events and not in the events themselves" (p. 75). In essence, he suggested, there is always a process of definition standing between external events and the internal understanding between external events and the internal understandings that guide human behavior.

There are a variety of approaches that have typically been grouped under the term *constructivist*, ranging from the most general idea that meanings are made by individuals based on their experiences past and present, to the more stringent philosophic movement called *constructivism* based on a mathematical rule that said that when the existence of some thing was mentioned it should be accompanied by a statement of the method of finding or constructing that thing (Parsons, 1967). At one extreme then we find a general epistemology; at the other we find a focus on epistemological procedures—the how's of observing.

Where these extremes meet in the stereotyped version of constructivism presented here, we find a de-emphasis on ontology. Without explicit attention, issues of ontology—the nature of reality—are set aside. Yet, references to such concepts as "events" imply an unstated acceptance of an externally ordered reality. Furthermore, the emphasis on individual constructings is itself assumed to be orderly (i.e., individual sense is made in orderly ways albeit orderly within individuals).

The result is that we have an orderly human with each individual human conceptualized as different. Theoretically, with such a set of assumptions, no standard of judgment for knowing is necessary beyond each individual. The ideological warrant, speaking on a theoretical level, is carried by each individual and is open equally to all members of the society. This implies that personal authority wields power, but it ignores the hidden way that power courses through society shaping individual choices.

Furthermore, Row 4 assumptions embed a subtle flaw in that with the implicit retention of an orderly ontology there is only one avenue open for handling the overbearing differences presented by an epistemology assumed to be orderly only within persons. Any kind of procedural negotiation is not only logically unnecessary, it is also logically impossible. The underlying assumptions provide no avenue for ameliorating difference, nor inviting difference into dialogue. Difference must be construed as babble and power, in an ironic sense, has as much unhampered access to control in the context of Row 4 assumptions as it does in Row 1 assumptions.

There are two important differences between Row 4 and the next row focusing on postmodernism: One is that the assumption of an orderly ontology is retained in Row 4; two is that the assumption of an orderly epistemology, albeit within persons, is retained. Unlike Row 2 assumptions where difference is conceptualized as error, in Row 4 assumptions difference is conceptualized as a host of complex personal realities that must be taken into account

Row 4 assumptions are particularly attractive to cultures that promote individualism and consumerism and account, in part, for top–down development programs that focus on attitude shifts as the basis for sparking social change. But, reliance on constructivist assumptions has not been limited to only top–down development approaches. Both top–down and alternative development approaches have, for example, pointed to the use of game shows as potentially effective strategies for involving individuals in active constructing activities relating to development. In such cases, of course, the arguments presented in support of essentially the same strategy vary.

There are also a variety of more philosophic moves within the Latin American participatory communication literature that point toward the belief system described under the label *constructivism*. This is evident in two of the key concepts arising from the Latin American literature. First, with the introduction of the concepts of *marginalization* and *internalized oppression*, Latin American writers paved the way for justifications of participatory communication resting on constructivist assumptions. The keys to development were presumed to reside within the minds of social actors, who, with enough time and persistence, would come to disentangle the real from the false. The psychological state described here could be interpreted as containing many of the assumptions described under the label of *naturalism*, but it differs in the exercise of the ideological warrant, which de-emphasizes expert authority in favor of each human subject "naming the world."

Second, the adoption of the notion of *praxis*, as the manifestation of dialogue, also represents a shift into the adoption of constructivist assumptions. Here, knowing is fully problematized as occurring in the dialectical unity of theorizing about and acting in the world. The nature of reality is bracketed in the praxis literature and primacy is granted to the lived experience in the world. Furthermore, humans are projected as knowing in intersubjective exchange with one another, exchange that results in transformed individuals and a "re-constructed reality." Reality, itself, is conceptualized as a mental phenomenon, not as a material condition marked by instability or constructedness.

This bracketing of reality, we propose, has stymied the ability of participatory communication research to advance theoretically. On the one hand, bracketing reality has seemed the only avenue open in the face of evidence regarding the highly individualistic and seemingly unpredictable ways in which people interpret texts, including texts relating to development. On the other hand, richocheting into assumptions of overbearing individuality defies the very idea of most development efforts so we see even in the alternative communication work a kind of schizophrenia, a belief in two positions that over time have become increasingly contradictory: structure versus process; process recipes versus process contingencies; product versus process. We propose that it is by journeying through the arguments stereotyped in Row 5 that we begin to develop insights allowing us to escape these increasingly paradoxical dualisms.

Postmodernism

Although on the surface it might seem that the Row 5 stereotype—postmodernism—presents a sterner challenge to assumptions of order than those in Row 4, in fact Row 5 assumptions are no test at all. Instead, they abandon the possibility of any kind of systematic development.[19] Here we have chaotic reality, chaotic knowing, and no possible universal standard of judgment. Different postmodern–poststructural theorists employ these assumptions in different ways so it is more useful to talk of postmodernisms than postmodernism. Most theorize that all knowing—all information—is defined by and within an episteme and the discourse of that episteme. Ontology as a central question is thus set aside. Rather, ontological reality is assumed to be manifest solely through interpretation--through discourse, as it is in the constructivist position. The difference between the postmodern and constructivist stereotypes presented here is that although neither one provides a direct ontological route to reality, postmodernism denies as well the methodological correction for indirect routes, the idea of systematic albeit differing epistemologies. Humans, when centered and ordered, are made so within and by the episteme. Humans are naturally chaotic, decentered, and unconscious.[20]

---

[19]For overviews of postmodern work, see Best and Kellner (1991), Lather (1991), Mukerji and Schudson (1991), and Rorty (1985). Particularly useful to this discussion were Barthes (1982/1985), Foucault (1965/1972), and Lyotard (1984). Fassbinder (personal communication, September 9, 1993) provided challenging comments, particularly helpful in thinking through this section.

[20]Although the term postmodernism and its frequent companions, poststructuralism and postparadigmatic, are used in a bewildering variety of contexts with a bewildering variety of meanings, for our purposes, the thrust of the movement is its intent on destabilizing all sources of truth, all grand narratives, whether assumed to be created by God, science, or the enlightened, reasoning human being. In an extreme version, the deconstruction called for by many labeled as postmodernists or postructuralists warns us that "nothing, whether deed, word, thought or text, ever happens in relation . . . to anything that precedes, follows, or exists elsewhere, but only as a random event whose power . . . is due to the randomness of its occurrence" (deMan, 1979, p. 69). From one perspective it can be challenged that most postmodernists are in fact not positing ontological

If such a set of assumptions were used to construct participatory communication programs, the project would be challenged as a contradiction to the very premises of many postmodernists. In such a deontologized[21] world, there would be no ideological warrant—no way for power to issue its claim—for it would be acknowledged that all systematic modes of knowing and acting are capricious impositions. On one hand, it would be assumed that no standard of judgment for knowing is possible; on the other, it would be assumed that if we found anything that might be called systematic knowing, oppressive power has been the sole standard used.

One of the main thrusts of the postmodern project has been to deconstruct the discourses that encapsulate power, to unravel the episteme. Thus, while ideally, in a postmodern world no power could gain a footing, postmodernists typically posit power in practice as operating everywhere, in all discourse, and therefore in all systems that pretend to generate knowledge through participatory actions. In essence, anything that orders human affairs is assumed to be imposed. To speak of systematic or planned participation as an egalitarian action is oxymoronic.

By and large, the communication for development literature has not been influenced by the philosophical contributions of postmodernism. Recent books in this field usually fail to mention postmodernism altogether (Jayaweera & Amunugama, 1987; Meyer, 1988; Nair & White, 1993; Traber, 1986; Vijaya Lakshmi, 1993). In the cases where postmodernism is mentioned, authors rarely engage the full philosophical and theoretical implications of postmodernism for development.[22]

One thoughtful, although indirect, engagement with postmodern ideas can be found in the work of Servaes (1989), who implicitly acknowledged notions of decenteredness, chaos, and fragmentation

---

chaos but rather an ontological order created and held in place through discourse and the power that is assumed to run pervasively through discourse. The implication at a higher level of abstraction is that there is no order given by reality. Hence, the characterization in this paper of postmodernism as positing a chaotic reality.

[21]The term *deontologized* is used here to refer to a setting aside or bracketing of ontological concerns. This use is becoming more common and relates to but is not equivalent to the dominant current usage in philosophy in reference to a deontological theory of ethics that "holds that at least some acts are morally obligated regardless of their consequences for human weal [sic] or woe." Etymologically, deontology means the science of duty (R. Olson, 1967, p. 343).

[22]For instance, in *The Passing of Modernity*, Mowlana and Wilson (1990) appear to take a swipe at Daniel Lerner's approach to development, rather than exploring the challenges posed by the end of a paradigm as the title might suggest. Their treatment of postmodernism is brief and nested wholly within cultural studies. The most radical aspects of postmodern thought seem to be dismissed as

when he advocated a contemporary paradigm shift in communication for development, which he called "multiplicity in one world." Rather than working with any specific or general postmodern notions, however, Servaes ended up drawing heavily on modernist ideas emerging from the work of Habermas, for example, to call for more pluralism in the development process. What he ended up with is essentially a cultural relativity approach albeit far better articulated than most such approaches in development communication work.[23]

S. Olson (1994) working in the arena of development communication has engaged postmodern ideas directly. He focused his attention on television and questioned its use for development or social change. Basing his arguments on Baudrillard's work—particularly the notion of hyperreality—S. Olson contended that television has an "essence" that renders attempts at development communication hopeless. The essence of television is a mixture of the following characteristics: iconic, immediate, intimate, "cool," pervasive, expensive, passive–aggressive, polysemic, and convergent. Whereas this essentializing of television implies a certain epistemological stability, S. Olson contended that the "nature of television" produces unstable meanings that cannot be controlled by human subjects or material objects in the communication process. Neither senders nor receivers nor referents can control or shape meaning that is mediated through television; rather images eclipse senders, receivers, and referents, and they create intense simulation of reality that replaces any notion of reality itself. S. Olson concluded, somewhat paradoxically, by suggesting that development communicators should explore ways to "control television," given that its effects are wholly unpredictable.

---

follows: "Mostly an intellectual exercise in the French social science tradition, this postmodernist writing is based in the esoteric realm of philosophy, language, and literature" (p. 90). The only contributions of postmodern thought to Mowlana and Wilson's "integrative theory" of global communication is a heightened sensitivity to cultural diversity, traditions, and uses of media, a sensitivity that, in fact, can be gleaned from various cultural approaches anchored in a cultural relativity.

[23]The idea that Servaes (1989) ended up with a cultural relativity approach is illustrated in his explicit explanation of his epistemological assumptions: "There are different kinds of knowledge: some regularities in human behavior are explainable on the basis of culture-specific laws, others on the basis of generally valid laws. Because their epistemological status differs, these two kinds of knowledge also imply two kinds of rules. In the case of culture-specific rules, one speaks of moral rules that have a normative character; the generally applicable laws have a more natural-scientific character" (p. 41). Servaes' mapping of the two kinds of epistemologies is somewhat analogous to the material versus ideational distinction for explaining cultural differences used by anthropologists inasmuch as it fails to draw a link from ontological status to epistemological status.

Our examples so far suggest that those who attempt to use post-modern ideas in development communication contexts either fail to realize them fully or assume that the ideas cannot be used, are in fact contradictory to the very ideas of participation and development. Yet, when the Latin American alternative communication work is examined, one finds a number of ingenious attempts, particularly when addressing practice, to incorporate postmodern ideas. Thus, for example, one can look at the recent emerging distinction between communication process versus communication product as an attempt to cope with the ways in which assumptions of orderly ontology or orderly epistemology simply are not sufficient for the communication task. Sometimes, the product–process distinction suggests we need to focus on stabilities and products, sometimes on instabilities and process. By focusing on both, the practitioner attempts to manage concerns growing out of the postmodernism label without sliding into the abyss of hopelessness that postmodernism implies.

Other researchers within Latin America have recognized the implications of postmodern notions of a chaotic reality for an empirical field such as development in a variety of ways (Fuenzalida & Hermosilla, 1989; García Canclini, 1990; Martín Barbero, 1988, 1993). These writers have pointed to concepts helpful at negotiating postmodern problems without abandoning development goals, ideas including: (a) the production of poly-discursive media texts through *una vinculacion horizontal*—a bringing together of grassroots audiences and media professionals in a mutually informative way (Fuenzalida & Hermosilla, 1989); (b) a shift from the study of media to mediations, from sender–receiver effects to the processes of appropriation, resignification, and reinscription of a wide array of beliefs and values in everyday life (Martín Barbero, 1988. 1993); (c) the introduction of the notion of hybrid cultures and transactions—spaces and moves that are neither wholly oppressive nor wholly liberating, but complex and negotiated by human action within historical, material constraints, and the freedom of their own lifeworlds (García Canclini, 1990).

In the most general sense, the postmodern stereotype is useful for displaying the consequences of the interplay of tensions, particularly within and between Rows 3 and 4. With each step down the Rows in Table 6.1, we move away from totalizing views of order. What if it turns out that cultural relativity is merely another kind of totalizing perspective heralding a never-ending clash within and between cultures, and if constructivism descends into overbearing solipsism or capricious tyranny with no communicative mandate? Some would assert only the postmodern abyss of total chaos remains.[24]

---

[24]It must also be noted that the charge can be made, as Hayles (1990) did, that postmodernism–poststructuralism is reaching for "a new globalizing imperative in its insistence that there can be no global theories" (p. 26). Lyotard (1984)

But this is a far too facile stereotype for there is another theme here, as well. In Row 5—postmodernism—is the first genuine introduction of an acceptance of a chaotic, decentered, unconscious human.[25] Row 2—naturalism—identifies the tendency but does not accept it as a proper state of being. Row 3—cultural relativity—suggests it by alleging that people differ across cultures, but does not handle the difficulty of differences within cultures, and therefore does not fundamentally deal with difference. Row 4—constructivism—points to the possibility but in fact deals primarily with the difficulties of understanding how humans know, given the constructivist view of human beings conceptualized as conscious, centered, and orderly, albeit different from each other in potentially infinite ways.

One way in which the projects of the various postmodern theorists can be understood is in their calls for social theories to incorporate theories of the subject that allow humans to be seen as less cognitive, less centered, less purposive, less conscious than theories that have their roots in naturalism. They reconceptualize the reach of power from that which constrains our material, informational, and symbolic worlds to that which interrupts and disturbs as well our very decenteredness. In this sense, postmodern projects provide a useful challenge as we attempt to move out of an episteme that privileges order toward an episteme that privileges chaos as well. In doing so, the diversity that is so troublesome to ontology in Rows 2, 3, and 4 begins to take on the potential of tool in Row 5. This is in essence what the Latin American researchers are reaching for when they mandate a focus on polydiscursive texts, mediations, and contexts that are both oppressive and freeing. Each of these moves is an attempt to ameliorate the old dualisms, to find a space between structure–staticness–product and agency–flux–process that does not require the connective "versus."

In general, it is our position that the failure to genuinely engage postmodern ideas on a fundamental level ultimately leads to a retreat to modernist ideas that are at best understood as cultural relativism. The consequences of such a retreat are a backsliding into notions of human subjectivity that are unable to advance the project of creating new communication strategies for development. Postmodern ideas are an essential challenge for us if we are to move to Row 6 assumptions, the assumptions that we label as *communitarianism*.

---

acknowledged this when he spoke paradoxically of postmodernism as the master narrative to end all master narratives.

[25]Particularly helpful in this section have been Deleuze and Guattari (1987), Gallop (1985), Holland (1988), Lacan (1977), and Theunissen (1984).

Communitarianism

A wave of cross-disciplinary writing has recently emerged under the umbrella term *communitarianism*. Because our use of the term does not represent its primary definitional focus in the literature, we review briefly here the primary emphasis so we can show how our use differs. Most of the work labeled *communitarian* refers to a perspective that emphasizes the idea that societies are made in communities. An example of this statement comes from communitarian movement founder Amity Etzioni (1995): "We believe that there can be no rights without responsibilities, and that the key to repairing our moral and civic culture is in strengthening the basis institutions of family, school, community, and the community of communities."

Recent work in this thrust has focused, for example, on the normative requirements of a community-based society. This branch of communitarianism has not left a major impression on our thinking about ontological and epistemological assumptions, but does represent a moment of openness, no matter how badly realized, in the search for alternatives to the dualisms presented thus far. In this line of work, for example, structure meets individual in community.[26]

We do not try to summarize in detail the major thrusts, hopes, weaknesses, or promises of this movement.[27] Instead we propose to leap into this intellectual opening in order to create a space where a new set of ontological and epistemological assumptions can be worked out—assumptions that center on communication dynamics as fundamental to the journey that humans travel, individually and collectively, between order and chaos, chaos and order. In essence, we switch the focus from community to communication. Rather than saying that society is made in community, we propose that society is made (and unmade) in communication.

Retaining the term *communitarian* for our project is useful for a number of reasons. First, the building (as well as maintaining, reinforcing, challenging, and destroying) of community in communication has direct implications for understandings and implementations of participatory communication for development. Second, the communitarianism literature threatens to dissolve into a combination of the stereotypes outlined thus far as it rails against the excesses of both individualism implic-

---

[26]For the purposes of demonstrating the recent interest in communitarianism, we offer this abridged list of authors: Barber (1984, 1992); Bellah, Madsen, Sullivan, Swidler, and Tipton (1985); Benhabib and Dallmayr (1990); Elshtain (1986); Etzioni (1993); MacIntyre (1981); Rorty (1989); Sandel (1982); Selznick (1992); Walzer (1983).

[27]See in particular the regular communitarian journal, *The Responsive Community*, as well as the reviews in Reynolds and Norman (1988).

it in liberal democratic politics finding a base in Row 1 and 2 assumptions and the relentless skepticism, deconstruction, and instability of social life evident in Row 3, 4, and 5 assumptions. In a sense, the communitarianism literature is traveling a communication path once identified in the work of John Dewey but not taken by mainstream research (Peters, 1989). Its failure to recognize communication as a central aspect in theorizing community, we suggest, is a major shortcoming and ultimate danger to the quest for theories able to reconcile the tensions identified in the stereotypes presented so far.[28]

The assumptions we build into our use of the term *communitarianism* rely on ideas developed in the sense-making approach, which calls for a methodological refocusing of attention from states and entities to processes and dynamics in an attempt to understand the nature of participatory communication.[29] This entails a shift from nouns to verbs, from nounings to verbings, from participatory communication to participating and communicating. It is argued that these moves are necessary in any communication theory of participatory communication processes. Furthermore, it is proposed that communication theorizing is essential if we are to find a way out of the dualistic traps inherent in the Row 1 to 5 assumptions. The stiltedness of the terms *nounings* and *verbings* all the more reinforces a fundamental assumption—that all modes of theorizing participation are consciously or unconsciously, formally or informally, explicitly or implicitly, focused on procedure. Participation is process. It involves moves. It involves making as well as confronting as well as unmaking order (i.e., structure, product, centered self). It involves brewing as well as challenging as well as taming chaos (i.e., diversity, decentered self).

In essence, this communitarian position formally incorporates both order and chaos as ontological and epistemological assumptions. It assumes both construction and deconstruction as aspects of knowing. It assumes that the standard for judgment of knowing focuses on recursivi-

---

[28]As one example, Rorty (1989) essentially developed an approach where he relegated to the pragmatic public arena all normative and ethical concerns and to a private arena of romanticism all creativity and dreaming. This seems to be his resolution of the tensions between structure and individual, common need and private dream. Fraser (1989) provided a useful analysis.

[29]Although this chapter provides a version of the communitarianism approach on the assumptions used in the Sense-Making approach, it does not present sense-making as such. For methodological discussions of Sense-Making, see Dervin (1989a); for development of the communitarian ideas on which Sense-Making is based, see Dervin (1991, 1993). For an application to the constitution of democracy in communication, see Dervin and Clark (1993). For another example of a communitarian approach with a strong theoretical and methodological focus, see Carter (1989, 1991), and Carter, Ruggels, Jackson, and Heffner (1973). Sense-Making owes a debt to Carter's project.

ties, consequences, contiguities, and intersubjectivities, rather than external immutable standards. It assumes that knowing is made and remade, reified and maintained, challenged and destroyed in communication, dialogue, contest, and negotiation. In contrast to the other positions, it focuses on how's, rather than whoops and whets.

The position proposed in Row 6 is one that accepts that humans sometimes implement assumptions of an orderly reality with useful outcomes, but also that the imposition of this as a universal assumption defies experiential and scientific understandings of the nature of human affairs. Chaos, accident, necessity, and contingency are as useful, in some circumstances more useful, explanations of events in both the natural and social worlds as are mechanisms, systems, and causalities. All explanations are assumed to be potentially useful fictions leading to the question, what do different explanations/fictions allow in terms of actions and possibilities? Notice that this approach does not negate any way of knowing on essentialist grounds, even totalizing modes of knowing. Rather it acknowledges that both the knowing and the standards of testing the knowing are made and contested in communication. Furthermore, in assuming both ontological as well as epistemological incompleteness, this approach provides not only epistemological justification for a view of participation as made in communication but also an ontological mandate. An epistemological mandate merely requires tolerance of difference; an ontological mandate suggests interdependency. It is in this way, in particular, that the communitarianism described here goes beyond the constructivist assumptions of Row 4.

The most significant aspect of Row 6 is the introduction of the privileging of process. It is assumed that by focusing on the process by which humans individually and collectively make and unmake both order and chaos, a basis for systematic study can begin to emerge out of what has been a dysfunctional ricochet (as exhibited in Rows 1–5) between order and chaos. In this sense, this perspective incorporates all of the perspectives that preceded it. Each element becomes a verb in a set of verbings: the how's by which humans make and remake order and chaos. Among the verbs: factizing, reasoning, observing, truthing, totalizing, challenging, averaging, exampling, authorizing, culturing, evidencing, generalizing, personalizing, imagining, experiencing, resisting, relating, picturing, trusting, centering, decentering, and so on. This particular set of verbings is listed here without any particular order to emphasize the enormous gap between noun conceptualizing (nouning) and verb conceptualizations (verbings).

There are, of course, a host of attendant concerns in making this conceptual move, such as breaking down conceptions of situation as a concept frozen in a particular time-space, and breaking down conceptions of people as different only between each other and not within themselves. Acknowledging the incompleteness of this presentation, the important point here is the call for reconceptualizing how participation is constructed, implemented, reified, and challenged—a call for reconceptualizing by enlarging, by encompassing all prior perspectives into a view allowing a more comprehensive vision of human possibilities—possibilities realized, destroyed, restrained, and envisioned; possibilities that come to good ends and those that come to bad.

In the context of these assumptions, the ideological warrant offered to power is either one of bracketed authority or disclosed authority. What this suggests is the possibility that power can be made a central focus of attention, either by bracketing (i.e., deliberately setting it aside) or disclosing (i.e., incorporating postmodernist deconstructing along with modernist constructing into the informational frame).

Because the communitarianism we propose here is a step beyond current theory and practice, there are no explicit examples of development communication practice that we can offer as illustrations. The examples we presented earlier as illustrations of efforts incorporating postmodern ideas are steps moving toward what we propose as a communitarian perspective. In the set of examples, we saw significant moves toward finding a purpose for diversity other than cultural challenge or cacophony. And, we saw an explicit recognition that we need to be attending to the in-between, to mediations, to spaces between order and chaos, structure and individual, product and process.

What the communitarian perspective as presented here offers is a call not merely to focus on the in-between but to see the in-between as the time-space where humans collectively and individually use a variety of communicating strategies for making and unmaking order (e.g., structure, community, facts, agreement, self) and chaos (e.g., diversity, conflict, cacophony, spontaneity, uniqueness).

CONCLUSION

What is important theoretically in the communitarian approach offered here is the fact that it emphasizes not order or chaos, but rather the making and unmaking, the in-between. One way of looking at the dualistic dilemmas presented by the assumptions in Table 6.1 is that they force us to choose between order and chaos. The choice is, of course, impossible, both theoretically and experientially. Communitarian assumptions, on the other hand, force us to accept both order and chaos and to focus on the in-between, the making and the unmaking. In this way, we are forced to accept not only diversity between people and cultures but within people and within cultures. By focusing on the unmaking and the making, rather than on the assumed to be overbearing chaos of diversity, the communitarian approach we offer assumes that we will be attending in essence to order of a different kind—an order than can be found hidden within chaos or emerging from it.[30]

Furthermore, in this approach, diversity is conceptualized as two-pronged in its origins. One prong is the incompleteness of reality—our ontological world could not, even if able to speak to us directly without the intermediaries of language, discourse, and power, fully instruct us. If we accept this assumption, then we must conclude that humans need to tap diverse perspectives, not merely to make peace across their differences, but as ontological necessity. This conclusion requires that we find a way to think of diversity of views as a step toward never-reachable ontological completeness and as a step away from the tyranny of epistemological completeness.

The other prong is to assume the incompleteness of the person—that we are not always centered, always conscious, always ordered; that we are sometimes unconscious, sometimes decentered, sometimes disordered; that we are in a constant state of moving between order and chaos; that it is just as much of a struggle to fall in line (i.e., to make ourselves fit our surroundings, our cultures, our societies), as it is to fall out of line (i.e., to resist and challenge our surroundings, our cultures, our societies). As individuals, we constitute and are constituted by our societies; our societies constitute and are constituted by us. This work is never done, never complete. To remain muddled, to refuse to choose, to dream, these can all be as relevant to problem solving and development as the most rigorous exercises in naming the world and proposing collective solutions to social problems.

What would be the consequences for the design, implementation, and assessment of participatory communication for development programs that adopted such a perspective? The answer to this question is already evident in some of the strategies emerging from Latin America, strategies that are moving toward a communitarian perspective by seriously addressing postmodern concerns. Participatory designs in journalism and television production, for example, have centered on the principle of diversity and maximal multiplicity when determining information sources, production formats and genres, language choices, and "artistic" talent (Fuenzalida & Hemmosilla, 1989; Fuenzalida Fernandez, 1990; Reyes Matta, 1986a, 1986b). Top–down formulas, expert sources, formal codes and language, and traditional talent are considered as vital

---

[30]Hayles (1990) reviewed the two major themes in chaos theories in terms of two metaphors—"the figure in the carpet," where pattern is found hidden in the complexities of chaos, and "something out of nothing," where pattern results from chaos.

as grassroots participants and horizontal structures within these programs. Furthermore, some communication strategies used to form social movements have relied on conceptual tools such as collective direction, proctorial representation by rotation, the "first among equals" principle to guide development workers, and parallel structures—such as neighborhood associations, political parties, and unions—that conserve integrity and autonomy of subgroups within a development program (Fals Borda, 1988, 1991).[31] "In this way the wise principle of redundancy in the cadres and in leaders is observed and there is no danger of falling into the temptation of the personality cult of supposedly indispensable leaders" (Fals Borda, 1991, p. 31). Rather than existing as a vague and benign notion, participation reconceptualized emerges as a communication and development mandate emphasizing the need for multiplicity, redundancy, iteration, recursiveness, and responsiveness at its core.

The few examples listed here should not be taken as prescriptions to be implemented across space and time. Rather, they should be interpreted as answers to questions arising from the ways in which engagement with Row 5 assumptions leads us toward Row 6 assumptions, questions such as: What are the different strategies people use to construct and deconstruct their worlds? What are the different ways in which humans conform to and resist order? How many alternative voices must speak to provide a framework within which people can make their own sense? How can journalistic, scientific, and development projects be designed so that diverse participants speak from the experiential and phenomenological contexts of their own world so that their voices are not ripped out of context and made uninterpretable? Can the deconstruction of power be systematically incorporated in systems, or is "systematic deconstruction" an oxymoron? How can diversity be invited into democratic participation without exhausting resources?

We propose that such questions require that we develop theoretical and methodological tools very different from those we use now. The communitarian approach offers promise to these tasks, promise founded on the possibility of incorporating chaos into our understandings of participatory communication processes and on the possibility of a new kind of order arising from or hidden within—an order based on the verbs by which people make and unmake ordered or unordered worlds. Communitarianism offers a middle course where both participatory communication and development are processes defined by tentative and humble human struggle and mediation. The nature of the struggle is at

---

[31]The word *proctorial* is used as it appeared verbatim in the text by Fals Borda (1991). We take the meaning to be the use of a proctor, or dispassionate third party, to monitor a popular organization and its administration and to enforce rules of turn-taking for the leadership positions.

least as informative as the resolutions stemming from it and more likely to serve diverse groups of people as they try to make community without sacrificing self, and make self without sacrificing community.

The important question now is how shall we build this tentativeness, struggle, elusiveness, and humility into our participatory communication for development programs? This chapter raises this final question without answering it.[32] Rather, it attempts to answer a different question: should the participation-development narrative be rejected? The answer offered here is both a yes and a no. Yes, if conceived in either totalizing, essentialist form; or in the form of a richochet between artificial dualisms. No, as reconceptualized in communitarian, recursive, dialogic form. This chapter is a mandate to rewrite the narrative.

REFERENCES

Abbagnano, N. (1967). Positivism. In P. Edwards (Ed.), *The encyclopedia of philosophy* (Vol. 6, pp. 414–419). New York: Macmillan.

Aguirre Alvis, J. L., & Abbott, E. A. (1991). Participatory radio in Bolivia. *Development Communication Report, 73*, 1-6.

Barber, B. (1984). *Strong democracy.* Berkeley: University of California Press.

Barber, B. (1992). *An aristocracy of everyone: The politics of education and the future of America.* New York: Ballantine.

Barlow, W. (1990). Rebel airways: Radio and revolution in Latin America. *Journal of Communications, 2*, 123–134.

Barthes, R. (1985). *The responsibility of forms: Critical essays on music, art, and representation.* (R. Howard, trans.). New York: Hill & Wang. (Original work published 1982)

Bellah, R. N., Madsen, R., Sullivan, W. M., Swidler, A., & Tipton, S. M. (1985). *Habits of the heart: Individualism and commitment in American life.* Berkeley: University of California Press.

Beltrán, L. R. (1975). Research ideologies in conflict. *Journal of Communication, 25*(3), 187–193.

Beltrán, L. R. (1980). A farewell to Aristotle: "Horizontal" communication. *Communication, 5*, 541.

Benhabib, S., & Dallmayr, F. (1990). *The communicative ethics controversy.* Cambridge, MA: MIT Press.

Berlo, D. (1960). *The process of communication: An introduction to theory and practice.* San Francisco: Holt, Rinehart & Winston.

Best, S., & Kellner, D. (1991). *Postmodern theory.* New York: Guilford.

Bottomore, T. (Ed.). (1983). *A dictionary of Marxist thought.* Cambridge, MA: Harvard University Press.

[32]See Dervin (1989a, 1989b) and Dervin and Clark (1993) for discussions that do address this question directly.

Bronowski, J. (1973). *The ascent of man.* Boston: Little, Brown.

Carter, R. F. (1989). Reinventing communication, scientifically. In *World community in post-industrial society: Continuity and change in communications in post-industrial society* (Vol. 2, pp. 120-142). Seoul, Korea: Wooseok.

Carter, R. F. (1991). Comparative analysis, theory, and cross-cultural communication. *Communication Theory, 1*(2), 151–158.

Carter, R. F., Ruggels, W. L., Jackson, K. M., & Heffner, M. B. (1972). Application of signaled stopping technique to communication research. In P. Clarke (Ed.), *New models for communication research* (pp. 15-43). Beverly Hills, CA: Sage.

Clifford, J. (1986). Introduction: Partial truths. In J. Clifford & G.E. Marcus (Eds.), *Writing culture: The poetics and politics of ethnography* (pp. 1–26). Berkeley: University of California Press.

Cornejo Portugal, I. (1993). "La Voz de la Mixteca": Diagnostico y perspectivas [The Voice of the Mixtec: Diagnoses and perspectives]. *Dialogos, 35,* 41–51.

Decker, P. (l988). *Portable video in grass-roots development.* Paper presented at the annual meeting of the Institute for Communication Research, Stanford University, Stanford, CA..

Deleuze, G., & Guattari, F. (1987). *A thousand plateaus.* Minneapolis: University of Minnesota Press.

Delia, J. G. (1977). Constructivism and the study of human communication. *Quarterly Journal of Speech, 63,* 66–83.

Delia, J. G. (1987). Communication research: A history. In C. R. Berger & S. H. Chaffee (Eds.), *Handbook of communication science* (pp. 20–97). Beverly Hills, CA: Sage.

deMan, P. (1979). *Allegories of reading figural language in Rousseau, Nietzche, Rilke, and Proust.* New Haven, CT: Yale University Press.

Dervin, B. (1989a). Audience as listener and learner, teacher and confidante: The sense-making approach. In R. Rice & C. Atkins (Eds.), *Public communication campaigns* (2nd ed., pp. 67–86). Norwood, NJ: Ablex.

Dervin, B. (1989b). Users as research inventions: How research categories perpetuate inequities. *Journal of Communication, 39*(3), 216–232.

Dervin, B. (1991). Comparative theory reconceptualized: From entities and states to processes and dynamics. *Communication Theory, 1*(1), 59–69.

Dervin, B. (1993). Verbing communication: Mandate for disciplinary invention. *Journal of Communication, 43*(3), 45–54.

Dervin, B. (1994). Information<-- -->democracy: An examination of underlying assumptions. *Journal of American Society for Information Science, 45*(6), 369–385.

Dervin, B., & Clark, K. (1993). Communication and democracy: A mandate for procedural invention. In S. Splichal & J. Wasko (Eds.), *Communication and democracy* (pp. 103–140). Norwood, NJ: Ablex.

Elshtain, J. B. (1986). *Mediations on modern political thought: Masculine/feminine themes from Luther to Arendt.* New York: Praeger.

Etzioni, A. (1993). *The spirit of community: Rights, responsibilities, and the communitarian agenda.* New York: Crown.

Etzioni, A. (1995, February 24). *Our second annual conference.* E-mail message on communitarians@civic.net.

Fals Borda, O. (1988). *Knowledge and people's power: Lessons with peasants in Nicaragua, Mexico and Colombia.* New Delhi: Indian Social Institute.

Fals Borda, O. (1991). *Knowledge and social movements.* Santa Cruz, CA: Merrill.

Flores Bedregal, T. (1989). Las Radios de los Mineros Bolivianos. [Radio of the Bolivian miners]. In A. R. Tealdo (Ed.), *Radio y democracia en América Latina* [Radio and democracy in Latin America] (pp. 41-63). Lima: Instituto Para America Latina.

Fontes, C. (1992, August). *Defining popular video: Emerging strategies in Latin America and the United States.* Paper presented at the International Association for Mass Communication Research, Guaruja, Sao Paolo, Brazil.

Foucault, M. (1972). *The archeology of knowledge* (A. M. Smith, trans.). New York: Pantheon. (Original work published 1965)

Fraser, N. (1989). Solidarity or singularity? In *Unruly practices: Power, discourse and gender in contemporary social theory* (pp. 93–110). Minneapolis: University of Minnesota.

Freire, P. (1970). *Pedagogy of the oppressed* (M. Bergman Ramos, trans.). New York: Herder & Herder.

Freire, P. (1973). *Extensión or comunicación?* [Extension or communication]. (L. Ronzoni, trans.). Buenos Aires: Siglo XXI.

Fuenzalida, V., & Hermosilla, M. E. (1989). *Visiones y ambiciones del televidente: Estudios de recepcion televisiva* [Visions and ambitions of TV viewers: Studies of television reception]. Santiago, Chile: CENECA.

Fuenzalida Fernandez, V. (1990) *La Television en Los '90* [Television in the '90s]. Santiago, Chile: Corporacion de Promocion Universitaria.

Gallop, J. (1985). *Reading Lacan.* Ithaca, NY: Cornell University Press.

García Canclini, N. (1990). *Culturas híbridas: Estrategias para entrar v salir de la modernidad.* [Hybrid cultures: Strategies for entering and leaving modernity]. Mexico: Editorial Grijalbo.

Gerbner, G., Mowlana, H., & Nordenstreng, K. (1993) *Global media debate: Its rise, fall and renewal.* Norwood, NJ: Ablex.

Geertz, C. (1975, January–February). On the nature of anthropological understanding. *American Scientist*, pp. 8-14.

Giddens, A. (1989). The orthodox consensus and the emerging synthesis. In B. Dervin, L. Grossberg, B. J. O'Keefe, & E. Wartella (Eds.), *Rethinking communication: Paradigm issues* (Vol. 1, pp. 53-65). Newbury Park, CA: Sage.

Gonzales, A., & Peterson, T. R. (1993). Enlarging conceptual boundaries: A critique of research in intercultural communication. In S. P. Bowen & N. Wyatt (Eds.), *Transforming visions: Feminist critiques in communication studies* (pp. 249-278). Cresskill, NJ: Hampton Press.

Gramsci, A. (1988). *A Gramsci reader: Selected writings, 1916–1935* (D. Forgacs, ed.). London: Lawrence & Wishart.

Hall, S. (1989). Ideology and communication theory. In B. Dervin, L. Grossberg, B. J. O'Keefe, & E. Wartella (Eds.), *Rethinking communication.* (Vol. 1, pp. 40–52). Newbury Park, CA: Sage.

Hamlyn, D. W. (1967). Empiricism. In P. Edwards (Ed.), *The encyclopedia of philosophy.* (Vol. 2, pp. 499–505). New York: Macmillan.

Hayles, K. N. (1990). *Chaos bound: Orderly disorder in contemporary literature and science.* Ithaca, NY: Cornell University Press.

Hein, K. (1984). Popular participation in rural radio: Radio Baha'i, Otavalo, Ecuador. *Studies in Latin American Popular Culture, 3,* 97–104.

Holland, E. (1988). Ideology of lack. In R. Merrill (Ed.), *Ethics/aesthetics: Postmodern* (pp. 86-107). Washington, DC: Maisonneuve.

Huesca, R., & Dervin, B. (1994). Theory and practice in Latin American alternative communication research. *Journal of Communication, 44*(4), 53-73.

Jayaweera, N., & Amunugama, S. (Eds.). (1987). *Rethinking development communication.* Singapore: Asian Mass Communication Research and Information Centre.

Kaplún, M. (1980, July 3). La comunicación participativa como praxis y como problema [Participatory vommunication as praxis and as problem]. *Comunicacao e Sociedade.*

Kaplún, M. (1985). *El comunicador popular* [Popular communicator]. Quito: Ciespal.

Kaplún, M. (1989). Video, comunicación y educación popular: Derroteros para una búsqueda [Video, communication and popular education: Searching for a past]. In P. Valdeavellano (Ed.), *El video en la educacion popular* [Video in popular education] (pp. 37–58). Lima: Instituto Para América Latina.

Lacan, J. (1977). *Ecrits.* New York: Norton.

Lather, P. (1991). *Getting smart. Feminist research and pedagogy with/in the postmodern.* New York: Routledge.

López Vigil, J. I. (1993). La nueva cara de nuestras radios en estos tiempos neoliberales [The new face of our radios in neoliberal times]. *Díalogos, 35,* 3-9.

Lukes, S. (1974). *Power: A radical view.* London: Macmillan.

Lyotard, J. F. (1984). *The postmodern condition: A report on knowledge.* (G. Bennington & B Massumi, trans.). Minneapolis: University of Minnesota.

MacIntyre, A. (1981). *After virtue: A study in moral theory.* Notre Dame, IN: University of Notre Dame Press.

Martín Barbero, J. (1988). Communication from culture: The crisis of the national and the emergence of the popular. *Media, Culture and Society, 10*(4), 447–455.

Martín Barbero, J. (1993). Latin America: Cultures in the communication media. *Journal of Communication, 43*(1), 18–41.

Meyer, W. H. (1988). *Transnational media and third world development: The structure and impact of imperialism.* New York: Greenwood.

Moemeka, A. A. (Ed.). (1994). *Communicating for development: A new pan-disciplinary perspective.* Albany: State University of New York Press.

Mowlana, H., & Wilson, L. J. (1990). *The passing of modernity: Communication and the transformation of society.* White Plains, NY: Longman.

Mukerji, C., & Schudson, M. (1991). *Rethinking popular culture: Contemporary perspectives in cultural studies.* Berkeley: University of California Press.

Nair, S. K., & White, S. A. (Eds.). (1993). *Perspectives on development communication.* Thousand Oaks, CA: Sage.

O'Connor, A. (1990). Radio is fundamental to democracy. *Media Development, 4,* 3-4.

Olson, R. G. (1967). Deontological ethics. In P. Edwards (Ed.), *The encyclopedia of philosophy:* (Vol. 2, p. 343). New York: Macmillan.

Olson, S. R. (1994). Television in social change and national development: Strategies and tactics. In A. A. Moemeka (Ed.), *Communicating for development: A new pan-disciplinary perspective* (pp. 77-100). Albany: State University of New York Press.

O'Sullivan-Ryan, J., & Kaplún, M. (1978). *Communication methods to promote grass-roots participation: A summary of research findings from Latin America, and an annotated bibliography.* Paris: Unseen.

Owen, H. P. (1967). Dogma. In P. Edwards (Ed.), *The encyclopedia of philosophy.* (Vol. 2, pp. 410-411). New York: Macmillan.

Parsons, C. (1967). Foundations of mathematics. In P. Edwards (Ed.), *The encyclopedia of philosophy* (Vol. 2, pp. 410-411). New York: Macmillan.

Pasquali, A. (1963). *Comunicación y cultura de masas* [Mass communication and mass culture]. Caracas: Universidad Central de Venezuela.

Peters, J. D. (1989). Democracy and American mass communication theory: Dewey, Lippman, Lazarsfeld. *Communication, 11,* 199–220.

Rakow, L. (1992). *Women making meaning.* New York. Routledge.

Reyes Matta, F. (1986a). Informe y propuesta sobre práctica periodística y renovación del mensaje [Report and proposal on the renewal of journalistic practice and production]. In F. R. Matta (Ed.), *Crítica v autocrítica en el periodismo joven* [Criticism and self-criticism of the new journalism] (pp. 133–149). Santiago, Chile: Instituto Latinoamericano de Estudios Transnacionales.

Reyes Matta, F. (1986b). Introducción: Autocritica y práctica periodística [Introduction: Self-criticism and journalistic practice]. In F. R. Matta (Ed.), *Crítica v autocrítica en el periodismo Joven* [Criticism and self-criticism of the new journalism] (pp. 25-31). Santiago, Chile: Instituto Latinoamericano de Estudios Transnacionales.

Reynolds, C. H., & Norman, R. V. (1988). *Community in America: The challenge of habits of the heart.* Berkeley: University of California Press.

Riaño, P. (Ed.). (1994). *Women in grassroots communication.* Thousand Oaks, CA: Sage.

Rodríguez, C. (1994). A process of identity deconstruction: Latin American women producing video stories. In P. Riaño (Ed.), *Women in grassroots communication* (pp. 149–160). Thousand Oaks, CA: Sage.

Roncagliolo, R. (1989). Distribución e intercambio: Hacia la conquista del espacio audiovisual Latin Americano [Distribution and exchange: Toward the conquest of Latin American audiovisual space]. In P. Valdeavellano (Ed.), *El video en la educación popular* [Videos in popular education] (pp. 59-71). Lima: IPAL.

Rorty, R. (1985). Habermas and Lyotard on postmodernity. In R. J. Bernstein (Ed.), *Habermas and modernity* (pp. 161-175). Cambridge, MA: MIT Press.

Rorty, R. (1989). *Contingency, irony, and solidarity.* Cambridge, UK & New York: Cambridge University Press.

Rorty, R. (1991). *Objectivisim, relativism, and truth: Philosophical papers* (Vol. 1). New York: Cambridge University Press.

Rosengren, K. E. (1989). Paradigms lost and regained. In B. Dervin, L. Grossberg, B. J. O'Keefe & E. Wartella (Eds.), *Rethinking communication.* (Vol. 1, pp. 21–39). Newbury Park, CA: Sage.

Sandel, M. (1982). *Liberalism and the limits of justice.* Cambridge: Cambridge University Press.

Santa Cruz, A. (1983). Mujer y comunicación: Nuevas voces en la busqueda de una democracia autentica [Women and communication: New voices in the search for authentic democracy]. In F. R. Matta (Ed.), *Comunicación alternativa y busquedas democraticas* [Alternative communication and the search for democracy] (pp. 71-85). Mexico: Instituto Latinoamericano de Estudios Transnacionales y Fundacion Friedrich Ebert.

Santoro, L. F. (1992, August). *Popular video in Brazil: Fever and mirages.* Paper presented at the annual meeting of the International Association of Mass Communication Researchers, Guarujá, Brazil.

Selznick, P. (1992). *The moral commonwealth: Social theory and the promise of community.* Berkeley: University of California Press.

Servaes, J. (1989). *One world, multiple cultures: A new paradigm on communication for development.* Leuven: Acco.

Simpson Grinberg, M. (1986a). Comunciación alternativa: Dimensiones, limites, posibilidades [Alternative communication: Dimensions, limits, possibilities]. In M. Simpson Grinberg (Ed.), *Comunicacion alternativa y cambio social* [Alternative communication and social change] (pp. 140-155). Tlahuapan, Puebla, Mexico: Premiá Editora de Libros.

Simpson Grinberg, M. (1986b).Trends in alternative communication research in Latin America. In R. Atwood & E. McAnany (Eds.), *Communication and Latin American society* (pp. 165-189). Madison: University of Wisconsin Press.

Theunissen, M. (1984). *The other: Studies in the social ontology of Husserl, Heidegger, Sartre, and Buber* (C. Macann, trans.). Cambridge, MA: MIT Press.

Toulmin, S., Rieke, R., & Janik, A. (1979). *An introduction to reasoning*. New York: Macmillan.

Traber, M. (Ed.). (1986). *The myth of the information revolution: Social and ethical implications of communication technology.* London: Sage.

Valdeavellano, P. (Ed.). (1989). *El video en la educación popular* [Video in popular education]. Lima Instituto Para America Latina

Vijaya Lakshmi, K. P. (1993). *Communications across the borders: The U.S., the non-aligned and the new information order.* New Delhi: Radiant.

Walzer, M. (1983). *Spheres of justice: A defense of pluralism and equality.* New York: Basic Books.

Weber, M. (1963). *Max Weber: Selections.* New York: Crowell.

Wollheim. R. (1967). Naturalism. In P. Edwards (Ed.), *The encyclopedia of philosophy* (Vol. 5, pp. 448–450). New York: Macmillan.

Zukav, G. (1979). *The dancing Wu Li masters: An overview of the new physics.* New York: Morrow.

7

Transcending the Limits of Traditional Research: Toward an Interpretative Approach to Development Communication and Education

Danny Wildemeersch
Katholieke Universiteit Leuven

Various disciplines and subdisciplines in the humanities currently investigate the taken-for-granted assumptions of their own discourse. Dominant worldviews that have underpinned research activities during the last decades are being questioned. Recently, I have had the opportunity to engage in a discussion with communication theorists. The introduction into their frames of reference was highly relevant, especially when I noticed the parallelism with ideas currently articulated in my own discipline which is concerned about the study of adult and continuing education. The striking similarities in the debates of both disciplines stimulated me to do some comparative work. In this chapter I present the result of these efforts, thereby focusing on theories and practices of community development. Community development aims at the systematic improvement of living and working conditions of underprivileged communities. Initiatives of community development came into existence some decades ago, both in the so-called developing and developed countries. In developing countries they aimed at bridging the gap with advanced industrial countries. In developed countries they were geared to the abolition of deprivation of specific populations or particular geographical areas. Over the years, an impressive body of knowledge has been elaborated in various disciplines with regard to economical, social, educational, and communication aspects of development. Hence, community development is a field of practice where various disciplines meet and influence each other. With regard to these interactions, I concentrate on the common features of two basic disciplines of community development.

First I present a synthesis of the insights concerning two major paradigms in communication theory as well as in (adult) education theory. Second, I clarify how the debates in both disciplines illustrate a deep crisis in the dominant conceptions of development. In my opinion, this crisis can be better understood by analyzing the way social scientists and practitioners have predominantly framed the meaning of participation within the context of development communication and education. In both the modernization and the dependency paradigm the potential of participants at the grassroots level with regard to the process of development has been strongly underestimated. In the former orientation, participants have been thought of as "laggards" who still have a long way to go on the road to genuine development. In contrast, the latter orientation conceives of participants at the grassroots level. Their potential has mainly been understood in negative terms.

A critical analysis of the discourse of social change reveals how this emphasis on deficiency is linked to the "mechanistic" epistemological and methodological traditions in the social sciences. If scientists and practitioners are to develop an alternative paradigm, they will necessarily have to question their own epistemological discourse. The multiplicity paradigm currently challenges some of the basic assumptions of traditional research. While discussing this approach, I outline some perspectives of social science. I conclude this contribution by critically assessing a research project in which I was personally involved some years ago. I hope this self-criticism leads one step further in improving research activities and practices in the field of development communication and education.

TWO CONTRASTING PARADIGMS ON DEVELOPMENT COMMUNICATION AND EDUCATION

The idea of relating epistemological issues to the concept of *paradigm* is exciting and stimulating. It shows how theoretical and empirical activities are embedded in schools of thought that frame the scientist's assumptions, methods, and goals in a taken-for-granted approach. As Kunneman (1986) made clear, scientific problem-solving patterns are by and large contaminated by what he calls the "funnels of truth" that direct the researcher's actions. Whatever problems are taken into consideration, they are funneled or canalized in such a way that a rational, scientifically legitimized solution emerges. Not only does the funnel canalize, it simultaneously transforms the problems that are processed. This relativizing insight, which was first made explicit by Kuhn (1970) with respect to practices in natural sciences, nowadays contributes in a productive way to the debate in social sciences. With reference to these insights, I investigate the self-evident assumptions of two funnels of truth that dominate the field of development communication and education. The reconstruction of the debate about communication theory is mainly based on Servaes (1989), whereas the analysis of the paradigm conflict in comparative education theory draws to a large extent on arguments developed by Puli (1988), Potemans (1989), and Carmen (1990).

In the modernization paradigm a gradual development of society toward more rationality is assumed. Change and development are the consequences of a growing adaptation and differentiation of the parts of a global system. Social change is conceived of as a unidirectional, gradual, and reasonable process. This process undergoes an inevitable evolution from a simple to a complex form of social organization, from diffuse to specific institutions, from a limited to a complex labor system, and from an attributive to a meritocratic stratification system. Development theorists who refer to this paradigm conceive of Western industrial and bureaucratic societies as attractive models for this evolutionary process. These societies are supposed to have reached the highest level of "advancement." Hence, their economic, social, and cultural organization standardizes the road to development for developing societies.

Communication for development that refers to this school of thought is very much concerned with the unidirectional diffusion of innovations from the "advanced" toward the "developing" societies. Theorists in this tradition, among whom Rogers (1970) was very influential, conceive of individuals, groups, and communities as receivers of valuable messages conveyed to them by well-intended development workers. In empirical research, much attention is paid to the processes of codification of the message by the senders and decodification by the receivers. As the message in itself is considered to be neutral and the receivers are the ones who are to be convinced, the analysis of the reception of the message is of foremost importance. Different stages of adoption and categories of adopters are distinguished. Furthermore, the mechanisms of resistance to change are examined. These empirically grounded insights form the base of the development of (mass) communication strategies. These strategies aim at the dissemination of scientific knowledge, which is expected to result in "freeing men and women from the shackles of superstition" (Chin & Benne, 1972, p. 235). "Traditional ways" are perceived as obstacles: "misguided, counterproductive, inferior, plain mistaken or whatever negative label one cares to attach to them, one thing is certain: they have to go" (Carmen, 1990, p. 17).

The same empirical rational strategies frame many educational development activities. Education and training are conceptualized as instruments for the proliferation of skills and knowledge that will stimulate economic productivity and hence, will enhance the process of economic development. Furthermore, education and training are expected to provoke change in the value and norm systems of the individual, who will gradually assimilate the characteristics of individual modernity such as entrepreneurial and commercial spirit, achievement motivation, future-directedness, and so on. Although these values are basic to the approach toward development education, the development strategies are considered to be value-neutral and technical. While characterizing the assumptions of the modernization paradigm in education, Carnoy (1986) remarked that "the problems of education are largely technical and financial; that is, the principal difficulties in resolving educational quality and equal educational opportunity are function of sufficient resources, good management, and access to better educational techniques" (p. 74).

The so called value-neutrality of the modernization paradigm has been strongly criticized by authors of an opposing school of thought who accentuate the position of dependency of developing societies with regard to the advanced societies. The advocates of the dependency paradigm argue that modernization reproduces and even reinforces the inequalities and the uneven distribution of means, as a consequence of the power exerted by the developed countries over the developing countries. "It is beginning to be widely acknowledged that there has been in the past and there is now a parasitic relationship which contributes significantly to the richness of the wealthy world and the poverty of the rest of the world" (Zachariah, 1986, p. 93). In this approach, the wealthy regions are described as the center or the metropolis, while the poorer regions are labeled as the *periphery* or the *hinterland*. These metaphors suggest that the most important obstacles to development are indeed external to the underdeveloped nations and are to be related to the position of economic and cultural hegemony of the developed nations. "Due to the fact that the Periphery is deprived of its surplus, development in the Center implies underdevelopment in the Periphery" (Servaes, 1989, p. 79).

Dependency theorists mainly understand development communication in terms of this very opposition between center and periphery. In their opinion, communication policy functions as an instrument of cultural imperialism or cultural synchronization. The exportation of Western media products both installs the supremacy of Western technology and reinforces the depreciation of the non-Western cultures. The Western hardware is predominantly conceived for one-way communication, while the software presents, both overtly and covertly, the Western way of life as a valuable model.

In the discipline of development education the same analysis is made. According to Bowles and Gintis' (1980) "correspondence theory," the social organization of schooling is structured such that it corresponds to the social relations of production. This is not only true as far as the organization in the center is concerned, it also applies to the relation between center and periphery. This correspondence is also manifest within the periphery. The class differences in most Third World countries are very much characterized by the power position of a small group that dominates both the economy and the bureaucratic apparatus of the state. This power relation is in its turn reproduced in the school system "as the dominant classes are surprisingly effective in using an allegedly meritocratic educational system to reproduce from generation to generation their highly overweighted representation in most lucrative professions" (Carnoy, 1986, p. 77). According to these theorists, this mechanism constitutes the hidden agenda of development education.

THE EMERGENCE OF A MULTIPLICITY PARADIGM

The dependency paradigm has invoked important questions that cannot be denied any longer by scientists and policymakers who are prepared to give the debate on development a fair chance. Yet, the paradigm shows some important shortcomings that need careful attention. Servaes (1989) pointed out that dependency, within this school of thought, is massively and almost exclusively explained in terms of external economic variables. As a consequence, the internal economic, cultural, and political processes are considered a mere "photocopy" of the external mechanisms. Hence, the developing regions and their inhabitants are considered entirely passive victims of new forms of colonization. The least one could say is that the process of development and dependency is a much more complex and subtle phenomenon. In the field of education, similar criticisms have been formulated by those who refute "the presumed or alleged implications in some dependency theories that the billions of people who live in the impoverished countries of Latin America, Africa and Asia are powerless marionettes manipulated by the rich countries" (Zachariah, 1986, p. 92).

With reference to the role of actors at the grassroots level, the two paradigms discussed earlier, have some important elements in common, that may be characterized as a product of "mechanistic thinking." Both the structural-functionalist approach and the dependency approach strongly emphasize the importance of external factors to explain processes of change. While conceiving "input–output models" to understand and examine development, they turn a blind eye on the internal processes, which they consider as irrelevant "black boxes." What goes on inside the box is not a relevant object of study, as the attention is primarily directed at "the more global and macro-economic considerations of rate of return on investment or, more radically the reproduction of the division of labor" (Apple, 1986, p. 61).

Although both paradigms fail to conceive of actors as creative participants, they inevitably consider them as "deficient." In the modernization paradigm, target groups are considered defective in many ways, because they do not (yet) meet the standards of development displayed by the "advanced" societies or cultures. Although stereotyping these target groups as indigent or in need of development, the advanced cultures fail to appreciate the creative potential of the former, and simultaneously present the level of development of the latter as intrinsically superior. Also, the dependency paradigm, in a particular way, considers the dominated culture as deficient, while describing it as merely reproducing the political, economic, and cultural patterns of the dominant societies. In other words, the dominated culture is again implicitly labeled as immature, due to its "false consciousness" or lack of insight in the nature of "true" development. Hence, both mechanistic approaches fail to understand education and communication as cultural processes in which people play an active role.

Understanding culture as a normative horizon that enables people to perceive and enact their natural and social world, may open new perspectives for a nuanced "actor orientation." "In the patterning of their social existence people make principally unconscious choices that are directed by the applicable intracultural values and options. The social reality can then be seen as a reality constituted and cultivated on the basis of particular values, a reality in which the value system and the social system are completely interwoven and imbued with the activity of each other" (Servaes, 1989, p. 42). While taking these arguments seriously, one must admit that there is a dialectical and not a unilateral or linear cause–effect relation among cultural control and socioeconomic structure.

With reference to this dialectical orientation, Giroux (1985) pointed to the importance of Freire in the domain of educational theory. He pictured Freire as the author who most creatively tried to step out of the one-sidedness of mechanistic thought in developing a discourse that bridges the relation between agency and structure. In this approach, human action is situated in constraints forged in historical and contemporary practices, while also pointing to the spaces, contradictions, and forms of resistance that raise the possibility of social struggle. Hence, Freire showed the way to a critical and creative alternative to the overwhelmingly pessimistic nature of left criticisms, which failed to provide a programmatic discourse through which contrasting practices could be established. "Consequently the language of critique was subsumed within the discourse of despair" (Giroux, 1985, p. xvi).

As an alternative to the mechanistic character of the two dominant orientations, Servaes discussed a more nuanced "multiplicity paradigm," which may help to transcend the previously mentioned shortcomings. In this paradigm, the interdependence of all nations and cultures is pictured. It is argued that especially the interrelatedness of internal as well as external factors, both in center and periphery, have to be studied. Additionally, more attention is required for the content of development, which implies a more normative approach. Finally, the idea of a universal model for development is left behind and is replaced by the idea that each society must develop its own development strategy.

In the domain of communication for development, the multiplicity paradigm bears witness to the emergence of a more horizontal, participative, and public-oriented model. It is argued that this dynamic has been enhanced by some global developments such as a steadily growing positive attitude toward democracy; the development of multicultural consciousness; a general increase in the degree of schooling; a growing sensitivity of the role and the position of the receiver in communication processes; the availability of cheap media such as transistor radios, television, and video; the creation of alternative communication networks, and so on. These developments give way to another understanding of communication that "rejects the necessity of uniform, centralized, 'expensive,' professional and institutionalized media, and argues for multidimensionality, horizontality, deprofessionalization, and diachronic communication exchange" (Servaes, 1989, p. 56).

As far as research and policymaking are concerned, advocates of the multiplicity paradigm are in favor of more dialectic "bottom–up" mobilization, and conscientization strategies that have in the past proved to clear the way for a better understanding of reality. Participatory research approaches could be interesting in that respect. With reference to these orientations the aforementioned educational and research concepts of Freire remain highly inspiring. They imply an active participation of the learners in the conception and realization of the process. Both education and research are considered active processes of meaning creation by all subjects involved. It is clear that this approach has much in common with recently developed ideas and strategies concerning action research. Here, I elaborate this matter further, and argue that an "interpretative" understanding of action research can fruitfully contribute to the multiplicity paradigm.

TOWARDS AN INTERPRETATIVE APPROACH TO ACTION
RESEARCH

In recent years, the methodological debate in the social sciences has been strongly influenced by the emergence of an interpretative understanding of reality. The "interpretative turn" shines a new light on our conceptions of how human beings understand the world and act on it (Rabinow & Sullivan, 1979). Contrary to what has long been taken for granted in the natural science paradigm, (social) reality does not exist as a reality in itself or as a world "out there." The world is essentially an "interpreted" reality and hence, constructed by active human beings. Action in this sense means that individuals "create" society through their practices and the meanings or understandings that they give them (Usher & Bryant, 1989). This insight implies that mere facts do not exist in themselves. Facts derive meaning from a certain "theoretical" angle, whereas theories simultaneously derive meaning from "interpreted" facts. Theory and facts relate to each other in a dialectical way. In other words, the meaning of the parts is determined by the meaning of the whole, whereas the knowledge of the whole is enriched by the knowledge of the parts. This process of understanding has been denoted as the "hermeneutic circle" by Gadamer (1965).

Human beings are related to the world in a hermeneutic way. This does not only apply to our understanding in everyday situations, but also to scientific understanding. According to Giddens (1976), social science is characterized by a "double hermeneutics." Scientific understanding is hermeneutic in a first sense, as it is based on a language form or an intersubjective frame of meaning that the scientist has to acquire as a basis for research. Moreover, social science is hermeneutic in a second sense, as it interprets a reality that has already been interpreted by social actors according to their frames of reference. Social scientists are simultaneously dealing with interpretations and interpretations of interpretations. This twofold process of understanding implies that the social scientist does not discover an already existing world, but creates an already interpreted world by interpreting it theoretically.

It is important to emphasize that this process of interpretation is not simply a subjective matter. Interpretation cannot be understood to be the ultimate product of self-consciousness. It is rather a process of taking over meanings that already exist, and changing them while taking them over. Just like the social scientist has been socialized within the meanings of his or her paradigm, an individual in everyday life has learned to take the meanings that are given and that he or she shares with others. This *habitus* (Bourdieu, 1979) or *lifeworld* (Habermas, 1981) is to be considered as a stock of taken-for-granted perspectives or a reservoir of interpretation patterns that are culturally transmitted and organized in a communicative way. The communicative organization of these patterns implies that the meanings on which human beings rely are intersubjective and hence, "are not reducible to individual psychological states, beliefs or propositions" (Rabinow & Sullivan, 1979, p. 6). Meanings are in the first place social realities or social constructions that are created and recreated in a permanent flow of communication with other subjects. Hence, human beings make their world by speaking the word (Freire, 1972).

The interpretative turn has enhanced a new awareness in social science for the position of human beings as "actors," in contrast to the dominant "factor" orientations. This means that they are not simply passive recipients of external stimuli that condition them. Does this approach mean a return to the former beliefs about the "intentional subject"? Servaes (1989) pointed to the fact that in communication theory this notion has never been left behind by the advocates of the modernization theory. He said, "The notion of intentionality is still considered to be a basic aspect of any definition of communication. This notion assumes implicitly . . . that each human activity can be explained on the basis of a subjective definition provided by the actors themselves" (p. 17). It should be emphasized that the interpretative approach, in contrast to this traditional understanding of the role of the subject, has amended and enriched the actor orientations while introducing the concept of intersubjectivity, which in its turn strongly relativizes the concept of the autonomous individual. Yet, the insights of the factor orientation should not be neglected in this enriched actor orientation. We should be aware of the fact that, although human beings interactively give meaning to their reality, this process is simultaneously constrained by factor mechanisms. Suffice it to refer to Habermas' analysis of the colonization of the lifeworld or Bourdieu's strong emphasis on the structural context of class that interferes with the development of the habitus. Earlier, I discussed the necessity to consider undogmatically the interaction of system mechanisms and intersubjective reality construction. This is one of the strongholds of the multiplicity paradigm.

The notion of "double hermeneutics" implies that social scientists are inevitably "participants" in the social practice of meaning construction and reconstruction. According to Habermas (1981), the communicative base of understanding necessarily implies that an "objectifying" position of the social scientist is insufficient. This position means that the observer limits his or her role to that of a "third person." If real understanding is to be the result of the research process, the observer has to actively engage in it. In doing so, he or she takes a "performative" stance, which implies that he or she takes the role of a "first person," establishing a relationship with a "second person." Hence, the social scientist acts as a "virtual" participant. He or she is not a "real" participant as he or she communicates with a second person, on other grounds than normally may be expected. But "taking this stance" implies that he or she also "takes a stand" and no longer can operate as a neutral observer. As the observer gives up the privileged position of an outsider, he or she faces the context dependency of his or her interpretation.

Conceiving understanding as a "performative" and not as a "contemplative" act gives rise to new perspectives concerning the theory and practice of research. Usher and Bryant (1989) also arrived at this conclusion with regard to the epistemology and methodology of action research. In contrast to some positivist applications, they argued that action research is not meant to add to the body of knowledge of the researcher, but is primarily concerned about improving the action capacity of practitioners. In their opinion, improving action is not to be restricted to the optimization of means to reach certain ends, but is predominantly concerned with the question of how actors (implicitly) frame their action patterns. As such, priority is given to the process of "problem setting" to the detriment of "problem solving." According to Schön (1983), to whom Usher and Bryant referred, "problem setting is a process in which, interactively, we name the things to which we will attend and frame the context in which we will attend to them" (p. 40).

In action research, the activity of naming and framing problems takes the form of cooperative inquiry into the situatedness of both researcher(s) and practitioner(s). For this reason, its purpose is one of widening the understanding rather than "discovering" knowledge. The subjects involved in this kind of inquiry need to become aware of their situatedness or historicity. Therefore, the process of action research will take the form of a dialogue. As Usher and Bryant (1989) stated "Through a participative openness, both the action researcher and those with whom he/she is researching attain a position where they are no longer divided into the subject and the object of research, researcher and researched. The recognition of 'historicity' on the part of both is therefore the first stage of the 'fusion of horizons' and the possibility of unconstrained dialogue" (p. 135). This interpretative concept of research strongly refers to the concept of *critical reflectivity* that has recently been identified as a central concept in adult education by several authors such as Freire (1972), Mezirow (1981), Schön (1983), Brookfield (1986), and Carr and Kemmis (1990). I contributed to a similar concept, when I described adult education as a process by which adults surface their taken-for-granted lifeworld, often as a result of a stagnation of everyday routines (in Wildemeersch, 1989; Wildemeersch & Leirman, 1988). These are all attempts to leave behind the dominant technological tradition in education, and to replace it by an approach that focuses on dialogue, which reveals the "disjunctions" (Jarvis, 1987) that affect the life perspectives of people.

The similarities between educational processes and interpretative action research processes, outlined by Usher and Bryant, are striking. In both cases, actors create a new reality by reflectively questioning their assumptions, prejudices, interests, and distortions that underlie several discourses. Although the actors cannot entirely step out of these often implicit prejudices, they can be consciously working toward the limits of situated horizons. In this process of research or education, "one's understanding of these limits will change and hence the judgement of possibilities of further action" (Usher & Bryant, 1989). Although I have emphasized the similarities among educational and research processes, I am well aware of the differences that mainly relate to the degree of systematization. I think, however, that in the context of this chapter, it is more important to first outline the similarities. In so doing, the contribution of education to a new understanding of research is taken into consideration. I now turn to a concrete example of action research in which educational and communication perspectives were combined. This allows further elaboration on the significance of the multiplicity paradigm.

LOOKING BACK AT A PARTICIPATORY EDUCATION AND COMMUNICATION PROJECT

As outlined earlier, the multiplicity paradigm implies a new perspective on research that breaks away from the mechanistic view about development and clears the way for a participatory, process-directed, and communicative approach. With reference to participatory communication research, Servaes suggested focusing on the practices of social movements that are involved in the public debate over themes such as social justice, peace, ecology, development, racial and gender discrimination, and so on. It is an invitation to pay attention to the active role of grassroots groups in the construction of social reality, in contrast to the more mechanistic, factor-oriented approaches that minimize that role. A multiplicity stance, however, also necessitates that additional attention is paid to factors or structural constraints that interact with cultural processes. Hence, cultural action for development at the level of grassroots movements should be related to structural determinants that operate on different levels (macro, meso, and micro).

Some years ago, I have tried to elaborate a research project that reveals some of the features of the multiplicity orientation (Wildemeersch, 1986). I first reconstruct the initiative and then assess critically the process and the results of the project with respect to the suggestions and insights of the interpretative approach. Inspired by Freire's ideas on participatory research, I executed a project of thematic investigation, together with community organization groups in a Belgian region. Thematic investigation is an approach by which the main themes that challenge a community are expressed in a systematic way in order to stimulate and deepen the debate within the community. The region in which the project was conducted was suffering from a multiplicity of problems among which industrial decay, unemployment, ecological disaster, and poor housing conditions were paramount. Several interest groups inside and outside the region conflicted with each other over the necessary economic and political measures. The relative consensus that had existed during the former decades had disappeared rapidly as a consequence of the crisis.

In order to elaborate the thematic investigation, I took the perspective of the grassroots groups that were actively involved in the struggle for better housing conditions and an ecologically sound environment as a point of departure. For several months, I attended all kinds of meetings, read about the history of the region, tried to understand the nature of the problems and conflicts, and contacted possible participants at the grassroots level in order to frame the action research project. After this introductory period, a group was formed that started the production of a video program about the region and its multiple problems. For 6 months, some 30 volunteers collaborated in the interviewing of inhabitants and in the decision-making process concerning the form and content of the program. In so doing, the group itself "decoded" and "recoded" reality. The final codification, which was called *Anger and Hope in the Rupelstreek*, was composed of complementary and contradictory images related to the visions expressed at the occasion of 40 filmed interviews with local inhabitants. It illustrated the major contradictory themes of the region as experienced by "the common man," such as economic decay and development, ecological struggle, urban renewal, regional policy, and community action. The program was meant to trigger further educational and action processes in the wider community via the discussion of the contradictory themes.

The distance over time allows me to picture more clearly the positive and negative elements of the project and to formulate some suggestions for the development of similar projects. Let me begin with the more positive aspects. The project succeeded in establishing an exciting climate of participation and collaboration. This probably was one of its strongest features. Many people were involved in an extraordinary way, over a longer period, apart from all other activities that simultaneously caught their attention. As a result of this engagement, a continuous debate took place, which revealed different assumptions and viewpoints concerning the development policy in the region. Yet, the debate was not restricted to themes of regional and national policy. It also concerned the nature of the research project. While looking for a balance among action goals, educational goals, and research goals, the power position of the researcher was questioned.

As a result, the project generated a truly participatory and hence, educational process. People were able to question their own and other's assumptions, to contrast them with other insights, and to evolve toward more grounded opinions. Apart from this rational process, some motivational aspects were of significance. The collaborators and the additional group of the interviewed, were enabled to "voice" their beliefs, hopes, and fears via the production of the program. In contrast to the traditional use of communication media, the participants seized the opportunity to use the medium for their own purposes. In so doing, they learned to understand better its language while using it creatively. During the events, the participants were assisted by some professional media specialists who supported them in the process of technical and interpretative action. One could say that the project had an empowering significance, stimulating critical reflectivity, especially among the participants who were involved in the research and production processes.

There were also some weaknesses. During the research and production processes different interpretations concerning the roots of the crisis and solutions were discussed. The debate was historical and political of nature. It surfaced some structural determinants of the problems people coped with in the region. Yet, we missed the opportunity to elaborate the arguments more deeply. When we began discussing the underlying mechanisms that caused the neglect of the region, outsider input could have given the learning and production processes some additional stimuli. Such outsiders could have been invited to give background information and interpretations concerning the dilemmas with which we were confronted. Also, we could have examined how similar problems in other areas had been solved. This would have given the process and the product a wider and richer scope. Due to the lack of additional information, experiences, and insights, the project was limited to the input of community insiders. I realize that this procedure resulted into a kind of experiential learning that I would disapprove of in other circumstances. The thematization and codification of experiences within a given community should be the point of departure, rather than the final step of the investigative process. Experiences at a grassroots level, however interesting they may be, need contextualization in order to be productive. The informal, and hence limited contextualization that came about, implied that learning opportunities and perspectives of alternative action were of a limited scope.

The reflection about the missed opportunities reveals two major causes. One has to do with some initial intentions of the community participants. The other is related to the position and intentions of the researcher. In the first place, some of the participants wanted to edit the

video program as a virulent pamphlet against the (regional) policymakers and industries who had, in their opinion, been at the basis of the
region's deterioration. Therefore, they wanted to give a voice to inhabitants of the region who had been silenced for a long time, as they had
no powerful communication medium at their disposal. The video program was thought to compensate for that uneven distribution of power.
In opposition to this point of view, it was argued that a pamphlet has
nothing to do with a critical analysis. As a result of the discussion, the
idea of the pamphlet diminished, although the idea of giving voice to the
inhabitants remained and was even reinforced, due to a deep mistrust
toward experts and outsiders.

My own, sometimes unclear, role as a researcher also contributed to the missed opportunities. Not only was I aiming at supporting
the learning and action process within the community, I also wanted to
produce some academically sound research. This academic concern,
which I discussed with the participants, related to the question of inhabitants giving meaning to the conditions in which they live. It was hoped
the research would contribute to the body of knowledge concerning adult
learning processes. Although my theoretical inspiration was drawn from
the interpretative paradigm, I did not quite succeed in translating these
theoretical insights into a corresponding methodology. Methodologically
spoken, I remained "infected" by the positivist tradition that suggested
taking an "objectifying" rather than a "performative" stance towards the
"objects" of research. This stance imposed some restrictions on the project. I was convinced that a reliable and valid analysis of the meaning
construction of the inhabitants needed a well-controlled methodology.
Hence, I considered the 40 interviews with the inhabitants as the only
valid base for scientific data collection and data processing. In my opinion, the additional activities, such as the debates among the volunteers
about the future form and content of the video program was only of secondary importance, as the conditions in which they came about seemed
to lack sufficient guarantees of control due to my own "performative"
presence. This is an additional reason why the interviews with the local
inhabitants became so predominant in the editing of the codification.

If I had a second chance, I would definitely implement the action
research methods differently. The ongoing discussion among the participants in the decodification and codification processes would now be a
central point of attention both in the research and in the action activities.
Hence, the research and the action objectives would have to converge
better than they actually did. I now better understand that research and
action do not necessarily refer to different rationalities. Earlier, I tried to
clarify that a researcher's performative stance not necessarily threatens
the validity of the insights resulting from the inquiry. On the contrary, I
am convinced that when researching the social construction of reality,

the position of a "virtual" participant is perfectly valid and probably contributing better to the kind of interpretative theory-building I claim to be valuable. As a consequence, the dynamic of research would put less constraints on the dynamic of praxis. Both dynamics would rather converge than diverge.

In the case of the video program, both the participants and the researcher could have felt more free to transcend the experiences of the local community in order to picture more profoundly and more widely the basic and structural mechanisms that limited the perspectives and actions of the community. As this freedom was limited in the initial program, the profound contextualization exercise only had a chance at the moment when the researcher solitarily wrote the report. Hence, the results of this academic contextualization were of no direct use for the practice in the field. Furthermore, it could be argued that if the discussions among participants had been considered a legitimate part of the research activities, they would have added additional value to the process of theory-building. A combination of both approaches would have been optimal. Hence, if research and action had been interconnected more fruitfully, a deeper understanding by all participants may have been the result.

CONCLUSIONS

I have tried to illustrate and assess a concrete example of a research project in the field of development communication and education. Although by the time it was executed, the multiplicity orientation did not yet exist as such, the project reveals some of the characteristics of this new paradigm. Media were used at the grassroots level to empower a social movement that tried to influence the public debate about the living conditions of a community. The approach was participatory in many respects. Community members were invited to cooperate actively in an inquiry about the history and future policy orientations concerning their region. The cooperation resulted in a reflective learning process concerning several conflicting discourses about the living conditions in the region. These discourses were codified by means of a video program that helped document the arguments of the community activists in contrast to the dominant technocratic and economic arguments of the policymakers. All these activities came about at the occasion of a project in which the researcher tried to challenge and transcend the traditional conceptions of research.

Nevertheless, this project showed some shortcomings that are now becoming evident in confrontation with the multiplicity paradigm on communication and some recent conceptions of participatory action research. The multiplicity paradigm suggests a dialectical understanding of factor dynamics and actor dynamics that determine the road to development. In the action research process, this dialectical relation was not sufficiently taken into consideration. The process of contextualization was too limited of scope due to the research design. Assumptions about valid research framed the research activities in such a way that the contribution of individualized inhabitants of the region was overemphasized. In other words, some important insights about the intersubjective character of human discourse were not sufficiently taken into consideration.

Here, I presented some new perspectives on communication, education, development, and research. I hope these insights, including the associated self-criticisms, will contribute to the critical debate about research designs and practices and hence will stimulate the process of critical reflection about the self-evidences that give direction to our actions. In this sense, the debate would be truly educational.

REFERENCES

Apple, M. (1986). Ideology, reproduction and educational reform. In P.G. Altbach & G.P. Kelly (Eds.), *New approaches to comparative education* (pp. 105-125). Chicago: University of Chicago Press.

Bourdieu, P. (1979). *La distinction. Critique sociale du jugement* [Distinction. A social critique of judgment]. Paris: Minuit.

Bowles, S., & Gintis, H. (1980). Education, class conflict, and uneven development. In J. Simmons (Ed.), *The education dilemma. Policy issues for developing countries in the 1980s* (pp. 205-231). Oxford: Pergamon.

Brookfield, S. (1986). *Understanding and facilitating adult learning.* Milton Keynes: Open University Press.

Carmen, R. (1990). *Communication, education and empowerment* (Manchester monographs). Manchester: University of Manchester, Centre for Adult and Higher Education.

Carnoy, M. (1986). Education for alternative development. In P.G. Altbach & G.P. Kelly (Eds.), *New approaches to comparative education.* (pp. 73-90). Chicago: University of Chicago Press.

Carr, W., & Kemmis, S (1990). *Becoming critical: Education, knowledge and action research.* Bascombe: Falmer.

Chin, R., & Benne, K.D. (1972). General strategies for effecting changes in human systems. In G. Zaltman, P. Kotler, & I. Kaufman (Eds.), *Creating social change* (pp. 233-254). New York: Holt, Rinehart & Winston.

Freire, P. (1972) *Pedagogy of the oppressed.* Harmondsworth: Penguin.

Gadamer, H.G. (1965). *Wahrheit und Methode.* Tübingen: Mohr.

Giddens, A. (1976). *New rules to sociological method.* London: Hutchinson.

Giroux, H. (1985). Introduction. In P. Freire *The politics of education* (pp. xi–xxv). London: Macmillan.

Habermas, J. (1981). *Theorie des Kommunikativen Handelns* [Theory of communicative action] (Vols. 1–2) Frankfurt: Suhrkamp.
Jarvis, P. (1987). *Adult learning in the social context.* London: Routledge.
Kuhn, T.S. (1970). *The structure of scientific revolutions* (2nd ed.). Chicago: University of Chicago Press.
Kunneman, H. (1986). *De Waarheidstrechter. Een Communicatietheoretisch Perspectief op Wetenschap en Samenleving* [The funnel of truth: A perspective of communication-theory concerning science and society]. Meppel: Boom.
Mezirow, J. (1981). A critical theory of adult learning and education. *Adult Education, 32*(1), 3-24.
Potemans, K. (1989). *Vergelijkend Kritisch Etnografisch Onderzoek van Klaspraktijken in Het Basisonderwijs in Burkina Faso* [Comparative critical ethnographic research concerning class-practices in basic-education in Burkina Fasso]. Unpublished manuscript, Catholic University of Leuven, Faculty of Psychology and Educational Sciences, Leuven.
Puli A. (1988). *Adult education and people-centred development. Analysis and case studies in the state of Andra Pradesh, India.* Unpublished doctoral dissertation, Catholic University of Leuven, Faculty of Psychology and Educational Sciences, Leuven.
Rabinow P., & Sullivan, W.M. (1979). The interpretative turn: Emergence of an approach. In P. Rabinow & W.M. Sullivan (Eds), *Interpretative social science* (pp.1-21). Berkeley: University of California Press.
Rogers, E. (1970). *Diffusion of innovation.* New York: Free.
Schön, D. (1983). *The reflective practitioner. How professionals think in action.* New York: Basic.
Servaes, J. (1989). *One world, multiple cultures. A new paradigm on communication for development.* Leuven: Acco.
Usher R., & Bryant, I. (1989). *Adult education as theory, practice and research.* London: Routledge.
Wildemeersch, D. (1986). Adult education and regional development in Flanders. In W. Leirman (Ed.), *Adult education and the challenges of the 1990s.* Leuven: Catholic Universtiy of Leuven, Faculty of Psychology and Educational Sciences.
Wildemeersch D., & Leirman, W. (1988). The facilitation of the life-world transformation. *Adult Education Quarterly, 39*(1), 19-30.
Wildemeersch, D. (1989). The principal meaning of dialogue for the construction and transformation of reality. In S.W. Weil & I. McGill (Eds.), *Making sense of experiential learning.* Milton Keynes: Open University.
Zachariah, M. (1986). Comparative education and international development policy. In P.G. Altbach, & G.P. Kelly (Eds.), *New approaches to comparative education* (pp. 91-104). Chicago: University of Chicago Press.

8

The Need for New Strategies of Research on the Democratization of Communication

Robert A. White
The Gregorian University

SHOULD THE DEMOCRATIZATION OF COMMUNICATION EXPECT ANY HELP FROM RESEARCHERS?

For researchers attempting to establish a pattern of more participatory communication, the democratization of communication is often a voyage into uncharted and hostile waters. All around them lie the wreckage of previous attempts that collapsed because of inexperience or that have been thwarted because they threatened the communication establishment. The public is, at best, skeptical. It is taken for granted that political, economic, or professional elites have the right to control communication unilaterally and hand down to passive receivers their own definition of reality. Authoritarian communication is protected by a rigid tradition of ideology, the organization of technology, and the structure of the political economic order.

The initiators of participatory communication generally know little about other successful experiences and have few expert guidelines to follow. Everything must be invented anew—at least in the particular context—and every traditional presupposition about communication must be questioned and re-examined. Survival demands constant effort toward building a secure space among the immediate constituency of a movement and strategies for moving out to the edge of what power elites will tolerate. Leaders generally have to train or retrain their own personnel because existing professional training is for conventional models of communication. All of this requires constant informal reflection and more formal evaluation and social analysis.

Moreover, many of the classical approaches to communication research have developed as a supportive tool of authoritarian communication (R. White, 1991). The invitation to academic researchers using conventional theory and methods to carry out evaluations has often led to bitterly frustrating disappointments once it becomes evident that these evaluators do not begin to understand participatory communication. If the hosts of the evaluation are not attentive, the evaluators may exert a deforming influence on the fragile attempts to implement more democratic communications. One must admit that some groups working in participatory communication have problems understanding and administering research even under optimum conditions. Nevertheless, the deep distrust of communication researchers by movements for participatory communication is often justified.

This chapter focuses on five problem areas which communication researchers must deal with in designing theory, methods and research strategies for assisting the democratization of communication. The areas are as follows:

1. Much policy-related research starts from the implicit premise that the felt need and popular aspiration for participatory communication is simply a given, always present. It is presumed that if planners can devise a set of rationally coherent policy objectives and provide the necessary political and economic support, it is possible to implement these objectives almost at will. Sufficient attention is not given to the fact that institutions of more participatory communication emerge within the structure of social movements and that these social movements arise in the context of historical, structural conditions. Both policy planning and research must look more closely at the efforts of popular communication in the movements of lower status urban or rural workers, in the artistic expression of enthusiasts for popular indigenous music, in various forms of political "undergrounds," or simply in the widespread indigna-

tion over the unrepresentativeness of a press or broadcasting system dominated by traditional elites. Planners place too much confidence in arbitrary external intervention and do not provide the protagonists of democratization with adequate tools of social analysis that would help these innovators relate their efforts to a broader social process.

2. Communication theory has developed largely as an explanation of the power and effects of mass communication and does not provide adequate explanation of the factors of social change leading toward democratization. Even the critical research tradition has been preoccupied with the rigidities of present communication systems and has produced relatively little comparative analysis of how the process of democratization occurs.

3. When researchers do offer models of social change and democratization, they are often far too utopian and urge a radical revolutionary change much more rapid than the social process permits. Often, this research does not throw much light on the slow, steady negotiation with reality which mass popular communication movements normally carry out.

4. Much research on participatory communication still follows the conventional strategy of (a) inviting an external research expert to gather data on audience use of media, (b) analyzing this data independently and then (c) submitting to media directors or managers a written report with conclusions and recommendations. This overlooks the fact that in participatory systems, the audience is also the owner-director and even the producer. Building a participatory communication system requires a parallel form of participatory research (R. White, 1991).

5. Developing a strong organization of participatory research is usually a long, slow evolutionary process (R. White, 1994). Academic researchers working from the base of a university or research institute are often separated from the reality of popular communication movements. Their primary concerns are the teaching of upwardly mobile middle-class students, the interests of academic colleagues, and the development of a logical body of theory. It is easy to treat an invitation to research as one more contract to carry out as quickly as possible with superficial survey methods. People working in popular communication resent being treated as guinea pigs for the curious academic dilettante adventuring into one more "bizarre ethnic tribe in a far-off place." Researchers are more helpful when they are willing to accompany these movements in their long, slow journey and share the same deep commitment and involvement held by those working in the movement.

SHIFTING FOCUS FROM POLICY OBJECTIVES TO EMERGING SOCIAL PROCESS

Recent research and writing on the democratization of communication has contributed significantly to defining policy objectives. Most of the summaries of policy include some version of the following, depending on the socioeconomic and political conditions and the history of a particular country:

1. More equitable access is needed to the information necessary for basic human needs of health, education, and personal development; occupations or significant participation in local or national public decisions (International Commission for the Study of Communication Problems, 1980; Somavia, 1981). This implies information that is not only available, but is also usable and applicable to socioeconomic conditions (McAnany, 1980). It also implies a radical change in our concepts of information and communication, from source-oriented to user-oriented communication (Dervin, 1980; Williams & Pavlik, 1994).

2. Communication systems should be reorganized to permit all sectors of the population to contribute to the pool of information that provides the basis for local or national decision making and the basis for the allocation of resources in society (International Commission, 1980; Reyes-Matta, 1981). The public should also have access to the tools of media production and the technical help to make their own programming (Berrigan, 1977a). Audiences should have the opportunity to collectively criticize, analyze and participate in the communication process from their own autonomous organizational base (Reyes-Matta, 1981).

3. The mechanisms should be established for broad consensual participation in the questions of general communication policy, the organization and management of media, decisions on media programming, and the evaluation of programming as well as other aspects of performance (International Commission, 1980; S. White, 1994). A basic principle is that communication is an individual and social right and that society only delegates the execution of this right to professionals (Fisher & Harms, 1983).

4. To ensure accountability of political and media professionals, the following kinds of measures are important:
   • The representative decision-making structures described in (3).

- Representative property structures, preferably beyond the simple dichotomy of private, commercial, or state ownership.
- The development of new concepts of public law governing information and communication systems and the legal definition of rights such as the right to participate in the public communication process.
- Forms of financing public communication that protect this from any minority monopoly interests.

5. A new public philosophy of communication (beyond 19th century libertarian and liberal social ideals) is needed that provides a better understanding of information and communication in human and social development and that defines access to information channels and public participation not just as an expediency to ensure an informed and docile labor force or a "stable democracy" but as basic social rights (Christians, Ferré, & Fackler, 1993; International Commission, 1980).

6. Finally, if the public is to exercise its basic rights and provide accountability for a social good, then education for more responsible use of the media and for participatory direction of public communications should become an integral part of basic education (Reyes-Matta, 1981).

The problem with much of this discussion of democratic communication is that it remains at the fairly abstract level of long-term objectives. There is much less clarification of how these objectives are realized in specific sociopolitical contexts.

There is growing consensus that democratization is rarely a simple matter of social engineering; it is part of a broader process of redistribution of social power and influence in society. New communication institutions are generated by and emerge out of the juncture of historical conditions and conflicting demands in a society (Somavia, 1981). More horizontal channels of communication, more participatory communication structures and the beginnings of new policy are forged within sociopolitical movements reacting to authoritarian control of communication. In so far as communication researchers are part of this historical process, they may contribute an element of more experienced planning and coherent direction (Policy Workshop, 1980).

In virtually all societies, we can observe tendencies toward the concentration of social power, and in some societies there is an immense concentration of power with a small elite controlling all central political, economic, and sociocultural functions. But in the same societies we can observe the simultaneous contrary reactive movements and proposals for re-distribution of social power and more participatory communication (Golding & Murdock, 1978).

There is a long tradition of communication research that analyses the factors within a given society that are contributing to concentration of power over communication networks: the studies of concentration of economic control over the press and other media; analysis of dominant ideologies in news, drama, and other programming; the unfavorable presentation of minorities and other less powerful groups in the media; the many studies of forms of cultural imperialism and multinational control of media products. The school of critical research has been developing progressively better conceptual and methodological tools for analyzing how dominant sociopolitical coalitions influence the structure and content of media.[1] Critical research has also exploded many of the myths of freedom and access held by the libertarian and social responsibility traditions of communication philosophy (Hall, 1977).

Critical research is important for those attempting to develop more participatory communication because it reveals the extent of the problems they face and calls attention to the danger that many of the models they are attempting to create may carry many traces of an authoritarian communication. This research is also a revelation of the inequities, the alienation, and the repression that suggest the need for change.

Although critical research has contributed significantly to our understanding of hegemonic control of communications, it has given much less attention to analyzing the factors leading toward redistribution of social power and democratization (Mattelart, 1979). One reason is that resistance to participation and the co-optation or repression of popular communication is a much more frequent fact in most societies. Halloran (1982) and others have rightly cautioned that it is difficult to generalize about critical research. However, there appear to be aspects of critical theory that limit its capacity to explain the democratization of communication.

Critical theory has correctly insisted on the organic interrelatedness of all institutions in a society and the tendency for dominant coalitions to absorb and reinterpret all new symbols and institutions in terms of their own drive for ideological control (Hall, 1977). However, this sort of analysis leads toward the inevitable conclusion that all societies are a hierarchical, monolithic control system, unchanging and unchangeable (Martín-Barbero, 1993). It is assumed that the mass media have virtually unlimited power to influence behavior uniformly throughout a society. The analysis does not easily detect the alternative subcultural patterns of communication and the dissident decodings that are occurring (Morley, 1992). It tends to dismiss resistance movements as unimportant unless

---

[1]For recent examples of the continually increasing sophistication of the concept of cultural imperialism and globalization of culture, see, for example Wallis and Malm (1984, 1994) and Martín-Barbero (1993).

they are a very exotic, eye-catching radical protest. Consequently, this analysis does not take seriously enough the small spaces of alternative communication at a group or local community level so that these can consolidate their ideas and grow slowly. Without intending to, perhaps, many critical studies actually revalidate the myth of the omnipotence and omniscience of hegemonic control (Mattelart, 1979).

As Enzenberger (1974) pointed out, the tendency to see communication systems as an organic, monolithic whole blinds many theorists of the left to the fact that media are more distributive, fragmented, and open to wide use than is generally suspected. Few of these theorists would have predicted that even though the Shah of Iran had complete control of the mass media and other forms of ideological propaganda, his government would be brought down by an alternative "mass" media based on audiocassettes, photocopiers, and local, small group meeting places (Mowlana, 1979). Most would have expected that only by getting control of the centralized mass-communication apparatus could a new climate of opinion have been crystallized. And, if the present Islamic government of Iran has not continued to develop the participatory infrastructure of communication, it is in part because this participatory process emerged within a popular movement and was largely a response to the logic of mobilization within the movement despite the equally monolithic concept of communication latent in this form of Islamic ideology.

Second, the rationalistic idealism and fascination with ideological control typical of some critical theorists lead to attempts to short-circuit the process of democratization of communication. The expectation is that if a new team of expert planners has access to the centralized economic and political power, they can reorganize communication systems along participatory lines almost at will. It is presumed that the motivation for participatory communication is always present in the masses and that this motivation only needs access to a well-planned structure of communication to blossom. This ignores the fact that democratization of communication is necessarily part of a broader process of redistribution of political power and productive resources (Jacobson, 1994). The social mobilization necessary to attain this redistribution involves building alternative channels of communication, developing a different explanation of social reality, and adaptation of media. The catalytic events, which motivate widespread participation in a movement mobilizing numbers as a power base, occur in the juncture of specific historical circumstances. The demand for a participatory structure of communication arises as part of the logic of a popular social movement, not from the logic in the mind of a planner no matter how perfect this may be.

A similar problem occurs in many small-scale projects to introduce participatory communication. O'Sullivan and Kaplun's (1982) study of a large sample of participatory communication experiences in Latin America shows that once the external agents and external funding were withdrawn, most of the projects ceased to function. Many were of too short a duration to develop adequately or suffered from insufficient training of participants. The lack of a broader supportive government policy or even repression by officials was a factor. The principal problem, however, was that many of these efforts did not build on an autonomous, mobilized and motivated organization that had initiated the project under its own leadership as an integral part of its own organizational existence. Too often, the project was started by external agents who saw an objective need and attempted to motivate ("conscientize") and train leaders to accept the ideas of the external agents.

Third, critical theorists who think largely in terms of a global, organic model of social systems tend to also think of the process of social change as global and organic. They are often overly optimistic and idealistic about what popular organizations can achieve in a given time span. For the theorist, everything must change simultaneously and in synchronization. In fact, it is difficult to predict just what kind of and in what time sequence an institutional organization of communication may emerge within a popular movement.

In brief, critical communication theorists have been largely concerned with explanations of why the democratization of communication has not occurred, and they have built up strong theories of monolithic ideological control. When they do attempt to explain how democratization of communication takes place, instead of thinking in terms of an emergent process of social change, they tend to rely on a powerful, arbitrary external intervention that reflects many aspects of their social model of monolithic ideological control.

This analysis suggests that a theory of democratization of communication must consider at least four central questions:

1. How do dissident social organizations emerge and develop within situations of high concentration of social power and hegemonic control in a way that permits autonomous communication channels and an autonomous ideology?
2. How do the institutions of participatory communication emerge within the social organization of movements in response to the internal logic of such a movements?
3. What political and economic conditions are necessary for the survival and growth of democratic institutions once they have begun to take shape?
4. What kind of research and policy strategies can contribute to the development of democratic communications?

THE DEMOCRATIZATION OF COMMUNICATION AS A PROCESS OF STRUCTURAL CHANGE

Developing a general model of the process of democratization of communication is difficult because there are so few explicit case studies. Much of the research on democratization has dealt with small, isolated experiments of participation in local media. Although these experiences may be of considerable significance within a longer process of change in communication institutions, taken individually they do not have a broad enough scope or duration to indicate the major points of relation between structural change and change in communication patterns.

The best methodology may be to begin by analyzing the reorganization of communication within broad, popularly based movements that have sought a profound redistribution of social power (Hollander, 1992; Mattelart, 1979). Some of the best examples of this are the peasant agrarian movements and national liberation movements of the 20th century out of which have developed so many new models of political, economic, and sociocultural organization. The analysis of these major movements indicates more clearly the major parameters of a model that can then be applied to more limited scattered cases of local participation that may have only a few very indistinct elements of the model.

The Emergence of a Dissident, Autonomous Structure of Communication

The beginnings of dissident movements are in situations where a fairly wide segment of the population has very unequal access to resources, low prestige, and little chance of individual amelioration because of very asymmetrical power relations. The specific issue is frequently the sharp deterioration in the allocation of resources for the aggrieved group and a sharp increase in exploitative conditions in a period of general socioeconomic improvement. For example, in a context of general agrarian modernization, large landholders begin to expel semi-subsistence farmers from land in order to take advantage of new markets and improved technology (R. White, 1977, 1980). Or, in a period of general prosperity, certain urban racial-ethnic groups find it more difficult to get employment. Often the key element in sparking off such a movement is that individuals or groups cannot get redress for their grievances or cannot solve economic problems through the existing vertical hierarchical structure of communication with the centers of administrative power. At a certain point, there is a collective awareness that there is no solution through the existing structure of power and communication. Or they may become aware that this pattern of communication extracts information for purposes of control, but gives no significant information in return. Or there may be an awareness that the whole symbol system denigrates their identity and their social opportunities. At this point, individuals and groups reject the hierarchical channels of communication and extend horizontal channels among other aggrieved groups to pool information and to mobilize the only powerful resource the poor may have: large numbers. Usually, these horizontal relations are between equals in power and represent an essential element in democratic communication: symmetrical exchange in power relation.

How the Logic of Popular Movements Demands Participatory Communication

The survival of lower status movements in the face of massive concentration of social power often depends on dissidence among elites. In this context the alliance of more sophisticated and powerful dissident elite groups with lower status groups can develop into important communication channels. Because dissident urban-technical groups need a mass base, the pattern of information exchange is more likely to be symmetrical, and lower status groups are more likely to obtain significant information and participation in decision making at a national level. These alliances are often the beginning of the integration of communication professionals into a popular movement and the basis for participatory structures for media policy and administration (Migdal, 1974).

Many of the characteristics of a democratic communication described in the section on policy objectives are evident in these movements. Access and participation are important for sustaining the cohesion of the movement because mass support is often the most important strategic resource to counterbalance the entrenched power of national elites, and participation may be the chief legitimating factor in this mass support. There is often, in these movements, a high value placed on the inherent right of every participant to be fully informed of decisions and to have the opportunity to be heard. New patterns of access and participation—indeed a new public philosophy of access—are embodied in the structure and ideology of these movements.

Because the network of communication in these movements develops on the periphery of the hierarchical structure of communication, the "center of gravity" of this alternative pattern of communication is decentralized so that there are many points of access and participation open to lower status people. It is radically different from a system of communication controlled from above that allows some token local access. In this case, the points of input are truly at the local, lower status level because this is where the locus of power and legitimacy lies. Lower status leadership and constituency also jealously maintain the control of their communication channels in order to guarantee the authenticity of information. There is concern that the kind of media used permit this local control. This is an attitude quite different from the alienation of passive consumers of a distant, foreign information source, and it is the basis for a continuing active involvement in the governance of a communication system.

Development of an Independent Culture and Discourse

Most important, these movements produce a new set of central symbols that redefine the perception of reality from a lower status perspective and form the basis of a new language or discourse (R. White, 1980). The new language re-evaluates the identity of the lower status people (Riaño, 1994). For example, peasants are redefined as the bearers of the true values and virtues of the nation, Black is beautiful, etc. This accentuates the positive role of this group in the development of the nation. The redefinition also legitimates the participation of these sectors in national decision-making and the major reallocation of all resources toward this group. If rural, peasant sectors have been defined as not being worth the educational opportunities, the land, or technical assistance, they now are seen as potentially very productive sectors. The new symbols and language cut across local and regional differences, status lines, ethnic and religious divisions, and other divisions to open up new possibilities of sharing meaning and communicating on a common basis. Although traditional elites tend to be internationally oriented in their culture and to take foreign cultures as their models, lower status groups are much more rooted in the ecology of their traditional habitat.

This new discourse becomes a revitalization culture because it establishes the basis for a national culture more congruent with the resources, geography and history of this place and turns the national culture inward. This undercuts the tendency of elites to prefer linkages with international organizations and international communication and provides the authentic foundation for a policy of self reliance and delinking from dependence on transnational economic ties (Hamelink, 1983).

Adaptation of Communication Technology to Participatory Communication

In the practice of social action such as described here, there may emerge very innovative uses of media appropriate to the channels of communication within these movements and appropriate for the resources available. The new horizontal interaction between lower status groups may activate the use of traditional, inexpensive "folk media," but, at the same time, give this a stronger social-change meaning. Perhaps more important than the technology itself are the symbol systems that define a new media language and the new social contexts that determine how these media are used.[2] Out of this combination develop entirely new programming formats that can be more participatory, embody kinds of news information that get at the deeper issues and foster a reflective liberating interaction with audiences. These efforts may start with very simple media such as mimeo newspapers, popular theater, local radio or audiocassettes, but, once these have taken on a different format, they can evolve into a very different national information system. Sympathetic media specialists may be involved, but with the delegation of the movement itself. Professionalism and technical expertise, which so often serve to separate the media from the people, are redefined and developed in a new mold (White, 1983).

The Dialectic of Opposition to Democratizing Movements

This general model of a popular movement indicates the basic relations between a process of structural change and major objectives in the democratization of communication. But, like many ideal types, it is extremely "optimistic," and does not take into consideration many of the problems that movements toward democratization have, especially in complex societies where control is exercised through very diffuse hegemonic coalitions:

1. The general model does not consider the strategies of opposition and structural restraint or repression that small, weak movements encounter in public regulatory policy, the rigidities of political systems in the name of national security, the lack of economic resources and the fierce competitive reactions of large multinational corporations, the lack of flexibility in the technology designed to support the established structure of communication, and the ability of the opposition to call on the immense resources of international economic and political systems.
2. The model ignores many of the internal problems that an initially "alternative" communication encounters as it gains a

[2]Solomon (1979), emphasized that a medium must be considered under four aspects: content, technology, symbol systems and the typical social context in which it is used. However, the most important communicative aspects are precisely the symbol systems that encode meaning within the potential offered by a particular technology.

broader popular base and begins to establish a general cultural trend. Once a movement becomes an organization that is expected to assume more routine public service responsibilities for the larger society, it is more of a support of the dominant hegemonic system. There are difficult decisions regarding the best way to respond to the close imitations of commercial culture industries, the forms of co-optation, the accommodation to a broader range of tastes, the problem of sustaining an organization with largely idealistic volunteer personnel, and the inevitable internal ideological divisions.

3. This model ignores time perspective and implies that change is a short triumphalistic drive to success. In fact, the development of democratic communications is at best a long, slow process of advances and defeats, bitter learning experiences, and working out of adaptations—a process that often must be sustained over several generations.

4. This particular model, as it stands, may be most useful for research from a post hoc, historical perspective but less useful as a guide to solving problems that require negotiation with restraints and limitations. The model outlines objectives within a process of social change, but says little about the mistakes that can be made along the way.

In recent years, a number of studies of social movements that seek an alternative and more participatory organization of communication, have outlined a different "natural history" that is less optimistic. In the area of the press, both Schiller's (1981) historical analysis of the evolution of the penny newspaper from alternative labor press to corporate conglomerate and the attempts in Peru to pass responsibility for the commercial press to popular organizations are illustrative (Atwood & Mattos, 1982). The many studies of the transformation of rock music from the voice of a counter-culture to mass popular muzak (Chapple & Garafalo, 1977; Frith, 1978) and the studies of efforts to sustain indigenous popular music in the face of multinational penetration outline clear stages of development (Wallis & Malm, 1984). Gitlin's (1980) analysis of the experience of the Students for a Democratic Society (SDS) movement with the media is also important. Rowland's (1982) analysis of media reform movements in the United States shows many of the inherent ideological and structural contradictions of attempts to at least modify public communications. Various studies of community radio and public access channels indicate the general tendency toward co-optation by elites (Berrigan, 1977b). In Latin America, numerous studies describe a flourishing multiplication of forms of popular communication—various types of revolutionary or alternative radio, networks of group communication and popular theater, documentation centers, and varieties of underground press (White, 1980). But already many cautious observers in Latin America are in a quandary as to how the participatory nature of these experiences can be maintained once they enter into a more institutionalized stage (Reyes-Matta, 1982).

Most of these studies analyze the emergence of an innovative, alternative media expression within the context of a political or cultural movement. A number of the studies explicitly link the development of new communication patterns and new forms of media with structural or cultural changes arising within the movement. The historical process described in these case studies generally starts with a new media form as a dissident voice and ends with this media form being absorbed and redefined as part of a powerful ideological control system. The process varies according to the medium, the country or the historical period, but it is possible to reconstruct four typical stages in this evolution:

1. Local, spontaneous communal expression (largely interpersonal communication).
2. Adaptation of this communal expression to a medium that links many such groups but also introduces participatory characteristics in the medium.
3. The growing popularity of the now cultural expression and the new medium with attempts by commercial media to imitate or co-opt this as a marketable product.
4. The expression is cut off from its local cultural base and is merged into a synthetic product capable of being marketed for mass tastes (Wallis & Malm, 1984).

The value of the more "pessimistic" model is that it adds a third dimension to the dimensions of long-term policy objectives and analysis of the historical process of social change. The third dimension is an analysis of the mechanisms of structural restraints. The three dimensions together form a model of democratization that combines policy objectives emerging within a process of structural change and negotiation with resistance to change. Most people trying to create a new pattern of communication must simultaneously manage these three dimensions: a clear concept of long-term, almost utopian goals; constant analysis of the historical process of which they are a part; and a realistic appraisal of the structural limitations they must face.

THE INFLUENCE OF STRUCTURAL RESTRAINTS IN THE STAGES OF MOVEMENTS TOWARD DEMOCRATIC COMMUNICATION

The Stage of Spontaneous Communal Expression

Most movements for an alternative, participatory communication begin within the context of small, relatively dispersed groups attempting to create a free space for a new cultural expression controlled directly by participants. The significant step beyond simple interpersonal discussion is the use of a format of music, popular theater, dance, oratory, or group discussion around an audiovisual presentation. This provides a more powerful emotional, symbolic, and celebratory expression. It also opens up a wide range of connotative and evocative communication that creates a transition from rational coping to performing arts and sets the stage for a broader public culture. The music, theater, or other form is a direct embodiment of dissent and goals of sociopolitical transformation that is characteristic of social movements. The expressive form is produced by the members of the group who are nonprofessionals, and the communicative technology employed is produced, owned, and controlled within the group.

Communication at this level is more likely to use local, "folk" formats that express local culture and language and is more interested in fashioning symbols that are emotionally powerful for this local group. The form of communication merges with a wide variety of symbols of the lifestyle of the group—the clothes, living conditions, economic employment, meeting places, and so on.

At this stage, there is little distinction between the creators and users of culture. The dream of most people working toward democratic communication is that they can somehow maintain the ecstasy and freedom of this small space of completely participatory communication. For this reason, most successful systems of participatory communication try to maintain and build on an infrastructure of small group communication.

Linking Local Groups in a Regional or National Network

A critical transition for many experiences of participatory communication occurs when many local groups discover that they have similar interests and ideals and wish to share the information, planning, or artistic expression of other groups. To overcome problems of distance and time, they must move to a medium: press, tape or disc recording, video cassettes, local broadcasting, and the like. A medium, however, requires reproduction equipment and some expertise not only in the technical aspects of reproduction but in the typical languages and formats of the medium. It also requires some commitment to systematic information gathering and regular distribution, some judgment about how to satisfy a broader range of interests beyond the local group and the maintenance of a distribution system. At this stage, these administrative tasks are assumed by volunteers who wish to exercise leadership in a movement. But support may come from outside noncommercial organizations such as religio-civic or service groups that wish to build an alliance with this movement and closely identify with the ideals of the movement. In some cases, small commercial recording studios or broadcasting stations provide the support.

In the transition from spontaneous communal expression to a medium, participatory communication immediately begins to experience a series of structural constraints. One of the most important modifications is the adaptation to the economic limitations and the marketing distribution conventions associated with a particular medium. For example, when the popular music movement in Sweden began to establish cooperatives and small independent commercial facilities for record production in the early 1970s, they found that large music producers had established certain expectations in recorded sound that required much more sophisticated and expensive production methods (e.g., blending of background music effects) than audiences expected from live performances. To compete, it was thought necessary to accept at least some of these commercial conventions (Wallis & Malm, 1984). Independent studios also found they could not support themselves only with music for youth subcultures and had to engage in other "sidelines" for other subcultures or had to modify some of their music for a broader market in order to support their primary line of records. Groups of musicians who go commercial find themselves catering to tourist spots and to the demands of concert circuits.

In Latin America popular radio, the "voice of the voiceless," has attempted to support itself with selected advertising, and some dependence on advertisers inevitably develops. Even when outside noncommercial support groups, such as the church or labor unions, provide funding, these organizations are themselves caught in a network of cross alliances that can condition support. Community radio stations in various parts of the world, which are run by volunteers and supported by direct subscriptions, find that the pressure to compete with other stations by improving the technical quality places ever greater demands for a wider range of financing that can compromise responsiveness to the basic constituency.

The technological and financial requirements of some media allow greater freedom. For example, the low level of investment required by small offset presses and cassette recordings makes it possible for small groups to maintain control. Radio licenses, however, are regulated by governments and only those recognized as having a cultural or public function can get their licenses. Record reproduction (especially discs) is more costly, and groups must rely on commercial producers who can mobilize the necessary capital.

One of the most crucial aspects of this transition to a medium is the effort to adapt the direct expression of groups to the demands of the medium without losing the authenticity, originality, and subjective meaning. Insofar as the medium is the voice of lower status people, it means picking up local folk expressions, the argot of neighborhood groups and other aspects of the popular culture. The continual search for adaptation of a medium to the popular communication style can gradually generate new formats. Such adaptation may bring into use neglected technologies, cause significant modifications in existing technologies, or encourage the development of new technologies. But at the same time, the images of the popular culture are modified by the underlying conventions of the medium and by the sheer physical limitations of sound, video, or print reproduction. Virtually any technology that participatory communication can use already has been designed for marketing with a mass, vertical type of communication in mind. It takes an unusual amount of questioning, creativity, and experimentation by groups working in participatory communication to redesign the technology for more democratic communication.

Characteristically, the production for media is carried out by volunteers or by people whose commercial interests are secondary and are willing to contribute a great deal of time on a noncommercial basis. The emphasis is on getting a direct expression of the views and values of those in the movement. In some cases, these movements insist on very simple inexpensive media that virtually everybody can use with a minimum of training. Often, however, volunteers cannot sustain this continued effort, especially at the level of central management. It is not always easy to find volunteers who can combine idealism with the necessary technical and managerial expertise. Translating the ideals of a movement into the language of a medium requires a great deal of sheer genius that is not always present. If not handled well, popular media can become so boring that even the most well-intentioned audiences are lost to competing media.

Few educational institutions are providing a technical training geared to popular, participatory communication. In any event, it may not be possible to provide formal training for this kind of media. Some networks of popular, participatory communication set up their own special training facilities directed by people who know how to combine idealism with artistic creativity. In order to guarantee some stable level of quality, however, there is danger that a sense of professional elitism gradually enters and separates the medium from the people. In societies with a highly defined class and status system, the entry of lower status groups into work with a medium—even when it is controlled by lower status groups—brings a loss of identification with their class background and an identification with professional media elites.

These are only a few examples of how the transition to the use of a medium can undermine the commitment to local control and to participatory characteristics of communication. If the evolution toward democratic communication is to be sustained in these movements, the following kind of measures are important:

1. An administrative structure that preserves direct popular control or at least control through an institution with a close identification with this movement.
2. A stable means of financing that avoids dependence on commercial income.
3. Training of nonprofessional producers so that these are able to adapt the medium to their own uses and exploit all of the artistic and entertainment potential of the particular medium.
4. A legal status that legitimizes participatory communications as normative or at least as a valued alternative within the national communication system.
5. A system of participation that can represent an increasingly pluralistic body of media user without allowing powerful minorities to dominate.
6. A philosophy of participatory communication that clearly distinguishes this communication system from conventional centralized communication but at the same time makes clear that participatory communication is consonant with the value traditions of a given national culture.

Competitive Imitation, Commercial Accommodation, and Co-optation

Once a movement of alternative and participatory communication begins to gain a wider popular base, entrepreneurs see in this an interesting popular trend that offers a potential market. These entrepreneurs know how to capture the novelty, authenticity, and naive creativity of a new music sound or media format and then package this in a form that is more smooth and attractive to a wide audience. Businesses also know how to win audiences with high-powered marketing techniques that creators of participatory communication abhor but are helpless to resist. Rarely are there attempts to directly suppress alternative media, but rather to develop a close competitive imitation that drives the participatory media out of the market.

Many commercial imitations begin by appealing to the same alternative dissident subculture this movement has created. Entrepreneurs will accommodate many of the images and heroes of protest in a way that appears to allow an authentic popular expression. But they will also move to isolate the more radical idealistic, politically oriented leadership and drain from theater, music, or information its power to symbolize and motivate. The entertainment, leisure, and relaxation value will be stressed. More radical views will be presented as an object of curiosity or as something people can romantically dream about but never realize. It all becomes framed as leisure activity, cut off from the hard world of productivity and pragmatic political and economic decisions. They are likely to define the innovativeness and creativity not in terms of the basic structures of power and economic relations, but change in styles, more efficient technology or a new range of consumer products.

Once alternative media begin to feel the competitive pressure of imitations and see their constituencies attracted away by these competitors, the stage is set for co-optation. Co-optation is rarely a well-coordinated conspiracy, but a series of structural restraints that resist, coerce, or channel "natural" developments. Talented writers, artists, and producers who have defined themselves as nonprofessionals facilitating popular participation will doubt whether their efforts are worth the sacrifice. The imitations seem to be offering the same as alternative communication, but with a much larger audience. They are offered a larger stage to present their ideals, with much more professional and administrative support. The change of emphasis from the expression of the ideals of a popular movement to the expression of personal, individualistic ideals is subtle but has significant consequences.

In the same way, popularly controlled cooperative media or small independent producers working with popular movements are tempted to sell out to large corporations. They lack the capital resources to grow and to compete. They expect that they will be able to serve their audiences better with more financial and managerial backing, and they will be able to attract the best talent.

The critical problem for many participatory communication movements is knowing how to grow slowly and solidly. Gitlin (1980) described how the SDS movement in the 1960s fell apart because it attempted to suddenly appeal to mass audiences instead of building more slowly. Wallis and Malm's (1984) analysis of the Swedish popular music movement in the 1970s shows that the groups that remained alternative and retained their grass-roots qualities with more meaningful songs survived the crisis of competition with multinational music producers. These groups opted for a gradual building up of loyal support of people who came to understand more fully the significance of authentic Swedish popular music. Over the years, the use of the Swedish language in music has won out over earlier

Anglo-American dominance. Locally owned resources for production have gradually increased their market, and the taste for the synthetic multinational music has waned. On the other hand, groups that tried to beat the multinational corporations at their own game by becoming more professional and technically sophisticated with appeals to a mass audience have disappeared (Wallis & Malm, 1984).

Transculturation: The Formation of a Synthetic Mass Culture

Many case histories of efforts toward popularly controlled communication end their story with what might be called a final, postmodern stage. The process of co-optation and absorption has finished its course. All organization of popular participation has been repressed or incorporated as simply one more division of a multinational corporation. What remains are traces of the cultural elements that originated in a particular subcultural movement. A classical case of this is the evolution of rock music from an expression of counterculture to the international sound of disco music (Chapple & Garafalo, 1977). In order to reach the widest possible spread of tastes, marketing specialists have fabricated a music made up of elements of many local cultural expressions but that has no ties with any spontaneous communal expression. The disturbing rough edges in rock music that were once a symbol of protest have been knocked off, and the elements that have meaning for a local subculture have been dropped.

Other case histories show that not only has the original social organization and cultural meaning been left behind, but that as the cultural element is absorbed into the ideology of dominant coalitions, the meaning is reversed. What was once a symbol of dissent and protest against elites has become a tool of ideological maneuvering. Schiller's (1981) analysis of the evolution of the concept of news objectivity in 19th-century America is one example of this. An insistence on objectivity was originally part of the strategy of a working-class, labor press to expose elite control of the legal system and courts. But later in the 19th century, as newspapers became an integral part of capitalistic finance, objectivity was used as an excuse to gather news from "responsible" elite sources.

The importance of this stage of the analysis is to demonstrate clearly the forms of ideological control that operate against movements of more popular, democratic communication from the beginning.

RESEARCH STRATEGIES FOR THE DEVELOPMENT OF PARTICIPATORY COMMUNICATION

As was noted earlier, the most difficult task faced by people working to build a participatory system of communication is to determine how to integrate an idealistic commitment to long-range policy objectives, a continuing analysis of the structural factors influencing their movement and response to structural constraints. In terms of the four-stage natural history of many movements toward a popularly controlled communication, the most critical stage is the transition from spontaneous communal expression to the linking of groups through a medium.

The invitation for outside research or evaluation might take various forms. The need might be for a type of feasibility study to determine what kind of medium would be best adapted for a particular type of local cultural expression and how to develop this medium within a participatory social organization. Or a medium such as a radio station might already exist as a service to lower status groups and the purpose of the research would be to determine how constituent groups could become more closely involved in setting policy, participating in the production of programs, and financing. In any event, the aim of research is to facilitate the development of a cooperative, participatory structure for a medium. The researcher must work with the social movement underlying the cultural expression of local groups and must help these groups forestall the problem of competition or co-optation by dominant elites that will unfold as soon as the movement has a greater cultural influence.

The Importance of Participatory Historical Analysis

The major objective of the research is to strengthen the capacity for cooperative data gathering and social analysis among the groups that constitute simultaneously both the audience and the production-management body. This calls for a research strategy significantly different from conventional media studies that assume that the owners and managers of the media will make all decisions. The purpose is not to produce a report about the audience needs and uses for a separate group of media controllers so that these directors can have a greater impact on the audience but rather to involve the audience in an active process of cultural production and communication. The research activity will center around a series of dialogues among constituent groups and between these groups and those delegated to administer the medium. The researcher is more of a group facilitator, coordinator and resource person.

In this chapter I have argued that the most appropriate theory for explaining the process of democratization is a general model of how participatory communication emerges within a historical process of social change and how this process is affected by structural constraints at different stages of its development. A research strategy must therefore attempt to operationalize in a participatory manner a type of historical analysis. Thus, an initial purpose of the dialogues mentioned here is to strengthen among constituent groups a deeper awareness of their role as protagonists of a historical process. Among people accustomed to passive reception of predetermined mass media messages, it is important to develop an identity and capacity for making cultural history. If they are to participate in a communication system, they must be convinced that they have something to say that is not only valuable in itself but important for the development of action in the community and/or nation.

This borrows very much from the concepts and methods of the Freirian "conscientization." One of the most important initial approaches is to help people reconstruct the history of their community and region; detect who have been the major actors in this history, pick out the critical turning points; and analyze the cultural, economic, and political influences in their lives. The participants can begin to contrast the accepted historical interpretation and their own deeply felt perspective. They can begin to contrast how it has actually happened and how it could have happened.

This process begins to reveal the talents and key cultural expressions they want to communicate. They see the powerful symbols and communication formats they can use in producing for a medium.

First, this strategy is very much different from the functionalist approach that starts with the scientist's own model of social or psychological behavior and gathers data for the purpose of prediction and control of audience behavior. The emphasis is on the awareness of the subjective meaning and organization of reality for purposes of greater self-determination.

Second, this historical analysis directs attention to the interrelation of the factors that have contributed to a particular historical outcome and different critical turns of history. It suggests who the powerful actors are and what are the structural constraints imposed by existing political, economic and cultural conditions.

Again, this is different from the statistical, cross-sectional survey that uses as the unit of analysis individual values, attitudes, or action preferences. This approach atomizes social facts and either spreads them out in a relatively meaningless quantitative description or aggregates them in terms of a sociopsychological construct that has little relation to the historical events. This prescinds from the real historical interrelation of events and the structural conditions that are determining the limits for free choices.

Third, the analysis of the interrelation of events and the process of collective decisions that have led to an historical outcome indicates the existing channels of information and lack of information. The analysis of power structure indicates the structure of communication channels and how various types of information flow within these channels. It may indicate, for example, the centralization of channels of information and the processes by which powerful elites extract information from dependent groups, pass this information to centralized ideological control groups and then releases a reformulated information through a structure of intermediaries. This hierarchical structure of intermediaries filters out all of the information that might be significant for helping lower status groups control outcomes.

Participants also begin to be aware of their horizontal channels of communication as well as their own "language" and significant symbols. All this is then consciously available to be picked up and expressed in a medium controlled by these participants. An awareness of the structural constraints may point to the need for an independent economic base for the medium (or adapting the choice of a medium to their financial possibilities), and the importance of strategies for gaining juridical, governmental legitimation to support this independence. The analysis will also suggest what kind of communication technology will permit participatory control and how they should (or should not) use available professional technical competence.

Fourth, these dialogues should reveal the sometimes striking differences of interest and different ways of expressing idealistic objectives within the groups. But the interchanges also set in motion a process of negotiation and attempts to codify a common vision. This definition clarifies who can function as part of this network and helps to avoid a heterogeneous pluralism that might eventually tear the movement apart.

Fifth, participatory research should help all involved to see the disjunction between idealistic models for an alternative participatory communication and the actual implementation of this model. Most have never experienced anything but vertical, authoritarian models, and they will be influenced by all of the structural constraints of political power, technology, problems of financing, and audience expectations that will tend to force them back into the model of conventional communication systems. It is especially important that the technical personnel responsible for managing a medium participate in these dialogues because many may bring with them a very conventional training and concept of how media should be run. It is important that participants understand well the particular characteristics of a medium and how they can translate their more direct interpersonal communication into the language of this medium.

Finally, the very act of constituting a participatory networking medium implies a commitment to a public action with important social change consequences. The constituent groups working with a medium thus become a major actor on the stage of change. To play this role adequately requires a sense of the historical junctures that will influence future history. One of the major advantages of this kind of historical analysis is that participants gain a kind of "map" of the sociopolitical process in which they are living and a clearer idea of how and when they should act within this process.

RESEARCH SUPPORT IN THE FACE OF COMPETING COMMERCIAL IMITATIONS AND PRESSURES TOWARD CO-OPTATION

Most reports of relatively successful experience of participatory communication show that these movements have been able to grow even in the face of various restraints primarily because they have resolutely maintained their identity as alternative, participatory, and volunteer movements (Schiller, 1981). At the same time, successful movements have skillfully avoided domination of the network by any one extremist group and have gained a deeper sense of their own ideological identity by continual dialogue among the groups. They have steadily improved their technical competence but more in the direction of developing a language to express their particular values and symbols than by expensive, sophisticated techniques. They have thus stayed close to their grassroots support and have not gone beyond the capacities of their volunteer personnel. By growing slowly but resolutely they have avoided causing alarm and repression so that they have carved out at least a space of tolerance for themselves within a society.

Especially important have been the formation of national and continental federations or other forms of coalitions for purposes of guaranteeing greater support from governments and other agencies. Federations can also maintain a secretariat that provides training, assistance in planning, help in research and evaluation, a series of publications that consolidate their cultural identity, and special support when any one member is facing a crisis.

THE PERSONAL COMMITMENT OF RESEARCHERS TO A PROCESS OF DEMOCRATIZATION OF COMMUNICATION

Researchers who come from a strongly academic university background often have a problem contributing to this process of gradual growth.

Those with a more radical background may perceive these movements that move slowly and cautiously as not really committed to social change. They may fail to see how alternative a given movement really is. On the other hand, if they come with a functionalist perspective, they may fail to see this as part of a long-term process of structural change. These latter researchers are likely to be satisfied with fairly superficial administrative and technical recommendations.

Too often, researchers of both radical and conservative tendencies tend to see a research project as just one more contract. They do not have the patience to commit themselves to a process of accompanying a particular movement in its long road toward firm establishment of participatory communications.

CONCLUSIONS: ADAPTING COMMUNICATION RESEARCH TO STRATEGIES OF SOCIAL CHANGE

The issues of freedom of speech, broader public access to media information, and diversity of opinions expressed in the media have been an integral part of the public philosophies of liberal democracies over the past several centuries. Much communication research has dealt, either directly or indirectly, with the proper implementation of these principles. Since the 1960s and 1970s, however, a series of economic, political, and sociocultural changes in many parts of the world have tended to extend the horizons of what is meant by participatory communication in democratic societies. These new concepts of participatory communication were sufficiently explicit and mature by the late 1970s to form the basic framework for the policy recommendations of the UNESCO-sponsored MacBride Commission Report, *Many Voices, One World* (1980). Indeed, the report introduced and gave a certain legitimacy to the term, *democratization of communication*. At first sight, many of the emphases of the MacBride Report seem innocuous enough: Communication is a basic individual and collective right, communication media should be decentralized to provide greater direct participation, there should be greater attention to the needs and rights of minorities and less powerful groups, participation in the management and policy making regarding communications is put forward as an ideal, and so on (International Commission for the Study of Communication Problems, 1980). These recommendations were intended for consideration as a part of national communication policies. In fact, there is little evidence of moves by governments to implement policies of democratization of communication, even by those governments that apparently supported the move toward a New World Information and Communication Order (NWICO). The elite groups who are closest to government-level decision making have too much to lose in such a process of democratization. Instead, most of the initiatives have been taken in local communities, in grassroots movements and by less powerful minorities—often, the very groups that do not feel they have a just access to and participation in communication systems. It is not unusual, of course, that the initiative for social change should come from outside the established system of communications. However, the fact that the initiatives are coming from "the grassroots" makes it more difficult for the communication research establishment to contribute to the democratization of communication.

Many groups working in innovative experiences of participatory communication have a greater need for various forms of social analysis, feasibility studies, and evaluations precisely because they are moving into uncharted waters. Indeed, one tends to find that people working in "alternative" communications have a greater openness to the more speculative, critical academic world. The administrators of conventional systems of media are more likely to be convinced they have "got it right" and do not need more basic research. In fact, one finds that communication researchers have not been able to provide much direct support to efforts toward democratic communications. This chapter has attempted to analyze three aspects of the limitations of communication research: (a) the lack of an adequate theory of social change and change in communication institutions; (b) the lack of an *empirical, operational framework* for systematic comparative analysis of experiences of democratic communication; and (c) the difficulty of adapting to an action *research strategy* that permits researchers to "accompany" groups initiating more democratic communication in their long-term negotiation of social change.

Theoretical Limitations in the Critical Research Tradition

Given the goals of social change and change of communication institutions implicit in the efforts toward democratization of communication, the most helpful conceptual and methodological approaches are likely to come out of the research tradition that is prepared to be consistently critical of a given organization of communication institutions. However, much research on democratic communication in the critical tradition is caught between a fascination with utopian models that, supposedly, are to be imposed in *deus ex machina* fashion and a preoccupation with social rigidities. Often, this research tells us very little about how social change might actually occur within specific social contexts that almost always carry their resistances to social change.

The root of the problem of much critical theory in the field of communications seems to lie, first, in an excessive reliance on an organ-

ic, monolithic model of societal organization, and insufficient development of a theory of dialectical social change explaining processes of
redistribution of social power and the emergence of participatory institutions (Bruck, 1990). Second, there is, in much critical research, an idealistic bias that sees new communication institutions as coming from rationalistic planning outside of the process of social change. Reinforcing this
bias is the tendency to analyze communications as powerful media or
hegemonic ideologies that have effects regardless of the social context
of audience use and various decodings of media.

A dialectical model of societal organization presupposes that
there are, in all societies, tendencies toward the concentration of social
power and social rigidities, but also reactive tendencies toward the redistribution of social power and the emergence of more participatory institutions. Communication institutions are seen as an integral part of social
organization. Such a model, emphasizing processes of social change,
calls attention to the social conditions that are generating alternative
structures of communication, new ideologies and media languages, and
new uses of communication technology all as part of a broader process
of democratization in a society.

Practitioners, who are negotiating the development of more
democratic communication institutions, need the clarification of long-
term, utopian models and they must be aware of the social rigidities with
which they are dealing. But more important is the continual social analysis of the possibilities for change within contexts of social rigidities
(Bruck & Raboy, 1989). In this chapter I have attempted to outline a conceptual framework that combines four dimensions in the democratization
of communications: (a) continued clarification of normative models
grounded in a social philosophy of democratic communication; (b) an
analysis of the economic, political, and sociocultural conditions that both
demand and support democratic communications; (c) an analysis of the
social rigidities, ideologies of power concentration and mechanisms that
thwart efforts toward democratic communications; and (d) an analysis of
how practitioners negotiate change in the face of social rigidities.

At the level of practical action, the social conditions and strategies for democratization of communication can vary immensely.
Theories of democratization of communication must develop a comparative framework for dealing with this complexity and diversity:

1. An awareness of the very different avenues and forms of
   democratization in societies with quite different stages and
   types of political, economic, and cultural development and with
   very different cultural histories.
2. A clarification of the meaning of democratization at different
   levels of societal organization: mass, public communication at

the national or international level; regional or local communication systems; communication systems within a particular social sector such as labor organizations or particular cultural interest groups; communication within small communities or face-to-face groups.

3. An analysis of the very different ways that protagonists of democratic communication negotiate change within the junctures of historical conditions.

All of this calls for a great deal more empirical data describing different expressions of democratic communication in different contexts.

A Framework for the Comparative Analysis of the Stages in the Development of Democratic Communications

As previously noted, the slowness of governments in initiating a comprehensive policy of more democratic communication has prompted many observers to place greater hope for initiatives in the spread of grassroots movements for participatory communications. The presupposition is that change is more likely to begin at the margins of society among groups that feel that the present system of communications is inadequate. A further presupposition is that these innovative experiences are not just a passing phenomenon, but rather are the beginnings of a new structure of communication or, at least, are establishing permanent alternatives within the established structure of a society's communication system. It is expected that the basic institutional form of more participatory communication will be developed at the local level, that the advantages of this will be demonstrated and that eventually there will be greater acceptance in the larger society. Proponents of this model of change would admit that often, unless there are fairly profound political and economic changes, it is not likely that a whole society would accept a thoroughly participatory system of communications. But they would argue that alternative forms of communication are an integral and essential part of the process of political and economic change. Thus, the transition from relatively isolated, idealistic experiments to incorporation into a national system of communications is becoming a concern among some research on democratic communication.[3] Is such a transition possible or likely in the

---

[3]One of the most thorough analyses of the resistance to efforts toward democratization of communication at the governmental level is that edited by Fox, Schmucler et al. (1982). The article by Reyes-Matta, "La comunicación alternativa como respuesta democratica" is a particularly insightful analysis right at the time that Latin Americans were making a thorough assessment of the previous 20 years.

face of social rigidities, and, if so, how does it occur? To analyze what permits grassroots initiatives to grow and survive, we must look at a longer term historical, comparative analysis of many such experiences.

This chapter contained a brief analysis of a sample of the more complete historical descriptions of attempts to introduce alternative communication systems that permitted greater access and participation to "disenfranchised" groups. There were varying degrees of "success" in the cases, and all of them left some permanent institutional changes in the communication systems of the countries where they have occurred or are occurring. But generally, the results were more pessimistic than many idealistic protagonists of democratic communication would like to expect.

What the analyses did reveal was a kind of natural history and a series of typical stages: (a) a new cultural expression at a local, spontaneous communal level; (b) adaptation of this communal expression to a medium, linking similar groups in a larger communication system; (c) once the alternative begins to attract a larger following and broader cultural significance, imitation, competition, and co-optation by established nondemocratic media systems; and (d) the transformation of the new cultural expression into a mass popular format, "marketable" in a pluralistic national or international society.

The value of a more systematic framework in terms of natural history stages is that it reveals not only the complex and often hidden way that structural restraints present themselves at each stage, but also the inherent weaknesses of some idealistic movements in responding to these restraints. The analysis in terms of stages also shows the problems inherent in the transitions, for example, the move from an "alternative" communication to acceptance among a broader, more pluralistic public with the greater public responsibilities that this entails. The natural history method also indicates that as a direct communal cultural expression moves through various stages of communication through a medium, the protagonists have to rethink what is meant by participation. The analysis of stages groups together a series of interrelated problems that can be studied as interacting variables. Finally, this analysis suggests the administrative and planning steps that are necessary if the innovation is to be successful in the transition to a stage of integration or "peaceful coexistence" with other approaches in a mixed system of media. Or it may suggest that the experience remain simply an alternative for a more restricted group.

The analytic framework presented here may have the disadvantage of projecting too pessimistic a process. The "successes" are often too negotiated, gradual, and partial to attract attention as "truly participatory." However, this framework can be modified as additional empirical cases are studied.

THE NEED FOR NEW STRATEGIES OF RESEARCH IN SUPPORT OF MORE DEMOCRATIC COMMUNICATION

Research is more than just a body of theory and systematic methodologies for collecting data to test theory. It is also an institutionalized professional establishment with its specialized organization, career ideals, and accepted modes of operation or strategies. Many of the conventions of communication research, borrowed from older scientific traditions, need to be adapted if research is to make contact with efforts toward democratic communication. Three areas of adaptation seem particularly important: (a) a different understanding of the objectives and procedures of communication, (b) a different relationship between the researcher and the host group, and (c) a different understanding of professional research organization and research careers.

Objectives and Procedures in Research on Democratic Communication

Because in participatory organizations, those who need information for decision making are the media users themselves, the primary objective of research is to increase the users' understanding of their cultural expression and their communication patterns so that they can determine more consciously what kind of culture they want to create and how they want to structure the use of media. The most adequate model of research is not that of the physical sciences where the subjects are not creators of culture but fields of force or variables that can be isolated for purposes of prediction and external control. Here "prediction and control" is greater individual and collective self-understanding and greater freedom in self-determination. A much better starting point is that of the humanistic or cultural sciences where the method is interpretation of meanings being created. The researcher becomes a participant-observer in an attempt to recreate the meanings from the point of view of the actors. In this case, however, the objective is not to draw up an external ethnographic model of the culture that can be reflected back to the group, but rather to help the group itself become aware of the culture they are creating and the role of a particular communication or media language in the creation of this culture. The group can then judge whether this culture is the richest expression of its own values, symbols, and myths or whether there are deeper resources of the human imagination in this historical tradition not being expressed. This method is closer to the concientization suggested by Freire (1990). This does not rule out quantitative survey or personality measurements of the behavioral sciences or external ethnographic description. But, in this case, the systematic analysis of cultural histories within a given political and economic context is more "objective" precisely because it can bring in more of the subjective intentionality (the world we want to create) than external observation. The subjective experience of cultural symbols and myths become part of the data for critical appreciation.

The Relationship of the Host Group and the Researcher

The researcher does bring "from the outside" tools of sociocultural interpretation, and the researcher does not (perhaps, ideally, should not) share totally the same cultural history as the host group. Like the psychoanalyst, the researcher should have already had the experience of conscious reflection on the ideologies and myths of his or her culture in order to lead (not direct) the host group in his or her own reflection. But the researcher must also share deeply and sympathetically the alienation and cultural goals of the host group. The researcher is also learning and experiencing the "liberation" of which Freire (1980) spoke. The researcher necessarily brings the knowledge of a different technical sphere, but he or she follows the leadership of the group and translates this technical knowledge into the language and goals of the group.

The Understanding of Professional Research Organization and Research Careers

For various reasons, the researcher must define the pace of research not simply in terms of the timing of a contract or development of a scientific field (or professional career), but according to the rhythm of the group itself. The process of self-awareness follows, as Illich (1970) noted, the pace of the "educable moment." Also, the host group is negotiating social change in the face of structural restraints and must be constantly analyzing the social process to determine the opportune moment for more participatory organization. The research organization must be ready to accompany the host group in its journey and must be ready to respond to the needs of the group as they arise.

All this implies a somewhat different career ideal for communication researchers, at least for those who wish to be associated with the democratization of communication. This research will undoubtedly bring a more intimate comparative knowledge of the immensely varied processes of democratization or communication, and this knowledge can be shared with professional colleagues. But the measure of "success" may not be the creation of external explanatory models that can be used by the masters of a society to make the media more effective. Rather, the norm is greater understanding within the host groups and is likely to be in the subjective intentional order: the experience of greater authenticity, integration and human satisfaction in cultural creation and in the communication of this culture. Only the protagonists of democratic communication can be the judge of this.

REFERENCES

Atwood, R., & Mattos, S. (1982). Mass media reform and social change: The Peruvian experience. *Journal of Communication, 32*(2), 33-45.
Berrigan, F. J. (Ed). (1977a). *Access: Some western models of community media*. Paris. UNESCO.
Berrigan, F. J. (1977b). Introduction. In F. J. Berrigan (Ed.), *Access: Some western models of community media*. Paris: UNESCO.
Bruck, P. (1990). Communication and the democratization of culture: Strategies for social theory, strategies for dialogue. In S. Splichal, J. Hockheimer, & K. Jakubowicz (Eds.). *Democratization and the media: An east-west dialogue* (pp. 56-72). Ljubljana: University of Ljubljana, Faculty of Sociology, Political Science and Journalism.
Bruck, P. A., & Raboy, M. (1989). The challenge of democratic communication. In M. Raboy & P. A. Bruck (Eds.), *Communication for and against democracy* (pp. 3-17). Montreal: Black Rose.
Chapple, S., & Garafalo, R. (1977). *Rock "n" roll is here to pay: The history and politics of the music industry*. Chicago: Nelson-Hall.
Christians, C. G., Ferré, J. P., & Fackler, P. M. (1993). *Good news: Social ethics and the press*. New York: Oxford University Press.
Dervin, B. (1980). Communication gaps and inequities: Moving toward a reconceptualization. In B. Dervin & M. J. Voigt (Eds.), *Progress in communication sciences* (Vol. 2, pp. 73-112). Norwood, NJ: Ablex.
Enzenberger, H. M. (1974). *The consciousness industry*. New York: Seabury.
Fisher, D., & Harms, L.S. (Eds.). (1983). *The right to communicate: A new human right*. Dublin: Boole.
Fox, E., Schmucler, H. et al. (Eds.). *Comunicación y democracia* [Communication and democracy]. Lima, Peru: Desco.
Freire, P. (1990). *Pedagogy of the oppressed*. New York: Continuum.
Frith, S. (1978). *The sociology of rock*. London: Constable & Company.
Gitlin, T. (1980). *The whole world is watching*. Berkeley: University of California Press.
Golding, P., & Murdock, G. (1978). Theories of communication and theories of society. *Communication Research, 5*(3), 339-356.
Grinberg, M. (1981). Comunicación alternativa: Dimensiones, limites, posibilidades. In M. Grinberg (Ed.), *Comunicación alternativa y cambio social* (pp. 109-129). Mexico: Universidad Nacional Autonoma de Mexico.

Hall, S. (1977). Culture, the media and the ideological effect. In J. Curran, M. Gurevitch, & J. Wollacott (Eds.), *Mass communication and society* (pp. 315-348). London: Edward Arnold in association with the Open University Press.

Halloran, J. D. (1982). The context of mass communication research. In C. Whitney & E. Wartella (Eds.), *Mass communication review yearbook* (Vol. 3, pp. 163-206). Beverly Hills, CA: Sage.

Hamelink, C. J. (1983). *Cultural autonomy in global communication: Planning national information policy.* New York: Longman.

Hollander, E. (1992). The emergence of small scale media,. In N. Jankowski, O. Prehn, & J. Stappers (Eds.), *The people's voice: Local radio and television in Europe.* London: John Libbey.

Illich, A. (1970). *Deschooling society.* New York: Harper & Row.

International Commission for the Study of Communication Problems. (1980). *Many voices, one world.* London: Kogan Page.

Jacobson, T. L. (1994). Modernization and post-modernization approaches to participatory communication for development. In S. A. White, K. S. Nair, & J. Ascroft (Eds.), *Participatory communication: Working for change and development* (pp. 60-75). New Delhi: Sage.

Malm, K., & Wallis, R. (1994). *Media policy & music activity.* London: Routledge.

Martin-Barbero, J. (1993). *Communication, culture and hegemony: From the media to the mediations.* London: Sage.

Mattelart, A. (1979). *Communication and class struggle, Vol I: Capitalism, imperialism.* New York: International General.

McAnany, E. G. (1980). The role of information in communication with the rural poor: Some reflections. In E. G. McAnany (Ed.), *Communication in the rural Third World* (pp. 3-18). New York: Praeger.

Migdal, J. (1974). *Peasants, politics and revolution.* Princeton, NJ: Princeton University Press.

Morley, D. (1992). *Television, audiences and cultural studies.* London: Routledge.

Mowlana, M. (1979). Technology versus tradition: Communication in the Iranian Revolution. *Journal of Communication, 29*(3), 107-112.

O'Sullivan-Ryan, J., & Kaplun, M. (1982). *Communication methods to promote grass-roots participation.* Paris: UNESCO.

Policy Workshop, Institute of Social Studies, The Hague. (1980, February). *Communications research and Third World realities,* pp. 2-26.

Reyes-Matta, F. (1981). A model for democratic communication. *Development Dialogue, 2*(1), 79-97.

Reyes-Matta, F. (1982). La communicación alternativa como respuesta democratica. In E. Fox, H. Schmucler et al. (Eds.), *Comunicación y democracia* (pp. 245-264). Lima, Peru: Desco.

Riaño, P. (Ed.). (1994). *Women in grassroots communications: Furthering social change.* Thousand Oaks, CA: Sage.

Rowland, W., Jr. (1982). The illusion of fulfillment: The broadcast reform movement. *Journalism Monographs, 79.*

Schiller, D. (1981). *Objectivity and the news: The public and the rise of commercial journalism.* Philadelphia: University of Pennsylvania Press.

Solomon, G. (1979). *Interaction of media, cognition and learning.* San Francisco: Jossey-Bass.

Somavia, J. (1981). The democratization of communications: From minority social monopoly to majority social representation. *Development Dialogue, 2,* 13-29.

Wallis, R., & Malm, K. (1984). *Big sounds from small peoples: The music industry in small countries.* London: Constable.

White, R. A. (1977). *Factors influencing the rise of an independent Campesino base of power* [Structural factors in rural development]. Unpublished doctoral dissertation, Cornell University, Ithaca, NY.

White, R. A. (1980). "Communicación Popular": Language of liberation. *Media Development Media Development, 27*(2), 3-9.

White, R. A. (1983). Communication strategies for social change: National television versus local public radio. In G. Gerbner & M. Siefert (Eds.), *World communication handbook* (pp. 279-293). New York: Oxford University Press.

White, R. A. (1991). Democratization of communication: Normative theory and sociopolitical process. In K. J. Greenberg (Ed.), *Conversations on communication ethics* (pp. 141-164). Norwood, NJ: Ablex.

White, R. A. (1994). Participatory development communication as a socio-cultural process. In S. A. White, K. S. Nair, & J. Ascroft (Eds.), *Participatory communication: Working for change and development* (pp. 95-116). New Delhi: Sage.

White, S. A. (1994). The concept of participation. In S. A. White, K. S. Nair, & J. Ascroft (Eds.), *Participatory communication: Working for change and development* (pp. 15-32). New Delhi: Sage.

Whyte, W. F. (Ed.). (1991). *Participatory action research.* Newbury Park, CA: Sage.

Williams, F., & J.V. Pavlik. (Eds.). (1994). *The people's right to know: Media, democracy, and the information highway.* Hillsdale, NJ: Lawrence Erlbaum Associates.

///

Theoretical Perspectives

9

Participatory Communication as Communicative Action

Thomas L. Jacobson
State University of New York at Buffalo

Satish Kolluri
University of Massachusetts at Amherst

The idea of participatory communication is central to one current formulation of the role of communication in national development. The classical paradigm in this subfield focused largely on information transfer processes from northern sources to southern recipients (Lerner, 1958; Rogers, 1962; Schramm, 1964). The idea of participatory communication focuses, instead, chiefly on communication among local community members engaged in development efforts. It has also been used to refer to communication between community members and outside experts, academics, and field workers, but in such instances information transfer is de-emphasized and the process of dialogue among participants is instead emphasized. Although the general idea of participatory communication is used increasingly often, it is used in a number of different ways, and further theoretical development is needed. The work of Freire (1970, 1973) has been prominent in its treatment of existential, political, and pedagogical elements of participatory communication, and has been widely embraced in the Third World. However, Freire's writings have not led to a body of derivative theory or research in the north, at least not one with the widespread acceptance of diffusion theory during the modernization era.

Although it has seldom been applied in this context, Habermas' (1984, 1987) work is of considerable relevance to the concerns of participatory communication. In a way that indicates sensitivity to cultural values Habermas' thinking relies heavily on philosophical hermeneutics. In a manner that parallels struggles for political freedom, his work is explicitly democratic. And, he recognizes with dependency and neodependency theorists that corporate and public interests are not entirely parallel. More importantly, at the foundation of this thinking lies a theory of communication. The *theory of communicative action* has been put forward as the centerpiece of Habermas' later work. And, notably, this formulation of communicative action strongly reflects processes that may be seen as participatory.

In this chapter, we argue that the theory of communicative action can be used to conceptualize participatory communication for development. A number of elements of Habermas' work can be used to this end. His analysis of the public sphere (Habermas, 1989a) could provide the basis for an analysis of media institutions insofar as they facilitate democratic participation through public discourse. Habermas' treatment of colonization of the lifeworld could more generally guide research into areas of the subjective lifeworld in which normative discourse has been marginalized by instrumental or theoretical discourse.

Here we focus on the theory of communicative action and discuss one element of this theory, the *ideal speech situation*. The ideal speech situation and the communicative action it typifies underlie Habermas' project as a whole, including his analysis of the public sphere and his analysis of lifeworld colonization. This chapter focuses on participatory communication in interaction between aid recipients and donors, or representatives of donors, in the development setting. Generally speaking, these relations can be thought of as being between local communities and outside development agents. But our discussion might also allude to communication among community members, and among development agents, as well. For the sake of practical convenience, and due to space restraints, questions related to press institutions and a variety of relevant cultural processes are not discussed here.

Briefly, we argue that the ideal speech situation can be used as a framework within which participatory communication can be both theoretically defined and evaluated. The definition consists in assigning various elements of participatory communication processes to their conceptual counterparts in the theory of the ideal speech situation, and in particular to one or more "validity claims." The evaluation consists in using the validity claims as a basis on which to judge ways in which particular communicative transactions are, or are not, participatory.

The argument begins with a review of participatory communication in the context of national development. It continues with an introduction to central elements of the theory of communicative action including the ideas of lifeworld colonization, universal pragmatics, the ideal speech situation, and validity claims. Participatory communication, as defined in the context of national development, is then reformulated in terms of communicative action. In the conclusion we review a number of challenges that can be raised against such an analysis, and we remark on the relevance of Habermas' work to development communication theory.

MODERNIZATION AND PARTICIPATION

To begin, it may be helpful to briefly review communication in both the participatory and modernization frameworks. Proceeding chronologically, recall the historical era in which modernization theory was developed. This was, of course, the era of the U.S. post-World War II rise to preeminence as a military superpower and a dominant force in global economics. It was an era of rapid evolution in communication technologies due to the widespread emergence of television and radio. And it was an era that saw the heyday of scientific social theory. Functionalist theories advanced universalistic accounts of macro-social processes encompassing the growth of nations. In the field, scientists both hard and soft, undertook to bring the benefits of theory testing to the Third World.

Accounts of communication's role in national development accorded with these historical preoccupations. The spread of mass media lead to an emphasis on the effects of mass media on the Third World, as associated with Lerner's (1958) theory of psychic mobility. The transference of expert know-how from north to south resulted in the great interest accorded to diffusion theory (Rogers, 1963).

Criticisms of modernization theory became numerous during the 1970s and 1980s (Hedebro, 1981; Jayaweera & Amunugama, 1987; Lerner & Schramm, 1976; McAnany, Schnitman, & Janus, 1981; Rogers, 1976), among them some that included calls for a new kind of people's participation. Rogers (1983) redefined development in a general way as participatory, in considering it "a widely participatory process of social change in society intended to bring about both social and material advancement for the majority of the people through gaining greater control over their environment" (p. 121). Cohen and Uphoff (1980) indicated a number of elements in each development program that involve participation, "participation includes people's involvement in the decision making process, in implementing programs . . . their sharing in benefits of development and their involvement in efforts to evaluate such programs" (p. 219). Tilakratna (1987) noted that participation is not limited to abstract principles or mere task assignments, but includes deeper levels of behavior:

> Participatory Rural Development's vision of human development as process of unfolding the creative potential of people embodies two inter-related central elements, namely self reliance and participation. The underlying promise is that these are fundamental human values that need to be promoted in order for people to develop as creative human beings, and that objectively generated processes possess an urge for liberation of these values. (p. 51)

DEFINITIONS OF PARTICIPATORY COMMUNICATION

In terms of communication, the participatory approach has tended to highlight small rather than large media, horizontal rather than vertical communication, collective self-reliance rather than dependence on outside experts, and action-rather than theory-oriented inquiry. This approach has influenced numerous project designs and field studies (Berrigan, 1979; O'Sullivan-Ryan & Kaplan, 1982) and has led to a growing body of academic theory and research (Jacobson, 1993; Melkote, 1991; Narula & Pearce, 1986; Servaes & Arnst, 1993; White, Nair, & Ascroft, 1995).

Specific definitions of participatory communication are highly varied. Diverse adjectives such as "popular," "participatory," "indigenous," "self-governing," and "emancipatory" are all used to characterize it. Fuglesang and Chandler (1986) argued that "recognition of shared interests, accountability, and facilitating decision making processes in a shared milieu of interests, constitute true communication and participation" (p. 62). Ascroft's (1987) definition of participatory communication emphasized "knowledge sharing and creating beneficiary comprehension of benefactor intentionalities".

According to Capriles (cited in Grinberg, 1986, p. 10), communication democratization is the "*conditio sine qua non* of all possible democracies: the permanent dialogue, the spontaneous and relevant participation, never arbitrary or conditional, generating collective decisions and the socialization of production and its fruits" (p. 176).

Nair and White (1993) defined from a transactional perspective *participatory development* as a two-way dynamic interaction between grassroots receivers and an information source mediated by the development communicators. Participatory communication is defined as, "The opening of dialogue, source and receiver interacting continuously, thinking constructively about the situation, identifying developmental needs and problems, deciding what is needed to improve the situation, and acting upon it" (Nair & White, 1993, p. 51)

These definitions have the virtue of broadly describing a new emphasis in development communication on two-way, dialogic processes. However, they overlap with one another only to varying degrees, each with a slightly different conceptual focus. No single definition has been both systematically elaborated and widely accepted.

THE THEORY OF COMMUNICATIVE ACTION

Habermas' general theoretical project involves an attempt to understand the historical development of human society within the framework of a critical theory. In addition to the theory of communicative action, this has produced a theory of social evolution, a theory of ethics, and other theoretical treatments of major social processes.

Habermas' system can be entered using any of these theories as a portal. For the purposes of this chapter, it is convenient to begin with analysis of the colonization of the lifeworld. This has the advantage of facilitating consideration of Habermas' relevance not only to participatory communication, but to other issues of interest in the field of national development.

Analysis of the lifeworld is founded on a selective use of the works of Max Weber, Talcott Parsons, Karl Marx, and other social theorists. Similar to the manner in which Marx analytically divided society into an economic base and an ideological superstructure, Habermas also identified two major societal spheres: "system" and "lifeworld." Habermas departed from Marx, following Weber, in arguing that neither of these spheres determines the others.

The system sphere generally refers to the activities of economics and administration. Each of these activities is treated as a further subsystem, and is conceptualized, using Parsonian thought, as a functionally self-regulating action context. The lifeworld sphere refers to collectively shared background convictions, to the preconscious, assumed "horizons" within which actors communicate with one another. This includes the processes in which tradition, social integration, and individual identity are produced and reproduced.

The system and lifeworld play distinguishable roles in constituting society, and hence they operate differently. System maintenance is achieved by orienting human action around "media" such as money or power. The mode of reasoning appropriate for such action is instrumental, technical, and achievement oriented—what is sometimes called means–ends reasoning. Alternatively, the lifeworld is reproduced through a different mode of reasoning, and comprises ongoing communicative processes of interpretation and dialogue. In other words, the means–ends rationality employed in system maintenance is not appropriate for forging and forming individual identity, facilitating social integration, or maintaining cultural tradition. Conversely, communicative processes central to the lifeworld are not sufficient to perform system maintenance.

Although Habermas made extensive use of Weber and Parsons, drawing on them to conceptualizing the differentiation of spheres in society, he departed from them in an attempt to account more adequately for social "pathologies," or contradictions, that result from the imperfect integration among social spheres. Habermas' diagnosis of modern society holds that an imbalance exists between the system and lifeworld. It is an imbalance in which technical system rationality dominates the lifeworld. It is this that is referred to as "colonization of the lifeworld." Briefly, the priorities and modes of reasoning appropriate for business and administration have marginalized and fragmented the processes proper to lifeworld maintenance. In the moral sphere, ethics are marginalized in numerous ways, in the name of capital accumulation, efficiency, and so on. In the aesthetic sphere, artistic appreciation is invaded by commercial priorities, to the extent that artistic expression is influenced by what is commercially viable. In the end, there is a deformation of social integration processes, a deformation that Habermas analyzed in countries of the north but may also be applicable to countries of the south.

The analysis of lifeworld colonization can be taken as a critical analysis of the effects of the commodification and bureaucratization of daily life. In order to justify this analysis, however, some kind of standard is necessary in terms of which lifeworld colonization can be negatively evaluated. This is the chief role played by the theory of communicative action. Why is this standard communicative? One way to answer this is by reference to the question of rationality. Rational assessment of what the most desirable life might be, and how to get there, has evaded philosophers. And without a basis for such rational assessment, technical, business, and bureaucratic ways of life cannot be judged better or worse than any other ways of life.

In personal terms, Habermas alluded to the Socratic credo, avowing that what is desirable is "pursuit of the good life." However, given that a rational philosophical foundation in support of this position is not possible, Habermas took a procedural approach. He argued that knowledge by which we might evaluate "the good" as a product can not be rationally assessed; however, the means by which knowledge is produced can be considered rational. In other words, knowledge is not a product that can be evaluated for truth or falsity. But, in the structure of necessary conditions for any communication, there is a basis for giving reasons with regard to knowledge claims. The "universal pragmatics" of communication constitute a communicative form of rationality.

In developing this communicative approach to reason, Habermas outlined in some detail the nature of these universal pragmatics. He has also distinguished various forms of expressive, verbal and nonverbal communication. And, he distinguished communication that is oriented toward reaching understanding from other forms of communication. Chiefly, this has been done to outline a program of research, and to focus his own analysis on verbal communication that is oriented toward reaching understanding.

Fundamental is the position that human communication has evolved a capability that presumes the intent to reach mutual understanding. Manipulative communication itself employs forms of violating the presumption of this intent. And, the intent embodied in this system can be summed up by referring to an "ideal speech situation," consisting in the assumption during communication of four "validity claims" (Habermas, 1979). These include:

1. Truth—the veracity of the propositional content in the speaker's utterance.
2. Rightness—the appropriateness of the statement made by the speaker in a context specific situation in accordance with cultural norms.
3. Sincerity—the authenticity of the speaker's good intentions in communicating.
4. Comprehensibility—whether the expression used is understood.[1]

All parties to a communicative transaction are said to make these validity claims implicitly. And it is through adjudicating disagreements over these claims that consensus is possible. If a hearer questions the validity of an implicit claim, he or she may ask for justification, and this can then lead to discussion through which the claim can be defended, or redeemed. If a hearer is not sure whether something is comprehended, he or she might ask, "I'm not sure whether I follow you. Could you please repeat

[1]Habermas' earlier formulations, such as the one presented in Habermas (1979) employed four validity claims. Later formulations refer to three validity claims because comprehensibility is actually a requirement of communication but not a validity claim in the technical sense (Horster, 1992). For the sake of convenience, we employ the fourfold framework here, however, because comprehensibility is often a very real problem in development communication settings.

that?" If the hearer is uncertain as to the truth of a statement he or she may ask, "Are you sure? How can that be?" If a hearer feels insulted at being addressed in a way that violates social norms, he or she might respond by asking the speaker to clarify the position from which he or she is speaking. And with regard to the communicative situation as a whole, the speaker is assumed to be speaking sincerely. Disingenuousness can be called into question by suggesting, "You don't really mean that."

In any of these cases, the question involves asking the speaker to redeem a validity claim that is normally assumed. As an instance of daily behavior this may take only a momentary pause. As a kind of communication, Habermas referred to it as the discursive justification of validity claims, which involves thematizing a validity claim and explicitly making it the subject of discussion.

This also comprises a definition of "discourse." Such discourse offers both speakers the opportunity to ground action in reasons. Put otherwise, it involves arriving at a rational consensus through the force of the better argument. To be fully realized it must allow all participants in discussion a "symmetrically distributed opportunity" to ask questions with the aim of determining, truth, rightfulness, and sincerity.

It is this specific form of discourse that defines *communicative action*. It is this process that Habermas characterized as rational and that may lead to knowledge around which action can be legitimately oriented. "It [rationality] refers to various forms of argumentation as possibilities of continuing communicative action with reflective means" (Habermas, 1984, p. 10).

Thus defined, the ideal speech situation can be approached in two ways. First, as an analysis of the preconditions of all communication. Second, as a set of criteria in terms of which manipulative and distorted communication can be evaluated. Habermas remarked:

> The ideal speech situation is neither an empirical phenomenon nor a mere construct, but rather an unavoidable supposition reciprocally made in discourse. This supposition can, but need not be counterfactual; but even if it is made counterfactually, it is a fiction that is operatively effective in the process of communication. Therefore I prefer to speak of an anticipation of an ideal speech situation . . . this anticipation alone is warrant which permits us to join to an actually attained consensus the claim of a rational consensus. At the same time it is a critical standard against which every actually realized consensus can be called into question and checked. (cited in Kemp, 1988, p. 188)

A RECONSTRUCTION OF PARTICIPATORY COMMUNICATION

The emergence of participation as a new approach to development communication has emphasized the importance of subjective experiences of people for whom development is supposedly meant. In this line of reflection, Habermas' formulations of the ideal speech situation and of communicative action draw a parallel to recent writing on participatory communication. Gonzalez (1989) argued that the ideal speech situation is suited to studying the social relations embodied in development communication situations. To take this general argument further, we review the definitions of participatory communication presented earlier, and then interpret each specifically within the framework of validity claims.

Fuglesang and Chandler (1986) suggested that "recognition of shared interests, accountability, and facilitating decision-making processes in a shared milieu of interests, constitute true communication and participation" (p. 62). In terms of the validity claims, we can say that accountability, or the willingness to be called on to redeem validity claims, suggests sincerity, as does acting in good faith. "A milieu of shared interests" implies, indirectly, rightness or appropriateness in terms of validity claims. However, validity claims related to truth and comprehensibility are not addressed.

Ascroft's (1987) definition of participatory communication emphasized "knowledge sharing and creating beneficiary comprehension of benefactor intentionalities" (p. 10). Theoretically, Ascroft's terms seem to suggest primarily the validity claim of comprehensibility. It seems indirectly to address sincerity, and even more indirectly normative rightness, but overlooks entirely the matter of truth.

For Capriles, participatory communication is "communication democratization characterized by permanent dialogue and participation that is never arbitrary or conditional, and collective decision making" (cited in Grinberg, 1986, p. 176). This definition reflected his intuitive understanding of the ideal speech situation, except that in the case of ideal speech there very much is a form of conditionality. This conditionality is the implicit need for justification of the validity claims, in both directions.

Returning to Nair and White (1993), their reconceptualization of participatory communication in the form of the "transactional perspective" requires, "The opening of dialogue, source and receiver interacting continuously, thinking constructively about the situation, identifying developmental needs and problems, deciding what is needed to improve the situation, and acting upon it" (p. 51). The term dialogue and the accompanying emphasis on cooperation suggest the practical spirit of communicative action, but they do not provide a framework explaining specifically what constitutes dialogue and how one might evaluate it as a communication process.

This exercise demonstrates that definitions of participatory communication overlap considerably with the communication process treated within the framework of ideal speech. Each of them represents one or more of the validity claims. Or, in other words, each of these definitions can be interpreted as specifying that for communication to be participatory, it is necessary that one or more of the validity claims is subject to challenge. At the same time, this exercise indicates that existing definitions under specify the participatory situation. None of them explicitly identifies all four validity claims, even though most of the definitions seem to reflect the ideal speech situation in spirit.

This suggests that communicative action may serve as a conceptualization of participatory communication, for both theoretical and practical purposes. For theoretical purposes the theory of communicative action is comprehensive. It is clear and systematic. And, it is also articulated within a larger theoretical system.

PROGRAM FORMULATION AND EVALUATION

At a practical level, the ideal speech situation provides a standard against which to evaluate practical communicative situations. Forester (1988) argued for an "applied turn" based in the theory of communicative action, and illustrated it in the field of urban planning. Application is performed by restating the validity claims as questions that are relevant to policy-oriented deliberations. A similar process could be used in community participation in national development settings.

Consider a hypothetical program evaluation involving interaction between outside experts or extension agents, and either an individual or group from a local population.

The questions are:

1. Is the communicator's communication correct, that is, is the information being offered undistorted and reliable? (Truth)
2. Is the communicator's role legitimate, given his or her role and the participation of other interested individuals, social groups, agencies, and nations who are party to the process of development? (Rightness)
3. Is the communication offered sincerely, in good faith without being manipulative, either on the part of the individual, or any organization from which the individual may have been sent? (Sincerity)
4. Is the communicator's communication comprehensible to others, that is, are idiom, cultural factors, and/or message design, adequately accounted for? (Comprehensibility)

In the tradition of participatory research, a negative answer to any of these questions should result in an adjustment of interpersonal relationships somehow to more fully reflect local wishes or questions. In theoretical terms, the outsiders must at least place a high priority on sensitivity to local questions, inviting challenges to any of the validity claims. As a matter of procedure in the field, the outsiders might thematize, or raise, the validity claims themselves, one by one. Of course, there are occasions in which validity claims are violated, consciously or otherwise, by locals, and in these cases the outsiders may challenge a validity claim.

The use of validity claims as a basis for evaluative questions can be illustrated with an example project. Again, the aims and statements employed in the project can be interpreted within the communicative action framework. In an agriculturally and economically backward region of rural western India, a nongovernmental organization in conjunction with outside researchers conducted several participatory research workshops. These workshops concentrated on attempts to organize farmers in dealing with localized problems in their villages (Tandon & Brown, 1981). Previous workshops had adopted the diffusionist approach in disseminating to the leaders of village farmer groups information pertinent to new farm practices. Relatively little change had taken place in the level and quality of production, and this had resulted in a lack of farmer initiative. The difference between benefactor intentions and beneficiary comprehension became apparent.

A participatory research workshop then made amends in that its training principles emphasized "increasing participant awareness, improving participant skills and information bases, and developing participants' ability to operate effectively as a group" (Tandon & Brown, 1981, p. 174). The design and implementation of the project explicitly assumed the following procedural aims:

1. Talk with participants about their situation.
2. Emphasize the concrete experience of participants as a focus for analysis and action.
3. Create a psychologically safe environment.
4. Develop the capacities of groups rather than individuals.
5. Develop concrete, well-understood steps that participants value and may realistically accomplish.

The resulting interaction between the local populace and outside researchers afforded a better understanding of problems and furthered deliberation on possible solutions to local problems.

This effort was conducted without any reference to the theory of communicative action. Nevertheless, it was conducted through a process in which some attempt was made to ensure that validity claims could at any time be called up for justification. "Creating a psychologically safe environment" is a rather nebulous and encompassing phrase but suggests sincerity and rightness in terms of the validity claims. The researchers' communication was offered in good faith, without being manipulative. Researchers dealt with local problems on local terms, which was likely to enhance comprehension, and furthermore legitimized their own sincerity because they demonstrated interest in the participation of the villagers, and in their concrete experience. In summary, the assumptions of the design and implementation of the research project employed participatory communication, or in Habermas' phrase communicative action.

This example illustrates how project statements and evaluations contain goal-oriented and operational guidelines that should, in the case of participatory communication, reflect ideal speech conditions. The importance of specific validity claims will vary from case to case. The theory of communicative action specifies that all four validity claims are always implicit in communication. However, one or some of them may be more problematic in a given situation, and one or some of them may be more likely to need justification.

Assuming that communicative action is a productive conceptualization of participatory communication then, it is a short step to employing validity claims explicitly in field work. There is not space here to explore such a possibility in more detail, but the manner in which this would be done seems clear. The validity claims would be used as guidelines. With regard to any given project, each validity claim could form a reference point for discussion, planning, or evaluation of interaction. In any given project one validity claim may be more problematic than another, and attention to the four claims need not be addressed in equal amounts.

CONCLUSION

The so-called demise of modernization led to the emergence of many paradigms that, over the years, constituted the field of development studies in the west and the Third World. Participation, as a postmodernization approach, is one of them. Although participation has not assumed the status of a full-fledged theory, it has been successful in expressing a different philosophical approach to the problem of so-called underdevelopment. Participatory communication is emblematic of this new approach in that it has been realized that dialogic communication is an important part of development. At the same time, one cannot help but note the diverse meanings, connotations, and conditionalities attached to the notion of participation. Therefore, the foregoing analysis uses Habermas' theory of communicative action as a conceptual framework with which to reconstruct and systematize the notion of participatory communication.

It should be noted that the examples used here would not seem to exhaust the communicative situations to which validity claims could be applied. We have focused on interaction between outsiders and locals. For another example, communicative action is the explicit *modus operandi* in community meetings where local goals are collectively argued over and hammered out. Validity claims could provide the basis for evaluation of communicative interactions between different individuals or power interests within community groups. Communicative action is also the stated modus operandi of "social marketing," given its stated attempt to earnestly assess local needs and to communicate in return knowledge about any available options that might satisfy local needs. Therefore, evaluation of social marketing programs could be structured on the basis of validity claims.

In closing, a number of difficulties involved in employing Habermas in the field of communication for national development should be raised. First, Habermas' work does not intersect well with any one contemporary school of thought on national development processes. For example, his theory of history is lineal, suggesting affinities with modernization theory. It does not suggest the tidy march toward wealth and modernism that writers such as W. W. Rostow (1952) seemed to suggest, but it does involve stages.

On a related matter, Habermas' thinking seems to include a brand of cultural universalism. He holds that some social formations embodied in Enlightenment values are superior to those that are organized around frameworks of religious or mythic values. Cultural sensitivity takes the form for many scholars today of a relativism holding that all social forms are of equivalent worth. Extreme skepticism regarding universals of any kind is common (Escobar, 1995; Spivak, 1987). Assessing these matters is not possible here due to space constraints, but Habermas' work seems too often to revisit Enlightenment values from the perspective of some postmodernist analysts.

On the other hand, the theory of communicative action is intended to comprise the foundation of a "critical theory." This aspect of Habermas' work should accord less favorably with modernization theory. For example, colonization of the lifeworld may be well suited to conceptualizing cultural imperialism.

Some additional challenges presented by Habermas are due not to schools of thought on development theory, but rather reflect common criticisms of Habermas' theory generally. One is the commonly leveled charge of idealism. Here, the ideal speech situation is seen as unrealistic, because such a considerable part of communication is not at all oriented toward attempts to reach understanding. The condition of deception is of course well recognized by Habermas, and anticipated in that the ideal speech situation does not refer to anything like intentions to reach agreement or to be honest. It refers instead to the conditions for communication, plainly speaking, of any kind, including attempts to deceive. Thus, Habermas specified various forms of action. "Strategic action" has as its aim the achievement of a goal without regard for the well being of any interlocutors, and may involve deception. "Communicative action" is reserved for action whose goal is expressly oriented toward reaching understanding.

These challenges, both those related to development theory and those more general, cannot be addressed here. We are attempting primarily to outline a communicative action approach to the study of participatory communication. Details and counterarguments can be attended to in the future. For now, the question is whether participatory communication scholars cannot find in Habermas' theory something beyond a friendly critical spirit. In fact, the heart of Habermas' work concerns participatory communication.

REFERENCES

Ascroft, J. (1987). *Communication in support of development: Lessons from theory and practice*. Paper presented at the Communication and Change: An Agenda for New Age Communication seminar. East–West Center, University of Hawaii, Honolulu.

Berrigan, F. (1979). Community communications: The role of community media in development. *Reports and chapters on mass communication* (Vol. 90). Paris: UNESCO.

Escobar, A. (1995). *Encountering development: The making and unmaking of the Third World*. Princeton, NJ: Princeton University Press.

Forester, J. (1988). Introduction: The applied turn in contemporary critical theory. In J. Forester (Ed.), *Critical theory and public life* (pp. ix-xxvi). Cambridge: MIT Press.

Freire, P. (1970). *Pedagogy of the oppressed*. New York: Continuum.

Freire, P. (1973). *Education for critical consciousness*. New York: Continuum.

Fuglesang, A., & Chandler, D. (1986). The open snuff-box: Communication as participation. *Media Development, 2*, 2-4.

Gonzalez, H. (1989). Interactivity and feedback in Third World development campaigns. *Critical Studies in Mass Communication, 6*(3), 295-314.

Grinberg, S. M. (1986). Trends in alternative communication research in Latin America. In R. Atwood & E. G. McAnany (Eds.), *Communication and Latin American society: Trends in critical research, 1960–1985* (pp. 165-189). Madison: University of Wisconsin Press.

Habermas, J. (1979). *Communication and the evolution of society*. Boston: Beacon.

Habermas, J. (1984). *The theory of communicative action Vol. 1: Reason and the rationalization of society.* Boston: Beacon.

Habermas, J. (1987). *The theory of communicative action Vol. 2: A critique of functionalist reason.* Boston: Beacon.

Habermas, J. (1989). *The structural transformation of the public sphere: An inquiry into a category of bourgeois society.* Cambridge: MIT Press.

Hedebro, G. A. (1981). *Communication and social change in developing nations: A critical view.* Ames: Iowa State University Press.

Horster, D. (1979). *Habermas: An introduction.* Philadelphia: Pennbridge.

Jacobson, T. L. (1993). A pragmatist account of participatory communication research for national development. *Communication Theory 3*(3), 214-230.

Jayaweera, N., & Amunagama, S. (1987). *Rethinking development communication.* Singapore: Asian Mass Communication Research and Information Centre.

Kemp, R. (1988). Planning, public hearings, and the politics of discourse. In J. Forester (Ed.), *Critical theory and public life* (pp. 177-202). Cambridge: MIT Press.

Lerner, D. (1958). *The passing of traditional society.* Glencoe, IL: The Free Press.

Lerner, D., & Schramm, W. (1976). *Communication and change: The last ten years and the next.* Honolulu: University of Hawaii Press.

McAnany, E. G., Schnitman, J., & Janus, N. (1981). *Communication and social structure: Critical studies in mass media research.* New York: Praeger.

Melkote, S. R. (1991). *Communication for development in the Third World: Theory and practice.* Newbury Park, CA: Sage.

Nair, K.S., & White, S.A. (1993). The development communication process: A reconceptualization. In K.S. Nair & S. A. White (Eds.), *Perspectives in development communication* (pp. 47-70). New Delhi: Sage.

Narula, U., & Pearce, B. (1986). *Development as communication: A perspective on India.* Carbondale: Southern Illinois Press.

O'Sullivan-Ryan, J., & Kaplan, M. (1982). Communication methods to promote grass-roots participation. *Communication and Society, 6.*

Rogers, E. M. (1963). *Diffusion of innovations.* Glencoe, IL: The Free Press.

Rogers, E. M. (1976). Communication and development: The passing of the dominant paradigm. *Communication Research, 3*(2), 213-240.

Rogers, E. M. (1983). *Diffusion of innovations.* New York: The Free Press.

Rostow, W. W. (1952). *The process of economic growth.* New York: Norton.

Schramm, W. (1964). *Mass media and national development: The role of information in the developing countries.* Stanford, CA: Stanford University Press.

Servaes, J., & Arnst, R. (1993). Participatory communication for social change: Reasons for optimism in the year 2000. *Development Communication Report, 79,* 18-20.

Spivak, G. (1987). *In other worlds: Essays in cultural politics.* New York: Methuen.

Tandon, R., & Brown, D. L. (1981). Organization-building for rural development: An experiment in India. *Journal of Applied Behavioral Science, 17*(2), 172-189.

Tilakratna, S. (1987). *The animator in participatory rural development: Concept and practice.* Geneva: World Employment Programme, International Labour Organization.

White, S., Nair. K. S., & Ascroft, J. (1995). *Participation: A key concept in development communication.* New Delhi: Sage.

10

Exploring the Links Between Structuration Theory and Participatory Action Research

Edith Friesen

RATIONALE

In this chapter I facilitate constructive dialogue in three areas of participatory action research (PAR)—namely between PAR and social science, between the two main and divergent schools of thought in PAR, and between theory and practice in PAR—through the application of structuration theory. Such an endeavor is admittedly problematic because structuration theory is an ontological metatheory and a work in progress, and PAR is primarily a collaborative process that unites inquiry, education, and social action. However, it may be worthwhile because there appears to be a basis for common ground. For example, both PAR and structuration theory reject the objectivist, value-free tenets of positivist social science. Both are also concerned with praxis, or the relation among knowledge, agency, and action. Finally, both are interested in the ability of social research to facilitate change. An examination of the links between PAR and structuration theory should lead to a creative and constructive dialogue within the diverse interests that constitute PAR and between PAR and the social science community.

PROBLEMS IN PAR

First, the need for a more constructive dialogue between PAR and social science is evident. One of the barriers, according to Jacobson (1991b), is the often antagonistic relationship between PAR and social science, a problem for which both sides bear some responsibility. Jacobson argued, "There should be a role for pursuit of knowledge, in addition to social change. And, there must be a metatheoretical or philosophical justification of this role" (p. 13). However, not all participatory researchers welcome rapprochement with the social science community. There are those like Hall (1984) who have argued that academic involvement may not be appropriate because the interests of the social science and lay communities are fundamentally different (i.e., PAR is dedicated to generating social change rather than generating scientific knowledge). Ironically, this view is also the reason why many social scientists do not consider PAR to be legitimate scientific activity. However, exclusion from the larger social science frame of reference, irrespective of the reasons for it, makes it difficult for PAR to engage in the kind of critical self-reflexiveness that could garner the respect of the social science community and generate theoretical improvements.

Second, a lack of productive dialogue between the two main and divergent schools of thought in PAR is evident in the writings of Whyte (1991) and Fals-Borda (1991). Whyte, who tends to emphasize inquiry into causal relations related to process changes in organizational, corporate, and agricultural settings, made no mention of Fals-Borda's more critical work, which emphasizes issues of unequal power relations related to structures of domination and oppression in developmental settings. Fals-Borda noted this omission and also stated that PAR is being co-opted by people who are diluting its emphasis on people's power. Although there are obviously fundamental differences between these two schools of thought, it is suggested here that there is little to be gained by sectarianism and much to be gained by better communication between participatory researchers with different perspectives and from the cross-fertilization of ideas.

Third, the need to improve the dialogue between theory and practice in PAR is also evident. As Le Gall stated, "Research professionals retreat to their ivory tower to engage in obscure theoretical speculations and, when they do emerge in the field, they are distanced by theory . . . [while practitioners] are too immersed in their daily practice to be able to distance themselves from it; all reflective work on their own practice can only lead them to confirm their own representation of it" (cited in Mayer, 1990, p. 209). A number of scholars interested in PAR have called for closer communication between theorists and practitioners in order to improve theory and practice (Einsiedel, 1992; Jacobson, 1991a, 1991b; Servaes, 1989; Whyte, Greenwood, & Lazes, 1991). They have argued that without careful and systematic documentation of practice or a broader theoretical framework for critical evaluation, it is difficult to improve either theory or practice.

CONTRIBUTIONS OF STRUCTURATION THEORY

Structuration theory, developed by Giddens during the past two decades, provides a useful metatheoretical framework for accounting for disparate views and establishing a discourse among divergent schools of thought. Although structuration theory provides an ontological framework for the study of human activities, that is, "the conceptual investigation of the nature of human action, social institutions and the interrelations between action and institutions" (Giddens, 1991, p. 201), it does not pretend to advance generalizations or laws about social reality. Giddens' critique of *functionalism, interpretivist sociologies,* and *critical inquiry* and his reframing of the subjectivist and objectivist, macro-and micro-leanings in various social science schools of thought, provides a way for PAR to engage in the larger theoretical discourse of the social sciences.

Furthermore, the concept of the *double hermeneutic* and the *dialogical model* developed by Giddens, represents a *legitimation* of involvement in social change activities by researchers and social scientists. As he stated: "Social science does not stand in a neutral relation to the social world, as an instrument of technological change. The implication of the double hermeneutic is that social scientists cannot but be alert to the transformative effects that their concepts and theories might have upon what it is they set out to analyze" (Giddens, 1989, p. 64).

The double hermeneutic also has implications for social change through policymaking. Giddens referred to the interactive application of the understandings of the lay community and scientific community as the dialogical model. It embodies the notion that "the most effective forms of connection between social research and policy making are forged through an extended process of communication between researchers, policy makers and those affected by whatever issues are under consideration" (Giddens, 1987, p. 47).

As well, structuration theory provides a useful analytical framework for building bridges between theory and practice because it emphasizes knowledgeable human agency and focuses on social practices. The concept of *structuration*—the processes by which structures, social systems, and institutions are produced and reproduced over time via the routinized and recursive social practices of human agents—offers a way of understanding how people are at the same time creators of society and yet created by it. Moreover, structuration theory provides an understanding of praxis that goes beyond epistemological concerns and links people with the social system.

Although structuration theory is an ongoing project with many aspects, only those ideas that are foundational to the theory or pertinent to this discussion are addressed here. The same applies to the discussion of PAR.

METATHEORETICAL FRAMEWORK FOR DIVERGENT SCHOOLS OF THOUGHT

Divergence

PAR is often defined as a process that unites inquiry, education, and social action, with roots in the pragmatic philosophy of Dewey and the action research of Lewin. It is an inquiry and educational process in which both facilitators and collaborators, usually referred to as participatory researchers, participate in order to learn about each other as well as about local social conditions. It is also an action process in which both facilitators and collaborators learn about and work toward improving social conditions. The process is based on the assumption that the way lay people see their lives and formulate their own interests is of central importance to inquiry and action and that collective inquiry produces new knowledge for participants.

However, this generalized definition of PAR is somewhat misleading because it glosses over the fact that PAR contains two very different schools of thought. The divergence of PAR into these schools of thought can be accounted for by the different economic, social, and political contexts in which PAR developed, and also by theories and developments that appeared relevant to those contexts. As a result, the assumptions about inquiry and social change in each of these schools of thought have become radically different. Both refer to themselves as PAR, and they are referred to here as *First World* and *Third World PAR* schools of thought because of their contextual origins. Although many PAR projects do not precisely conform to either of these schools of thought, they are nonetheless presented here as ideal types for analytical purposes. A brief examination of some of the ideas about inquiry, theory and practice, participation, and communication in each school of thought prepares the ground for the application of structuration theory.

First World PAR

Although First World PAR emerged in North America, it is currently in evidence throughout the world in both developed and developing contexts. First World PAR, according to Whyte (1991), derived its impetus from three developments. First, there was a shift in thinking that a participatory and hands-on approach to applied research was, in many cases, more powerful than the applied social research model in which a professional expert simply reported findings to the decision makers. Second, there was a shift in thinking that recognized the value of participation of workers in decision making, first in industry and later in agriculture. These first two developments echo the practical concerns of action research. Third, the development of sociotechnical systems thinking provided a site for exploring the relation between social and technical processes in a participative context. This third and more recent development has led to the incorporation of systems theory into First World PAR.

Influenced by these developments, First World PAR has become what Mayer (1990) referred to as

> a collective undertaking that integrates both a research strategy and an action strategy; it is accomplished by . . . researchers [facilitators] and actors [collaborators] in a cooperative relation; it is centered on a concrete problematic situation, inserted into real social relations and tied to an action for social change; it aims to increase knowledge about conditions and results of the action experimented with in order to pinpoint advantages that can be generalized; it requires the intellectual and emotional commitment of each participant, an openness to criticism and reevaluation, and the ability to evolve one's conceptions, one's practice, and one's interpersonal relationships as the project develops. (p. 208)

Inquiry in this school of thought is informed by an implicit utilitarian ideology (Vandenberg & Fear, 1983). This school of thought is most common in fields of agriculture, organizational development and community development, and seeks to improve rational and intelligent decision making through the intervention of the PAR facilitator. There are two important aims of inquiry. The first aim is instrumental and focuses on bringing about social change for the benefit of the collaborators who are involved in implementing the change or who will be affected by the change. The second aim is theoretical and involves the interface between theory and practice; more particularly, theory building for the benefit of the PAR practitioner or facilitator (Vandenberg & Fear, 1983). The ultimate goal is to produce objective knowledge that can be effectively used in applied and policy contexts to stimulate the participation of communities of people in studying, analyzing, and devising solutions to their problems. There is considerable emphasis on people's rational capabilities to deal intelligently with complex problems and to bring about change by manipulating social events and reforming social structures. However, the transformation of conditions is always accomplished within the existing social order and questions of domination, unequal power relations, and conflict are noticeably absent in the literature (Vandenberg & Fear, 1983).

This PAR school of thought emphasizes a strong relation between theory and practice and the value of PAR for testing existing theoretical hypotheses, formulating new hypotheses, developing local theory, and generating grounded theory. Whyte (1991) explained: "As I see it, PAR focuses more heavily on social structures and processes. Without rejecting the value of preformed hypotheses, PAR is likely to depend more on what I call 'creative surprises'—new ideas that arise unexpectedly during the intervention process" (p. 97).

Going even further, Whyte et al. (1991) suggested that PAR, as a method, is also helpful for theoretical development in the social sciences since it

has important qualities as a method for examining the plausibility of theories. . . . It is also productive in formulating new hypotheses about key relationships, hypotheses testable by either further . . . research or through conventional research methodologies. It is not, therefore, an alternative to existing social science but a way of dramatically enhancing our achievement of the goals of theoretical understanding and social betterment by widening the range of strategies at our disposal. Active involvement with practitioners struggling to solve important practical problems is highly likely to open up researchers' minds to new information and new ideas, leading to advances in theory as well as in practice. (p. 54)

Furthermore, Elden and Levin (1991) viewed the PAR process as important for the development of local theory that they defined as "the most direct, simple, and elegant context-bound explanation of cause-and-effect relations in a given situation that makes sense to those with the most local experience. It could be described as a causally focused, group cognitive map . . ." (p. 138). In addition, PAR provides a site for the development of grounded theory, or generating new knowledge based on data obtained through practice. For example, Whyte (1991) developed a new theory of worker participation when it became apparent that there was a contradiction between his observations on participation in a Xerox plant and existing theories of worker participation. It appears that in First World PAR, there is a considerable interest in improving theory and practice, in the development of grounded theory and an openness to a closer and mutually beneficial relation with the social science community.

It becomes clear, then, that this PAR school of thought is primarily interested in inquiry concerning issues related to causality and in contributing to both the theory and practice of PAR. It also favors an instrumental approach, with the assumption that social theory is powerful for predicting or producing a desired event or preventing its occurrence. Although it runs the risk of being manipulative or authoritarian, Vandenberg and Fear (1983) argued that this trap is avoided through a strong emphasis on participation. However, it should be noted that the facilitator is often in control of the process and the extent of participation by collaborators varies considerably (Beausoleil, 1990).

Joint participation between facilitators and collaborators raises issues around scientific rigor and objectivity, and issues concerning the practical implications of inquiry. It involves considerable risk for those who participate, as indicated by Beausoleil's (1990) description of several projects undertaken by the Participatory Research Group on Support Networks and Institutional Practices in Montreal:

> The university team [facilitators] risked not being in a position to contribute to the development of new fundamental knowledge about community care, not receiving the recognition of the scientific community which values quantitative research copied from the natural science model, not satisfying their university's evaluative criteria, and finally, risked having trouble raising funding. Practitioners [collaborators] risked having trouble surmounting the dichotomy that separates academics from field workers. They feared being accused of lacking thoroughness and objectivity by the scientific as well as the professional community, worried that planning organizations might consider a collective undertaking threatening and finally, risked seeing their results taken up by government organizations who would use them to impose rigid evaluative norms. (p. 162)

This suggests that the traditional notion of objectivity and rigor is held up as a standard, even though it does not apply to PAR. Rather, the definition of rigor for this PAR school of thought is intertwined with the notion of participation that is similar to that of interpretivist sociology. Whyte et al. (1991) elaborated on the interrelationship when they stated:

> According to conventional wisdom, no other research strategy can match the standard model for rigor. Whether this is true depends upon how we define rigor. In the standard model, the subjects of our studies have little or no opportunity to check facts or to offer alternative explanations. If we feed back our research reports and publications to members of the organization we studied, they often argue that we have made serious errors in facts and in interpretations. If the standard social science researcher hears such criticisms, he or she can shrug them off, telling colleagues that the subjects are just being defensive—defensiveness apparently being a characteristic of the subjects but not of social scientists themselves. PAR forces researchers to go through a rigorous process of checking the facts with those with firsthand knowledge before any reports are written. (p. 41)

Elden and Levin (1991) proposed a model, referred to as *cogenerative dialogue*, that places these issues in a framework emphasizing the value of participation and the confluence of two types of knowledge and expertise. Although they recognize the differences between expert and processed knowledge, they postulate that equal and full participation between collaborators and facilitators creates new understanding and new interpretive frameworks. As they stated:

> Insiders [collaborators] . . . are expert in the specifics of the setting or situation and know from personal experience how things work and how the elements are connected to each other and about values and attitudes, local company culture, and so on. . . . They want to solve practical problems and achieve personal and organizational goals. The initial framework of what will become local theory comes from how individual organization members make sense out of their situation. They are experts in the particular situation but their theories are not systematically tested.

> Outsiders [facilitators] . . . have what's missing: training in systematic inquiry and analysis, in designing and carrying out research, and in recognizing patterns and creating new knowledge irrespective of content. . . . The researcher's initial framework of what will become local theory is based on general theory or a particular way of thinking about the problem at hand.

> The insider comes to the inquiry because of a personal interest in a specific practical problem. The outsider, in contrast, comes because of an interest in solving particular kinds of problems (in theory and/or practice), methods, general knowledge, or values. (Elden & Levin, 1991, p. 132)

Through the interaction of these two frameworks, or the process of cogenerative dialogue, empowering participation occurs between the insiders and outsiders. According to Elden and Levin, "Both insiders and outsiders operate out of their initial frames of reference but communicate at a level where frames can be changed and new frames generated. Exchange on a level that affects one's frame of reference is a much more demanding form of communication than mere information exchange" (p. 34).

It appears that although Elden and Levin are still interested in the formulation of causal explanations, they explicitly address and introduce the idea of the social construction of meaning systems and the development of shared meaning systems to this PAR school of thought. Of interest here is how they interrelate the concepts of participative inquiry, equal participation, and the development of new frames of meaning, a decidedly *communications* issue.

Another communications issue, critical reflection through discussion, was addressed by Beausoleil (1990). He provided an interesting account of this dynamic process that occurred among the academics who facilitated a community care PAR project, and the health and social services administrators and representatives of community organizations who collaborated in the project.

> Discussions were rational but also emotional, reflecting the values and convictions of individuals. From meeting to meeting, the group approached the global situation via different themes, passed from one aspect to another in a spiraling motion and ended by unearthing a statement that explained and integrated a series of ideas, events, lived experiences, failures and successes. The analysis thus turned on itself. Spiral upon spiral, intersecting and merging in a continuous process, helped us arrive at a more coherent definition and explanation of the phenomena discussed, incorporating both the nature of events and the convictions and commitments of individuals and groups. (Beausoleil, 1990, p. 181)

This description suggests that although First World PAR emphasizes the rational elements of decision making, there is a recognition that critical reflection also involves open communication about convictions, values, and commitments and not merely the exchange of information. As a result, First World PAR is both goal- and value-committed.

In summary, First World PAR focuses inquiry primarily on *causal relations* related to social change, and combines an interest in social betterment with a practical and scholarly interest in learning about and implementing action. Furthermore, PAR is sensitive to *meaning frameworks*, also a concern of interpretivist sociologies. However, it is apparent that issues of unequal power relations within a broader sociohistorical framework are usually ignored by First World PAR. Such is not the case for Third World PAR.

Third World PAR

Although Third World PAR emerged in Latin and South America, it is also currently in evidence throughout the world primarily in developing but also in developed countries. Even though Third World PAR addresses issues of unequal power relations, it was initially influenced by action research. Fals-Borda (1991) explained that Third World PAR deviated from action research when the latter became preoccupied with small-group processes in industrial and organizational contexts and attempted to reinforce and perfect the status quo, and when the former became more militant in contexts of oppression and more concerned with broader issues of participation.

Third World PAR developed as a reaction to the failure of paternalistic Third World development methods for improving social and economic conditions and in response to new alternatives that promised the oppressed classes economic and political emancipation and the development of self-reliance (Latapi, 1988). More specifically, it developed as a reaction to the failure of conventional approaches to adult education, modernization and development, and the failure of sociology to transform society (Fals-Borda, 1979). On the other hand, it was influenced by Paulo Freire's conceptual approach to adult education; Catholicism's liberation theology; the rise of dependency theory; a revitalization of the neo-Marxian view of Gramsci; and the emergence of cultural revolutions (Latapi, 1988). These developments contributed to the emergence of a utopian liberation ideal that emphasized the participation of the oppressed in changing their conditions.

Third World PAR developed through several stages. According to Rahman (1991), it now combines a micro- and a macro-level focus: "At the micro level, PAR is a philosophy and style of work with the people to promote people's empowerment for changing their immediate environment—social and physical—in their favor" (p. 16). Rahman added: "However, in terms of macro-social transformation, PAR at this stage may be viewed more as a cultural movement, independent of (in some countries in link with) political movements for people's liberation rather than a political alternative itself" (p. 19).

It is apparent that *inquiry* in this school of thought, unlike First World PAR, is informed by an explicit emancipatory ideology designed to challenge status quo power relations. Inquiry is viewed as a political act through which the power inherent in knowledge is wrested away from the privileged and returned to the oppressed. This school's primary aim is to generate social change for the benefit of the oppressed and under-privileged, who are also the instigators of change, and is most common in Third World development work (Latapi, 1988). Unlike in First World PAR, the transformation of social conditions is often achieved by con-fronting the existing social order and either transforming the social sys-tem or replacing existing social structures. The aims of this school of thought are often framed in the context of a liberation or Marxian ideolo-gy (Himmelstrand, 1982). However, there appears to be some confusion over the extent to which supporters of Third World PAR are committed to a Marxist stance because according to Latapi, some authors may use Marxian terminology without necessarily committing themselves to Marxian philosophy. Rahman (1985) noted that historical materialism has "passed through many hands" and there no longer seems to be a broad consensus as to its operational meaning (p. 118).

This school's conception of what is meant by *theory and practice* differs sharply not only from that of traditional social science but also from First World PAR. Because the science of the people, rather than that of the scientific community, is paramount, theory consists of what the local people think and perceive and practice consists of how they act on this knowledge. According to Fals-Borda (1979):

> Within the context of regional field work, what was considered "theory" meant preconceived or preliminary ideas or exogenous information, related to "things-in-themselves," processes, events or trends observed in reality . . . "practice" meant the application of principles or information gained through observation, application carried out primarily, by orga-nized, basic groups as actors and controllers of the process. (p. 41)

Moreover, this union of theory and practice constitutes what is meant by praxis in this PAR school of thought. Praxis is political action designed to generate knowledge and change the structure of society and Fals-Borda contrasts this with the positivist notion of praxis that he interpreted as knowledge to manipulate and control social processes.

In Third World PAR, *participation* is viewed as the key to increasing the knowledge, solidarity, and self-reliance of the oppressed through the collaborative PAR process. In this collaborative context, the PAR facilitator must closely identify with the social justice aims of the oppressed people who are collaborators. As Fernandes and Tandon (1981) explained:

The foremost implication for participatory social research is its clear attempt at power equalization, by eliminating the distinction between the researcher and the people. This power equalization assumes that research becomes an action-reflection-action process of interaction between the outsider who functions no more as a scholar but as a catalyst, and the local people. (p. 11)

However, Latapi (1988) noted that an equal power relationship between the facilitator and collaborators is often difficult to achieve because

The professional researcher [facilitator] maintains a directive role that cannot be denied. The researchers have an overall understanding of the research process, they are more familiar with abstract thinking, and they are expected to assist the group [collaborators] and to provide the necessary tools. All this supports the existence of a certain superiority and entails the risk of paternalism and manipulation. (p. 317)

It is of interest that although the risks of joint participation between facilitators and collaborators in First World PAR are more connected to issues of scientific rigor and practical implications, in Third World PAR they are more connected to issues of manipulation and domination. Despite these difficulties, both schools of thought view participation as critical to building knowledge.

Although participation is the key to increasing the knowledge, solidarity, and self-reliance of the oppressed, *communication* is the key process through which the coordination and exchange of information or "knowledge empowerment" take place. As in action research and First World PAR, the action-reflection spiral in this school of thought is critical to the PAR process. According to Latapi (1988), this involves research, or the gradual discovery of new knowledge; action, as the component that spirals between practice and reflection; and education because through this process, the collaborators not only gain a better understanding of the social facts, but also improve their capacity for further reflection and analysis. Furthermore, he suggested that this process can only develop in the context of dialogue. In addition, de Roux (1991) provided an account of how this process worked in a Third World PAR project. His account echoed Elden and Levin's (1991) discussion of cogenerative dialogue:

Collectively producing knowledge meant that many actors, coming from their own individuality, at different times and in different situations, and based on their own perceptions and ways of communicating them, contributed a variety of experiences to what became a common vision of the situation. These meetings, wherein everyone was given the floor, were a context for bringing forth their everyday experience, their significant images and common sense, all of which yielded a collective reading of reality, not from the confines of academic disciplines but from a holistic perspective. The possibility of forging new common ground—based on the people's analytical categories, their own interpretations, their cultural prism, their collective outlook and their traditions—made it possible for the people's subjugated wisdom to rise up while empowering them to transcend it to forge a liberating vision capable of stirring emotions and translating shared concerns into actions. (de Roux, 1991, pp. 45–46)

Although de Roux was primarily interested in unequal knowledge and power relations, he explicitly addressed the idea of the social construction of meaning systems and the development of a shared meaning system. It is of interest that, like Elden and Levin, de Roux also interrelated the concepts of participative inquiry, equal participation, and the development of new frames of meaning. For de Roux, this type of dialogue constitutes the beginning of a process that ultimately leads to the people gaining control over decision-making power.

It is apparent that Third World PAR focuses inquiry primarily on issues of *unequal power relations* and social transformation that are also concerns of critical analysis. However, there is also evidence of a concern with *meaning frameworks* in this school of thought, which is also a concern of interpretivist sociologies. Although issues of causality are addressed in this school of thought, a sociohistorical framework is usually imposed on them.

Critique in Structuration Theory

Because structuration theory critiques schools of thought that emphasize causal relations, meaning frameworks and unequal power relations, it may be helpful for theoretical development in PAR. The basic tenets of structuration theory constitute a rejection of the assumptions of the orthodox consensus of social science, that is, the notion of positivism that the social sciences should be modeled after the natural sciences; the idea that the role of the social sciences is to explicate elements of social causation of which actors are unaware; and the functionalist view that social systems can be studied like biological systems (Giddens, 1989). Instead, Giddens offered a selective synthesis of concepts drawn from a diversity of disciplines. The theory is rooted in the phenomenology of Schutz, the ethnomethodology of Goffman, the conversational analysis of Sacks, and the understanding of structure in structuralism. It also includes reformulations of the time geography of Hagerstrand, the psychoanalytic theory of Freud, the functionalist conception of consequences by Merton, and the historical materialism of Marx. However, structuration theory avoids the deterministic tendencies of structuralism and functionalism and the voluntaristic leanings of interpretive sociologies by focusing on how knowledgeable human agents, through repetitive social practices, produce and reproduce the social conditions that affect them.

Reframing Causal Relations

Giddens' critique of functionalism provides a way of reframing the understanding of causal relations. Giddens (1984) had no quarrel with the functionalist emphasis on analyzing the unintended consequences of institutionalized practices or individual activities and stated that "the work of functionalist authors has been very important in social research precisely because it has directed attention to the disparities between what actors intended to do and the consequences which ensue from what they do" (p. 296). However, he maintained that functionalists have not accorded enough importance to intentional or purposive action and often see causality in a deterministic manner. Alternatively, Giddens suggested that inquiry should explain how the social activities that are carried on in an intentional way by people, create unintended consequences for people and society. These consequences then course back into society to create the conditions that form the basis for subsequent social activities. This focus on the creation and recreation of society through the social practices of people lessens the force of the functionalist argument that powerful social forces, operating like the laws of nature, determine the activities of people and the nature of society.

Giddens' notion of intended and unintended consequences is of value for PAR because it grounds the discussion of causal relations in a framework that emphasizes the ability of people to create and recreate society, although in often unpredictable ways. By focusing inquiry on the intended and unintended consequences of human action implicated in the creation and recreation of society, participatory researchers gain the ability to not only describe but also to explain complex causal relations in a way that is not deterministic because human agency is at the core of action. This is important for both PAR schools of thought because it emphasizes that social change cannot be predicted or controlled because both intended and unintended (or unpredictable) consequences of knowledgeable human agency generate social change.

Reframing Meaning Frameworks

Giddens' critique of interpretivist sociology provides a way of reframing its descriptive, subjectivistic, and relativistic emphases. Giddens relied heavily on Schutz's understanding of social actors' stocks of knowledge, knowledge that is practical and is inherent in the capability of people to go on with the routines of social life. However, he criticized the interpretivist sociologies for regarding "society as the plastic creation of human subjects" (Giddens, 1984, p. 26). As he stated, for interpretivist sociologies:

> Subjectivity is the preconstituted center of the experience of culture and history and as such provides the basic foundation of the social or human sciences. Outside the realm of subjective experience, and alien to it, lies the material world, governed by impersonal relations of cause and effect. . . . In interpretive sociologies, action and meaning are accorded primacy in the explication of human conduct; structural concepts are not notably prominent, and there is not much talk of constraint. (p. 2)

What is lacking, according to Giddens, is the understanding that human interaction is linked to the implicit knowledge of rules or abstract structures that make it possible for people to go on in life. These social rules are procedures that people apply in the creation and recreation of social practices. They are not the same as formally expressed rules and operate more like the deep and implicit rules that govern language production and reproduction.

Giddens then linked the implicit rules that guide human interaction with social accountability and with the interpretive schemes that make communication possible between people. According to Giddens, "'Interpretive schemes' are the modes of typification incorporated within actors' stocks of knowledge, applied reflexively in the sustaining of communication. These stocks of knowledge which actors draw upon in the production and reproduction of interaction are the same as those whereby they are able to make accounts, offer reasons, etc." (p. 29). Giddens also added:

> To be a human being is to be a purposive agent, who both has reasons for his or her activities and is able, if asked, to elaborate discursively upon those reasons. . . .[However] purposive action is not composed of an aggregate or series of separate intentions, reasons and motives. Thus it is useful to speak of reflexivity as grounded in the continuous monitoring of action which human beings display and expect others to display. (p. 3)

By linking interpretive schemes with implicit structural rules on the one hand and social practices on the other, Giddens provided a corrective to the subjectivism of the interpretivist sociologies. This is of value to both PAR schools of thought because it anchors the concept of meaning frameworks in structure.

Reframing Power Relations

Giddens' critique of critical science provides a way of reframing the understanding of power and conflict relations. Acknowledging the contributions of Marx in bringing the notion of power into sociological discourse, Giddens (1984) stated:

> Anyone who reflects upon the phrase 'human beings make history,' particularly within the broader scope of Marx's writings, is inevitably led to consider questions of conflict and power. For in Marx's view, the making of history is done not just in relation to the natural world but also through the struggles which some human beings wage against others in circumstances of domination. (p. 256)

However, he maintained that although power is sometimes linked with oppression, class struggle, and conflict in the sense of active struggle, it is a mistake to treat power as inherently divisive. Rather, power struggles should be seen as efforts by some groups of actors to influence the circumstances or actions of others. Although the historical materialist view may be attractive to those who struggle for emancipation of the oppressed, it should be avoided because "the interests of the oppressed are not cut of whole cloth and frequently clash, while beneficial social changes often demand the use of differential power held only by the privileged" (Giddens, 1990, p. 155).

Alternatively, Giddens (1984) suggested that power should be reframed as "the capacity to achieve outcomes; whether or not these are connected to purely sectional interests is not germane to its definition. Power is not, as such, an obstacle to freedom or emancipation but is their very medium—although it would be foolish, of course, to ignore its constraining properties" (p. 257).

It is important to note that power is not in itself a resource; rather power is used by human agents to draw on other resources. In addition, the constraining properties of power are contextually derived and involve those things that place boundaries around the range of options open to people in a particular set of circumstances. One important constraint is how power is used to draw on resources, either those involving material goods or authority, rather than the fact that it is used. This type of constraint is often expressed as sanctions of various kinds that may range from the direct application of force or violence, or the threat of such application, to the mild expression of disapproval. Giddens emphasized that constraints should always be considered alongside enablements because these operate in tandem and one person's constraint is often another person's enablement. In this way, Giddens reconceptualized the dualism of power.

In a similar vein, Giddens (1984) suggested that power in social systems "presumes regularized relations of autonomy and dependence between actors and collectivities in contexts of social interaction" and referred to this concept as the dialectic of control (p. 16). The implication is that even forms of dependence that appear to exhibit a lack of power offer some resources whereby those who are subordinate can influence and even control the activities of those who are superordinate.

Giddens' notion of power is helpful for PAR because it emphasizes the capacity for action in the context of both constraints and enablements and autonomy and dependence. This is particularly important for Third World PAR because it has implications for the analysis of power relations in PAR contexts.

ANALYTICAL FRAMEWORK FOR THEORY AND PRACTICE

Social Conditions

Although First World PAR is keenly interested in developing links between theory and practice, the same cannot be said of Third World PAR. In fact, the research generated by the latter often does not go beyond the documentation of social conditions and rarely do facilitators record and analyze the types of action involved (Cassara, 1987; Latapi, 1988). Latapi, a supporter of Third World PAR, noted that many of its supporters fail to adequately define their concept of science and this gives the impression that any type of knowledge is scientific. Furthermore, he questioned whether the inquiry done by this school of thought can be called science because:

> The process of scientific knowledge requires synthesis, systematization, and accumulation. It is a difficulty, to say the least, that PAR carried out by local groups on isolated concrete topics may reach the levels of integration and synthesis required so as to supplant the knowledge obtained by established social research. In other words, PAR may be suitable for reaching conclusions on local situations, but such conclusions require a further treatment in order to obtain broader validity. (Latapi, 1988, p. 317)

Although it is not necessary or even desirable for all participatory researchers to engage in theoretical work, it appears there is room for the development of an analytical framework that can guide theory and practice in both PAR schools of thought.

Knowledgeable Human Agency

Structuration theory offers PAR a rich theoretical understanding of knowledgeable human agency. The concept of knowledgeable human agency is central to structuration theory and it stands in opposition to that of the orthodox consensus of social science, which, according to Giddens treats human agents as though behavior is derived directly from social forces of which they are unaware. Although this is not completely wrong, it is a false notion of human agency (Giddens, 1989). According to Giddens, all people are knowledgeable agents even though they may not be able to discursively provide reasons or accounts that satisfy social scientists or tell everything they know. He stated that: "Human agents . . . have as an inherent aspect of what they do, the capacity to understand what they do while they do it. The reflexive capacities of the human actor are characteristically involved in a continuous manner within the flow of day-to-day conduct in the contexts of social activity" (Giddens, 1984, p. xxii). In other words, the knowledge human agents have about the conditions of their activity is not merely contingent upon what they do, but constitutive of it.

Knowledgeability is evidenced by the fact that human agents have a complex understanding of what it takes to go on with their lives. It involves two types of consciousness; practical and discursive. The understanding of what it takes to go on with life is rooted in the practical consciousness of human agents. This is the core of knowledgeability and it consists of implicit knowledge of conventions or structures that guide human interaction. These conventions are techniques or generalizable procedures that human agents apply in the enactment of and the reproduction of social practices (Giddens, 1984, p. 21). Only some of the conventions inherent in practical consciousness can be expressed discursively. When human agents explicitly state the conventions, it is usually in response to others who question or want to know the reasons for their actions. The line between practical and discursive consciousness is permeable and fluctuating and the researcher should be aware that what lay people say only forms a small part of what they know. A misunderstanding of the relation between these two types of consciousness may be why deterministic and functionalist approaches have not accorded human agents the knowledgeability they deserve. Both practical and discursive consciousness allow human agents to reflexively monitor interaction and make choices for future action. The reflexive monitoring of action depends on rationalization, which is a process rather than a state, and it is the form of knowledgeability most deeply involved in the recursiveness of social practices.

Although knowledgeability is richly complex and deep, it has limitations. One of the boundaries of knowledgeability is the unconscious, which is separated from other forms of consciousness by a barrier. Motivation is located in the unconscious and it should be noted that motives are not the same as reasons. Reasons provide the grounds or rationalization for action, whereas motives refer to wants that have the potential for action and that provide the overall plans for actions (Giddens, 1984). According to Giddens, the primary motivation of people engaged in social activity is the desire for ontological security or trust. Trust in turn is based on the security that comes with regularized responses.

Yet another boundary of knowledgeability is the conditions of which people are not aware. The factors that influence these conditions, according to Giddens, include the means by which individuals, in the context of their social location, access knowledge; the modes in which knowledge is claimed or articulated; circumstances relating to whether belief claims are valid or not; and factors to do with the means of disseminating available knowledge (Giddens, 1984).

This leads to the final boundary of knowledgeability; the unintended consequences of action. Although day-to-day life occurs as a flow of intentional action, discrete acts have unintended consequences that feed back into the unacknowledged conditions of further acts (Giddens, 1984). Unintended consequences are important because they occur in a regular way and are involved in the reproduction of society. However, unintended consequences can only be examined from the perspective of intentional action.

The intent to act is not the same as agency, which refers to the ability and capacity of people to do things in the first place (Giddens, 1984). Furthermore, action is a process that occurs in a continuous flow and "depends upon the capability of the individual to 'make a difference' to a pre-existing state of affairs or course of events" (p. 14). Power is central to the capability of agents to make a difference and to bring about intended consequences of action. In other words, action is contingent on power, and human agency presumes the ability to deploy a range of causal power.

Giddens (1984) specified three forms of constraint (and enablements) on human agency. The first has to do with aspects of the body and relevant features of the physical environment. The second constraint has already been referred to and concerns the constraining aspects of power. The third involves structural constraint that derives from the contextuality of action. However, structural constraint is not imposed on human agents. According to Giddens (1984):

> Structural constraint is not expressed in terms of the implacable causal forces which structural sociologists have in mind when they emphasize so strongly the association of "structure" with "constraint." Structural constraints do not operate independently of the motives and reasons that agents have for what they do. . . . The structural properties of social systems do not act, or "act on," anyone like forces of nature to "compel" him or her to behave in any particular way. The only moving objects in human social relations are individual agents who employ resources to make things happen, intentionally or otherwise. (p. 181)

The concept of knowledgeable human agency offers some possibilities for the interaction between theory and practice in PAR. For example, an examination of the boundaries of knowledgeability is helpful not only for theoretical development but also in the field. As Giddens (1984) stated, "Studying practical consciousness means investigating what agents already know, but by definition it is normally illuminating to them if this is expressed discursively, in the metalanguage of social science . . ." (p. 328). As well, the manner in which social conditions result from spatial or vertical segregation, the way belief claims are articulated and the way information is disseminated may also be of interest for those engaged in theory and practice. Furthermore, there may be some merit in studying how intentional actions have created the unintended consequences that are now part of a particular social condition.

By balancing constraint with enablement, structuration theory can help both practitioners and theorists avoid the trap of dualistic thinking (i.e., that the social system, as an impersonal object, imposes constraint on human agents on the one hand, or that human agents have unlimited capabilities to change the social system on the other). Because constraints and enablements are contextually situated in settings of interaction and are the result of what human agents do, an examination of them is particularly useful for theoretical and practical developments in PAR.

Social Practices

Although structuration theory is helpful for understanding human agency, it is also helpful for analyzing agency in a larger social framework. Giddens explained that the focus on social practices is the primary concern of structuration theory: "The basic domain of study of the social sciences, according to the theory of structuration, is neither the experience of the individual actor, nor the existence of any form of societal totality, but social practices ordered across space and time" (p. 2).

The continuity of social practices, according to Giddens, is made possible by the reflexivity of knowledgeable human agents. Reflexivity is a continuous process rather than a state and involves the monitoring of action in the ongoing flow of social life. According to Giddens:

> The reflexive monitoring of activity is a chronic feature of everyday action and involves the conduct not just of the individual but also of others. That is to say, actors not only monitor continuously the flow of their activities and expect others to do the same for their own; they also routinely monitor aspects, social and physical, of the contexts in which they move. (p. 5)

At the same time, the existence of regularized social practices is made possible by the abstract structures or generalizable rules on which human agents routinely draw to go on with their lives. What ensue from these social practices are not only intentional consequences of action but also unintentional by-products. Both types of consequences then feed back into the ongoing flow of social life and directly or indirectly further influence the conditions of action in the original context. Therefore, a focus on social practices dissolves the macro/micro dualism of other theoretical approaches because it is the recursive social practices of people that constitute the link between abstract structures and social conditions.

The analysis of social practices is valuable for PAR since it goes beyond a description of the local context and incorporates a broader understanding of how social conditions are produced and reproduced. This provides the basis for analysis along both historical lines and across spatial contexts. Perhaps most importantly, the concept of social practices provides the theory and practice of PAR with a powerful lens to analyze many concerns in PAR, including causal relations, meaning systems, power relations, participation, communication and inquiry.

LEGITIMATION FOR INVOLVEMENT IN SOCIAL ACTION

Academic Marginalization

It is primarily around the issue of praxis that PAR has been marginalized in social science circles. There are several possible explanations. One reason is generated from within PAR and concerns what Latapi (1988) referred to as a strong anti-intellectual component and lack of scholarly work in Third World PAR. Many supporters of this school of thought believe that knowledge leads to power and that only people's knowledge or the knowledge produced by the oppressed classes is valid. Therefore, the legitimation of academic knowledge only serves to perpetuate the domination of intellectuals and suppress the people's knowledge. However, Gaventa (1991), a supporter of this school of thought, suggested that isolation from other knowledge production systems may be counterproductive:

> To the extent that it relies upon the peoples' experience as the basis of knowledge, how does it develop knowledge within the people that may be in their interest to know but is outside of their experience? . . . Are there not circumstances, even for the oppressed, in which there is a need for a science which is democratic, but which does not require all of the people to become scientists in order to control and benefit from it? Is direct participation in all aspects of the knowledge production system the only form of its popular control? (p. 129)

Another explanation for academic marginalization is that social scientists have tended to look askance at both PAR schools of thought, but for different reasons. For example, the instrumental agenda and applied nature of First World PAR may be why social scientists have regarded PAR as primarily policy research. By the same token, the emancipatory emphasis of Third World PAR, may be why it is sometimes seen as primarily political activity.

Structuration theory addresses these concerns indirectly through the concepts of the double hermeneutic and the dialogical model. These concepts concern the interaction between the social science community and the lay community and address issues of inquiry, participation, and communication.

Double Hermeneutic

The concept of the double hermeneutic is central to understanding the relation between inquiry in the social science community and inquiry in the lay community. Giddens (1984) argued that *all* social actors, whether they are scholars or lay people, are social theorists or inquirers. Although social scientists are more concerned with developing theoretical knowledge about social phenomena, lay people are more concerned with applying practical knowledge in their daily social activities.

Lay knowledge and social science knowledge come together in a process that Giddens refers to as the *double hermeneutic*. Lay knowledge consists of what people consider socially meaningful. Social science or processed knowledge consists of the metalanguages invented by the social sciences. The intersection of these two types of knowledge and frames of meaning is a logically necessary part of the social sciences. According to Giddens (1987), the development of processed knowledge depends on experiential knowledge.

> The social sciences operate within a double hermeneutic, involving two-way ties with the actions and institutions of those they study. Sociological observers depend upon lay concepts to generate accurate descriptions of social processes; and agents regularly appropriate theories and concepts of social science within their behavior, thus potentially changing its character. (pp. 30–31)

Giddens (1984) also added, "The theorizing of human beings about their action means that just as social theory was not an invention of professional social theorists, so the ideas produced by those theorists inevitably tend to be fed back into social life" (p. 27).

There is also constant slippage between these two types of knowledge and, according to Giddens (1984), no absolute dividing line between them.

> The concepts that sociological observers invent are "second-order" concepts in so far as they presume certain conceptual capabilities on the part of the actors to whose conduct they refer. But it is the nature of social science that these can become "first-order" concepts by being appropriated within social life itself. What is "hermeneutic" about the double hermeneutic? The appropriateness of the term derives from the double process of translation or interpretation which is involved. Sociological descriptions have the task of mediating the frames of meaning within which the actors orient their conduct. But such descriptions are interpretive categories which also demand an effort of translation in and out of the frames of meaning involved in sociological theories. (p. 284)

The practical side of the double hermeneutic is reflected in organizations and social movements, "the two ways in which reflexive appropriation of knowledge about the social world is mobilized . . ." (Giddens, 1987, p. 48). The double hermeneutic then, has implications for communication and participation as well as for inquiry.

It appears that processed social science knowledge and experiential lay knowledge are interdependent, interactive, mutually influential, and natural. Because PAR takes the double hermeneutic to its logical and practical conclusion, its marginalization in academic circles appears indefensible. From this perspective, the joint participation of researchers and lay people in the inquiry, education, and social action process of PAR is simply an instantiation of the interaction between processed and experiential knowledge in society.

Dialogical Model

The interactive application of the double hermeneutic also finds practical expression through what Giddens called the dialogical model, which is based on three suppositions:

> First, social research cannot just be "applied" to an independently given subject matter, but has to be linked to the potentiality of persuading actors to expand or modify the forms of knowledge of belief they draw upon in organizing their contexts of action. . . . Second, . . . "the mediation of cultural settings," coupled with conceptual innovation, are at least as significant for the practical outcomes of social research as is the establishing of generalizations. . . . Third, the practical implications of the double-hermeneutic should be underscored. The most far-reaching practical consequences of social science do not involve the creation of sets of generalizations that can be used to generate instrumental control over the social world. They concern instead the constant absorption of concepts and theories into that "subject-matter" they seek to analyze, constituting and reconstituting what the "subject-matter" is. (Giddens, 1987, pp. 47–48)

The implication here is that when knowledge about cultural settings or social conditions is communicated via social research to policymakers, and when it is linked to innovation, there is the possibility of changing things for the better. However, even in the absence of direct intervention, "theories and findings in social sciences are likely to have practical (and political) consequences regardless of whether or not the sociological observer or policy-maker decides that they can be 'applied' to a given practical issue" (Giddens, 1984, p. xxxv).

It is not surprising then, that Giddens rejected the notion that systematic social research can directly bring about a more desirable social order when it is used in an instrumental fashion geared toward restricted policy objectives. Rather,

> [The dialogical model] tends to reverse the traditional view that specified policy objectives should determine the character of research carried out. Primacy instead tends to be given to the process of research over the formulation of policy objectives, which this influences as much as the other way around. In a rapidly changing world, continuing processes of social research help indicate where the most urgent practical questions cluster, at the same time as they offer frameworks for seeking to cope with them. (Giddens, 1987, pp. 46–47)

Although there is a clear role for the researcher to influence policy, it cannot be envisioned, according to Giddens, as instrumental to achieving predetermined objectives but rather as mediating differing frames of reference. In fact, Giddens described the social scientist as a communicator who introduces frames of meaning associated with certain contexts of social life to people in other contexts. This "mediation of cultural settings" coupled with conceptual innovation has significant practical implications although the outcomes can never be predicted (Giddens, 1987).

The dialogical model indicates how inquiry into meaning frameworks can help PAR move beyond the description of social conditions and offer explanations regarding divergent and often unintelligible frames of meaning. Questions about divergent frames of meaning can be explored across the varying contexts of individual societies as well as between. In other words, explanations of the interpretive frameworks of particular groups of people, to others outside those groups, carry the possibility of creating greater understanding. This is important for PAR because the mediation of frames of meaning between different groups of people is one of the ways that social change is generated. Furthermore, by focusing inquiry on the explanation of the interpretive frameworks of some groups of people to others, PAR is firmly rooted in the communications mandate of the social sciences.

CONCLUSION

Limitations

Applying structuration theory to PAR is difficult for a number of reasons. First, structuration theory does not fit into any particular tradition or ideological framework nor can it be mapped directly onto PAR. In addition, many concepts are irrelevant for PAR. Rather, as Giddens himself stated, the concept of structuration should be used as a sensitizing device. Consequently, a very careful reading and critical review of what structuration theory has to offer PAR is imperative. Second, structuration is still a loose and unfinished theoretical work. Some of the basic relations, such as those between social practices and structures, are not adequately clarified. As well, very little is said about organizations and institutions, other than that they are produced and reproduced via structuration. This raises the possibility of applications that are themselves not complete or that constitute unwarranted extrapolations. Third, structuration theory is not easily accessible. For example, structuration's terminology, which is at times an invention or a reformulation by Giddens, can be difficult to understand. Often the explanations are not precise and become more clear only after many readings. Consequently, it takes time and patience to work through the material. As well, some of the concepts are not systematically developed. Concepts are sometimes brought together briefly and then recombined in different ways later on. Fourth, structuration theory is not a critical social theory nor does it address change in a substantive manner. As such, it may not appeal to participatory researchers who are looking for a formula for change.

In addition, structuration theory may represent a contradiction for participatory researchers who are ideologically entrenched. For example, Giddens' dialogical model, which gives precedence to the process of research over the formulation of policy objectives, runs counter to a utilitarian ideology which emphasizes inquiry for the purpose of rational decision making. As well, his understanding that power is not a resource in itself may not sit well with those who are committed to an emancipatory ideology.

Possibilities

On the other hand, structuration theory may have much to offer participatory researchers who are looking for a balanced approach that allows for the development of common ground between divergent schools of thought, one that provides an analytical framework for building bridges between theory and practice, and one that positions PAR within a social science framework. At the very least, structuration theory shows participatory researchers how to reframe dualisms that divide—micro versus macro, autonomy versus dependence, constraint versus enablement—into dualities that unite.

Even though structuration theory does not show how to predict, control or manipulate social change, it does provide an approach to understanding how society is produced and reproduced—through the social practices of knowledgeable human agents. Moreover, it acknowledges that the social scientist is capable of bringing about social change, although in unpredictable ways. Such an understanding can help participatory researchers better understand the complexity of change and the potential for creating it.

The aspects of structuration theory that show some promise for PAR include Giddens' critique of functionalism, interpretivist sociologies and critical theory; analysis of knowledgeable human agency and emphasis on social practices; and explanation of the double hermeneutic and the dialogical model. These aspects directly address some of the inquiry issues that PAR is concerned with, namely causal relations, power relations, and frames of meaning. They are also implied in PAR concerns about theory and practice, participation, and communication. Finally, it appears that the concepts of knowledgeable human agency and the double hermeneutic may provide the most fertile ground for PAR because they speak eloquently to the relation between lay and expert knowledge, and communication in the context of participation. On this basis alone, it is suggested here that a fuller investigation of the relation between structuration theory and PAR is warranted.

REFERENCES

Beausoleil, J. (1990). Participatory research: An instrument in communi-ty care. In J. Alary (Ed.), *Community care and participatory research* (pp. 155-198). Montreal: Nu-Age Editions.

Cassara, B. (1987). The how and why of preparing graduate students to carry out participatory research. *Educational Considerations, 14*(2), 39-42.

de Roux, G. I. (1991). Together against the computer: PAR and the struggle of Afro-Colombians for public service. In O. Fals-Borda & M. A. Rahman (Eds.), *Action and knowledge: Breaking the monop-oly with participatory action-research* (pp. 37-53). New York: Apex.

Einsiedel, E. F. (1992, August). *Action research: Theoretical and methodological considerations for development communications.* Paper presented at the International Association for Mass Communication Research, Sao Paolo, Brazil.

Elden, M., & Levin, M. (1991). Cogenerative learning: Bringing participa-tion into action research. In W. F. Whyte (Ed.), *Participatory action research* (pp. 127-141). Newbury Park, CA: Sage.

Fals-Borda, O. (1979). Investigating reality in order to transform it: The Colombian experience. *Dialectical Anthropology, 4*(1), 33-55.

Fals-Borda, O. (1991). Remaking knowledge. In O. Fals-Borda & M. A. Rahman (Eds.), *Action and knowledge: Breaking the monopoly with participatory action-research* (pp. 146-164). New York: Apex.

Fernandes, W., & Tandon, R. (Eds.). (1981). *Participatory research and evaluation: Experiences in research as a process of liberation.* New Delhi: Indian Social Institute.

Gaventa, J. (1991). Toward a knowledge democracy: Viewpoints on par-ticipatory research in North America. In O. Fals-Borda & M. A. Rahman (Eds.), *Action and knowledge: Breaking the monopoly with participatory action-research* (pp. 121-131). New York: Apex.

Giddens, A. (1984). *The constitution of society: Outline of the theory of structuration.* Berkeley: University of California Press.

Giddens, A. (1987). *Social theory and modern sociology.* Cambridge: Polity.

Giddens, A. (1989). The orthodox consensus and the emerging synthesis. In B. Dervin, L. Grossberg, B.J. O' Keefe, & E. Wartella (Eds.), *Rethinking communication: Paradigm issues* (Vol. 1, pp. 53-65). Newbury Park, CA: Sage.

Giddens, A. (1990). *The consequences of modernity.* Stanford, CA: Stanford University Press.

Giddens, A. (1991). Structuration theory: Past, present and future. In C.G.A Bryant & D. Jary (Eds.), *Giddens' theory of structuration: A critical appreciation* (pp. 201-221). London: Routledge.

Hall, B. (1984). Research, commitment and action: The role of participatory research. *International Review of Education, 30*(3), 289-299.

Himmelstrand, U. (1982). Innovative processes in social change: Theory, method and social practice. In T. Bottomore, S. Nowak, & M. Sokolowka (Eds.), *Sociology: State of the art* (pp. 227-247). London: Sage.

Jacobson, T. L. (1991a, May). *Methodological concerns in participatory research.* Paper presented at the annual conference of the Canadian Communication Association, Kingston.

Jacobson, T. L. (1991b, May) *A pragmatist account of participatory communication research for national development.* Paper presented at the annual conference of the International Communication Association, Chicago.

Latapi, P. (1988). Participatory research: A new research paradigm? In *The Alberta Journal of Educational Research, 34*(3), 310-319.

Mayer, R. (1990). Participatory research: Theory and practice. In J. Alary (Ed.), *Community care & participatory research* (pp. 201-242). Montreal: Nu-Age Editions.

Rahman, M. A. (1985). The theory and practice of participatory action-research. In O. Fals-Borda (Ed.), *The challenge of social change* (pp. 107-132). Beverly Hills, CA: Sage.

Rahman, M. A. (1991). The theoretical standpoint of PAR. In O. Fals-Borda & M. A. Rahman (Eds.), *Action and knowledge: Breaking the monopoly with participatory action-research* (pp. 13-23). New York: Apex .

Servaes, J. (1989). *One world, multiple cultures: A new paradigm on communication for development.* Leuven: Acco.

Vandenberg, L., & Fear, F. A. (1983). Participatory research: A comparative analysis of two approaches. *Journal of Voluntary Action Research, 12*(4), 11-28.

Whyte, W. F. (1991). Introduction. In W. F. Whyte (Ed.), *Participatory action research* (pp. 7-15). Newbury Park, CA: Sage.

Whyte, W. F., Greenwood, D. J., & Lazes, P. (1991). Participatory action research: Through practice to science in social research. In W. F. Whyte (Ed.) *Participatory action research.* Newbury Park, CA: Sage.

11

Discourse and Power in Development: Michel Foucault and the Relevance of His Work to the Third World

Arturo Escobar
University of Massachusetts at Amherst

There is a sense in which rapid economic progress is impossible without painful adjustments. Ancient philosophies have to be scrapped; old social institutions have to disintegrate; bonds of caste, creed, and race have to burst; and large numbers of persons who cannot keep up with progress have to have their expectations of a comfortable life frustrated. Very few communities are willing to pay the full price of economic progress.
—United Nations, Department of Economic Affairs (1951)

Michel Foucault's fundamental insights into the nature and dynamics of discourse, power, and knowledge in Western societies enable us to conduct similar inquiries regarding the present situation of the Third World in at least two important respects: the extension to the Third World of Western disciplinary and normalizing mechanisms in a variety of fields; and the production of discourses by Western countries about the Third

World as a means of effecting domination over it. During the last four decades, these discourses have crystallized in a strategy of unprecedented scope, namely, the strategy for dealing with the problems of "underdevelopment" that emerged and became consolidated in the span of a few years after World War II. After presenting the rudiments of such discourse of development, it is concluded that not only does the deployment of development contribute significantly to maintaining domination and economic exploitation, but that the discourse itself has to be dismantled if the countries of the "Third World" want to pursue a different type of development. The implications in terms of strategies of resistance are then explored briefly.

Foucault's work was restricted to European societies. While acknowledging his ignorance of societies other than his own, he enthusiastically encouraged people to undertake similar inquiries concerning other places and cultures, such as Third World societies. He himself referred at times to the importance of studying the transfer of technology to the Third World, its potentially positive effects, its problems and dangers.

One might ask, "Why the Third World?" A number of reasons arise from Foucault's work itself. The first reason is that the totalizing character of power and the will to knowledge—Foucault's fundamental preoccupations—and their tendency to assume increasingly global forms make almost inevitable their steady and insidious spread to all societies. Second, the very tools he developed to analyze power and the will to knowledge make it possible to study how this is happening in the Third World as well. Third, the Third World is the realm par excellence of all forms of power in today's world (from the most brutal forms of torture to sophisticated power techniques). Finally, there are important connections between the processes through which power is exercised (and resisted) in both the Third World and the developed countries.

In the following sections I sketch out, in a very general and provisional manner, a response to the following questions: How do we relate, in both theory and practice, the critique of disciplinary society and normalizing technologies provided by Foucault—as well as his insights into the workings of discourse and power—with the situation and struggles in the Third World? In what ways are disciplinary and normalizing tendencies contributing to the domination of the Third World? Finally, what implications does Foucault's view of power have for strategies of resistance in the Third World?

FOUCAULT'S "HISTORY OF THE PRESENT"

Very broadly, Foucault's interest lies in the study of those practices by which people govern themselves and others through the establishment of domains in which the distinction between true and false is made. For him, these practices lead to the development of modes of objectification that transform human beings into subjects, and to the production of a disciplinary society for the sake of welfare. Individualizing techniques (in military barracks, schools, factories, and hospitals) lead to the production of "docile bodies"; the practices of surveillance, examination, and scientific classification, on the other hand, result in the production of "normalized subjects." Finally, confessional techniques and processes of self-subjection (e.g., as in psychiatry, psychoanalysis, and sexuality) lead to objectifying processes in which people turn themselves into objects. An "anatomo-politics of the human body" that operates through disciplines, and a "bio-politics of populations" that operates through regulatory controls are established and they constitute the poles around which a new form of power, "bio-power," is deployed. These processes of disciplining and normalization were constitutive of, and indispensable for, the development of capitalism. The subjugation of bodies and the control of populations are the objectives of this type of power today.

Foucault's investigations are intended to develop an understanding of the specific ways in which these processes of discipline, normalization, and the deployment of power have taken place within the field of certain fundamental experiences (madness, illness, knowledge in the human sciences, crime, sexuality). To this end, he directed his attention to the discursive practices associated with these experiences, in the belief that the manifold operations of power are at once most visible and most difficult to identify in such practices and that, moreover, it is in discourse that power and knowledge are joined together. It is Foucault's fundamental contention that in every society the production of discourse is controlled, organized and redistributed according to a certain number of procedures. His aim is thus to study the specificity of the production of discourses and discursive practices in Western society.

Discourses, according to Foucault, have systematic structures and they should be studied archeologically (i.e., by identifying the different elements of which they are composed, and the system of relations by which these elements form wholes). More importantly, they should be studied genealogically. Genealogy is concerned with the effective formation of discourse by nondiscursive practices, such as socioeconomic factors, institution administrative requirements, and the like. The genealogist undertakes a diagnosis of a current situation by concentrating on the political technologies constituted by the interrelation of contemporary forms of power and knowledge. The objective of the genealogist's study are those practices of modern culture embodied in specific technologies, their localization in different discourses, institutions and disciplines, and the processes by which they arise and develop. This is what Foucault called "writing the history of the present." His detailed studies of madness, medicine, the human sciences, the prison, and sexuality are part of this history of the present.[1]

A STRATEGY OF RESISTANCE

It is only by writing this history of the present that we can develop "a historical awareness of our present circumstance," that we can "know the historical conditions which motivate our conceptualization" (Foucault, 1982, p. 209). Moreover, only through this type of history, through the struggles to which it should lead, will we be able to develop "a new economy of power relations." We can work toward this new economy of power by taking the forms of resistance against different kinds of power as a starting point (i.e., to study those forms of resistance that question the status of the individual, the privileges of knowledge, the misrepresentations imposed on people, as well as various forms of exploitation, domination, and subjection).

Foucault distinguished between three major types of struggle: (a) against forms of exploitation (which separate individuals from what they produce), led by the working classes; (b) against forms of domination (social, ethnic, sexual, religious, professional, etc.), conducted by individuals and groups in their own terrain; and (c) against modern forms of subjection (i.e. those forms of subjection, subjectivity, and submission that tie the individual him or herself and submit the individual to others as an individual, such as psychiatry and sexuality). Although the mechanisms of subjection have to be studied in relation to the mechanisms of exploitation and domination, the former are not merely the "terminal" manifestation of the latter.

These three forms coexist in various ways in any given society, although one of them usually prevails. In modern European societies, for instance, the struggles against forms of subjection—which question the status of the individual, the right to be different—are becoming more and

---

[1]See especially the following books by Foucault: *Madness and Civilization* (1965), *The Birth of the Clinic* (1975), *The Order of Things* (1971), *The Archaeology of Knowledge* (1972), *Discipline and Punish* (1978), *The History of Sexuality* (1980a). For an excellent presentation of Foucault's work, see Rabinow and Dreyfus (1982).

more important, although struggles against domination and exploitation have by no means disappeared.[2]

In other words, power relations are immanent in other types of relations (economic, sexual, familial, of knowledge, etc.); they are the result of the disequilibria of the latter—and, at the same time, the basis of their transformation. They are not in a superstructural position, but have a directly productive role of their own. Moreover, it is the interweaving of power relations with those other types of relations that "sketches out the general facts of domination . . . [which] is organized in a more or less coherent and unitary strategy" (Foucault, 1979, p. 55).[3] Thus,what needs to be studied is the proliferation of "local centers" of power knowledge, their patterns of transformation, the ways in which they enter into an overall strategy and, finally, the ways in which the latter finds support in the former.

Thus, for Foucault, any strategy that overlooks this manifold structure of power is self-defeating. To the multiplicity of forms of power, we must respond with a multiplicity of localized resistances and counteroffensives. These localized resistances, however, must be of a radical and uncompromising character if they are to confront the totality of power. Rather than a massive revolutionary process, the strategy must be aimed at developing a network of struggles, points of resistance, and popular bases. This does not mean, however, that global processes should be abandoned. Like power, the multiplicity of resistances may be integrated into global strategies. Although radical ruptures are occasionally possible, "it is doubtless the strategic codification of points of resistance that makes a revolution possible, somewhat similar to the ways in which the state relies on the institutional integration of power relationships" (Foucault, 1980a, p. 96). The important question, then, is to analyze the specificity of power (among individuals, groups, activities, and so on) in order to develop a knowledge of strategies, and to bring about new schemes of politicization of individuals, intellectuals, workers, and oppressed groups on whom power is exercised.

---

[2]This threefold character of the struggles of resistance is introduced by Foucault (1982).

[3]Foucault's thoughts on power are found in most of the writings he produced during the 1970s, as well as in numerous short essays and interviews. See, for instance, *The History of Sexuality* (1980b), and Gordon (1980, especially pp. 92-102). See also the article by Daudi (1983), which is very much concerned with Foucault's thoughts on power.

SOME GLOBAL FACTS OF THE PROBLEMATIZATION OF LIFE AND CULTURE

The history of Western and, increasingly, non-Western societies, especially during the modern period, is of a steady process of appropriation
and consequent disposition of societal background practices, common
social meanings, and cultural contents through a series of discourses,
institutions, and practices[4]—a process by which the material conditions
of life and the unspoken mechanisms of culture are brought into the
realm of explicit calculations and subjected to an infinite number of forms
of power knowledge.

It is perhaps within the context of this continuous appropriation
and disposition that we can most adequately and fruitfully understand
Foucault's work. By studying the ways in which certain behaviors, situations, or ideas became problematized in Western society at specific
points in time, and the discourses, institutions, and practices associated
with such problematizations, Foucault shed invaluable light on crucial
processes of appropriation and disposition. By studying, for instance,
how and why certain behaviors or conditions were, after the
Renaissance, seen as a problem, brought together and analyzed as
"madness," and the ways in which medicine and psychiatry took charge

[4]The notion of "background of shared practices" is Dreyfus' way of explaining what
Heidegger (1963) called "primordial understanding." These background practices
embody a cultural interpretation of what it means to be a human being, what
counts as real, and so on. For Heidegger, there were three major ways in which
understanding and interpretation (e.g., in the sciences) involve what he called a
preunderstanding, namely, fore-having (roughly, the background practices), foresight and fore-conception. (see M. Heidegger, 1963, p. 191); see also the section
on "Involvement and Significance: The Worldhood of the World," pp. 114-123.

Taylor's (1979) notion of "intersubjective meanings" or constitutive self-
interpretations (i.e., those ideas, norms, beliefs, implicit in society's practices) is
akin to Dreyfus' notion of background practices. Out of these practices, communities and groups define what Taylor called "common meanings." One corollary
of this conceptualization is that our social sciences, based on an epistemology
that gives primacy to the individual, cannot account for the realm of "common
meanings" (i.e., for the communal) that is the basis of all human action. Another
consequence of utmost importance is that it is impossible to have "normal"
human or social sciences by following the model of the natural sciences:
Although in the former the background of practices is internal to them, in the natural sciences the background is external and theory may thus succeed by
decontextualizing. The background is so pervasive that it cannot be accounted
for by theory. Moreover, in the human sciences, meaning plays an essential role
in determining what counts as an event, but it is precisely the contextual meaning that theory must ignore. For a full account of these arguments, see Dreyfus,
(1980, 1984). See also Taylor (1979).

of the mad person by producing endless discourses about him or her, Foucault helped us understand—with invaluable precision and detail— the appropriation of the fundamental experiences of the human mind, the governing of the psychic phenomena, and their disposition through institutionalizing a regime of reason and truth.[5]

Habermas contributed another set of elements for understanding the global rationality that characterizes these processes in advanced industrial societies. In these societies, according to Habermas, state intervention shifts the crisis tendencies of the system originating in the economic realm—obeying the imperatives of capital accumulation—to the administrative, political, and sociocultural systems—in order to ensure the continued existence of the mode of production. Politically, the system takes over the task of ideology planning. The cultural system is thus invaded by the political; a number of cultural aspects, usually taken for granted (implicit social knowledge, background practices, and shared meanings) are brought into the realm of public, scientific, and political discourses. Once long-established cultural contents are unsettled, they can be stabilized only through discourse; the culture's capacity for self-definition is thus progressively eroded. Administrative planning encroaches on schools, hospitals, factories, cities, media, and so forth. Cultural meanings become scarce, whereas consumable values rise. Norms are altered and theoretical and practical discourses are institutionalized and controlled (see Habermas, 1975).

---

[5]In a similar vein, Foucault (1991) argued that we can no longer comprehend power as the guarantee of a mode of production; in fact, power is one of the constituent elements of the form of production, it functions at the heart of the mode of production. We have seen that the functioning of the instruments of sequestration (factory, prison, bank, asylum, etc.) was not the guarantee of a mode of production, but precisely the constitution of the mode of production. In fact, the primary aim of sequestration consisted in the subjection of time to this time of production. . . . Instead of this penal system we must speak properly of the disciplinary system, that is, of a society equipped with an apparatus whose form is sequestration, whose aim is the constitution of labor-power and whose instrument is the acquisition of discipline and customs habits. Since the nineteenth century there has developed and passed into the shadows a series of apparatuses whose aim was the manufacture of discipline, the imposition of compulsions, the forming of habits . . . the modern sequestration manufactures norms. Constitution of labor-power, apparatus of sequestration: disciplinary society, permanent function of normalisation. That is the series that characterizes our type of society (pp. 61, 64, 65).

A VIEW OF THE THIRD WORLD

How can we see the situation and struggles of the Third World from this perspective? At a very general level, we can say that new types of power and knowledge are being deployed in the Third World that try to ensure the conformity of its peoples to a certain type of economic and cultural behavior (broadly speaking, that are embodied in "the American way of life"). Through this process, not only the economic, but increasingly also the sociocultural and political systems are being progressively permeated and appropriated by the socioeconomic and cultural systems of the "advanced" countries, obeying chiefly, although not exclusively, economic imperatives. Noneconomic spheres thus acquire a growing importance vis-à-vis the economic sphere, in relation to the processes by which exploitation and domination are effected and maintained.

Within this general perspective, a strategy of resistance by Third World peoples should be based on the recognition of the following three major factors:

1.   There still exist important areas of cultural meanings and practices that have not yet fallen under the sway of Western disciplinary and normalizing processes. Among these areas, those considered important and positive should be defended, strengthened, and strategically opposed to the appropriating and appropriated forms by developing new ways of cultural politicization, the strategic use of the past and of national and subnational traditions, and so on.[6]

---

[6]A similar contention is found in late Heidegger, and can also be thought to be implicit in Foucault's work. For Heidegger, there still exist practices that are nonsubjectifying and nonobjectifying, which have resisted the advance of technological society. An alternative understanding of being human may lie embedded in these micro-practices. Heidegger thus envisaged a threefold process by which (a) empirical studies produce a concrete demonstration of ways in which human beings are formed by cultural practices that cannot be totally objectified; (b) our current cultural situation is interpreted by finding a paradigm (a technological device for Heidegger, the prison or the confessional for Foucault) in which the dominant objectifying practices can be focused and visualized; and (c) evidence is assembled at the same time of the existence of (micro-) practices not yet under the control of the dominant rationality. These latter practices have the potential to become the focus of a new cultural paradigm. Foucault's project, in this way, can be seen as very similar to Heidegger's (see Heidegger, 1971, pp. 33-35); see also the articles by Dreyfus, 1980, 1984). The defense and strengthening of those forms which have resisted appropriation are seen as perhaps the only hopeful alternative presently viable in advanced industrial societies. The conclusion to a recent study of U.S. psychiatry, for instance, reads as follows:

2. Although class compromise takes place at some levels, class struggle and class conflict are by no means latent (as they tend to be in more industrialized societies). Any strategy of resistance must thus be conscious of the class structure of the society in which it takes place. In the Third World, mechanisms of exploitation and domination prevail, although contemporary forms of subjection (from Coca-Cola as a cultural item to therapies for the middle classes, consumer values, lifestyles, and so forth) are increasingly gaining importance and contributing to the maintenance of exploitation and class differentials. Given the fact that power is exercised chiefly to maintain economic exploitation, localized struggles against forms of domination and subjection, carried out by individuals and groups in the terrain of their own activities, enter into a class-revolutionary process insofar as they are uncompromising and nonreformist struggles against specific forms of power. These localized strategies may cover a wide range of issues, such as political activities, professional practices, repression in terms of ethnicity, sexual preferences, opposition to specific programs and technologies, educational strategies, and so forth.

3. There exist several grand strategies constructed by the developed countries that play a crucial role in maintaining domination over the Third World. Two of these are discussed here, although only one is elaborated on. The first is the discourse on the underdevelopment of the Third World constructed by the developed countries. This discourse is associated with the whole apparatus of development (from international organizations, such as the World Bank and the International Monetary Fund, to local-level development agencies) as well as the large number of theories of development produced especially by international organizations and by scholars at North American and European campuses. I elaborate on this discourse in the next section.

A second grand contemporary strategy for the penetration and control of the Third World is embodied in communication and information

---

To anyone who regards this analysis as pessimistic, we can only answer that it is better to understand how a mechanism operates than to endure its effects in ignorance. One must know that nobody is exempt from the growing importance of social controls before one can prepare to work against them by mapping out and hopefully adding to the last remaining territory not yet fallen under the sway of the old guardians of law and order and the new engineers of the mind. (See Castell, Castell, & Lovell, 1982, p. 320) technologies, especially the mass media, television and commercial cinema. Although it would be of great value to analyze these mechanisms in terms of power and knowledge, such an analysis is well beyond the scope of this chapter.[7]

THE DISCOURSE OF DEVELOPMENT

Foucault's insights into the control of the production of discourse and the workings of power and knowledge enable us to conduct a radical reinterpretation of development theory and practice. The overall contention of such reinterpretation can be stated as follows: Without examining development as discourse we cannot understand the systematic ways in which the Western developed countries have been able to manage and control and, in many ways, even create the Third World politically, economically, sociologically, and culturally;[8] and that, although underdevelopment is a very real historical formation, it has given rise to a series of practices (promoted by the discourses of the West) that constitute one of the most powerful mechanisms for ensuring domination over the Third World today.

The aim of this approach should be to investigate the formation of this discourse of development and, more specifically, to identify the appearance, development and articulation of a general strategy for dealing with problems of underdevelopment, the practices generated by such a strate-

---

[7]The emergence of the new communication technologies and their impact were the subject of a recent UNESCO conference held in conjunction with the Istituto della Enciclopedia Italiana in Rome (see *Symposium on the Cultural, Social and Economic Impact of the New Communication Technologies*, Final Report, UNESCO COM84/WS/11, Paris, March 1984).

[8]A similar contention informs Said's (1979) book, *Orientalism*, an excellent study of the systematic creation of the "Orient" by the discourses of writers, colonial authorities. scholars, and so forth. According to Said, this discourse is based on a predicated ontological distinction between East and West, whereby the "Orient" is essentialized and assigned a homogeneous character, very much in the same manner in which the "Third World" is assumed to have a homogeneous nature (despite the enormous differences exhibited by the countries of Asia, Africa, and Latin America that compose it). Said also pointed out that for this discourse of orientalism to make sense depends more on the culture that produces it (viz. the "developed" countries) than on the "Orient"/"Third World" itself. In a similar vein, we can say that the Third World is "underdeveloped" not only because it was discovered to be so, but also because, through this discourse of development, it was made susceptible to underdevelopment. In many ways, the discourse of development is more a sign of power over the Third World than a truth about it.

gy, the mechanisms by which these practices operate and, in general, the ways in which development enters into a nexus of power and knowledge, that is, the ways in which development is "put into discourse" (Foucault, 1980a, p. 11). In this way, development will be seen, not as a matter of scientific knowledge, a body of theories and programs concerned with the achievement of true progress, but rather as a series of political technologies intended to manage and give shape to the reality of the Third World.

Three major factors should be considered in this type of analysis: the historical conditions under which the discourse arose, the structure of the discourse itself, and the relations of power and knowledge made possible by the deployment of development. Only a very succinct account of these three factors is given here.[9] Finally, the appearance of counterdiscourses is also analyzed briefly.

Historical Conditions

European and, more recently, North American interest in much of Asia, Africa, and Latin America dates back to the discovery and conquest of "new worlds." This interest has gone through a series of identifiable stages up to the present. Before 1945, it barely revealed a general and explicit strategy for dealing with what came to be known after the war as "the underdeveloped world." Between 1945 and 1955, in the climate of the great postwar transformations, a whole new strategy for dealing with the problems of what came to be known during this period as "the underdeveloped world" emerged and took definite shape. The character of the relations between rich and poor countries, the scope they occupied, the form they acquired, the mechanisms by which they operated, all were subjected to a substantial mutation. All that was important in the economic, social, political, and cultural life of the poor countries (their population, processes of capital accumulation, agriculture and trade, natural resources, administration and cultural values, etc.) entered into this new strategy. The first "missions" sent to the underdeveloped world by the International Bank for Reconstruction and Development during the late 1940s and early 1950s, with the purpose of formulating "comprehensive" development programs, were one of the first concrete expressions of this new strategy. So, too, were the array of international organizations concerned with development, as well as the profusion of "experts" in all types of development fields, all of which appeared during this period.

Very broadly stated, the historical context under which the new strategy arose can be summarized as follows. There was a reorganiza-

---

[9]This section on "The Discourse of Development" forms part of my dissertation (Escobar, 1987). A more detailed account of this section can be found in Escobar (1983).

tion of power at the world level (which included the break down of old colonial systems in Asia and Africa, the successful march of Chinese communists to power, and the beginning of the "cold war"), the final result of which was far from clear. Important changes had occurred in the structure of production, and they had to be made to fit the requirements of accumulation of a capitalist system in which the countries of the "Third World" occupied an increasingly important, even if not yet fully defined, role. These countries could forge alliances with any pole of power. In the light of expanding communism, the steady deterioration of their life conditions, and the alarming increase of their populations, the direction in which they would go will depend largely on actions that are urgent in character and unprecedented in scope.

Rich countries, on the other hand, were believed to have the financial and technological capacity to secure their brand of progress the world over. A look at their own past instilled in them the conviction, magnified by the success of the Marshall Plan, that this was not only possible, let alone desirable, but perhaps even inevitable. Sooner or later, the poor countries would become rich, and the underdeveloped world would be developed. International organizations had been set up to help these countries pursue their goals. A new type of economic knowledge (e.g., the reentry of economic growth into the scope of economic analysis) and an enriched experience with the design and management of complex systems (e.g., the Tennessee Valley Authority and a variety of planning mechanisms) made this goal seem even more plausible. It was only a matter of adopting the appropriate strategy to do it, of setting in motion the right forces to ensure progress and global happiness.

This was achieved for the poor countries at the cost of much greater intervention. Behind the humanitarian concern and the positive outlook of the new strategy, new forms of power and control, more subtle and refined, were put into operation. The poor countries became the target of ever more sophisticated practices, of a variety of programs that seemed to be inescapable. From the new institutions of power in the United States and Europe, from the offices of the new international organizations and lending institutions, from North American and European campuses, research centers and foundations, from the new planning offices of the big capitals of the underdeveloped world, this was the type of development that was actively promoted and that, in a few years, was to extend its reach to all aspects of the social body.[10]

---

[10]For a more complete account of these historical conditions, as well as a list of works from this period, see Escobar (1983). The first mission sent by the International Bank for Reconstruction and Development to the Third World was the one that visited Colombia from July 11 to November 5, 1949. The mission included 14 international advisors in a large variety of fields: economics, trans-

The Structure of Discourse

A survey of the few general treatises on economic development written before 1958, along with the reports of the missions sent by international organizations to Third World countries, reveals the broad structure of the discourse to which the new strategy gave rise. The elements with which development began to deal were numerous and varied, encompassing all economic, social, and political aspects of importance, at all levels: rural and urban; local, regional, and national; sectoral and integrated; and so on.[11]

Development, however, was not merely the result of these elements, or of their combination and gradual elaboration; nor was it the product of the practices to which they gave rise or of the introduction of new knowledge and ideas. It was not the effect of the new international organizations, or of a new sensibility to poverty, or of the success of the Marshall Plan. It was rather the result of the establishment and systematization of a set of relations among these elements, institutions, and practices, of the particular type of organization of these various elements made possible by this set of relations. The discourse of development was not constituted by the array of possible objects included under its domain, but by the way in which, thanks to this set of relations, it was able to form systematically the objects of which it spoke, to group them and arrange them in certain ways, to give them a unity of their own.[12]

---

portation, industry, highways and waterways, railroads, petroleum refineries, national accounts, community facilities, agriculture and health, and so on. Working closely with the mission was a similar group of Colombian advisors and experts. Based on the large body of information collected, the mission elaborated a detailed and comprehensive development plan for the country, including concrete goals, quantifiable targets, and so on. Its report embodied the totally new scale and style of assistance that was then emerging. (see International Bank for Reconstruction and Development, 1950).

[11]For a substantial list of works written during this period, see Escobar (1983). See also the excellent article by Pletsch (1981). His article traces the origin of the notion of "three worlds" within the context or the "cold war" and modernization theory. A few of the works of the period can be mentioned here: United Nations (1951), Milbank Memorial Fund (1948), United Nations (1949), Nurkse (1953), Lewis (1949); esp. Appendix 11: "On Planning in Backward Countries, Leibenstein (1954), United Nations (1953), Frankel (1953), Lewis (1955), Buchanan and Ellis (1955). Studies that deal with factors such as population and food are too numerous to list here. On the other hand, a number of works on economic development, although not dealing explicitly with underdevelopment, were published during the early 1950s by authors such as Rostow and Clark. The writing of economic development treatises took off in the late 1950s.

[12]The methodological approach of this subsection draws heavily on Foucault's (1972) *The Archaeology of Knowledge*.

The basic organization of this discourse (i.e., the basic system of relations between the key variables of capital, technology, and certain institutions) laid down during the period between 1945 and 1955, has remained for the most part invariant, although it allowed the system to undergo a series of changes. It includes new elements and variables, develops new modes of operation, and so forth. It was the systemization of these relations that conferred on this discourse its great dynamic quality: its immanent adaptability to changing conditions, which allowed it to survive, indeed to thrive, up to the present. The result has been the uninterrupted succession of "development strategies" and substrategies, always within the confines of the same discursive space in which we are still encapsulated.

The Deployment of Development

The discourse of development described briefly here has made possible an endless number of practices through which new mechanisms of control (i.e., new forms of power and knowledge) are deployed. The deployment of development has operated through three major strategies, all of which carry with them disciplinary and normalizing elements. These strategies are discussed here.

The Progressive Incorporation of Problems. The discourse formed after the war brought with it the multiplication of problems with which to deal. Once a problem was incorporated into the domain of development, it had to be categorized and further specified. In many ways, development was preceded by the creation of "abnormalities" such as the "underdeveloped," the "malnourished," the "illiterate"—which it would later treat and reform. The specification of problems required detailed observations in Third World households, villages, regions, and countries. Complete dossiers were elaborated, and information gathering and dissemination designed and constantly refined. It constituted a whole political anatomy of the Third World that sought not so much to illuminate problems and possible solutions as to give them a visible reality amenable to specific treatments. This first strategy resulted in the formation of *a field of intervention of power*, the establishment of an ever more encompassing domain of intervention.

The Professionalization of Development. This was effected through the proliferation of development disciplines and subdisciplines. Such professionalization (or, better perhaps, "technification") allowed experts to remove from the political realm problems that would otherwise be political, and to recast them into the apparently more neutral realm of science. It would lead in a few years to the consolidation of "development studies" in most major universities of the developed world. The policies and programs that originated out of this vast field of knowledge inevitably carried with them strong normative and teleological components. What was at stake was a type of knowledge that sought to establish the nature of Third World countries, to classify their problems and formulate policies, to pass judgment on them and visualize their future—to produce, in short, a regime of truth and norms about development. This second strategy sought the formation of *a field of control of knowledge*, through which "truth" (and, so, power) was produced.

Within this second major strategy, special attention should be given to the ways in which development economics was able to "economize" development. This process of "economization," by which all realities and development subdisciplines were subjected to the rationality espoused by development economists, is undoubtedly of crucial importance. Its specificity, however, must be analyzed within the context of the establishment of economics as a "positive," "objective," science, thanks in part to the development—during the past 200 years—of a culture in which a specific economic rationality (based on certain institutions such as money, markets, banks, etc.) became dominant. This process, which one can perhaps call "the economization of life," was intimately linked to the development of capitalism; it entailed as necessary prerequisites the establishment of the normative discourse of classical political economy, the adoption of certain principles of government, and the introduction of new forms of discipline and control.[13]

The Institutionalization of Development. This process took place at various levels, ranging from the international organizations and national planning bodies to local-level development agencies. These institutions became the agents of the deployment of development, the network of new sites that, taken as a whole, constituted the apparatus of development. It was (and still is) largely through this network and system of regulatory controls that people and communities are bound to certain cycles of production, certain behaviors and rationalities. This strategy resulted in *the dispersion of local centers of power knowledge* (i.e., the establishment of a multiplicity of sites of power that made possible the disciplinary system of development).

---

[13]An analysis of the basis on which economics achieved its scientific status is found in Taylor (1985, see also Sanz de Santamaria, 1984). For the evolution of the "art of government" since the 16th century and its relation to political economy and disciplinary forms, see Foucault (1991, see also Donzelot, 1979). An interesting account of "The Histories of Economic Discourse," with special reference to the identification of the founding of political economy with the publication of Adam Smith's *Wealth of Nations*, is found in Tribe (1981). A similar line is pursued by Gudeman (1984, pp. 90-110).

The analysis of the deployment of development through these three great strategies leads to the conclusion that development has been successful to the extent that it has been able to penetrate, integrate, manage, and control countries and populations in increasingly detailed and encompassing ways. If it has failed to solve the problems of underdevelopment, it can also be said, perhaps with greater pertinence, that it has succeeded well in creating a type of underdevelopment that has been until now, for the most part, politically and economically manageable.

After four decades of "new knowledge," we still hold to the same basic tenets. The forms of power that have appeared act not so much by repression as by normalization; not by ignorance, but according to carefully regulated knowledge; not by humanitarian concern, but by the moralization of issues. As the conditions that gave rise to it become more pressing, it can only increase its hold, refine its methods, extend its reach even further.

The analysis here has been restricted to a short period, but one that saw a crucial threshold for the Third World and a number of fundamental changes in the international sphere. These changes were not the result of a radical epistemological or political breakthrough (this has yet to occur), but of a reorganization of a number of factors that allowed the "Third World" to display a new visibility and to erupt into a new realm of language. This new space was carved up out of the vast and dense surface of the Third World, placing it into a new field of power. It constituted the historical conditions of the possibility of a number of development sciences accepted as positive and true. Through them, underdevelopment became the subject of political technologies that sought to erase it from the face of the earth, but that ended up, instead, multiplying it to infinity.

I have tried to show that this discourse has a validity of its own that goes beyond the materiality of "underdevelopment" itself, and in fact profoundly affects it. That this materiality is not conjured up by an "objective" body of knowledge, but rather that it is charted out by the rational discourses of economists, politicians, and development experts should already be clear. What has been achieved is a specific configuration of factors and forces in which the new language of development finds its support. Thus, *development* (as discourse) is a very real historical formation, albeit articulated around a fictitious construct (*underdevelopment*) and on a certain materiality (i.e., certain conditions of life baptized as *underdevelopment*), which we must seek to conceptualize in different ways.

To be sure, there is a situation of economic exploitation that must be recognized and dealt with. Power is too cynical at the level of exploitation and should be resisted on its own terms. The requirements of capital accumulation on a world scale, and the contradictions inherent in such a process, on the other hand, determine the specificity of exploitation and greatly affect the constitution of the discourse itself. The conditions of social and sectoral disarticulation prevailing in Third World countries, for instance, influence the strategies adopted as regards the patterns of capital accumulation, labor policies, promotion of certain crops, and so on.[14] Yet the ways in which the discourse organizes these elements go beyond the economic realm and cannot be easily analyzed in terms of direct causal relations.

To be sure, too, there is a certain materiality (of life conditions) that is extremely preoccupying and that requires continuous effort and attention. But we have long ago lost sight of this materiality by building on it a new reality that has haunted us for decades. Why, for instance, and by what processes, did the experience of hunger (lack of adequate food intake) become successively green revolution, agrarian reform, single cell protein, integrated rural development, comprehensive food and nutrition planning, and sectoral food policies? Why such a host of food and applied nutrition programs, of nutritional, agricultural, and economic sciences devoted to this problem? What has been their impact? Should we not examine instead the ways in which the fundamental experience of hunger has been invested by Western forms of power (and, in this way, see the body of the malnourished as the most pathetic sign of power over the Third World)? And, in relation to all other development problems, why and by what processes did specific political technologies arise in response to local objectives, themselves linked to welfare concerns?

Finally, at the same time that we write the history of the investment of the Third World by Western forms of power and rationality, should we not start to look at that materiality—at those basic conditions of life that characterize the "Third World"—with new eyes and new categories, perhaps different from the ones in vogue today?

Counterdiscourses and Resistance

It was a given historical conjunction that made necessary the deployment of development. If it is true that this deployment made possible the advance of social control over the Third World, it is also true that at the same time it made possible the emergence of opposing discourses. The leaders and intellectuals of the countries of the Third World began to speak on behalf of their own people, to use similar weapons in order to pursue their own interests, often times with the same vocabulary and

---

[14]For an elaboration of the concepts of social and sectoral disarticulation in Peripheral capitalist societies, see Amin (1974, 1976). The specificity and implications of this disarticulation for the agricultural sector has been explored by de Janvry (1981).

espousing the same goals. These counterdiscourses (some more or less accommodating or susceptible to co-optation, some more or less radical than others) operated for the most part within the same discursive space and within the same field of power of the dominant strategy. To what extent did they undermine power, forcing it to bend its arm in their own favor? Or, conversely, to what extent and in what ways were they circumvented, appropriated and subverted by the prevailing discourse? The answer to these questions would undoubtedly be of great importance for new strategies of resistance.

A number of notions linked to development, some of which might have otherwise played a positive role, were easily co-opted by the established system and rendered ineffective or counterproductive. Some of these notions did not originate within the most powerful institutions, but were soon appropriated by them (e.g., the notion of basic needs, adopted by the World Bank as a major policy instrument). Other types of notions or approaches, transposed from other locations or historical contexts where they perhaps originally had a liberating character, met a similar fate. Such was the case, for instance, with rural cooperatives (conceived on European models) in Latin America during the 1960s, with popular education and literacy programs during the 1960s and 1970s (some of which succeeded in subverting the Freirian pedagogical principles by linking oppression to production and low productivity in what was called *functional literacy*), and with the notion of participation in development—promoted by international organizations and universities in the developed world—strictly conceived in an utilitarian fashion while denying the political character of participation.[15] As in the case of the rural cooperatives, the experience of participation in development is another eloquent proof of the fact that the importation of models or ideological doctrines from a different cultural and historical context is often times a counterproductive or diversionary strategy as far as development is concerned.[16]

Somewhat related to the notion of participation, but conceived in an entirely different manner, is the notion of participatory action research

[15]The experience of rural cooperatives as a case of "intellectual colonialism" has been interestingly analyzed by Fals-Borda (1972). For an analysis of literacy approaches during the past three decades, see Pedrosa (1981). A lucid analysis of the myth of participation in Third World politics and development is found in Kothari (1984). Finally, within the field of development proper, the themes of participation and local organizations were the subject of large research projects in the 1970s and early 1980s in U.S. universities (e.g., Cornell and Berkeley).

[16]This point is forcefully made by Kothari (1984) in relation to participation. He also pointed out how, paradoxically, "The more the economics of development and the politics of development are kept out of reach of the masses, the more they (the masses) are asked to 'participate' in them. For they are told that it is for them that 'development' takes place" (p. 542).

(PAR). PAR grew out of experiences in popular education and grassroots activism in a number of countries in Latin America, Asia, and Africa during the 1970s, and continues to be today one of the most hopeful lines of research and action in the Third World. Central to the PAR philosophy is the question of popular power (i.e., the investigation of the mechanisms necessary to develop popular counterpower for social transformation and their relation to the production of knowledge). Thus, it seeks to generate popular power, not only "to develop." PAR projects combine techniques of adult education, social science research, and political activism. Some of the methods that have been successfully used in these projects include collective research (between external agents or intellectuals and the popular groups concerned, always taking popular knowledge as the starting point for research and action), the critical reconstruction of local or regional histories (geared towards preparing for action and correcting official histories), the restoration and use of popular cultures (including the use of people's feelings, imagination and artistic capabilities, activist tendencies, popular language), and the use of novel means of diffusing knowledge (all knowledge being considered the property of the community). Achievements of PAR projects have included, for instance, legal or forcible repossession of land, participation in existing local or regional institutions, creation of new local organizations, production of local history books, audio-visuals, community newsletters, theater, and so on. In a few cases, PAR projects have already formed networks that have led to the emergence of important nonparty regional movements.[17]

From a philosophical point of view, PAR constitutes a radical departure from traditional Western philosophy. By its very nature, PAR rejects the subject–object division, central to Western philosophy and empiricist social science, and transforms it into a subject-subject project. First of all, PAR creates a dialectical tension between the local people (problematizing their alienation and feelings of inferiority by emphasizing popular culture) and the external agents or intellectuals (who are led to overcome their class position and any illusion of vanguardism). Second, by sharing with the popular groups their goals of social transformation and their political commitment, the external agents do not create relations of submission and dependence. Third, this mutual commitment tends to produce open-ended projects, which may branch out in various directions and last a good number of years (contrary to the practice of

---

[17]PAR was launched internationally at a world symposium held in Cartagena, Colombia in 1977. See *Ciencia y Crítica en las Ciencias Sociales* (Bogotá: Fundación Punta de Lanza. 1978), 2 vols. An excellent review of a number of important PAR projects in Colombia, Nicaragua and Mexico has recently been completed and will be published shortly by the International Labor Organization (see Fals-Borda, 1985). On PAR, see also, for instance, Rahman (1985), Kassam and Mustafa (1982), Grossi et al. (1982), and Hall (1979).

traditional research projects). Finally, PAR projects are assessed in terms of the quality of the practices or actions they enable, including their pluralistic and truly democratic character, and not in terms of some abstract criteria "objective" knowledge.[18]

Because one of the major foundations of power is truth, the knowledge of that truth (i.e., its invention and confirmation) becomes a major mechanism for the legitimation of the hegemonic forms of power within a given system. Discourse thus seeks its legitimacy in a carefully controlled definition of science and truth. The counterdiscourse of participatory research, initiated in the Third World, conceives of popular science as the result of an endogenous process in which theory-building and popular organization for action are combined. Within this process of social theory as practice, not only existing social conditions, but science itself, are permanently transformed. In this way, it constitutes a radical challenge to the regime of knowledge and truth that has ruled discourse and life up to the present—which brings us back to the main subject of this chapter.

SOME GENERAL PROPOSITIONS

PAR is not an isolated instance of counterdiscourse and resistance. Although perhaps still somewhat dispersed, other similar offensives against hegemonic powers and theories are also taking place the world over. Some of these are grassroots movements, whereas others have a more global character.[19] Perhaps these movements can be related to what Foucault called "the insurrection of subjugated knowledges" that has taken place since the early 1980s, or the reactivation of local knowledges, a variety of "popular knowledges" that defies the authority of any arbitrary idea of science and truth. At the center of his genealogical project is an investigation of these subjugated knowledges in such a way that their critical contents are tactically released in local struggles (Foucault, 1980b). Besides the local character of these struggles, what matters is their autonomous, noncentralized and nonhierarchical character and the fact that their validity has ceased to depend on the approval of the established regimes of thought.

[18]A first reaction of many people participating in PAR projects is that "we are not afraid of speaking any longer." This liberating assertion also highlights the important role of language, usually emphasized by oppressed groups in their processes of liberation (think, for instance, of the feminist insistence on "naming" the world).

[19]The issue of grassroots activism and nonparty formations is discussed by Kothari (1984). See also Alger and Mendlovitz (1984), for a discussion of the possibilities of strategic cooperation between "globalists" and "localists."

In summary, a Foucauldian perspective on the Third World would begin with conceptualization of development on the basis of the system and techniques constructed for the deployment of power in its midst. Besides giving an account of the problems (economic progress or dependency, etc.), one must investigate the investment of the Third World by Western forms of rationality (political, economic, cultural), the use of forms of power and knowledge, the establishment of mechanisms of control, and the constitution of discourses and practices. One must reconstruct the "strategic connection" of these discourses and practices in order to make visible the very fine web laid out by them throughout history. More specifically, I postulate the following provisional hypotheses, for further exploration and refinement:

1. Parallel to the global process of capital accumulation (and closely associated with, although not reduced to it), there is a global process of domination defined by the system of power and the accumulation of normalized individuals. This process, which spreads throughout the world out of the centers of the developed countries, must be studied in its historical and geographical specificity. Thus, the Third World should be seen as an integral part of this global process, aimed at understanding the particular aspects taken by the introduced disciplinary and normalizing forms.

2. In the Third World, the new forms of domination and subjection (concerning areas such as education, demography, housing, psychiatry, cultural values, ethnic oppression, etc.) are progressively increasing their hold and contributing to the maintenance of economic exploitation. The specific rationalities of these various forms of domination, as well as the forms of resistance presented to them throughout history, should be studied. Moreover, a strategy of resistance must develop, alongside working-class and liberation struggles, that consists of localized actions—a plurality of struggles based upon the plurality of interests of those who are the object of power—that take into account those positive cultural practices which have resisted, or that have not yet been invaded by normalizing tendencies.

3. The discourse of development must be dismantled if Third World countries hope (by working with their various material, social, and cultural resources) to counteract the penetration of power and to overcome poverty, unemployment, and inequality. Detailed studies of specific development practices (e.g., programs or institutions) are likely to contribute to this dismantling process by providing the context for modifying current

practices. Also needed is a language that enables the conceptualization of "developing" social systems in a new manner. Otherwise, there is the risk of not saying anything new because the language does not permit it. It is only by saying no to development (i.e., to the power it creates and the language that supports it) that Third World countries can fruitfully attack adverse conditions with new discourse and knowledge, new ways of fulfilling basic needs, of realizing the possibilities of human beings.

I have attempted to answer the question of why the situation of poor countries was problematized during the postwar period, in what ways, and with what consequences—in short, why these various elements were brought together and analyzed as underdevelopment. This process was associated with new socioeconomic and political factors, new institutions and knowledge, and so forth, but the problematization was not so much a result of this situation as a response to it. This response can also be seen as part of a wider strategy—dating as far back as the discovery and conquest of "new worlds"—which has systematically sought to create in these new worlds the idea that Westernization (presently along capitalist lines) is a fundamental problem for all societies. It is for this reason that the domain mapped out by development must be studied not only on the basis of Western notions of rationality—science, representation, and so forth—but also within the space created by the trajectories followed by these philosophical and anthropological categories in relation to the three major strategies through which development has been deployed.[20]

---

[20]A complete genealogy of the construction of the Third World would have to start with the discovery and conquest of the new territories during the first phase of European expansion. The three major strategies of the deployment of development undoubtedly have their antecedents in a number of colonial (and, in the case of Latin America, postcolonial) enterprises, institutions, fields of knowledge, and so forth. One may think, for instance, of the enormous body of travel narratives that, from the 16th century on, constituted one of the main discursive spaces in which Europe represented the rest of the world to itself as an ideological weapon for its own economic and political expansion. One can also think of the emergence of the notions of "primitive" or "archaic" societies, associated with the development of Western ethnography, or of the transference or voluntary adoption, since an early date in the colonial period, of techniques (e.g., of city planning, public hygiene, education, administration, etc.) with high disciplinary and normalizing contents or, finally, of the crucial influence exerted by European ideas or movements (e. g., positivism and modernism) on the thought and movements of, say, Latin American countries. This genealogy (which would necessar-

CONCLUSION

It was in the name of modernization and development that an entire productive apparatus took charge of the management of the life of the "new" nations, replacing the older and more visible forms of colonial oppression and bringing forth at the same time a different disposition of the factors of life.

At times, development became so important for these countries that it was acceptable to subject our populations to an infinite variety of interventions, to more powerful forms of power and systems of control; so important that we accepted the price of massive impoverishment, of selling our resources to the most convenient bidder, of degrading our physical and human ecologies, of killing and torturing, of condemning our native populations to near extinction; so important that we began to think of ourselves as "inferior," as "underdeveloped," as "ignorant," that we began to doubt the value of our own cultures and decided to pledge allegiance to the banners of reason and faith; so important, finally, that the realization of such "development" clouded the awareness of the impossibility of fulfilling the promises that "development" itself seemed to be making.

It is in this historical sense that underdevelopment can be said to be rooted in a Westernization process whose genealogy spans a period of several centuries, and whose latest phase—beginning roughly in 1945—is characterized by a strategy of unprecedented proportions. It is thus confused with the history of the West, and marked by movements of penetration and resistance. But it is not Western forms per se to which one should object, nor to the need to preserve the productive achievements of civilizations, but rather to the types of rationality linked to them, to the forms of power and knowledge that characterize them and, finally, to the ways in which they assume responsibility for the conditions of life

---

ily have to cross philosophical, anthropological, and economico-political trajectories) would undoubtedly be of great value and interest.

For an account of travel narratives within this context, see Defert (1982), and Pratts (1983). Columbus' discourse about the "New World" is interestingly analyzed by Rabasa (n.d.), whose analysis contains a detailed textual analysis of Columbus' travel journals.

Some examples of studies of the penetration or adoption of forms of discipline and normalization in the Third World prior to 1945 are Abu-Lughod (1980), for the practices of urban planning by French colonial authorities as a means of controlling the Arab population; Machado (1978), whose study is one of the development of social medicine and psychiatry in Brazil, following a Foucauldian perspective; and two studies of pedagogical discourses and practices in Colombia since the 17th century: Zualuaga de E (1984) and Martinez and Silva (1983).

in order to manage and contain them. At the end of the first volume of *The History of Sexuality*, Foucault (1980a, pp. 157-159) mused on the possibility of a future in which our modern preoccupation with sex would be a strange trait of the past. Perhaps we can also think of our preoccupation with development in a similar manner when we read these lucid paragraphs:

> Perhaps one day people will wonder at this. They will not be able to understand how a civilization so intent on developing enormous instruments of production and destruction found the time and the infinite patience to inquire so anxiously concerning the actual state of sex; people will smile perhaps when they recall that here were men—meaning ourselves—who believed that therein resided a truth every bit as precious as the one they had already demanded from the earth, the stars, and the pure forms of their thought; people will be surprised at the eagerness with which we went about pretending to rouse from its slumber a sexuality which everything—our discourses, our customs, our institutions, our regulations, our knowledges—was busy producing in the light of day and broadcasting to noisy accompaniment. . . . People will wonder what could have made us so presumptuous; they will look for the reasons that might explain why we prided ourselves on being the first to grant sex the importance we say is its due. . . .
>
> Let us consider the stratagems by which we were induced to apply all our skills to discovering its secrets, by which we were attached to the obligation to draw out its truth, and made guilty for having failed to recognize it for so long. These devices are what ought to make us wonder today. Moreover, we need to consider the possibility that one day, perhaps in a different economy of bodies and pleasures, people will no longer quite understand how the ruses of sexuality, and the power that sustains its organization, were able to subject us to that austere monarchy of sex, so that we became dedicated to the endless task of forcing its secret, exacting the truest of confessions from a shadow.
>
> *The irony of this deployment is in having us believe that our "liberation" is in balance.* (Foucault, 1980a, pp. 157–159)

ACKNOWLEDGEMENTS:

My thanks are extended to Professors Sheldon Margen, Paul Rabinow, and Hubert Dreyfus for their helpful comments and invaluable support. The material on the discourse of development was largely developed as part of Foucault's working seminar at Berkley in the Fall of 1983. The reader acquainted with Foucault's work will be well aware of its crucial importance for the work presented here.

REFERENCES

Abu-Lughod, J. L. (1980). *Rabat: Urban apartheid in Morocco*. Princeton, NJ: Princeton University.

Alger, C.F., & Mendlovitz, S. (1984). Grass-roots activism in the United States: Global implications? *Alternatives, 9*(4), 447-474.

Amin, S. (1974). *Accumulation on a world scale*. New York: Monthly Review.

Amin, S. *Unequal development*. New York: Monthly Review.

Buchanan, N. S., & Ellis, H. S. (1955). *Approaches to economic development*. New York: Twentieth Century Fund.

Castell, M., Castell, F., & Lovell, A. (1982). *The psychiatric society*. New York: Columbia University Press.

Daudi, P. (1983). The discourse of power or the power of discourse. *Alternatives, 9*(2), 317-325.

de E., O. L. Zualuaga (1984). *El maestro y el saber pedagógico en Colombia, 1821-1848* [The teacher and pedagogical knowledge in Columbia, 1821-1848]. Medellín: Colombia Universidad de Antioquia, Facultad de Educacion.

Defert, D. (1982). The collection of the world accounts of voyages from the sixteenth to the eighteenth centuries. *Dialectical Anthropology, 7*, 11-20.

de Janvry, A. (1981). *The agrarian question and reformism in Latin America*. Baltimore, MD: Johns Hopkins University Press.

Donzelot, J. (1979). *The policing of families*. New York: Pantheon..

Dreyfus, H. (1980). Holism and hermeneutics. *Review of Metaphysics, 34*(1), 3-23.

Dreyfus, H. (1984). Why current studies of human capacities can never be scientific. *Cognitive Science Report Series* (No 11). Berkeley: University of California.

Escobar, A. (1983). *Discourse and power: A historical perspective on the formation of development theory and practice (1945-1955)*. Paper presented at UNESCO's meeting on Philosophical Investigations of the Fundamental Problems of Endogenous Development, Libreville, Gabon.

Escobar, A. (1987) *Power and visibility: The invention and management of development in the Third World*. Unpublished doctoral dissertation, University of California, Berkeley.

Fals-Borda, O. (1972). *Ciencia propia y colonialismo intelectual* [Autonomous science and intellectual colonialism]. Bogotá: Carlos Valencia ed.

Fals-Borda, O. (1985). *Knowledge and people's power*. Geneva: ILO.

Foucault, M. (1965). *Madness and civilization*. New York: Pantheon Books.

Foucault, M. (1971). *The order of things*. New York: Pantheon Books.

Foucault, M. (1972). *The archaeology of knowledge*. New York: Pantheon.

Foucault, M. (1975). *The birth of the clinic*. New York: Random House.

Foucault, M. (1978). *Discipline and punish*. New York: Pantheon Books.

Foucault, M. (1979). Power and strategies. In M. Morris & P. Patton (Eds.), *Michel Foucalt: Power, truth, strategy*. Sidney: Federal Publications.

Foucault, M. (1980a). *The history of sexuality*. New York: Pantheon Books.

Foucault, M. (1980b). *Power/knowledge: Selected interviews and other writings*. New York: Pantheon.

Foucault, M. (1982). Afterword: The subject and power. In P. Rabinow & H. Dreyfus (Eds.), *Michel Foucault: Beyond structuralism and hermeneutics* (pp. 208-228). Chicago: University of Chicago Press.

Foucault, M. (1991). Governmentality. In G. Burchill, C. Gordon, & P. Miller (Eds.), *The Foucault effect* (pp. 87-104). Chicago: University of Chicago Press.

Frankel, H. (1953). *The economic impact on underdeveloped societies*. Cambridge, MA: Harvard University Press.

Gordon, C. (Ed.). (1980). *Power/knowledge: Selected interviews and other writings by Michel Foucault*. New York: Pantheon Books.

Grossi, V. et al. (1982). *Investigación participativa y praxis rural* [Participatory research and rural praxis]. Lima: Rosca Azul ed.

Gudeman, S. (1984). Ricardo's representations. *Representations, 5*, 90-110.

Habermas, J. (1975). *Legitimation crisis*. Boston: Beacon.

Hall, B. (1979). Knowledge as a commodity and participatory research. *Prospects, 9*(4), 393-408.

Heideger, M. (1963). *Being and time*. New York: Harper and Row.

Heideger, M. (1971). *The question concerning technology*. New York: Harper & Row.

Kassam, Y., & Mustafa, K. (1982). *Participatory research: An emerging alternative methodology in social science research*. New Delhi: Society for Participatory Research in Asia.

Kothari, R. (1984). Party and state in our times: The rise of non-party political formations. *Alternatives, 9*(4), 541-564.

Leibenstein, H. (1954). *A theory of economic-demographic development*. Princeton, NJ: Princeton University Press.

Lewis, W. A. (1949). *The principles of economic planning*. London: D. Dobson.

Lewis, W. A. (1955). *The theory of economic growth*. Homewood, IL: Irwin.

Machado, R. (1978). *Danação da Norma: Medicina Social e Constituição da Psiquiatria no Basil*. Rio de Janeiro: Edições Graal.

Martinez, A., & Silva, R. (1983). *Dos estudios sobre educación en la colonia*. [Two studies on education during the colonial period]. Bogotá: Université Pedagógica Nacional.

Milbank Memorial Fund. (1948). *International approaches to problems of underdeveloped countries*. New York: Author.

Nurkse, R. (1953). *Problems of capital formation in underdeveloped countries*. Oxford: Oxford University Press.

Pedrosa, A. (1981). El trabajo alfabetizador entre los sectores populares [Literacy work with popular groups]. *Revista Cleba* (No. 4).

Pletsch, C. E. (1981).The three worlds, or the division of social scientific labor, circa 1950-1975. *Comparative Studies in Society and History, 23*(4), 565-590.

Pratts, M. (1983). *Peripheral vision travel writing and the ideologies of imperialism*. Unpublished manuscript, Department of Spanish and Portuguese, Stanford University.

Rabinow, P., & Dreyfus, H. (1982). *Michel Foucault: Beyond structuralism and hermeneutics*. Chicago: University of Chicago Press.

Rahman, M. A. (1985). The theory and practice of participatory action research. In O. Fals-Borda (Ed.), *The challenge of social change*. London: Sage.

Said, E. (1979). *Orientalism*. New York: Vintage.

Sanz de Santamaria, A. (1984). Discurso economico y poder [Economic discourse and power]. *Texto y Contexto, 1*(2).

Taylor, C. (1979). Interpretation and the sciences of man. In P. Rabinow & M. Sullivan (Eds.), *Interpretative social sciences* (pp. 25-73). Berkeley: University of California Press.

Taylor, C. (1985). Social theory as practice. In *The Philosophy of the human sciences* (pp. 91-115). Cambridge: Cambridge University Press.

Tribe, K. (1981). *Genealogies of capitalism*. Atlantic Highlands, NJ: Humanities. (Original work published in *Economy and Society, 6*, 314-345)

United Nations, Department of Economic Affairs. (1949). *Methods of financing economic development in underdeveloped countries*. New York: Author.

United Nations, Department of Economic Affairs. (1951). *Measures for the economic develeptment of underdeveloped countries*. New York: Author.

United Nations, Department of Economic Affairs. (1953). *The determinants and consequences of population change*. New York: Author.

12

Popular Culture, Discourse, and Development: Rethinking Entertainment-Education From a Participatory Perspective

J. Douglas Storey
Johns Hopkins University

The literature on development communication is replete with compelling arguments against positivist communication. Many of these critiques portray mass media and planned communication as forms of monologue by resource-rich, politically, and economically advantaged forces in society aimed at managing the trajectory of social change. Although it is true that top–down communication has been the dominant mode historically, emerging theories of popular culture and discourse—although rarely applied in the development context—suggest that the relationships among media, audiences, and social change need to be re-examined and the uses of communication for development re-evaluated. In short, cultural studies and discourse theory suggest that even the most authoritatively managed communication systems are more participatory than previously conceptualized.

Entertainment-education—the use of popular forms of entertainment such as radio and television drama, popular theater, or popular music as vehicles for information, role modeling, and behavioral appeals in social change programs—is a case in point. Entertainment-education has traditionally been informed by social scientific theories of communication and behavior change aimed at predicting and maximizing specific behavioral responses desired by program designers. Although some "enter-educate" projects employ grassroots media to foster community activism (e.g., Conquergood, 1988), the majority are high-profile mass media productions with explicit attitude and behavior-change objectives defined by donor and implementing agencies, with little apparent participation by intended beneficiaries. Popular "participation" in such projects typically takes the form of audience research during the message design phase and fan mail sent to the broadcast station.

Yet, theories of popular culture and discourse suggest that entertainment-education may have a participatory dimension despite its instrumental and positivist origins. Popular culture, the domain within which entertainment-education operates by definition, is highly involving, emotionally engaging, continually evolving, and inherently participatory. By attempting to operate within the sphere of popular culture, development communication—in the form of entertainment-education—becomes subject to the free play of popular discourse that reworks it in ways its producers may never have imagined. Accommodating both social science and popular culture perspectives in the practice of development communication is possible but will require some changes in the way we think about media, audiences, and the goals and effects of development communication.

The objectives of this chapter are to explore some of the opportunities presented by recent scholarship on popular culture and discourse—particularly the work of Mikhail Bakhtin—for theorizing about participatory communication, and to indicate with examples how a discourse perspective enriches analysis of entertainment-education as a form of development communication, while highlighting its participatory aspects. The discussion is illustrated with examples drawn primarily from reproductive health programs, a discursively rich domain of applied development communication, which has used entertainment-education in a variety of ways.

POPULAR CULTURE

Fiske (1994) described popular culture as follows:

> Culture is the social circulation of meanings, pleasures, and values, and the cultural order that results is inextricably connected with the social order within which it circulates. Culture may secure the social

order and help to hold it in place or it may destabilize it and work toward changing it, but is never either neutral or detached. The social circulation of meanings is always a maelstrom, full of conflicting currents, whirlpools, and eddies. (p. 193)

The interplay of commercial, political, public, and individual forces generate the messages and meanings of popular culture. Public consumption of media content; individual-level feedback in the forms of discussion within families and among friends, purchase and use of advertised or modeled products, and adoption or rejection of modeled behaviors; policy statements and legislation pertaining to media and public issues appearing in the media; and commercial and public service activities and investments of media organizations are all forms of pop-cultural activity. Under the rubric described by Fiske, these are all aspects of popular culture which is, first and foremost, a *communication* phenomenon.

Theoretical approaches to popular culture had been, until the mid-to-late 1980s, heavily influenced by structural–materialist critiques of media institutions and mass culture that tended to paint a picture of hegemonic media manipulating a compliant audience. More recent scholarship strikes a better balance of power by recognizing that audience members actively interpret and use media content according to their own sensibilities and purposes. The interpretive acts of the audience are not completely independent of the institutional forces that shape media content and influence media behavior, but neither do media institutions operate independently of audience agendas, tastes, and needs on which the media must depend to generate interest for its programming. From this perspective, popular culture must be seen as a form of discourse or, more accurately, as a discursive system (see section on discourse).

Audience studies of the type just described, provide many examples of rich multidisciplinary theorizing and research about popular culture (see e.g., Ang, 1991; Fiske, 1994; Katz & Liebes, 1987; Livingstone, 1990; Morley, 1993; Rosengren, 1993). Audience studies like these bring together elements of the effects tradition (which typically focuses on the attitudinal and behavioral impact of messages on individuals) with the reception tradition (which typically focuses on the interpretation of texts by audiences). From this convergence emerge theories of the relationship between audiences/readers/viewers and texts/media. Within this new synthesis, mass communication is seen as an ongoing, sociocultural, and historical process, rather than as a series of discrete broadcast activities or message events. From this perspective, the communication process involves an array of interrelated elements: individuals, the communities in which they live, the social structures and institutions such as media systems that interpenetrate lives and communities, and the messages or texts generated by the various social actors. None of these elements can be studied in isolation from the others. All of these elements are posited to affect and be effected by each other through public discourse.

DISCOURSE

The contemporary notion of discourse owes much to the work of the Russian literary theorist, Mikhail Bakhtin (1895-1975). Bakhtin has become known gradually to communication theorists (far less so to communication practitioners, except novelists) through a growing number of translations of his work on a theory of the novel—his views of authorship/readership/text as a social phenomenon, in particular—and through interpretation of his work by cultural studies theorists who apply it to the analysis of media systems, media texts, and audiences. His work is voluminous and complex and an extended discussion of his theory is far beyond the scope of this chapter. However, certain concepts from Bakhtin and his interpreters can be introduced here to indicate how they might inform perspectives on participation and popular culture.

For Bakhtin, *dialogue* is the process by which an *utterance* (defined broadly to include speech acts as well as words, messages, images, texts) interacts with the greater social and ideological whole. An utterance,

> having taken meaning and shape at a particular historical moment in a socially specific environment, cannot fail to brush up against thousands of living dialogic threads, woven by socio-ideological consciousness around the given object of [the] utterance; it cannot fail to become an active participant in social dialogue. After all, the utterance arises out of this dialogue as a continuation of it and as a rejoinder to it—it does not approach the object from the sidelines. (Bakhtin, 1981, p. 277)

The preexistence of a *language world* from which the utterance emerges ensures that the utterance will be "relativized" or juxtaposed against other competing definitions for the same things. Furthermore, the language world is *heteroglot.* It encompasses multiple languages, each of which is informed by histories of experience and socioideological contradiction that predate and will survive any particular users of the language. Language, as a "matrix of forces practically impossible to recoup and therefore impossible to resolve" (Bakhtin, 1981, p. 428), causes every word, message, and image to be constantly reworked through dialogue.

According to Bakhtin (Morson & Emerson, 1990), dialogue is an open-ended, undominated, unfinalizable web of communicative (i.e., symbolic) interaction. As Bakhtin used the term, dialogue cannot be trivialized as "mere" interaction or conversation between individuals. People (as well as social groups and social institutions) are not regarded as bounded selves or entities except in a physical sense. The historical reality of each entity is better regarded as a "cultural field" of richly intersecting temporalities and identities. People cannot be said to "enter into" dialogue because existence cannot be separated from the ongoing process of communication (Morson & Emerson, 1990). Dialogue involves "the constant redefinition of its participants, develops and creates numerous potentials in each of them separately and between them interactively and dialogically" (p. 52).

Bakhtin's image of the novel as an open system of interacting meanings is evocative. As his work became more widely available, cultural studies scholars were quick to pick up on its implications for the study of media systems and media "texts." Newcomb (1984) argued that dialogue can be seen among audiences, community formations, governmental bodies, and media, with each entity generating texts (e.g., conversations, behavioral norms, policy statements, program offerings, social activities, value assertions, and so on) that reveal the unfinished and unfinishable nature of social change.

However, following Hall, Willis, Hobson, and Lowe (1980) and Morley (1980), cultural studies scholars have preferred to use the term *discourse* rather than *dialogue* to avoid some of the latter term's associations with speech and rhetorical studies. For Bakhtin, discourse had a narrower sense (meaning forms of speech—literally, "word"—including mediated and direct or unmediated, passive and active, unidirectional and varidirectional; Morson & Emerson, 1990) than dialogue (meaning the process of interaction), whereas cultural studies tends to inscribe *discourse* with the broader Bakhtinian sense of *dialogue*.

For example, in his book on audience interpretation of a popular British television show, Morley (1980) referred to the locus of *dialogue* as a *discourse system*, by which he meant the system of interactions among readers (audience members), texts (words, images, utterances), and social forms (media systems, a circle of friends, one's workplace, the commercial market) of which both readers/audiences and texts are parts. A discursive system is defined "by reference to the area of social experience that it makes sense of, to the social location from which that sense is made, and to the linguistic or signifying systems by which that sense is both made and circulated" (Fiske, 1987; see also Morley, 1993; Newcomb, 1984). From this perspective, mass communication begins to take on a new more interactive or participatory character.

If discourse is, by definition, uncontained (Newcomb, 1984), it is not, therefore, amenable to manipulation. Domination of discourse, such as occurs in persuasive attempts by authoritative media, involves the creation of boundaries or limits ("Buy this!" [Not that.] "Vote for me!" [Not for her.]). To try to create such boundaries in discourse is to deny discursive opportunities. It is in the nature of discourse that when powerful voices (e.g., government media) attempt to dominate, the discourse either shifts to other sites, or the attempt at domination itself becomes a subject of discourse, is deconstructed, and defused (Hall et al., 1980).

Discourse informs all its participants; therefore, it is antithetical to suppose that only some participants inform the others. To achieve discourse in development communication, then, all parties to the communication must be committed to engaging (rather than dominating) each other. Popular culture (and entertainment-education as a form of popular culture) may be the ideal venue for this engagement, because it is largely beyond the control of any particular party and is the site of ongoing construction, deconstruction and reconstruction of social realities.

ENTERTAINMENT-EDUCATION

The use of entertainment-education (or enter-educate) strategies to foster social change is gaining recognition as a viable option for health promotion, and applications of these strategies grow increasingly sophisticated. Among many cases that could be cited, Piotrow et al. (1990) reported successful uses of entertainment-education media for family planning promotion in Africa, Singhal and Rogers (1989) documented the success of Indian soap operas at conveying family planning themes, popular music has been used successfully to promote teenage sexual responsibility in Mexico (Coleman, 1988) and in the Philippines (Rimon et al., 1994), and Lozare et al. (1993) reported increases in positive attitudes toward and adoption of family planning among viewers of a prosocial television drama in Pakistan.

Analyses of entertainment-education programs (e.g., Kincaid, 1993; Kincaid, Jara, Coleman, & Segura, 1988) indicate that this approach maximizes audience attention, message appeal, and message recall by using strong emotional appeals, humor, music and attractive— even sexy—role models to attract and hold an audience. Interpersonal communication, particularly between spouses, is another documented effect of entertainment-education. Interspousal communication in turn, leads to health-clinic attendance and contraceptive adoption (Lozare et al., 1993). Note that all of these processes and effects are of the short-term, individual-level variety. Longer term effects are sometimes sought, as well, but for the most part are also individual-level effects (e.g., confirmation of behavioral decisions and/or behavioral reinforcement).

In contrast, McAnany and Potter (1993), based on a review and reanalysis of Brazilian data, assumed an historical perspective to argue that mass communication—television soap operas, in particular—may have long-term demographic consequences by virtue of their cumulative effects on communication processes within the family and community and on social values over time. Short-term individual-level behavior change may in turn result from shifts in social values at the family level. These propositions are supported by evidence from cultivation research (Gerbner 1973; Gerbner, Gross, Morgan, & Signorelli, 1980) that perceived social reality is affected by long term exposure to the ubiquitous symbolic environment of mass media. Still, the processes by which such effects occur are little understood.

A short-term perspective results, at least in part, from the theoretical frameworks that are used to study and design entertainment-education programs. For example, message learning and persuasion perspectives (see McGuire, 1987; Petty & Cacciopo, 1981, for reviews of this literature) tend to focus on messages as discrete packages of information which audiences quickly apprehend, evaluate, and respond to. Another common framework for analyzing persuasive communications programs is social learning theory. Social learning theory suggests that people learn new behaviors by observing how role models (either fictional or real) behave and what consequences occur (Bandura, 1986). Classical formulations of social learning theory indicate that role models must clearly act out the steps or components of a given behavior. Only if a behavior is clearly and unambiguously modeled can a viewer learn the steps, rehearse them mentally, attempt to reproduce them, and observe whether the consequences he or she experiences match those experienced by the role model. As far as the learning process is concerned, the theory describes a largely rational process involving a linear and fairly predictable sequence of causes (enacted behaviors) and effects (consequences, good and/or bad).

Often paired in practice with social learning is value-expectancy theory (Fishbein & Ajzen, 1980), which posits that behavioral intentions are affected by one's beliefs and attitudes toward a behavior and its consequences. These beliefs and attitudes include beliefs about and evaluations of social support for the behavior in question. Social drama or other entertainment-education formats can be used to influence perceptions of social support for a behavior and to change evaluations or expectations of the consequences of that behavior.

Although these frameworks help explain individual-level change in knowledge, attitudes, and behaviors, they do not adequately capture either the richness and complexity of entertainment-education or its potential for long-term change, neither do they deal very well with the volatility of meaning and the sensemaking process engaged in by audiences who are exposed to and use entertainment-education material. For example, social dramas (especially lengthier ones that develop a narrative plot over weeks or months) cannot be single-mindedly didactic, otherwise they lose the aesthetic, dramatic, entertaining qualities that make them interesting to audiences in the first place. Consequently, in dramas that work as entertainment, the prosocial messages are embedded in the larger structure of the narrative and may not be so easily recognized as discrete message units or appeals. Behaviors appear in context, motives are imputed, not all conflicts are neatly resolved—as in life itself. Furthermore, individuals and communities of viewers bring diverse interpretive frames to their viewing; this leads to a wide range of interpretations and uses of the already richly layered and nuanced symbolic content. So far, research and theory about entertainment and education have not dealt very effectively with how audiences identify, interpret, and use narratively structured information; or how entertainment-education operates within the larger social, cultural, and historical context of media systems and audiences.

In contrast, theories of communication that draw on semiotics (see Hawkes, 1977, for a comprehensive review) and cultural studies (e.g., Foucault, 1980) emphasize that messages derive much of their meaning from context and use (Fiske, 1987, 1994; Newcomb, 1984): Any given message has meaning *in relation to* the larger text in which it is located, the historical characteristics of the message vehicle or medium, and the experiences and social situation of receivers as they engage with symbolic material. Individuals impose shades of meaning on messages they apprehend, influenced by past experiences and present sociocultural conditions. These meanings are often socially constructed; that is, an individual makes sense of something he or she has seen or heard through subsequent interaction with others and in relation to personal history and social experience. Furthermore, the meaning that an individual derives from a message must be seen as volatile because new information or experiences will result in revised meaning. Theoretical development in entertainment-education has so far dealt very little with the issue of meaning.

Nor has there been much theoretical elaboration of the organizational and institutional aspects of entertainment-education, that is, how it operates in relation to existing media and other socio-political institutions. With the exception of a few studies (Singhal, Rogers, & Obregon, 1994; Faria & Potter, 1994), these aspects have been largely overlooked. One institutional effect of entertainment-education that has been studied is increased support for health promotion programs in the form of political support, financing, and advocacy by opinion leaders and other influentials (Piotrow & Coleman, 1992). For example, entertainment-education programs often garner support for health promotion programs from commercial and political quarters because they are perceived to be (a) *profitable*—through corporate tie-ins and product endorsements; (b) *cost-effective*—through cost-sharing, resale to commercial broadcasters and video outlets, and because of the size of the audience generated; and (c) *highly visible*—making them a politically attractive, high profile component of a national health program.

Yet, even advocacy is underdeveloped theoretically, in part because the frameworks commonly used in entertainment-education research and practice, however insightful they are regarding individual-level psychological and behavior changes, are insufficiently elaborated regarding the larger political, cultural, and historical context of communication. Policy activity and decision making at an institutional level, and the interactions among political, economic, and cultural institutions are not typically viewed as communication phenomena. Not that the broader context has gone completely unacknowledged. Kincaid (1993) noted that "[The entertainment-education approach] has the capacity to influence culture because it becomes part of a country's own popular culture (not an outside influence), competing with other sources of culture for attention and influence" (p. 5).

Entertainment-education, dealing as it does with popular culture, needs to be analyzed within a broader framework, provided by elements of popular culture and discourse theories.

SYNTHESIS: POPULAR CULTURE, DISCOURSE, AND ENTERTAINMENT-EDUCATION

The marriage of social scientific and cultural studies perspectives is in some ways an uneasy match, not least because of the historical antipathy between critical cultural studies and positivist social scientific theories and methods. To make this marriage work, the theories and practices need to be reevaluated in two important ways.

Systematicity

One change will have to be an epistemic shift in the way the task is conceptualized. Fiske (1994) argued that:

> Systemic theories of structure go further than do positivist ones, for systemic structures, such as language are generative, whereas positivist structures are descriptive. Systemic structures generate the

practices by which they are used and are, in their turn, modified by those practices. Positivist structures, however, have effects, not practices, and the relationship between structure and effect is one-way. (p. 195)

To illustrate this distinction in the context of mass communication, Fiske also said that

> [Television p]rograms, the industry that makes them, and the people who watch them are all active agents in the circulation of meanings, and the relationships among them are not ones of cause and effect, in which one precedes the other, but of systematicity. . . . The relationships between [audience and text] are not ones of cause and effect, in which one spatially, temporally, or epistemologically takes precedence over the other; the relations are systemic ones of a complex of reciprocities in which contradictions and complicities struggle to gain ground over one another. (p. 196)

Yet, even projects with anti-positivist goals often do seek to "intervene," for example, to facilitate participation, to empower communities, and to con-scienticize citizens as a first step toward democratic engagement. From this perspective, development communication becomes a partnership of media institutions, development agencies, donor organizations, and the audience, all of whom desire to improve the public welfare. Of course, single-minded devotion to public welfare rarely occurs. Institutions in the partnership have their own economic, political, and social priorities, all of which contend discursively with each other and with public welfare to shape and color the goals and strategies of entertainment-education. To the extent that these contending priorities can be kept in the open, development communication programs can serve as sites of discourse. Bakhtin suggested that this is unavoidable, particularly when the format engages popular culture, as in entertainment-education programs.

Participation

A second change, which goes to the core issue of this book, is in the way the communicator–audience relationship is conceptualized. Popular culture is not something one can readily manipulate, even with concerted effort. Instead, popular culture is something in which one can participate. This suggests a need to adopt a participatory mentality among those who would tap popular culture as a vehicle for development or social change programs. For example, the aim of much communication in the area of reproductive health is to expand discourse (we usually speak of increasing spousal or client–provider interaction—but expanding discourse is the underlying goal) in order to open up the possibilities women and men have to control their own fertility and reproductive health. This communication takes place in the larger context of cultural imperatives and historical traditions of reproductive rights and gender relations, such as within the ethnic and nationalist politics of newly independent states, in which family size becomes an expression of awakened ethnic pride.

Campaign theory and research (Rogers & Storey, 1987) tell us to select the channel or medium that is the most appropriate vehicle of the message for the audience we wish to reach. Although we usually take advantage of the visual or auditory power of television or radio to command attention, raise interest, or maximize involvement, we have yet to take advantage of the power of media as open, participatory, discursive systems. One of the most powerful effects of development communication that uses the entertainment-education approach may be the creation of discursive space for the discussion of health and development issues. Within such a strategy, the effect of discourse is more discourse.

An added benefit of conceptualizing entertainment-education as a participatory, discursive process is that the discourse of popular culture is ongoing; that is, it is inherently—in fact, unavoidably—sustainable. The cultural discourse perspective outlined here suggests that sustained public communication about health and development issues already exists and that entertainment-education must merge with or participate in that discourse, rather than intervene into and change that discourse. Especially useful may be longer serial forms of entertainment-education (television soap opera, talk radio, weekly public affairs programming) that present more open and fluid discursive opportunities and that have the potential for interaction with audience members over time. A popular serial could become a major and ongoing part of development discourse.

EXAMPLES

Presented here are two brief examples of reproductive health programs that used entertainment-education formats, and that interpret aspects of them from the perspective of discourse and popular culture previously outlined.

Reproductive health itself is a discursively rich area of development. In the late 1950s and early 1960s, this field focused mainly on family planning and the promotion of contraceptive use as a way to reduce population pressure and to avoid food shortages. As population programs mature, they have incorporated a wider range of interrelated issues including child survival, maternal health, environmental quality, sexually transmitted disease, and gender relationships. The International Conference on Population and Development held in Cairo in 1994 and the Fourth United Nations World Conference on Women held in Beijing in 1995 fostered this expanded view of reproductive health. Both conferences tried, not without controversy, to position population programs away from the narrow technological perspectives on fertility control toward broader integrated perspectives on population growth, poverty, and patterns of consumption and production as they relate to comprehensive reproductive health, reproductive rights, and the status of women and children (Garcia-Moreno & Turmen, 1995). Two enter-educate projects that reflect expanded perspectives on reproductive health are the Reproductive Health Drama Project in Pakistan and the *Alang-Alang* Project in Indonesia.[1]

Pakistan: Discourse begins at home

An important discursive system in its own right is spousal interaction. In health promotion programs, the degree of interaction between husband and wife is often associated with increased health knowledge and behavior change. Especially in the area of reproductive health, husbands and wives influence each other's contraceptive behaviors (sometimes positively, sometimes negatively), so understanding the nature of this process is crucial to the study of community and family health. At the same time, interpersonal interaction is an important site of inquiry into the communication process itself. This was the focus of a series of social dramas in Pakistan supported by Johns Hopkins University/Population Communication Services (JHU/PCS) in the early 1990s.

Prior to 1990, population communication efforts in Pakistan had been limited to spot advertising campaigns promoting the small family norm. Such indirect approaches (no explicit reference to contraception was made) were considered necessary to avoid provoking conservative religious opposition. Yet, research indicated strong latent demand for contraception. According to the Pakistan Contraceptive Prevalence Survey of 1986, 35% of nonusing couples of reproductive age favored spacing births whereas another 23% favored limiting births. Additional research by the National Institute of Population Studies indicated that, for 63% of women, the spouse was the most important motivator of contraceptive adoption. Finally, a series of individual case studies revealed that the woman was most often the one to obtain family planning sup-

[1]Both projects were funded by the United States Agency for International Development (USAID) under Cooperative Agreement DPE-3052-A-00-0014-00 with Johns Hopkins University Center for Communication Programs.

plies, but her action had to be sanctioned by her husband. Many women reported fear of their husband's disapproval, but lacked the skills to negotiate successfully for approval.

Between May 1990 and October 1993, the national broadcasting authority, Pakistan Television (PTV), produced and aired three television sociodramas on reproductive health. *Aahat* (An Approaching Sound) aired from October to November 1991. The six-episode drama aimed at increasing husband-wife communication regarding reproductive and family health issues, approval of spacing and family planning, clinic attendance, and adoption of family planning. *Aahat* was followed by a single-episode television film, *Aik Hi Rastha* (The Only Way) in July 1993 and the 13-part *Nijaat* (Deliverance), which aired from July to October 1993.

Public response to all three dramas was positive and press coverage extensive: More than 50 articles about *Aahat* alone appeared in the national and regional press. Thus, at the macro-level, the drama entered into and influenced public discourse on family planning.

At the micro-level—that of individuals and the family—research indicated substantial impact, as well: Of *Aahat* viewers surveyed (n = 2,118) 12% said the program had prompted them to take steps to space-out the births of their children, and 9% said they had visited a family planning clinic after viewing the drama (Lozare et al., 1993).

Consistent with the themes of the drama, spousal communication was closely linked with family planning behavior. Of the 9% of viewers who said they went to a clinic after watching the series, almost all of them (98%) had discussed family planning with his or her spouse. Put another way, 81% of those exposed to *Aahat* who discussed family planning methods with their spouses visited a clinic.

In general, the National Family Planning Program, especially its communication component, had been historically constrained by lack of political support. Yet, public and political support for televised population information lead PTV to continue its participation in public discourse around population and family planning by developing and airing *Aik Hi Rastha* and *Nijaat*.

Nijaat was launched by PTV on July 19, 1993 amid highly favorable press reports. It aired every Monday at 8:30 p.m. (prime time) through October 11. The story once more focused on husband–wife communication but was pitched more toward a rural male audience. Hazoor Baksh, a financially stressed small businessman; his wife Sajida; their two sons, Kashi (aged 7) and Tari (aged 5); and a baby are the main characters. Zareena is a nurse at the understaffed hospital in their small town; she is a friend of Sajida, having treated her through poor health and a series of miscarriages. Over time, Zareena convinces Sajida that she must talk to her husband about waiting to have another child. Hazoor, despite his softening attitude toward the adoption of family planning, fails to make a decision. Sajida discovers that she is again expecting, a condition that Zareena tells her is life-threatening. When the time comes, the delivery is very difficult, the baby is lost, and Hazoor finally decides they need to practice contraception. In the concluding episodes, Sajida and Hazoor struggle to bring their family together again.

A national television ratings service in Pakistan reported 60% to 75% viewership of *Nijaat* in the major cities of Karachi, Lahore, and Islamabad/Rawalpindi, giving it the highest reach by a large margin in its time slot.

The impact of *Nijaat* was evaluated using qualitative methods (in-depth interviews with men, women, and female service providers) designed to explore how discourse functioned around the drama.

Viewers clearly used the characters and situations in *Nijaat* as jumping off points for discussion of their own concerns and experiences as shown in the following passage from an interview with the 30-year-old wife of a welder (Aftab Associates, 1994):

> Q. Did you talk about the drama [while you watched]?
>
> A. My husband watched [parts of the drama]. He doesn't normally talk much. Only sometimes while watching the play he would say, "What is the A.C. doing to his wife?" or "What is Hazoor Baksh doing?" He would pass these short comments.
>
> Q. Didn't you talk about the main subjects in the play?
>
> A. No. We mostly talked about our own problems. Well, once he said that there is a cold war going on between the A.C. and his wife: "Two people, [when] they live under one roof, develop some kind of relationship after all." And I said, "We had the same problem, didn't we?" And he said, "That was before, not now. It's something of the past; now we understand each other." (p. 8)

The research on Aahat and Nijaat confirms a discursive link between the social drama, interspousal communication, and visits to the clinic. Television social dramas such as Aahat and Nijaat influence ideation (Cleland & Wilson, 1987), that is, how people think and talk about reproductive health. Witnessing the experiences of a couple on the television screen and hearing what they say to each other in the intimacy of their bedroom alters the boundaries of what is thinkable, the limits of what is speakable. Viewers acquire a vocabulary of characters, dialogue, and images from the drama that they subsequently incorporate into family conversations about family planning. New words, ideas, and strategies for negotiation between husband and wife enter family discourse.

Indonesia: Aesthetics and Social Change

Alang-Alang (Wild Grass), a three-part television drama promoting the education of female children, was a project of the Indonesian Family Planning Coordinating Board (BKKBN) with technical support from the JHU/PCS project. The drama was directed by Teguh Karya, one of Indonesia's and Asia's most experienced and respected film directors. Broadcast in December 1994, the drama tells the story of Ipah, the young motherless daughter of a trash scavenger living on the margins of the great garbage dumps of Jakarta. Ipah's father, Pak Rengga, fails to understand Ipah's desire for education and a better life, and withholds the money she needs for her school fees, causing Ipah to seek odd jobs and to work long hours to pay for her own education. Through the help of neighbors and her own diligence, Ipah eventually sways her father's opinion, completes her schooling, and becomes a teacher.

The drama was seen by 25% to 30% of the Indonesian television audience in major cities in Java and was the subject of several dozen newspaper and magazine articles in the Jakarta area. The discourse that occurred among Ipah, her father, their neighbors, and school staff, and the media coverage of the broadcast are only a few facets of the discursive quality of the entire project. Examining the effects of *Alang-Alang* from a discursive perspective indicates that numerous valuable and constructive discursive outcomes occurred as a result of this popular culture event.

Teguh Karya himself illustrates the intersection of or discourse among aesthetic priorities, commercial forces, social activism, government policy, health promotion, and foreign aid. As a renowned artist and activist (he has run a grassroots theater company, *Teater Populer*, for many years), Teguh struggled constantly with the tensions between art and delivering a message and reached accommodation between his priorities as a filmmaker and the government's wish for him to use his art in support of its family welfare (*keluarga sejahtera*) program. He embraced the creative tension between artistic expression and social scientific health communication by participating in focus group research used to inform the story development process. He accommodated JHU/PCS requests for explicit population themes by adding a female character who dies as a result of repeated high-risk childbirth. And by following up an earlier collaboration with BKKBN and JHU/PCS (*The Equatorial Trilogy*), Teguh continues to set an example as a socially active artist.

The television industry also played a role in the discourse surrounding *Alang-Alang*. Originally planned for broadcast on a parastatal television channel, a major commercial television station (SCTV) bought the series instead and aired it, knowing of its prosocial content and purpose, in part because they recognized the popularity of social dramas (drama with a message) and the artistic quality of the director's work. This was the first time that SCTV had aired such a program.

BKKBN was enthusiastic about female education as a subcomponent of its *keluarga sejahtera* program and saw Teguh Karya's interest in the issue as an opportunity for collaboration. Through their involvement with and support for social dramas like *The Equatorial Trilogy* and *Alang-Alang*, BKKBN continues to build relations with the artistic community and to support popular culture as a site where health discourse can occur.

Reaction to the drama was also discursive: Using focus groups, a qualitative evaluation of audience response to the drama revealed multiple interpretations of what the drama's main messages were. This finding, in turn, generated discussion within JHU/PCS and between JHU/PCS and BKKBN about the specificity of and relations among BKKBN's *keluarga sejahtera* program goals and the clarity with which those goals were or could be represented in television drama. In addition, mother–daughter interaction was stimulated by the drama. References to characters in the narrative occurred in mother–daughter interactions following the broadcasts. For example, one mother reported asking her daughter, "Why can't you be more like Ipah?" The mother did not relate her daughter's response, but it probably reflected themes inherent in discourse among adolescent females and their parents in Indonesia.

Discourse changes the institutions as well as the audiences who participate in it. JHU/PCS, while hoping to make the family planning and population themes as explicit as possible, supported the broad theme of girl-child education as consistent with its aims to expand reproductive health options for women in Indonesian society. This reflects a gradual shift within JHU/PCS, and within the larger structure of U.S. and international population programs following the Cairo and Beijing conferences in 1994–1995, toward a broader conceptualization of population issues in terms of reproductive health and women's rights.

A further institutional change is revealed in the choice of evaluation methodology. *Alang-Alang* impact evaluation had a qualitative component aimed at discovering what viewers had to say about their understanding of and response to the story. This is in contrast to an historical preference (within the donor community in general) for quantitative assessment of program impact. JHU/PCS has undertaken several qualitative evaluations of entertainment-education projects in the past few years.

Generalizations About Popular Culture, Discourse, and Development

Attempting to use popular culture for educational purposes, as entertainment-education proposes to do, may not be easy, although it is ripe with potential. This review of theories and entertainment-education projects suggests that we must revise the way we think about it if we would use it effectively to foster social change. Looking at entertainment-education as a manifestation of popular culture, and at popular culture as a communication process, a number of generalizations emerge.

Generalization 1: Popular Culture is Localized and Difficult to Know Very Completely or Quickly. The use of entertainment-education may require more reliance on qualitative research than has typically been the case with other types of media-based health and development projects. Furthermore, because the entertainment-education process is still little understood, more qualitative research may be needed before reliable and meaningful quantitative impact evaluation techniques can be developed.

Generalization 2: Popular Culture Has Its Own Dynamic That Resists External Control. This is not to say that popular culture does not change; in fact popular culture is often highly syncretic. But it is unrealistic to expect entertainment-education to have only predictable, direct, short-term effects on individual attitudes and behavior.

Generalization 3: By Adopting a Popular Culture Perspective, Entertainment-Education Must Take a Long-Term View of Social Change. Popular culture is an ongoing discursive process. Therefore, efforts to promote change within popular culture must recognize that historical forces have helped to shape the current forms and content of cultural expression. It also suggests that popular culture surrounding health issues, for example, will unfold over time in response to changing social, cultural, and political conditions. Entertainment-education is only one element among many that shape and are shaped by popular culture.

Generalization 4: Entertainment-Education Is Not Just Another Vehicle for Health and Development Messages. Entertainment-education is certainly capable of carrying discrete messages or appeals and of generating attitudinal and behavioral effects, but it is also part of the rich and dynamic discursive system of popular culture. Longer narrative and dramatic forms of entertainment-education such as serial drama have a particular capacity to bear sociocultural information that far exceeds the capacity of shorter forms such as spot advertisements, print materials, and other channels, which are typical of social marketing strategies and common in development campaigns.

Generalization 5: Entertainment-Education Is a Point of Engagement, a Site of Discourse, Not Just Another Message. Entertainment-education can be used for more than just role modeling; it can be a powerful impetus for negotiation within families about family roles, responsibilities, and priorities. It can also provide a forum for interaction between audiences, media, and health institutions over social priorities and values.

Generalization 6: Entertainment-Education May Be Most Useful for Initiating Discussion and Debate and Influencing the Public Agenda. Not that entertainment-education cannot motivate behavior change, but it may be best paired with advocacy efforts, public service announcements, and other more focused appeals, rather than being expected to accomplish behavior change in and of itself. Because well-done serials become absorbed into the stream of popular culture, they can be a powerful means for getting issues onto the public agenda.

Generalization 7: Entertainment-Education Encourages Less Emphasis on the Message Per Se and More Emphasis on the Audience. Entertainment programming cannot be effective unless its producers respond to the sensibilities of their audience. The effective use of humor and emotion requires close attention to the origins of those narrative devices in the audience's culture.

Generalization 8: The Audience for Entertainment-Education Is a Participant, Not a Target. Because entertainment-education is discursive, the audience must be regarded as a full partner in the communication process. This means that entertainment-education programs must make a special effort to involve audiences in the program development and scripting process through research and pretesting. The more participatory this research can be made, the better, as it will increase the veracity and relevance of the material for its audience. Also, as an entertainment-education program gains acceptance and becomes a part of popular discourse, health communicators must be prepared to engage with the discourse that emerges around the program, using its language and responding to it, even if that discourse diverges from the program's original objectives.

Generalization 9: The Institutions Involved in Entertainment-Education Also Change Because They Are Participants in the Discourse as Much as is the Audience. For example, some US foreign assistance agencies, as exemplified by JHU/PCS and USAID, are changing in response to the discourse of which they are a part. This is indicated by shifts in terminology toward reproductive health and women's rights and away from family planning per se, increased attention to the institutions and contexts of population programs, and an increased acceptance of qualitative methods.

CONCLUSION

Taking a discursive approach will encourage practitioners to assume a less instrumental but more functional stance toward the people and communities they attempt to serve. That is, communication will be used less to manipulate and more to participate in what people in their communities and societies wish to achieve. By recognizing the discursively integrated nature of people and social systems, and the dynamic and unfinishable historical process of communication in which they are continuously engaged, we are forced to assume a more modest position regarding our ability to create change. Instead, we become (or, according to Bakhtin, we already are unavoidably) participants in a development dialogue that links the many individual, group, and institutional entities in a social system.

This should not render us powerless as practitioners, but we must be more modest and cautious about choosing our goals. I have argued elsewhere (Storey, 1990, 1991, 1993) that the most challenging first step in many development projects, especially projects with a strong participatory element, may be simply to start people talking to one another about needs, goals, resources, and strategies. By entering into the ongoing process of social discourse of the people and societies we encounter in our work, we bring ourselves closer to, and perhaps into, the public space where people have been operating all along. By becoming participants, ourselves, in the discourse of those we try to serve, we meet them at their own points of engagement with their own public and private concerns. As practitioners, we cannot, any more than our clients, be disintegrated from the social and cultural environment. It is this participation in the discursive systems surrounding health that will have the most sustained impact on health behavior and health status and development in general.

REFERENCES

Aftab Associates, Ltd. (1994). *A qualitative evaluation of the impact of Nijaat in the rural vicinity of Lahore, Pakistan.* Unpublished research report to the International Development Research Center (IDRC). Ontario, Canada and Karachi, Pakistan.

Ajzen, I. (1989). Attitude structure and behavior. In A. R. Pratkanis et al. (Eds.), *Attitude structure and function* (pp. 241–274). Hillsdale, NJ: Lawrence Erlbaum Associates.

Ang, I. (1991). *Desperately seeking the audience.* London: Routledge.

Bakhtin, M. (1981). *The dialogic imagination.* Austin: University of Texas Press.

Bandura, A. (1986). *Social foundations of thought and action.* Englewood Cliffs, NJ: Prentice-Hall.

Cleland, J., & Wilson, C. (1987). Demand theories of the fertility transition: An iconoclastic view. *Population Studies, 41,* 5-30.

Coleman, P. (1988). Enter-educate: A new word from Johns Hopkins. *JOICFP Review, 15,* 28-31.

Conquergood, D. (1988). Health theatre in a Hmong refugee camp: Performance, communication, and culture. *TDR: The Drama Review, 38* (1), 174-208.

Faria, V., & Potter, J. (1994, February). *Television, telenovelas, and fertility change in Northeast Brazil.* Paper presented to the IUSSP seminar on values and fertility change, Sion, Switzerland.

Fishbein, M., & Ajzen, I. (1980). *The theory of reasoned action.* Englewood Cliffs, NJ: Prentice-Hall.

Fiske, J. (1987). British cultural studies and television. In B. Allen (Ed.), *Channels of discourse: Television and contemporary criticism* (pp. 254-289). Chapel Hill: University of North Carolina Press.

Fiske, J. (1994). Audiencing: Cultural practice and cultural studies. In N. Denzin & E. Lincoln (Eds.), *Handbook of qualitative research* (pp. 189-198). Newbury Park, CA: Sage.

Foucault, M. 1980. *Power/knowledge: Selected interviews and other writings.* Brighton: Harvester.

Garcia-Moreno, C., & Turmen, T. (1995). International perspectives on women's reproductive health. *Science, 269,* 790-792.

Gerbner, G. (1973). Cultural indicators—the third voice. In G. Gerbner, L. Gross, & W. Melody (Eds.), *Communication technology and social policy* (pp. 553-573). New York: Wiley.

Gerbner, G., Gross, L., Morgan, M., & Signorelli, N. (1980). The mainstreaming of America: Violence profile no. 2. *Journal of Communication, 30,* 10-27.

Hall, S., Willis, P., Hobson, D., & Lowe, A. (Eds.). (1980). *Culture, media, language.* London: Hutchinson.

Hawkes, T. (1977). *Structuralism and semiotics.* Berkeley: University of California Press.

Katz, E., & Liebes, T. (1987). Decoding Dallas: Notes from a cross-cultural study. In H. Newcomb (Ed.), *Television: The critical view* (pp. 419-432). New York: Oxford University Press.,

Kincaid, L. (1993, May). *Using television dramas to accelerate social change: The enter-educate approach to family planning promotion in Turkey, Pakistan, and Egypt.* Paper presented at the annual conference of the International Communication Association, Washington, DC.

Kincaid, L., Jara, J., Coleman, P., & Segura, F. (1988). *Getting the message: The communication for young people project.* (USAID Special Study 56). Washington, DC: USAID.

Livingstone, S. (1990). *Making sense of television: The psychology of audience interpretation.* London: Routledge.

Lozare, B., Hess, R., Yun, S., Gill-Bailey, A., Valmadrid, C., Livesay, A., Khan, S., & Siddigni, N. (1993, October–November). *Effects of Aahat: A family planning television drama in Pakistan.* Paper presented at the annual conference of the American Public Health Association, Washington, DC.

McAnany, E., & Potter, J. (1993, May). *Entertainment television, public policy and fertility change: Brazilian telenovelas as sites for research.* Paper presented at the annual conference of the International Communication Association, Washington, DC.

McGuire, W. (1987). Theoretical foundations of campaigns. In R.E. Rice & C.K. Atkin (Eds.), *Public communication campaigns* (pp. 43-66). Newbury Park, CA: Sage.

Morley, D. (1980). *The "nationwide" audience.* London: BFI.

Morley, D. (1993). *Television, audiences and cultural studies.* London: Routledge.

Morson, G., & Emerson, C. (1990). *Mikhail Bakhtin: Creation of a prosaics.* Stanford, CA: Stanford University Press.

Newcomb, H. (1984). On the dialogic aspects of mass communication. *Critical Studies in Mass Communication, 1*(1), 34-50.

Petty, R., & Cacioppo, J. (1981). *Attitudes and persuasion: Classic and contemporary approaches.* Dubuque, IA: Wm. Brown.

Piotrow, P., & Coleman, P. (1992). The enter-educate approach. *Integration, 31,* 4-6.

Piotrow, P., Rimon, J., Winnard, K., Kincaid, L., Huntington, D., & Conviser, J. (1990). Mass media family planning promotion in three Nigerian Cities. *Studies in Family Planning, 21*(5), 265-274.

Rimon, J., Treiman, K., Kincaid, L., Silayan-Go, A., Camacho-Reyes, M., Abejuela, R., & Coleman, P. (1994). *Promoting sexual responsibility in the Philippines through music: An enter-educate approach* (Occasional Paper Series #3). Baltimore: Johns Hopkins Center for Communication Programs.

Rogers, E., & Storey, D. (1987). Communication campaigns. In C. Berger & S. Chaffee (Eds.), *Handbook of communication science* (pp. 817-845). Newbury Park, CA: Sage.

Rosengren, K. (1993). Audience research: Back to square one—At a higher level of insight? *Poetics, 21*, 239-241.

Singhal, A., & Rogers, E. (1989). Television soap operas for development in India. *Gazette, 41*, 109-126.

Singhal, A., Rogers, E., & Obregon, R. (1994, October–November). *Simplemente Maria and the formation of the entertainment-education strategy.* Paper presented at the annual conference of the American Public Health Association, Washington, DC.

Storey, D. (1990, August). *Motivating participation in participatory research: Lessons from research on interpersonal communication and intragroup processes.* Paper presented to the Participatory Research Working Group of the International Association for Mass Communication Research, Bled, Yugoslavia.

Storey, D. (1991). History and homogeneity: Effects of perceptions of membership groups on interpersonal communication. *Communication Research, 18*(2), 199-221.

Storey, D. (1993). Mythology, narrative and discourse in Javanese wayang: Toward cross-level theories for the new development paradigm. *Asian Journal of Communication, 3*(2), 30-53.

13

Action Research: Theoretical and Methodological Considerations for Development Communications

Edna F. Einsiedel
University of Calgary

Since the 1970s, a growing literature has developed around participatory action research (PAR), also known as participatory research. Recent attempts to bring to bear the PAR framework to development communications have stressed the importance of developing theory, of linking theory to development communications practice, and, more importantly, of examining such a linkage in the context of social transformation.

Efforts to encourage theory development in this area exemplified by the work of Jacobson (1993) and Servaes (1989) have usefully focused on the notions of participation and participatory communications as potential sites for theory development. Jacobson, for example, emphasized the theoretical task of identifying common dimensions among different types of participation. Drawing on Habermas' concept of consensual dialogue in the ideal speech situation, both Jacobson and Servaes proposed that this concept provides a useful framework for analyzing "processes of horizontal communication in a way reflecting ideals of participatory decision-making and conscientization" (Jacobson, 1993, p. 221).

In this chapter, I suggest that a second prong in the process of theory development for participatory communications can be developed by looking at the potential contribution offered by development practice. Here I explore this second avenue by examining the *action research* tradition as a means of understanding the reflexive relation between theory and practice and as a means of *building theory from practice in the context of social change*. I further propose using grounded theory as an analytical framework for this task. Despite the interchangeable nature of the terms *participatory research* and *participatory action research*, I use the latter if only to emphasize the action research component in this chapter. I discuss in the words of Rahman (1985), "action research that is participatory, and participatory research that unites with action for [transforming reality]" (p. 108).

WHAT IS ACTION RESEARCH?

Action research has been described in various ways and the following statements are illustrative rather than comprehensive:

> Action research is distinguished by its adherence to a collaborative ethic. Action research is a collaborative endeavor in which groups of practitioners work together to understand better their own practice, to increase their awareness of the effects of their practice, and of their control over the situation in which they work. (Brown, Henry, Henry, & McTaggart, 1988, p. 4)

> Inevitably, the action researcher becomes involved in creating change not in artificial settings where effects can be studied and reported dispassionately, but in the real world of *social practice*. In action research, the intention to affect social practice stands shoulder to shoulder with the intention to understand it. (Kemmis & McTaggart, 1988, p. 33, italics added)

> Action science is an inquiry into how human beings design and implement action in relation to one another. Hence, it is a science of *practice* (which) calls for basic research and theory building that are intimately related to social intervention. (Argyris, Putnam, & Smith, 1985, p. 4)

The focus on social practices and the ways that research and reflection leading to theoretical insight might inform the process of social change is called *praxis*. Notwithstanding Habermas' (1974) comprehensive analysis, action research's historical roots extend much further to Aristotle and his notion of self-reflection as a way of informing practice (Grundy, 1982). The term *praxis* introduced by the Greeks, was equated with the idea of "critically informed practice." Praxis requires reflection on three levels: the exact nature of the action as conducted (and as it is perceived and understood by its practitioners), the impact or consequences of the action, and its context. This reflection is meant to transform the knowledge base in order to guide further action.

Another important dimension to praxis is its guidance by a moral disposition to act for the enhancement of truth and justice, a disposition labeled *phronesis* by the Greeks. Without such a moral imperative, one is left with technique and the possibility of perpetuating self-deception and injustice (Grundy, 1982).

In summary, praxis involves six interrelated steps. Step 1 is the identification of a social goal that may arise from particular problems ("What is it we would like to achieve?"). Step 2 is the critical examination of one's social practices ("What is it we do?"). Step 3 is the search for explanations and alternatives for those practices in need of change ("Why do we do what we do?" "What can we do to change things?"). The fourth step is testing alternative modes of doing things ("What happens when we try this?"). Step 5 involves revising strategies and step 6 calls for further testing and reflecting on these until the goal is obtained. Praxis, as outlined in these steps, is in essence building "theories" of understanding from practice for social transformation.

It is the praxis dimension of action research that distinguishes the latter from applied social science. An applied science is normally the counterpart to basic science and the applied scientist is typically seen as one who puts into practice the principles uncovered by basic scientists. Argyris et al. (1985) argued that "this division of labor reinforces a pernicious separation of theory and practice" (p. 5). What action research emphasizes instead is the importance of practical knowledge, the knowledge of the practitioners or the community of individuals with whom the researcher interacts, and the need for harnessing this knowledge to inform social theory and to achieve social change.

ORIGINS OF ACTION RESEARCH

It is important to understand the historical origins of action research as a precursor to making the case for building theory from practice. This historical understanding is designed to show the venerable tradition behind a theory-from-practice approach, and the basis for arguing that practice for social transformation can contribute to theory-building.

The North American Stream

The educational philosopher John Dewey (1938) provided an early impetus for action research by suggesting that a philosophy isolated from the rest of life is sterile and that social practice is an important focus of scientific inquiry. His argument that teachers, educational researchers, and community members might collectively address educational problems to bring about reform is a way of demystifying and democratizing the conduct of research. In this regard, it is his contention that practical judgments share common attributes with theoretical judgments. Foreshadowing the action-reflection process of action research, Dewey viewed inquiry as a continuous, self-corrective process, with every contention or knowledge claim open to further criticism and discussion (Bernstein, 1971).

For Dewey (1929), the usefulness of research findings in the realm of practice is the final arbiter of the research's "value":

> Educational practices provide the data, the subject matter, which form the problems of inquiry. . . . These educational practices are also the final test of value and test the worth of scientific results. They may be scientific in some other field, but not in education until they serve educational purposes, and whether they really serve educational purposes can be found out only in practice. (p. 47)

Viewed from this perspective, Dewey's analysis of scientific inquiry was clearly not value-neutral. Moreover, he saw praxis as a base for genuine social reconstruction.

Another social scientist often associated with action research is Kurt Lewin, who invented the term *action research* to describe a process whereby social scientists worked collaboratively with a group, an organization, or a community. His vision of action research embodied a dynamic relation between knowing and doing. He had in mind the process of improving understanding in dialectical relation with the process of improving action. Lewin (1946) maintained that "Research that produces nothing but books will not suffice" (p. 34).

For Lewin (1946, 1947), action research "consisted in analysis, fact-finding, conceptualization, planning, execution, more fact-finding or evaluation; and then a repetition of this whole circle of activities; indeed a spiral of such circles" (p. 33). Such a plan is geared toward a program of social action, and participants in the community or group are to be involved in every stage of the action research cycle. Learning within the group is dependent on everyone's participation in information seeking and diagnosis; moreover, freedom of choice was imperative for the selection of and engagement in new kinds of action.[1]

Clearly, Lewin was impelled by the principles of knowledge sharing, rational analysis, and democratic participation. He further believed these values to be compelling for the social actors involved. He also recognized that "expertise" and the capacity for learning are resident in both the researcher and the group.

His work on group decision-making as a means of collaboratively generating knowledge with social actors and creating a basis for social theory was well illustrated by his attempt to help U.S. housewives increase their use of alternative meals such as kidneys, beefhearts, and sweetbreads during the food-rationing period. The social scientist's better understanding of group dynamics and motivation was concomitant with and grew out of housewives' better understanding of nutritious preparation of alternative meals (see Lewin, 1952).

His work in the area of minority relations reflected his acceptance of the practice of social science as an advocacy activity. As a German Jew driven from Germany by widespread persecution, he was, not surprisingly, deeply concerned with social issues such as the social conditions from which prejudice evolved (Marrow, 1969). His desire to understand these conditions became the foundation for the desire to bring about change, putting his work squarely within an advocacy mode.

Lewin's influence was evident in the outpouring of reports from the Research Center for Group Dynamics, which he founded, and the Tavistock Institute of Human Relations in Great Britain. Much of the work of these institutes was evident in the pages of the early issues of *Journal of Human Relations* and *Journal of Social Issues* in the 1940s. The debates between the Gestalt and behaviorist approaches to psychology were raging at the time and Lewin's call for action research and the need for understanding the dynamic nature of change in the context of real social events outside of the laboratory reflected his Gestaltist leanings (Marrow, 1969).

Lewin was not naive about the challenges of initiating and sustaining change within the group. He maintained that social scientists and practitioners "should consider action, research and training as a triangle that should be kept together for the sake of any of its corners" (Lewin, 1946, p. 44).

The essence of Lewin's conception of action research might be summarized as having the following attributes: It is an effort that focuses

---

[1]Lewin was, of course, recognized in communications for his concepts of the "gatekeeper" and force-field analysis.

specifically on the amelioration of some social problem; such a focus also provides the impulse for inquiry and the articulation of social theory; the effort was a collaborative one, or a "joint project" between social actors and researchers; its process was characterized by cyclical elements of action reflection, consisting of analysis, fact-finding, conceptualization, planning, execution, more fact-finding and evaluation. However, the successful maintenance of this process and resolution is one that requires systematic efforts at training.

Both Dewey and Lewin contributed to the growth of action research in the fields of education and organizational development. It is beyond the scope of this chapter to describe, except in passing, the development of action research in these fields.[2] In the field of organization development in Britain, strategies for worker cooperation and management were explored. The role of the action researcher consultants and their relationships with the workers and managers is seen as central to problem solving and theory articulation (see Foster, 1972). Similar approaches in industrial settings were applied by Elden and his colleagues in Norway (see, e.g., Elden & Levin, 1991).

THE CONTRIBUTIONS OF CRITICAL SOCIAL SCIENCE

Habermas' elaboration of a critical social science has been seen as an attempt to reconcile "interpretive understanding" and causal explanations (Carr & Kemmis, 1986). Dissatisfied with mainstream positivist approaches to science and the interpretive approach's traditional concern with the uncritical reproduction of individuals' self-understanding, he pushed for the illumination of the causes of distortions in perceptions and overcoming these causes.

It was Habermas' (1984) main contention that in order for critical social science to be a viable and rationale enterprise, it required normative foundations that, in turn, could be derived from an analysis of ordinary discourse. Thus, his theory of communicative competence and the "ideal speech situation" are key to the emancipator dimension of a critical social science.

Habermas (1970) contended that the conditions for democratic discussion are the same as those which nurture "truth-telling":

---

[2]For fuller accounts, see Gustavsen and Hunnius (1981), Kemmis and McTaggart, (1988), Whyte (1991). These sources provide a good overview of the applications of action research to settings as varied as the workplace, education, and community development.

No matter how the intersubjectivity of mutual understanding may be deformed, the design of an ideal speech situation is necessarily implied in the structure of potential speech, since all speech, even intentional deception, is oriented toward the ideal of truth. This idea can be analyzed with regard to a consensus achieved in unrestrained and universal discourse. Insofar as we master the means for the construction of the ideal speech situation, we can conceive the ideas of truth, freedom and justice, which interpenetrate each other. (p. 372)

This freedom from constraint is possible only when there is true equality in opportunities to speak, question, and reason. Such conditions for an ideal discourse are clearly the same as those conditions that make for an ideal form of life.

For Habermas, a critical social science is a social process that combines a collaborative effort at critique with the political will to overcome the structural constraints (e.g., existing institutions, unjust social practices) that bring about injustices. It is one that evolves from critique to critical praxis, or one in which the actors involved bring their enlightenment to bear on transformative activities.

How is this to happen? Habermas failed to offer a useful explanation for the accomplishment of this aim. As Bernstein (1976) observed: "The very idea of practical discourse—of individuals engaged in argumentation directed towards rational will formation—can easily degenerate into a mere ideal, unless and until the material conditions required for such discourse are concretely realized and objectively realized" (p. 46).

Although Habermas' major contribution may be in the illumination of the action-reflection cycle, or "the organization of enlightenment," which is the precursor for organizing action, this criticism offers a real opportunity for better theoretical elaboration. We remain unfamiliar, for instance, with how the processes of discourse proceeds under different power relations.

Many of the ideas of PAR in the Third World can be described within the framework of critical social science. Freire's (1970) notion of conscientization, referring to a process of raising self-awareness via collective inquiry and reflection to promote empowerment and change is one such example. The work of Fals-Borda (1991) similarly rests on the action-reflection principle and the importance of praxis, with its twin prongs of practice or experience, and commitment. According to Fals-Borda, "Through the actual experience of something, we intuitively apprehend its essence. . . . In participatory action research, such an experience, called *vivencias* in Spanish, is complemented by another idea: that of authentic commitment" (p. 4).

Finally, the contributions of feminist research in the area of gender and development need to be recognized as a further significant exemplar of critically oriented action research. The omission of women from the development picture prompted feminist researchers to ask some key questions that transformed development policy and practice: "Where are the women?" "If they are present in the development arena, what do we know about what they are doing? If they are absent, why is this so?" (Einsiedel, in press). Examinations of women's place in the development picture (see, e.g., Boserup, 1970) led to policy changes that resulted in changes in development policy and practice (see Moser, 1993) and new ways of theorizing that could not have come about without the fruitful collaboration among researchers, policymakers, development practitioners, and women at the grassroots.

The parallels between action research and critical social science are clear. First, there is a shared focus on and concern with the practical: The examination of social practice by social scientists and the community involved becomes the basis for developing better practice and, in the process, building some theoretical understanding. Second, both depend heavily on perceptions and understanding of self-reflective practitioners. Third, both require critical processes of self-reflection in order to build knowledge that is emancipatory.

THE DEMISE OF ACTION RESEARCH

"Whatever happened to action research?" This was the question posed by Sanford in 1970 in an article that bemoaned the decline of action research. By this time, observed Sanford, "I would say that we have separated—and then institutionalized the separation of—everything that, from the point of view of action research . . . belongs together" (p. 7). The decline of action research came about in the 1970s for a number of reasons.

First, the attempt by the social sciences to model themselves after the natural sciences (in approach, rigor, paradigms) led to the adoption of the same "biases." Second, the general tendency toward specialization in modern science and scholarship (Sanford, 1970), including intradisciplinary specialization, resulted in what Sanford called "a fantastic proliferation of bitsy and disconnected and essentially unusable research" (p. 8), and contributed further to this decline.

Finally, the progressive focus on the individual and the technologization of the modern world paralleled—some would say contributed to—the increasing focus on behavior and its atomistic parts, resulting in a fragmented and externalized conception of the individual. This development opposed the more holistic and communitarian tendencies of action research.

Happily, the demise was not a permanent one. Current revival has received impetus from a number of directions: (a) the questioning of the dominant paradigm in much of the traditional social sciences, including its assumptions of knowledge for its own sake and the appropriateness of the natural science approach to generation of social laws and theory testing; (b) additional impetus within development studies came from critiques of failed development models; (c) a corollary thrust of grassroots movements to promote localized and self-reliant development carried with it a recognition of the validity of indigenous knowledge and challenges to expert claims to ownership of knowledge.

This climate of social changes contributed to an increasing "revival" of action research from a number of directions including development studies (see Fals-Borda, 1991; Freire, 1970), education (Kemmis & McTaggart, 1988), and organizational development (Argyris et al., 1985).

IMPLICATIONS FOR DEVELOPMENT COMMUNICATIONS

In the preceding discussion, we made the case that action research's foundation of viewing *practice* as the base for theoretical understanding offers another useful arena for theory-building on development and, more particularly, on development communications.

I begin this section by briefly going beyond theory-building to address paradigm-level issues. Gildart (1993) contended that the field of development and PAR in particular will benefit greatly from a multiparadigm perspective. I agree with this position for three reasons. First, action research is considered one of the areas that bridges paradigm boundaries (see Argyris, Smith, & Putnam, 1985; Gioia & Pitre, 1990). Second, the very nature of development study and practice requires a comprehensive view that can be gained only when differing perspectives have been examined, evaluated, and juxtaposed. "The multiple perspectives view implies a kind of metatriangulation not across methods within a single theory or paradigm . . . but across theories and paradigms" (Gioia & Pitre, 1990, p. 597). Third, this perspective allows us to get beyond the heated debates on theory, method, and worldviews that have characterized much of PAR literature, debates that have been extensions of the paradigm incommensurability battles and that have left little room for expanding theoretical understanding.

This multiparadigmatic approach has implications for theory and method that are explored here.

In examining numerous case studies under the rubric of PAR, it was found that many of the cases provide good descriptive bases for development work that incorporate various degrees of participation or describe participation in specific phases of a development project (e.g., the evaluation phase). Very few, however, have provided sufficient detail on the communication aspects that allow inferences about potential theoretical postulates.

THEORY-BUILDING FROM PRACTICE: APPLYING GROUNDED THEORY

Some key questions remain in need of elaboration. How do we build praxis-based theory for development communications? More generally, how might the theoretical and methodological map be drawn? How can action research be conceptualized so that the community of inquirers can begin to work on development issues broadly articulated, but still bear on the particular problems of development communication practice? For action researchers, the task is one of relating dialectically the issues of meta-theory to theories of practice. Because our conceptual and theoretical templates are meager, we can only begin to propose ideas on how these issues might be addressed.

The general approach that might be useful in this context is that of *grounded theory*, which describes how theory might evolve from "data," systematically obtained and analyzed (Glaser & Strauss, 1967). The emphasis of this approach is on theory generation as opposed to theory testing.[3] As Glaser and Strauss (1967) observed: "Many social scientists have been diverted from theory generation in their zeal to test either existing theories or a theory that they have barely started to generate" (p. 262). They further emphasized that the adequacy of a theory cannot be divorced from the process by which it is generated (Glaser & Strauss, 1967, p. 31).

Grounded theory may take different forms. Although the *process* of generating theory is related to its subsequent use and effectiveness, the *form* in which the theory is presented can be independent of this process by which it is generated. In terms of process, grounded theory can be presented as a "running theoretical discussion" (Glaser & Strauss, 1967, p. 32), using conceptual categories and their properties as a way of theory building from the ground up. "Theory as process . . . renders quite well the reality of social interaction and its structural context" (p. 32), a point that captures the essence of the communication processes.

Case studies from development practice can offer insights into communication processes. However, in examining case studies, insights

---

[3]Glaser and Strauss (1967), in fact, argued that "not finding the data for testing a speculative theory should be sufficient grounds to disqualify its further use" (p. 262).

can be of little use unless the theorist proceeds from anecdote to theory-building (Glaser & Strauss, 1967). This can proceed by means of comparative analysis, for example, by comparing across cases or by pitting specific cases against current wisdom (i.e., current "theory").

If we attempt to build theory from the ground up, what do we then observe? In light of the preceding discussion, on what aspects of development practice do we focus? We suggest three potential sites for examination: communication as social process, or communication as dialogue; communication as social practice; and communication as a social right.

Communication as Dialogue

If action for change is to develop from the reflective and self-critical processes of inquiry and dialogue, as earlier described, then the first site must be within these group interaction situations. It may arise among social scientists working with nongovernmental organizations (NGOs) and with villagers, or with social groups mobilizing for development. What communication patterns are evident in the dialogic processes surrounding learning for social transformation? A number of action researchers have depicted this dynamic and participatory learning process with parallel concepts. Argyris and Schon (1978), for example, suggested "deutero-learning" as a concept describing participants learning how to learn. Elden and Levin (1991) proposed "cogenerative learning" and "cogenerative dialogue" to depict ideas of empowering participation. Freire (1972) argued for a dialogic relationship characterized by "subjects who meet to name the world in order to transform it" (p. 136).

Although many have echoed Habermas' call for unfettered speech in the ideal speech situation, few attempted to describe communication patterns within this context and the conditions that promote such a situation. As a starting point, Gustavsen (1985) proposed nine criteria for evaluating the degree of democracy in a dialogue aimed at democratizing work:

1. The dialogue is a process of exchange: Points and arguments move to and fro between participants.
2. All concerned must have the possibility to participate.
3. Possibilities for participation are, however, not enough: Everybody should also be active in the discourse.
4. As a point of departure, all participants are equal.
5. Work experience is the foundation for participation.
6. At least some of the experience that each participant has when he or she enters the dialogue must be considered legitimate.

7. It must be possible for everybody to develop an understanding of the issue at stake.
8. All arguments that pertain to issues under discussion are—as a point of departure—legitimate.
9. The dialogue must continuously produce agreements that can provide a platform for investigation and practical action.

What happens to the learning process when these "rules" are in place? How do communication processes and the construal of meaning under these conditions proceed? These are important questions to ask as part of organizing our understanding at the micro level. At the same time, it is important to recognize that these nine criteria may reflect particular cultural contexts as participation in the Western sense may entail different values and behaviors from those demonstrated in other cultural contexts:

> From a western perspective, participation involves the open exchange of arguments and ideas, it sanctions the right to question, and it legitimates the prerogative to be different, to conduct experiments and to make mistakes. In many rural regions of sub-Saharan Africa, however, direct questioning and open dialogue among different subgroups are shunned, and, in subsistence economies, experimentation and mistakes are often regarded as conveying unacceptable risk. (Fernandez, cited in Maclure & Bassey, 1991, p. 202)

It is thus important to raise the issue of what forms of participation under what contextual conditions promote emancipatory communications? And how, do these patterns differ in different cultural contexts?

Korten (1981) used the notion of "social learning" in an organizational sense to describe "a well developed capacity for responsive and anticipatory adaptation" (p. 498), a capacity that involves recognizing and learning from errors, collaboration with community groups, and joining knowledge building with action. A case in which he was closely involved illustrates this experience.

As part of the Philippine drive for self-sufficiency in rice production, the National Irrigation Administration (NIA) was established in 1964 with the charge of overseeing the design and construction of irrigation systems. A number of myths prevailed within the bureaucracy that, in turn, influenced the way its management of the water systems and interactions with farmers were conducted (Korten & Siy, 1989). Such myths included the following: (a) farmers had little knowledge relevant to the construction and management of an irrigation system; (b) small irrigation systems constructed by farmers using traditional methods were less effective at water control than high-tech engineered systems; (c) no resources are available among poor villagers that might be useful for the construction and maintenance of an efficient irrigation system; (d) it is usually farmers' ignorance of proper water management practice that is at fault when an irrigation system is not working efficiently.

By the early 1970s, serious problems in irrigation system operation and maintenance were being encountered. Irrigated areas fell short of their design targets and there were consistent problems with fee collections that were often insufficient to cover maintenance and operation costs (Korten & Siy, 1989).

The commitment of key agency managers to find solutions, the collaboration of social scientists with these managers and with farmer groups, and support from an aid agency, provided the joint catalyst that set in motion social transformation at the grassroots level as well as institutional transformation. In-depth analyses of local culture, farming, and water management practices involving farmers themselves led to a change in institutional practices, with the NIA developing more participatory approaches to irrigation construction projects. Examination of the effectiveness of these approaches demonstrated that 24 systems in which the NIA had used participatory methods showed an array of benefits not evident in 22 systems where "conventional" methods had been used. The former areas showed more functional physical facilities, higher rice production, stronger water user organizations, and greater contributions from farmers toward construction costs (Korten & Siy, 1988).

As subsequently analyzed, these positive changes were products of "a carefully tailored mix of national level policies, field level methods, and internal management systems" (Korten and Siy, 1988, p. 146). Such a mix of larger social-structural factors and participatory approaches for effecting social change was crucial. As Korten & Siy (1988) observed:

> The participatory approach as introduced in the NIA was only one element of a much broader organizational transformation which touched on nearly every aspect of the agency's structure and function. Each of these changes constituted an integral element of the whole—all contributing to the overall improvement of the NIA's performance as an agency. Each change involved an institutional learning episode in which errors were detected and embraced, alternative solutions examined and tested, adjustments made, and competing interests confronted and negotiated. (p. 142)

Frank and open communications were important throughout and the changes obtained would not have been possible without such a condition. The case also richly illustrates the spiral of action and reflection, the accounting of errors as part of this inquiry process, and the process of transformative learning that characterizes participatory action research.

Communications as Social Practice

In many development projects, the communication issue has been reduced to a technical one: "What messages, through which channels, for which audiences?" Even those sensitive to the use of appropriate information technologies have sometimes tended to isolate the communication process. I suggest that a second exploratory arena is afforded by interpretivist ethnographic accounts of communication practices that exist within a community. These practices serve as inhibiting conditions for change, or alternatively, may serve to enrich efforts at information diffusion. Freire (1970) described this process as "codification," or the selection of appropriate ways of communicating based on a thorough cultural understanding.

The experience of a health program in India (Chand & Soni, 1981) is illustrative. Health professionals and villagers in 21 communities illustrated the evolution of the process of dialogue wherein this community of inquirers attempted to define the health issues in the villages. This required a thorough understanding of social practices surrounding health and nutrition. The *dais*, or village birth attendants, became key participants in the project and an important channel for integrating health professionals' knowledge with traditional knowledge. During the process of identifying the appropriate tools of communication, learning from previous mistakes occurred. It was learned that methods such as puppet shows and tape recording distracted the viewers and led them to ignoring the messages. Finally, the villagers and the villages' traditional birth attendants, the *dais*, came up with pictures they drew themselves to accompany the messages that had also been modified according to their suggestions. Committees were formed with a representative from each caste and the task of each was to spread the health messages and to arrange a health post in each village. The case illustrates the mistakes made, the learning that resulted from reflection and discussion, and the changes that took place as a result. The social changes effected included the raised status of women and particularly, that of the scheduled caste women. However, success has not been achieved in all areas. For example, the project has not been as successful in changing the sex bias in the village's outlook on children, a dimension that will require more time and further effort.

In general, there are two ways that communication social practices have been employed. The traditional approach has been to incorporate them in a mix of channels, basically a top–down approach. A second approach is closer to a participatory approach, where indigenous communication channels are employed by members of the community in the dissemination of ideas. The consequences of using indigenous communication practices appear to be three fold. First, they are used specifically to impart information. Second, their efficacy in helping people develop a critical awareness of their situation and stimulating discussion has been demonstrated (see Kemp, 1995, for a fuller discussion of alternative communication forms such as popular theater for social consciousness raising and mobilization). Finally, they may be helpful in social mobilization and agitation for social change.

Mlama (1991) described the use of popular theater for development as incorporating a number of stages:

1. Members of the community research the development problems that they have defined for themselves.
2. They analyze their data, identify root causes of the problems, and propose possible solutions.
3. The people themselves then concretize these problems and causes by transforming them into a dramatic performance that draws on the community's own theatrical conventions.
4. Suggestions for solving the problem are also woven into the performances.
5. After the performances, the entire community discusses strategies for coping with identified problems.
6. The whole process is conducted with the assistance of facilitators who have both theater and social mobilization experience; these people act as catalysts, and attempt to encourage maximum community participation in all stages of the process.

Such uses of indigenous forms of communication have already been incorporated by development agencies for public education and social mobilization programs (see, e.g., Sherry, 1997).

Communication as a Social Right.

This arena for investigating development communication problems reflects PAR's concerns for issues of information availability, access to information, ownership of information, and knowledge validity. It surrounds such questions as knowledge for what, knowledge for whom, and whose knowledge? In a sense, we are talking here about communication as a process of "knowledge reconstruction" (Fals-Borda, 1991).[4]

---

[4]In a brief discussion with Fals-Borda (personal communication, May 19, 1992), he suggested that the role of communications was very much within this area of knowledge sharing and reconstruction. (Fals-Borda, personal communication, May I9, 1992). Much of his writing does tend to reflect this emphasis on knowledge restructuring toward a knowledge democracy. Unlike Freire or Lewin, he

Gaventa's (1991; Gaventa & Horton, 1981) accounts of Appalachian citizens' efforts for obtaining access to information and for learning research skills to produce additional information to solve an environmental pollution problem (and, in the process, challenging "expert" knowledge) illustrate the achievement of what he called a "knowledge democracy" (see also Chambers, 1983).

How is the right to communicate to be conceptualized and, more importantly, what are its consequences? Such notions as communication access, communication equity, and democratic communications have been theorized, but the need to develop theoretical propositions arising from practice remains. Within feminist studies, the idea of access to literacy skills has been represented as being more than just a skill; it is in essence the key to "the practice of freedom," to borrow a phrase from Freire. Access to such basic skills goes beyond the provision of a bridge to the pleasures of reading and writing; it means one has access to ideas, to the development of imagination, and to the growth of critical thinking skills: "An individual's access through reading a variety of interpretations of reality increases that person's capacity to think for herself, to go against the norms of the culture, and to conceive of alternatives for society—all of which are fundamental to acting politically" (Bunch, 1979, p. 2).

Underlying these three communication sites is the need to look at communication issues at the micro-and macro-levels. Communications as social practice, as dialogic process, or as a social right might be examined more fully within the larger context of macro structures. The Philippine irrigation system case illustrates just such a point (Korten & Siy, 1989). That is, community patterns of communication and participation were successful because they were facilitated by processes at the institutional/bureaucratic levels. In a development project we were involved in a Philippine coastal region,[5] we learned that fisherfolk's fishing practices and nutritional habits were very much enhanced or constrained by fishing regulations, the international market for seafood, or the lack of government action on pesticide runoff (Armstrong, 1991). It was difficult to talk about public education programs without this larger context in perspective.

---

assumes the importance of dialogue and does not spend as much time elaborating on the process as a socially transformative activity.

[5]This was a Food Systems Development Project in Aklan province, central Philippines funded by the Canadian International Development Agency, with McGill University and the University of the Philippines in the Visayas as partner institutions.

METHODOLOGICAL ISSUES

The nature of action research, the effort to build theory from a multiparadigm perspective, and the nature of development problems demand of the researcher a range of skills and methodological approaches. Most important is an ethnographic understanding of the community and an in-depth process-oriented understanding of group interactions where the action-reflection spiral is at work. A major element in the process of reflexive learning from the action-reflection spiral is understanding how this process occurs. The only way this process can be understood in its entirety and complexity is through observation and intensive documentation. Although this may seem intuitively obvious, much documentation in development projects is done retrospectively (e.g., during mid-term or final evaluations). The danger here is explained by Karl Weick (cited in Korten, 1989):

> Retrospective explanations are poor guides to prospective action. We know relatively little about how we actually get things done. We don't know what works, because we misremember the process of accomplishment. We will always underestimate the number of false starts that went into the outcome. Furthermore, even though there were dead ends, we probably did learn from them—we learned more about the environment and our capabilities. Keep good records during process, because hindsight will gloss over most of the difficulties you had while striving for the outcome. Failure to see the difficulties may result in unrealistic expectations about how fast and how easily the next goal can be achieved. (p. 45).

It is also the case, as Boulding observed, that conventional bureaucratic organizations operate with built-in mechanisms that inhibit reality testing, filtering the flow of information, particularly negative information. Process documentation research (PDR) helps to bypass this process.

PDR is an intensive reporting/data-gathering approach. It requires keeping intensive fieldnotes on the part of participants (e.g., through activity logs, diaries, field reports, minutes), including notes on decision-making and problem-solving processes. The nature and process of PDR is documented more fully in Veneracion (1989).

To some extent, this discussion comes full circle when considering what Lewin (1947) similarly described much earlier:

> To understand why the workshop produced whatever change or lack of change would be found, it is obviously necessary to record scientifically the essential happenings during the workshop. Here, I feel research

faces its most difficult task. To record the content of the lecture would by no means suffice. Description of the form of leadership has to take into account the amount of initiative shown by individuals and subgroups, the division of the trainees into subgroups, the frictions within and between these subgroups, the crises and their outcome, and, above all, the total management pattern as it changes from day to day. . . . The task which social scientists have to face in objectively recording these data is not too different from that of the historian. (p. 40)

The approaches of participant observation and process documentation discussed here are crucial to the task of focusing on the *process* of change. Particularly when embedded in detailed community ethnographies, these approaches can be extremely powerful research tools (see Heath, 1983). However, these are not the only approaches that are viable.

At a more general level, the importance of intertwining a variety of approaches, both qualitative and quantitative, needs to be stressed. Although earlier formulations of PAR tended to show a preoccupation with attacking the tools of traditional social science, particularly survey research (see, e.g., Bryceson, Manicom, & Kassam, 1981; Fals-Borda, 1979; Hall, 1979), such attacks might also be understood in the context of the larger battle to gain ownership and control over knowledge production and generation. Survey research particularly came in for bitter attack, with critics suggesting the method was inherently oppressive, alienating and dominating. As Conchelos and Kassam (1981) pointed out, it is a misdirected criticism and only identifies instances of researchers' misuse of the method (see also Burt & Code, 1995, for similar arguments). It is certainly possible to conceive of a survey research approach which involves the subjects in its planning, design and implementation. As Patel (1988) demonstrated in her description of slum dwellers' participation in planning and carrying out a census, it can, in fact, be empowering when communities learn how to identify and describe themselves and their neighborhoods: The information collected via the census by people in these urban slum communities was utilized to rationalize formation of a cooperative, gain housing assistance, civic amenities, and eventually, land tenure. Efforts to systematize community information bases to monitor the status of the entire community have also been successfully established in the Philippines (Polestico, 1988).

As an extension of this issue, the distinction between quantitative and qualitative methods is one that can be considered trivial. Theory as process and theory that springs from practice require approaches that reflect structural conditions, consequences, deviations, norms, processes, patterns, and systems. In short, what is called for is a broad range of methods that allow an understanding of the richness and complexities of communication in the context of development.

It is clear that much work needs to be done in aligning communication issues within the action research framework and its intellectual offspring, PAR. My proposal to base this work on grounded theory arose from its utility in the context of theory-building from practice; that is, its applicability in situations as well as to them. I suggest that these efforts be grounded in the examination of communication as a social practice. This means that development practitioners and researchers should investigate communication processes within conditions of democratic participation, and the analysis of the larger structural context for participatory communications offers one starting arena.

REFERENCES

Argyris, C., Putnam, R., & Smith, D.M. (1985). *Action science*. San Francisco, CA: Jossey-Bass

Argyris, C., & Schon, D. (1978). *Organizational learning*. Reading, MA: Addison-Wesley.

Armstrong, N. (1991). *The food systems development project*. Unpublished paper. University of the Philippines, Visayas.

Bernstein, R. J. (1971). *Praxis and action*. Philadelphia: University of Pennsylvania Press.

Bernstein, R.J. (1976). *The restructuring of social and political theory*. New York: Harcourt Brace Jovanovich.

Boserup, E. (1970). *Woman's role in economic development*. London: George Allen & Unwin.

Brown, L., Henry, C., Henry, J., & McTaggart, R. (1988). Action research: Notes on the national seminar. In S. Kemmis & R. McTaggart (Eds.), *The action research reader* (pp. 337-352). Victoria: Deakin University Press.

Bryceson, D., Manicom, L., & Kassam, Y. (1981). The methodology of the participatory research approach. In T. Erasmie & J. de Vries (Eds.), *Research for the people, research by the people*. Sweden: Linkoping University.

Bunch, C. (1979). Feminism and education: Not by degrees. *Quest, 5*(1), 1-7.

Burt, S., & Code, L. (1995). *Changing methods: Feminists transforming practice*. Peterborough, Ontario: Broadview.

Carr, W., & Kemmis, S. (1986). *Becoming critical: Education, knowledge and action research*. London: Falmer.

Chambers, R. (1983). *Rural development: Putting the last first*. London: Longman.

Chand, L., & Soni, S. (1981). Participatory research and health. *Convergence, 14*(2), 64-78.

Conchelos, G., & Kassam, Y. (1981). A brief review of critical opinions and responses on issues facing participatory research. *Convergence, 14*(2), 52-63.

Dewey, J. (1929). *The sources of a science of education.* New York: Livewright.

Dewey, J. (1938). *Logic: The theory of inquiry.* New York: Henry Holt.

Einsiedel, E.F. (1996). Action research: Implications for gender, development, and communications. In D. Allen, R. Rush, & S. Kaufman (Eds.), *Women transforming communications.* Newbury Park, CA: Sage.

Elden, M., & Levin, M. (1991). Cogenerative learning: Bringing participation into action research. In W.F. Whyte (Ed.), *Participatory action research.* Newbury Park, CA: Sage.

Fals-Borda, O. (1979). Investigating reality in order to transform it: The Colombian experience. *Dialectical Anthropology, 4*, 33-55.

Fals-Borda, O. (1991). Remaking knowledge. In O. Fals-Borda & M.A. Rahman (Eds.), *Action and knowledge: Breaking the monopoly with participatory action research.* New York: Apex.

Foster, M. (1972). An introduction to the theory and practice of action research in work organizations. *Human Relations, 25*(6), 529-556.

Freire, P. (1972). *Pedagogy of the oppressed.* New York: Herder & Herder.

Gaventa, J. (1991). Towards a knowledge democracy: Viewpoints on participatory action research in North America. In O. Fals-Borda & M.A. Rahman (Eds.), *Action and knowledge: Breaking the monopoly with participatory action research.* New York: Apex.

Gaventa, J., & Horton, B. (1981). A citizens' research project in Appalachia, U.S.A. *Convergence, 14*, 3.

Gildart, E. (1993). *Innovations for participatory research: Communication implications for paradigmatic triangulation.* Unpublished master's thesis. University of Calgary, Calgary, Alberta.

Gioia, D.A., & Pitre, E.(1990). Multiparadigm perspectives on theory building. *Academy of Management Review, 15*(4), 584-602.

Glaser, B., & Strauss, A. (1967). *The discovery of grounded theory.* Chicago, IL: Aldine Atherton.

Grundy, S. (1982). Three modes of action research *Curriculum Perspectives, 2*(3), 23-34.

Gustavsen, S., & Hunnius, G. (1981). *New patterns of work reform: The case of Norway Oslo.* Norway: University Press.

Habermas, J. (1974). *Theory and practice.* Boston: Prentice-Hall.

Habermas, J. (1984). *The theory of communicative action.* Boston, MA: Beacon.

Hall, B. (1979). Knowledge as a commodity and participatory research. *Prospects, 9*(4), 393-408.

Heath, S.B. (1983). *Ways with words.* Cambridge, MA: Cambridge University Press.

Jacobson, T. (1993). A pragmatist account of participatory communication research for national development *Communication Theory, 3*(3), 214-230.

Kemmis, S., & McTaggart, R. (1988). *The action research reader* (3rd ed.). Victoria, Australia: Deakin University Press.

Kemp, M. (1995). *Acting up! The use of alternative media in community development and education.* Unpublished master's thesis. University of Calgary, Calgary, Alberta.

Korten, D. (1989). Social science in the service of social transformation. In C. Veneracion (Ed.), *A decade of process documentation research* (pp. 43-56). Quezon City, Philippines: Institute of Philippine Culture.

Korten, F., & Siy, R. (1989). *Transforming a bureaucracy: The experience of the Philippine National Immigration Administration.* West Hartford, CT: Kumarian.

Lewin, K. (1946). Action research and minority problems. *Journal of Social Issues, 2*(4), 34-46.

Lewin, K. (1947). Feedback problems of social diagnosis and action. *Human Relations, 1*(3), 147-153.

Lewin, K. (1952). Group decision and social change. In T. Newcombe & E. Hartley (Eds.), *Readings in social psychology* (pp. 459-473). New York: Holt.

Maclure, R., & Bassey, M. (1991). Participatory action research in Togo: An inquiry into maize storage systems. In W. F. Whyte (Ed.), *Participatory action research.* Newbury Park, CA: Sage.

Marrow, A.J. (1969). *The practical theorist: The life and works of Kurt Lewin.* New York: Basic.

Mlama, P. M. (1991). Women's participation in communication for development: The popular theater alternative in Africa. *Research in African Literatures, 22*(3), 41-53.

Moser, C. (1993). *Gender planning and development: Theory, practice, and training.* London: Routledge.

Patel, S. (1988). Enumeration as a tool for mass mobilization: Dharavi Census. *Convergence, 21*(2-3), 120-135.

Polestico, R. (1988). *Framework and operation of community information planning systems* (CIPS). Makati, Philippines: Philippine Partnership for the Development of Human Resources in Rural Areas.

Rahman, M. (1985). The theory and practice of participatory action research. In O. Fals-Borda (Ed.), *The challenge of social change.* London: Sage.

Sanford, N. (1970). Whatever happened to action research? *Journal of Social Issues, 26*, 3-23.

Servaes, J. (1989). *One world, multiple cultures: A new paradigm on communication for development.* Leuven: Acco.

Sherry, J. (1997). Prosocial soap operas for development: A review of research and theory. *Journal of International Communication, 4*(2), 75-101.

Veneracion, C. (1989). *A decade of process documentation research.* Quezon City, Philippines: Institute of Philippine Culture.

Whyte, W. (1991). *Participatory action research.* Newbury Park, CA: Sage.

Author Index

Subject Index

A

Action research, 110, 219, 220, 359, 360, 362-364, 364, 366-367, 375
and interpretive methods, 218-219, 221, 225-226
Adult and continuing education, 7, 211
Africa, 17, 30, 36-39, 319-320, 327, 369
Agenda setting, 27, 82, 90
Apartheid, 94
Asia, 319-320, 327
Audiences, 232, 240, 249, 339

B

Bakhtin, 340-342
Bio-power, 311
Bolivia, 67
Botswana, 17
Brazil, 162, 331, 343
Broadcasting stations, 244

C

Canadian International Development Agency, 374
Capital accumulation, 315, 324, 329
Catholicism and the Catholic Church, 172, 290
Causal relations, 290, 294
Chiapas, 65-66
China, 32, 320
Collective processes, 78, 97, 176, 327, 365
and expression, 242-244, 248, 257
Colombia, 331
Comilla project, 117, 119
Communication,
alternative, 179,192, 196, 238, 240, 241, 243, 247, 254-255, 257, 373
authoritarian, 229-230
centralized, 246, 251

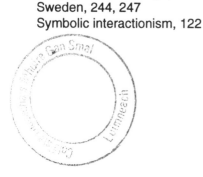